Walter Besant

My little girl

A Novel

Walter Besant

My little girl
A Novel

ISBN/EAN: 9783337050443

Printed in Europe, USA, Canada, Australia, Japan

Cover: Foto ©ninafisch / pixelio.de

More available books at **www.hansebooks.com**

MY LITTLE GIRL.

A Novel.

BY THE AUTHORS OF "READY-MONEY MORTIBOY."

BOSTON:
JAMES R. OSGOOD AND COMPANY,
(LATE TICKNOR & FIELDS, AND FIELDS, OSGOOD, & CO.,)
124 TREMONT STREET.
1873.

MY LITTLE GIRL.

BOOK I.— IN THE ISLAND.

CHAPTER I.

IN the great stormy ocean — that part of it which is bounded by the Bay of Bengal on the west, and the coast of Mexico on the east (or thereabouts) — lies the island which the French, when they had it, called Ile des Palmistes; but which the English, on taking it at the beginning of this century, patriotically named after their great and good regent, Prince George. The geography books call it Prince George's Island still; but no one out of England knows it by any other name than the Ile des Palmistes : and all English people, with the exception of the Colonial Office, know it by the name of Palmiste Island. It lies, in its rounded and graceful curves, like a maiden at rest, within a silver ring of surf, breaking over the coral reef, in latitude 18° S., — a latitude, which I take to be the most delightful in the world, especially in a country where you can get highlands to live in, and a constant sea-breeze to fan you. In Palmiste Island the sea-breeze blows all the year round, sometimes giving way to a warm west wind, which comes from the neighboring continent, and sometimes lashing itself to fury, no one knows why, and performing prodigies as a hurricane. It is bad at these times to be at sea, because all the ships go down : but it is perhaps worse to be on shore; for there the roads are mere rushing rivers, down which the wayfarer is hurried by the flood to meet an untimely fate. The gardens are stormy lakes, trees are blown about like leaves, roofs of houses are lifted like sheets of paper, and men, if they are so unlucky as not to get shelter, are sometimes take up towards heaven, like Elijah; only, like the prophet, they generally come down again with the breakage of a good many legs, arms, ribs, and whatever bones happen to be most easily fractured. If the hurricane lasts long enough, the people, shut in their houses, are starved for want of provisions; and, while it blows, there is no means of cooking what they have. It has its advantages; for, after it is over, all the planters, who were shaky before take the earliest opportunity of going through the form of bankruptcy, and excite universal commiseration for their hard fate, as they enlarge on the thousands of pounds' worth of canes or coffee that the hurricane has destroyed. Once clear of debt, they go on again with light hearts and renewed hope. By some curious inversion of the laws of political and social economy, very few, either debtors or creditors, unless they are English, seem the worse for their calamities. I have some idea, though not in this place, of putting forth a treatise on this important subject from a novel and tropical point of view. My readers will perhaps bear this in mind, and buy me, when I do appear, on "The Northern and Temperate Zone System."

After the hurricane, the papers — there are six daily organs of opinion in the island, two on straw paper, two on a peculiar fabric something stiffer than tissue, and something coarser than homespun, and two on real paper — live for a fortnight at least on the correspondence which pours in. An "Occasional Correspondent" writes to detail the effects in his town, an important centre of at least three hundred people; a

"Special" narrates the effects in the adjoining hamlet, half a mile removed; "Our Own" writes from the other end of the island, fully thirty miles away: they all sign their names, and run up to town the next day to receive the congratulations of their friends. They arrive with folded arms and brows knit. This illustrates the majesty of literature, since even these small dallyings with the muse produce such mighty throes of the mental system. And in a month all is repaired: the fields move again with the yellow-green canes, the dark coffee bushes blacken the hillsides, the roofs are all put on brand-new, the bankrupts have got fresh estates, or retain their old ones through the clemency of their creditors, and all is as it was. And in the Ile des Palmistes nothing changes but the men.

These are a heterogeneous race. They lie like a parti-colored pyramid, the single stone at the top representing his Excellency the Governor. The lowest stratum is composed of Coolies. These excellent beasts of burden supply the place of the old slaves. I do not think they are exactly kidnapped; but I believe it is demonstrable that very few of them have distinct ideas of their future when they embark on board the emigrant ship off Calcutta or Madras. On the other hand, their condition is certainly improved by the step. They get better wages and a larger access to drink; they do not work very hard; they are well fed; and, if they are beaten with sticks, they may, if they like, have up their employer for assault. To be beaten with sticks carries, however, no sense of personal degradation with it, and generally hurts little, much less than the docking of wages, which is the only alternative. Consequently, despite laws and fines, Old Father Stick, the first lawgiver, still retains a certain amount of authority. Then, again, their children can go to school, if there happens to be a school near; and, when they are taught to write, come in handy at forging leaves of absence, passes, and such-like small helps to making life pleasant. At least once in six months, too, a missionary comes their way, and beguiles the time for half an hour after sundown by telling them they are going to that place where they will find all their good resolutions. This raises an animated discussion for the evening, and helps to fill up the missionary's trimestrial letter. He writes this the next morning, after a comfortable dinner at the planter's house, with half a dozen cigars, and two or three goes of brandy and soda. The English collector of those stray shillings which go to make up the million a year spent in this noble work may read the half-hour described as follows:

"Tuesday. Rose half an hour before dawn. Thought of Zech. li. 32. Rode, on my journeying, through the gigantic forest to the estate of Fontainebleau. Having obtained permission to preach the Word, spent a long time in deeply interesting conversation with the laborers in the village. All were eager to learn. Alamoodee, an aged Tamul man of sixty-five, was particularly anxious to hear the good tidings. And I was greatly pleased with the intelligent look of Mounia and Cassis, two young Indian women of about sixteen. I left them a few tracts, and they laughed, putting their fingers in their mouths in the artless Indian manner. They cannot read, but others can read to them. In the evening news came that the husband of Mounia was beating her for some alleged misconduct. How sweet it is to sow the seed! Alamoodee, poor fellow, was brought in next morning on a charge of drunkenness, but dismissed with a fine and caution. I have reason to believe it was a conspiracy. The hard toils of the humble missionary have often no reward but hope."

The next stratum on our pyramid is coal-black. This is composed of all the negroes now left alive. Thirty-six years ago they were emancipated, — a hundred thousand, of all ages. There are now about ten thousand. For receiving their freedom with a joy which argued well for the future, as their admirers said, they proceeded to make a solemn covenant and agreement; not on paper, for they had none, and could not write; nor by special Parliament, for they never met; nor by mutual exhortation, for they never talked about it, — but by that more certain method, the silent consent of the nation, the inarticulate vox populi. They agreed, one with the other, that they would never do any more work at all. And they never have done any. They have kept this resolution with the unbending obstinacy of the medical student who promised his aunt that he would lay aside his studies on the sabbath. It has been a pleasant time with them, but somehow they have not prospered. They are dying out. They live in little patches of garden, where they plant potatoes and lettuces, bananas, beans, and such things as grow by themselves, and cost little trouble. What they cannot eat themselves, they sell for rice and rum. When they desire to make a feast, the nearest planter's poultry-yard supplies the materials. They smoke their pipes in great peace, while the vertical sun strikes upon their roofless hats, and penetrates pleasantly through the woolly protection of nature; they talk but little, and then of soothing subjects, such as the cheapness of rum, the excellence of their bananas, and their own amazing sagacity; and they laugh on small provocation, seeing great jokes and effects of humor when graver men look on with a smile. Sometimes they call themselves — all out of the gayety of their hearts — carpenters; and, if you trust them, will build you a house whose windows are of unequal height and differing dimensions. They laugh when you point out this incongruity of things; and, if you foolishly get into a rage, they only laugh the more — but at a distance. When they marry, they buy a large mosquito curtain as a proof of respectability; and their highest ambition is to have a piano.

Their wives and daughters love to go to church in white kid gloves and a parasol. Their husbands follow, walking behind in bare feet, battered straw hats, and blue stuff coats. Or, if they are richer, they have a black coat and blue stuff trousers. The ladies are mightily devout, and go through the external part of religion with great fervency. The men kneel down, and continue kneeling, with what is called the sweet, sad intelligence of the African race, till they catch the eye of a friend; then you may see two frames convulsed with a mighty struggle. Finally, quite overcome, they go out into the churchyard, and laugh on a tombstone till the service is over; taking turns to laugh at each other, like an Aristophanic chorus.

By degrees they get old: their wool becomes gray; the fine calf which once adorned that part of the leg with us called shin, shrinks and shrivels; the heel projects another two inches or so behind, the frame gets bent, but the man is the same. He does not know that he is old; he does not know how long he has lived, or how long men usually live. Presently, to his utter amazement, he positively dies; and thinks himself cut off prematurely, although he has numbered eighty summers. Certainly he has had no winters, because there is no winter there.

The best of them go fishing, and are very handy with their boats. Some few have been pushed on in the world; but their patrons generally drop them, on account of defects which make them a little lower than those angels we English once took the race to be. The half-educated fellows are very bad specimens indeed. A hog in black clothes, a monkey with a book before him, would be fair types of their morals and philosophy. As a rule, they drink themselves to death; and as there are, fortunately, but few of them, they hardly count.

Let us get a step higher. The next stratum is the oddest of all: it is the Chinese layer. I have the greatest liking for this folk. There is a profundity, coupled with cynicism, in their look, that few English philosophers possess. They seldom laugh, they despise all people but themselves, they make money diligently, live laboriously, fare badly, drink little, are clever artisans, can be relied upon in matters of work; and, with all these virtues, are so clogged and burdened with vice that they cannot rise. To smoke opium, to gamble all day, and to do one or two other things that Western civilization denounces, form their ideal heaven. They are convivial too. Their gravity is the result of education, not of nature; it is grafted, not indigenous. Witness the air of suppressed fun, inseparable from the nature of the action, with which two of them carry a pig between them on a pole, or attend a pork-devouring religious ceremony, or let off crackers at the funeral of a friend, or sell you a box of sardines. And more remarkable still, they are all alike. I do not know how they get over the possible complications that might be caused by this circumstance. I suppose care is taken so far as the rights of property and the domestic relations are concerned. At least, I never heard but once of any case in which the national likeness was taken advantage of. This was when Ah-Kang — I knew him well; a good fellow, but deficient in the finer shades of moral principle — going into the shop of Kong-Fow, found his poor friend lying dead behind his own counter. He thereupon conceived the brilliant notion of burying him in the garden, and taking his place. This plan he carried into effect, and for three months drove a good trade, his friend's name and titles, painted by an imperfectly educated Creole, being all the time on the door-post as follows:—

<blockquote>
Mr Kongfow Esquire Licensd Deeler in Tobacco Retailer of Spirruts

N.B. — Day and Martin's Best Blacking.
</blockquote>

Then he was found out. I forget how. Another step. We are among the mulattoes. I suppose this is the most intelligent class in the community, because they are always saying so. For the same reason, they are the most truthful, the least addicted to the ordinary frailties and backslidings of human nature, the most religious, the most trustworthy, the most enterprising, the most polished, and the bravest.

That no one else says so is a clear proof of the malignity of other people. Scandal hints that they hate their fathers for being white, and despise their mothers for being black: their enemies maintain that they have the vices of both races, and the virtues of neither; and, though they have barristers, physicians, and lawyers of their own, assert that their science is worthless, their eloquence froth, and their law chicanery. When all is told, I dare say, if they could forget their black blood, they would not be a bad set. The thing that rankles in their bosoms, the injustice that sets their blood aglow, is that white people, who shake hands with them on the Exchange, and meet them on terms of equality in the courts of law, will neither enter their houses, nor sit at meat with them, nor introduce them to their wives. The law, which formerly forbade them to wear boots, has given them all the rights of civic equality; but no law can remove the prejudices of caste. Are they worse off than we in Europe? Are there not houses where we, who grace the district of W.C., enter only on a kind of sufferance? Does not the Faubourg St. Germain still exist, eighty years after the Revolution? Would the Duke of St. Smithfield, whose grandfather began life as a journeyman baker, and ended as an earl, sully his blue blood by letting his fair daughter marry me — me, the author? And are we, therefore, dear inhabitants of Bloomsbury, to eat out our hearts in malice?

Our pyramid narrows. Next we come to the planters and the merchants, the English and the French. With the merchants we have nothing to do. Let me try to show you a planter's house. But first, for I am tired of my pyramid, let me clear it off and have done with it. The next stratum is the governing body, — the officers sent out by England. Palmiste Island is a Crown colony. Therefore, the officers are generally men of good family, if of small means. Their posts do not enable them, as a rule, to save much, but they save a little; and, when the time comes for retiring, they have something more than their pension to fall back upon. They are not usually a remarkably brilliant set of men; but they are generally well-bred, and possessed of tact. The Government cart goes on smoothly enough. There are few real grievances, and there would be no imaginary ones were it not for the daily papers. The judges are just; the Crown law-officers have sufficient ability; the bishop is pious and bland; the Colonial Secretary is cautious: things get put by for a more favorable opportunity, and then right themselves. And the top story, the apex, the crown of the building, his Excellency the Governor-General of Prince George's Island and its dependencies, gives dinners to the *élite*, balls to society in general, receives whom the Colonial Secretary sends to him, and composes long despatches recommending reforms which will make the colony a paradise. He is obliged to write them, to show his zeal, though it must be a fearful bore. And, when they come home, some young clerk in the Colonial Office, who knows as much of Palmiste as of Timbuctoo, annotates the labored thoughts of the experienced statesman, and snubs him. This done, according to rule, the despatches are put in a book, and carefully bound up to be preserved forever. There are now so many of these hapless children of thought, smothered as soon as born, and kept as calf-bound mummies in Downing Street, that a few years since they were compelled to move them all to the cellars. Their weight was pressing out and crushing down the walls; and it was feared that their presence, longer continued, might possibly result in the demolition of the whole fabric. Shades of departed governors, pensionless wanderers by Brighton sands, consider with gratitude the Nemesis that waits on the contempt of your labors!

CHAPTER II.

THE estate I am going to take you to is called Fontainebleau. All the estates in the Ile des Palmistes have these pretty French names. One is called Mon Songe, another Mon Rêve. There is a Trianon, a St. Cloud, a Sorèze, an Amboise, a Chenonceux: there are Beau Plan, Belle Vue, Riche en Eaux, Belle Rivière, Savanne; there are Lucie, Eugénie, Adrienne, and Louise. All the poetry in the heart of the owner is lavished on the name of his estate. "All the same," as a wandering jockey once observed to me, "as the owners of the 'orses in the Derby," — a remark which seems to throw a new and very pretty light upon horse-racing.

Fontainebleau lay on the confines of the great forest that filled the centre of the island. On one side rose hills — not the round, indolent hills of England; but sharp, eager, ambitious little mountains, scarped with precipices fifty and a hundred feet high, jagged with peaks, and cut with passes, for all the world like a row of Alps. These pretentious elevations tower upwards at least five hundred feet, and are covered with wood, except in small spaces cleared for coffee. They look down upon the broad fields of Fontainebleau. Planted with canes, the acres stretch down the sloping land towards the sea, kindly mother earth rounding, as it were, into a breast of fertility. As the sun takes his swift, long course midway in the heavens, the yellow-green crops wear a thousand different shades of light: now as the wind turns up the dark hidden side of the leaf, — now as it flutters out the bright upper part; now when the cane is in flower, when it blows about the feathery beauty like the trappings of a helmet; or now, when the clouds fly here and there in dark shadows along the glorious colors; and always the sea-breeze raises the gentle waves of the field, like the sweet unrest of a sea which never knows a storm.

An English corn-field, when the sun shines upon it, is a sight to admire; but an estate planted with canes, in all their richness of color and beauty of form, is one to fill the eye with those tears which rise at the contemplation of nature at its best, — tears from no divine despair, but perhaps from a sense of the unfitness of man for the earth. In the cities, it is not felt; but in the lonely corners of the world, in those tiny spots of the ocean where God's finger seems to have lingered longest, delicately shaping sweet river-courses, shady glens, ravines, cascades, and quaint mountain tops, where nature is most productive and man most out of sight, the heart is saddened, the eyes dimmed.

Fontainebleau was a very quiet place, and a lonely. To north and east lay the great silent forest. To south only, it opened out; and, standing in the road, one could see ten miles of land — ten miles, rather, of waving canes — before the ocean seemed to rise up like a wall, and bar the prospect. Looking over the sailless sea — for no ships ever came that way — the misanthrope might derive a sense of freedom from feeling, that, far and wide, no land interposed between the headland beneath him and the barren peaks of the Antarctic shores, far to the south; but the broad fields looked hot, thirsty, and parched. It was better to turn northwards, and, climbing over the wall which kept out the deer, and was a nightly gymnasium for the monkeys, dive into the glades and recesses of the forest.

I suppose it would have been difficult to lose one's self in it. One might, perhaps, wander about in it for a few days; but sooner or later the end of it must have been reached. It is not very large, — ten miles one way, by perhaps thirty another. There are few paths in it; but a man has only to keep going by the sun to arrive somewhere near his destination. And then there are no perils in it. Nothing more harmful lurks in its recesses than the monkey, — a gigantic beast, — species, say, ourang-outang — of at least a foot and a half high. There are also deer, the little bristly jungle pig, and perhaps a wild cat or two, — that is, a tame cat gone wild; not a panther or a leopard, or any thing of that nature, understand. There was a tiger. He got away from a menagerie, and betook himself to the woods. Of his end there are two legends. For some maintain that he died of indigestion, having eaten an old negro who disagreed with him; others, with greater plausibility, affirm that his nature has been changed, — animum cum cælo, mutavit, — that he has been distinctly visible in the gray of the morning, filing his teeth in bowlders, and that he lives retired in the mountains, — a vegetarian, shunning the sight of man. And this they allege as a proof of the mildness and placability induced by the climate of Palmiste Island. There was once, also, a crocodile. He, too, escaped, being yet quite young, and unfortunately mistook a water-pipe for a cavern or retreat made specially for his behoof. There, many weeks afterwards, he was discovered, choked, — a gruesome body; and Englishmen must needs take consecutive sodas and b.'s as a corrective and preservative against any small matter of putrefaction that may have entered their bodies through incautiously drinking the water unmixed, — a thing quite improbable on the face of it, and entirely contrary to their known habits. Lastly, there was once found — as the ballads say, I do not lie — *half a snake*, the tail half. How it got there, where the other half was, whether he had a sister or a brother, a father or a mother, or a dearer and nearer one still, in the jungle, was never ascertained. And in all the annals of Palmiste, no other snake, crocodile, or tiger was ever found in the whole island.

As a set-off against this immunity from danger, the forest is almost silent and inexpressibly dreary. Save here and there the faint chatter of a monkey, or the occasional cry of a coq-de-bois, the silence is profound and oppressive. Few birds are there in Palmiste, — very few in the forest. They have two natural enemies, — monkeys and hurricanes. The former take down their nests, and destroy their eggs, — all out of pure mischief; and the latter blow their nests and eggs and all into the sea.

But besides the mournfulness of its silence, the mere aspect of the forest saddens if you stay in it too long. For a bright, cheery, glorious wood, where you may picnic, wander, or build castles of future greatness, I prefer the New Forest; for a poetical, dreamy place, where you may make poetry and *chansons de geste* that of Fontainebleau — in France, I mean; for a sweet-smelling, sentimental wood, a place where one can walk with one's love, and fall into tender talk of eternity and heaven, and all sweet hopes and confiding trusts, I prefer a pine forest on the lower slopes of a Tyrolese Alp. But for a place where death and decay stare you in the face, — where if you stay your steps, you fall presently to musing on a misspent life, go to the forest in the centre of Palmiste. There, when you mark the giant creeper crushing the life out of some great monarch of the wood, curling round him like the prieve, with its countless arms, think of evil habits, and remind yourself how man never shakes them off, and how the soul is choked with them. Then remember your own, and abandon hope. Or when you see the dense mass of trees, — so thick that they press against one another, so close together that they never dream of such a thing as leaves till they are thirty or forty feet high, — think of men in great cities, how thick they are, and how they fight for life, and give up all prospect of aught but toil and labor and oblivion, till the end comes. Presently you will come — it lies in your path — upon a large pillow-like mass of green, soft moss; put your foot upon it — it sinks through to the hip. This was once a great tree. It lies where it has fallen; its wood is rotten and wasted; no one ever noticed its beauty, and it served no purpose in life or in death. Then draw your moral, sitting in the shade.

I extract most of this description from a discourse I once pronounced in my friend Venn's rooms. He maintains that such a forest as I have described would affect him with a lively joy; and points out how all that I have named would but serve to raise his spirits, and fill him with gratitude and hope. Nature can be read in two ways. In all her moods there are joy and hope, and in all there are mockery and despair. I tell of the forest as it affected me.

There are two or three little water-courses running out of the forest through the estate, which the simple islanders call rivers. These bubbling streams speedily cut out little ravines for themselves, and go brawling about among the bowlders at the bottom as if most important business, not to be deferred a moment, hurried them down. Here and there they disappear, and you may hear them grumbling below. When they emerge, it is to make a great leap, as if for joy, into a basin where the water runs round and round in a mighty hurry to get away. These ravines are dark and narrow; the steep, sloping banks crowded with trees and brambles. Rich and rare ferns lurk under the shadows, orchids almost priceless are found in the branches; and you never by any chance meet any one if you care to wander down the ravines except perhaps a bevy of Indian damsels with their hair down, performing their ablutions, like Bathsheba of old, in the open.

By one of these rivers stands the residence of Fontainebleau. It is a large, deeply-veraudcd wooden house, with wooden tiles for roofs, all on one floor. All the rooms open into each other, and on the veranda. They are furnished with a curious mixture of things costly and things rude. There is a rough, common table side by side with chairs that might do duty in Belgravia. A piano-forte which has never been tuned, and never been opened for no one knows how many years, is in one corner, littered with powder-flasks and shooting gear; a tall bookcase, filled with volumes whose bindings have once been splendid, but which are now dropping off the books from damp; a few pictures, a great pile of newspapers, and a general air of comfort and negligence, — mark a drawing-room where there has been no lady for many years. The dining-room is behind: it has a great table and a side-board, both of which were once, it may be presumed, new, but which are now mere monuments of neglected mahogany. It has no other furniture, because the chairs of the house have generally succumbed to time the destroyer; and now at dinner-time they take them out of the drawing-room, and bring them back after dinner. Not that they are ever wanted; for easy chairs stand on the veranda, and cigars are best smoked in the cool night air.

At the back of the house, outside, stands the kitchen of the Indian cook, — a place whence come savory things, but within which no one was ever known to penetrate, except one man. He came out with pale face and trembling limbs. They gave him brandy. Presently he recovered; but he never afterwards was known to touch pudding in Palmiste. I believe too, that he died young. And the bedrooms, each furnished with gay little iron bedsteads and mosquito curtains, are, like the sitting-rooms, made to open on the veranda. There are not many of these inhabited now; for the gay days of Fontainebleau are over, and the gray-haired man who lives there now has little companionship save that of his son and his nephew. The society of the town twenty-five miles away has nothing to do with him. He is out of it now, and forgotten; save once or twice a year, when at some great hunting party in the forest, he appears pale and melancholy, and old men whisper that poor George Durnford is the ghost of himself. Time was, they tell you, when George was the soul of the island. The ex-calvary officer, who got into such a devil of a mess with his colonel, and had to sell out; who came to Palmiste twenty years ago, and bought Fontainebleau; who married Adrienne — la belle Adrienne — niece and ward of Henri de Rosnay; who led the life of the place, and was foremost in every thing social and genial, — can it be the same person?

More of him hereafter. Let me finish with the house.

About the veranda, or in the dining-room, or about the kitchen, are the boys—Indians — who belong to the service of the house. There are some half-dozen of them, dressed in a sort of tight cotton jacket, with little caps, looking, as they are, full of intelligence and life. These, with the bright, fearless look in the eyes, and the slender grace of the limbs, vanish when the boy passes the threshold of manhood; and he becomes heavy, sluggish, and sensual. At present, however, the boys are from eight to twelve years old, and make the best servants in the world. Mendacious they are, it is true, and as destructive as monkeys; but, if one is going to be thrashed for breaking a glass, it is just as well to say that another did it. You get no more if you are found out. Logically, and with respect to immediate results, they are quite right. It has not yet entered into the heads of the residents of Palmiste that they might Christianize their servants. Certainly the specimens turned out by the missionaries are not encouraging. The converted Hindoo is, in most cases, precisely the kind of man that *no one* will employ; and though things may be better in those districts of Southern India which have been largely Christianized, I think that the least said about missionary labor among the Indians the better.

At the side of the house stretches its great garden, filled with all sorts of English vegetables, and all kinds of tropical fruits. Here are rows of pines which Covent Garden cannot hope to equal. There are too many for eating, and they are rotting on stalk. Here is an orchard of Letchi trees, the fruit that Warren Hastings tried to acclimatize in England, but failed. I would he had succeeded. Here are mangoes, with vanilla trained upon the trees. Here are custard apples, oranges, citrons, and guavas. Here, too, are strawberries, peaches, mulberries, and grapes. You may look, however, in vain for apples, pears, and such things. These grow not in Palmiste; and Englishmen, eating fruits more delicious far than these, grumble that they cannot get a pear, and would almost go back to England to get a plum.

In front of the house lies its lawn, — a broad, rolling piece of ground, set with flower-beds, mostly neglected, and planted round with rose-trees. Side by side with English flowers are others which remind you of greenhouses, Kew Gardens, and the Crystal Palace. They are not, however, so sweet as our own; and yonder bed of mignionette fills the air with a perfume far more delicate than any of the heavy-laden tropical plants. Here is a sensitive plant. Touch it: all the leaflets near your finger close, and shrink together in a kind of fear. Here is a gorgeous dracæna. You remember one like it in the Palm House. Here is a honeysuckle climbing up the wall of the house; and here, in heavy masses over the veranda, are creepers, which, if left unchecked, would climb over and embrace the whole house, and tear all down together.

My picture of still life must finish. Throw into the background a row of slender palms; put in, if you can, that glimpse to the right of a miniature gorge, some fifty feet deep; mark its tree ferns, tall and symmetrical, with their circled glory of leaves; throw in for light, the soft, white rays of a sun that wants yet half an hour of setting; let your air be warm and mild; let a breeze, cool and crisp, from the south-east, blow through the branches; while, from the camp of the Indians, not far away, imagine — for you cannot paint it — a confused murmur of tongues, cries of children, an occasional quarrel among the women, the monotonous beat of the tumtum, and the drone of the Indian story-teller. Then try to fancy that you have lived in all this so long that Europe with its noisy politics, and England with its fierce battle for life, and London with its fevered pleasures and bitter sorrows, seem all dreams of a former existence: that the soft lassitude of the climate has eaten into your very marrow; and that you no longer care to think, or to work, or to do any thing violent or in a hurry; that your chief pleasure is to sit at early dawn on the veranda, with a cigar, and see the day rise over the hills; or, at evening, watching the southern cross, and letting your thoughts roam here and there unchecked; your chief hope, — save at moments when a sickness for home comes on you, and a yearning for the life and vigor of England, — always to go on like this : to have no sickness, to feel no sorrows, to be tormented by no sympathy, to make no alteration or improvement, to dream life away, to eat the lotus day by day, in a land where it is, indeed, always afternoon.

CHAPTER III.

COME back with me ten years before my tale begins. We are still at Fontainebleau. It is a dark, dreary night in January, — cold, though it is the middle of the hot season. A fierce gale, to which the wind blowing about the trees is a sort of fringe or outside robe, is raging somewhere at sea. The rain falls at intervals in a continuous sheet of water; doors and windows are closed; and George Durnford is sitting alone in his dining-room, with an untasted bottle of claret before him, and a bitter sorrow at his heart. That morning he had followed to the grave the wife who but two days ago was alive and well. From a room close by comes the prattle of two children, in bed, but not yet asleep. To them the dismal ceremony of the morning was a pageant which conveyed no meaning. One of them has lost his mother; and he sits now on his little white bed, a great-eyed, fair-haired, solemn boy of two, with an uneasy sense of something wrong, and a growing wonder that the familiar hands do not come to smooth his sheets, and the familiar lips to kiss his good-night. The other, — a year or two older, with blacker hair and darker complexion, — in the opposite bed, is singing and laughing, regardless of the nurse's injunction to make no noise and go to sleep. He is Cousin Phil, and the little two-year-old is Arthur Durnford.

The baby voices do not rouse the lonely mourner in the room outside them. He sits musing on his brief three years of love and happiness; on the dreary scene of the stormy morning's funeral; of death and of sorrows that come to mar the brightest promise. He thinks of the day when he brought home his young bride, flushed with joy and hope; and of her cold waxen features when he took the last look at the fair face that had nestled at his heart. The hope and vigor of his life seem suddenly taken out of him; and he shudders as he remembers the long years to come, — perhaps thirty or forty, — alone in misery. For all sorrow seems to be endless when it begins; and, when the pain dies away into a sad regret, its very poignancy is remembered as a kind of evil dream.

The storm outside increases. Roused by the crash of thunder, he raises his head; and then, for the first time, he sees that he is not alone.

How long she has been sitting there, when she came in, and how, he knows not.

She is a young mulatto woman, not darker than many a black-haired woman of Provence, apparently about twenty years of age. Her jet black hair is rolled up in a wavy mass. She holds her hat in her hand. Her dress is wet and draggled, but her hands are not rough. In her face, as she gazes steadfastly on Durnford, there is a look of mingled triumph and pity.

He starts with surprise.

"Marie! why do you come here? I thought you were in England."

She does not answer for a while, and then begins in a sort of slow, measured way — speaking English fluently, but with something of a foreign accent.

"Why do I come to-night, George Durnford? I think I came to triumph over your sorrow, because I heard about it in the town when I landed yesterday; but I heard things when I came along which forbid me to triumph any longer. Why should I triumph? You, who loved me once, would love me again if I chose. You, who deserted me for that good, dead girl — you see, George, I can be just — would, if I chose, take me again to be your plaything."

"Never," said Durnford. "Woman, can you not understand that a man can cease to do evil?"

"But," she went on, as if he had not spoken, "I do not choose. I will be no man's plaything. You taught me something, George. You taught me that a woman, to be what a woman should be, must learn many things. We, the daughters of a despised race, are good enough to be the mistress of an hour, but not good enough to be the companions of a life. We have our year of fondness, and think, poor fools, it will last forever. We have but one thing to give you, — our love. You take it, and trample on it. We have nothing but ourselves. That is yours; and when you are tired of the toy, you throw it away in the dirt. As I am only one of the many, — only a mulatto girl, — I ought not to complain. It has been my fate, and I accept it. Besides, you are a gentleman. Not every girl gets an Englishman for a lover. You were kind to me; you put ideas into my head; you taught me things; you made me feel, without meaning it, how great a gulf there is between your race and mine; and you showed me how to pass the gulf. You did more, not as a salve for your own conscience, because I suppose your conscience never pricked you about it; nor as a bribe for me to go away and never trouble you again — you gave me money on that day — the day before you married — when you bade me farewell. I used the money well, George. Even you will confess I used it well. I have been to your great city, — your big, cold, dreary London. I put myself to school there. I have learned all that a woman should learn, and more. Shall I play to you?

Shall I sing to you? Shall I prove to you that even your cast-off mistress can be, if she pleases, as perfect a lady as — No, George, I will make no comparison. Adrienne, my mistress — my poor darling — whom I played with and loved, I shall never be like you!"

Durnford made an impatient gesture.

"I must say what I have to say. I want to say a good deal. Besides, it pleases me to talk. I have talked to no one since I left England, and you must listen. Don't think, to begin with, that I love you any more. The poor, ignorant creature that trusted you, and thought herself honored by having your arm about her, is gone. George, she is dead. All that is left of her and her life is a memory and an experience, I remember, and I know. She could have done neither. She would have gone away, back to her own cousins, — the swine who live in the huts by the seaside, and scramble once a week for the wretched fish that will keep them till another week. She would have married some black clown, as ignorant as herself, and far more brutal, and would have brought her children up like their father. George, where is my boy?"

Durnford pointed to the bedroom door.

She snatched a light, and came back directly with little Phil, still asleep, in her arms — kissing and crying over him like a madwoman.

"O Phil, Phil! my darling, my darling! Could I leave you all alone? Speak to your mother, my son — my son! Will you never know her? Will you never be proud of her, and cling to her, and be good to her?"

The child opened his eyes, looked up sleepily, and then heavily turned his face from her, and was asleep again in a moment.

She took him back, and placed him again in his cot, and took the light, and looked long and steadfastly at the other. She returned, and sat down again, sighing deeply.

"Your child is mine, Marie," said Durnford. "What I swore to you then, I swear to you now. He will be brought up like the other, educated with him, and shall share with him."

"Will he never know the story of his birth?" asked the girl.

"It is my hope that he never will. He will be called — he is already called — my nephew. I told all to my wife. She had forgiven."

"When you die, will he, or will the other, have this estate?"

Dunford hesitated. At last he looked steadily at her, and said, —

"My lawful son will be my heir. What wealth I have shall be his. Your son will have a competence; but I will not — I cannot Marie — defraud my heir of what is his."

Marie sat silent for a time.

Then she began to walk about the room. "I am not myself to-night, George. I was angry as I walked here through the forest. I am only repentant now. The love for my poor Adrienne drowns the resentment that filled my heart an hour ago. I came to upbraid you — I cannot. Her spirit is in this house. I felt her breath as I leaned over the face of her boy. I saw her face as I came in at the door. I feel her here now, George. If I think more of her, I shall see her. I do see her! She is here — before me. Adrienne," — she bent forward with streaming eyes and supplicating hands — "forgive me. Forgive the poor, passionate girl that never did you any harm, but whose heart has been filled with bitterness against you. You did not wrong me, my poor dear; and as for him who did — here, in your presence, I forgive him. George, for three long years, far away from here, among strangers, I have had but one prayer every night, I have prayed that misery might fall on you and yours. Adrienne, Adrienne, speak to me if you can. Give me some sign that my prayer was not answered. Let me go away at least forgiven."

As she spoke, the hurricane swept with all its fury against the house. The wind howled like an accusing spirit. George rose from his chair, pale and trembling.

"Woman," he cried, "you are answered."

But as suddenly the wind dropped, and with one last effort blew back the shutter of the window. Durnford hurried to replace it; and, with the driving rain that came in, like tears of wild repentance, a poor dying dove was blown through the window, straight to Marie's bosom.

"I am answered," she said, folding the creature in her hands.

Neither spoke. Presently Marie fell on her knees, with the dove in her hand, and prayed aloud. Great tears rolled down Durnford's face. When she had finished, he lifted up his voice and wept, saying, —

"God have mercy upon me a sinner."

. . . .

It was midnight. Marie rose from her knees, another Magdalene.

"I must go," she said; "but first, George, aid me to carry out my plan of life. I am going back to London. I have got a great voice, — a splendid voice, George, — a voice that will bring me, they say, more money than I can spend. I shall save it for the boy. To make it useful, I must study and work. Let me have some more money. I don't think it degrades me to ask it of you, does it? My real degradation no one knows over there. You must give me money, George."

He told her how he would help her in England, and give her what he had. They were both very quiet and subdued.

"I have seen you," she said, "and I have not cursed you. But, ah! my heart misgives me. I came through the lonely forest to-night, and heard sounds that mean misfortune."

"Marie, it is superstition."

"Perhaps. I cannot help it. It is in my blood. And a voice whispered in my ear, as I came along, that I should have no joy with my boy; and that you would have no more pleasure in life; that my fortune was to come, but my misery and punishment with it. George, was it no bad omen that my child turned away his face from me? Is it good to come to a house of sudden death and mourning? Shall I begin the world afresh with a brighter spirit for this night of tears and repentance?"

"You are shaken. Stay to-night. Take the child to sleep with you. In the morning you can go, if you will."

"No — now, now," she said. "I cannot stay here. Take care of him, George — take care of him. Some day, perhaps"—

"You cannot go through the forest to-night."

"I must — I cannot stay here. Farewell, George. I think I shall never see you again. Pray God to forgive us both. I will pray every day. They say God hears if you go on praying. And write to me sometimes to tell me of the boy."

They stood one moment, face to face. George took her hand; and then their faces met. There was no passion now, in that last embrace. The memory of the wife came between them like a spirit. They kissed each other, like children, in token of forgiveness and in self-abasement; and then, lifting the latch, Marie went out into the darkness, and disappeared.

George Durnford, lighting a cigar mechanically, went outside to the veranda. The Indian guardian, whose duty it was to make the rounds, and keep off nocturnal thieves, was coiled up in a corner, fast asleep. The storm had died away. A pure sky, bright with the southern constellations and with a clear half-moon, was overhead. George's eye fell on the cross of the south, — that heavenly sign that once filled the sailors with hope. He felt the warm, soft air of the summer night. Sitting down, he presently fell asleep. When he awoke the day was breaking; the mill was lighted up; the day's work was begun; and he pondered in his mind whether he had not dreamt it all.

Little Philip, coming to him at six o'clock, began to ask who had taken him out of bed. And lying on the floor George Durnford found a handkerchief with the name of Marie on it. Then he knew that he had not dreamed this thing. And he kept it in his heart.

CHAPTER IV.

Mr. Alexander MacIntyre used to describe himself, as a dingy card on Mr. Durnford's table testified, as Professor of the Classics and Mathematics, Instructor in Foreign Languages, Fencing, Fortification, Hindustani, and the Fine Arts. He was a most accomplished man. With the exception of the last-named department of learning, — which I fancy he inserted rather with a view to the effect and roundness of the sentence than with any intention of instructing in the Fine Arts, — he really knew, and could teach, the things he professed. He was not a Porson in Greek, but he made boys fairly good in Greek scholarship. He would not have become senior wrangler, but he knew a good lot of school mathematics. He could really fence; he could talk Italian or French or German with equal fluency; and he could and did swear horribly in Hindustani. Finally, on occasion, he talked about fortification as glibly as Capt. Shandy.

This great luminary of science was engaged for some years as private tutor to the two boys at Fontainebleau. He used to ride over on a little pony from his house, some two miles off, and ride back again in the evening. Sometimes when he staid to dinner, Mr. Durnford would leave him on the veranda, smoking and sitting in friendly proximity to the brandy bottle. Then it was the delight of the two boys — for Mr. Durnford had got into a habit, of late years, of going to his own room about nine o'clock — to observe their revered instructor drink tumbler after tumbler of brandy and water, getting more thirsty after each, and more rapid in his despatch of the next. At the opportune moment, — that is to say, when he was not too far gone, — they would emerge upon the scene, and engage him in talk. He would then make a laudable effort to give the conversation a philosophical and improving turn. Getting into difficulties, he would try to help himself out by another pull at the brandy; and when, as always happened, he got into fresh complications, he would fall back in his chair, and make use of a regular and invariable formula. He would say, quite clearly and distinctly, "I am a Master of Arts of the University of Aberdeen — I'm the MacIntyre!" Then he would become speechless; and the boys, with a huge delight, would carry him neck and heels to bed. In the morning he would rise at six, and emerge with unclouded brow. Perhaps, in the course of the day, he would find occasion for a few remarks on temperance, with an excursus on his own moderation in spirituous liquors.

He was a small, spare man, in glasses, with sandy hair, a pale face, and a red nose. He lived by himself, in a little house of three rooms, two miles down the road. He had no pupils except the two Durnfords; and, at odd moments, an uneasy consciousness would seize him, that, when these went, he would starve. Nor had he any friends to help him. The voice of rumor, which aggravates a man's vices and subtracts from his virtues, said that he went drunk to bed every night. As to his antecedents, there were many reports. Some said that he had been in the army, but was cashiered for embezzlement while he was adjutant; others, that he had been a courier, a billiard-maker, all sorts of things. Rumor lied, of course. He had been none of those things. He had, after a laborious and meritorious career at Aberdeen, "gone in" for Scotch mission-work in Constantinople. Here he preached the gospel to the Jews, till he preached his belief away. This becoming known to his employers, he was turned out with ignominy. Then he wandered about the Levant, living no one knew how. After a few years, he turned up again in England, and became a lecturer to some society. Difficulties about the money ensued, and Mr. MacIntyre once more left his native shores. This time he came to Palmiste, with a letter to Mr. Durnford, and set up as a public teacher of every thing in the principal town. Troubles of all sorts fell upon him, and he removed to the other end of the island, partly to escape them, and partly to coach Mr. Durnford's boys. He had a way of introducing remarks — which at first appeared to be of the profoundest wisdom, and took in the unwary — with a magisterial and Aberdonian "obsairve." He was sententious and deferent. He had no morals, no principles, no self-will, no self-control. All his better qualities were wrecked on the quicksand of drink; and, of the hard-working, hopeful days of Aberdeen, nothing was left but the knowledge he had acquired, and a habit of industry which never deserted him. He was not, it must be confessed, the best tutor possible for boys; but education in Palmiste is difficult.

Mr. Durnford liked to keep his boys at home. There was less harm to be learned there, at all events, than in the hot, unhealthy town where the college stood. And even Mr. MacIntyre could teach them mere book learning. So they staid at home, and grew in years and stature.

In appearance they were as different as in manners: for Philip, the elder, was strong, sturdy, and overbearing; Arthur was slight, delicate, and yielding. If Philip wanted any thing, he always had it. Philip, too, wanted every thing. The best pony was his, the best dogs, the best gun. He was the cleverer, — the favorite with Mr. MacIntyre, sharp of tongue, and cool of temperament; but he was not popular. Arthur was. By his soft, feminine ways; by the gentle sympathy which he showed for all alike; by the kindly grace of his manner, which he inherited from his mother, — he won affection where his cousin only gained fear. The children ran after him when he walked through the village; the women came to him to adjust their differences; the Indians, when they had a petition to offer or a point to gain, which was nearly every day, waited till they could get hold of the chota sahib, — the little master. Philip, though he pretended to despise this popularity, was secretly annoyed at it. It rankled in his heart that he, for his part, commanded no man's affection. By degrees, too, as he grew up, he began to ask questions about himself. These his uncle put aside, quietly but firmly. And gradually a sort of feeling of inferiority took possession of him. There was something — what, he never guessed — that was not to be told him something that had better not be spoken of, something that made him different from his cousin. It was the germ of what was to grow into a great tree, — a tree whose fruit was poison, and whose very shade was noxious. But at this time it only stimulated him. It made him more eager to surpass his cousin; threw him with fresh vigor into his studies; and urged him to practise more and more the arts which he thought would lead to success in life. These — for the boy's knowledge of life was very small — he imagined to be chiefly skill at shooting and riding. He did both splendidly. Arthur did both indifferently.

Mr. Durnford seemed to take but little notice of their progress. Still, from a word here and there, they knew that he watched them. Nor could Philip complain, when his uncle gave him the best horse and the costliest gun that could be got in the island, that he was overlooked. There were few times when the grave man conversed much with them. Sometimes, at breakfast, —, that meal which means, in a planter's house, an early dinner at half-past eleven, when the work of the day, which has gone on for five or six hours, is more than half over, which is followed by two or three hours of rest and lazy talk, — he would relax, and tell them long stories of English life and youthful adventure, at which their faces were set aglow, and their hearts beating with excitement. Or he would set forth the perils of a young man's course; hiding little; letting them know some of the temptations that lie in the way of life; telling them something of the battle that lay before them; and — for George Durnford was now a religious man — backing up his pictures with a homily on duty. Surely there is but one thing needful to teach boys, — to do their duty; and one thing above all to train in them, — the power of will that will help them to do it. On Sunday mornings they would read the service of the Church, the three together, — Phil taking the first lesson, and Arthur the second. By this arrangement, the younger boy seemed to get all the teaching of Christ, and the elder all the passion and rebellious self-will of the Israelites.

Once a week or so they generally rode, the two boys together, but sometimes Mr. Durnford with them, to see Madeleine.

Madeleine, some three years older than Arthur, was the one thing that kept the boys alive to a sense of the social side of life. She, like them, was motherless; and, like them, lived with her father, M. De Villeroy, on a sugar estate, his property. She was everybody's pet and plaything, — a bright little black-haired beauty, whose laughter kept the house gay, and whose wilful ways were law. M. de Villeroy was one of those grand Frenchmen — some day we shall see them all in their proper place again — whose manners are the perfection of courtesy, and whose ideas chiefly date from a time when Louis the Sixteenth was king, or, to speak more truly, from a time when Francis the First was king. Not that his own birth dated from either of those reigns. He and his were colonists in Palmiste Island, from very early in the last century. The Marshal de Villeroy he spoke of as his cousin. He had the right, if he wished, to call himself marquis. He had a profound contempt for roturiers, and held that gentleman was a name that belonged to him by divine right; but he held, too, that the name involved duties, and truth, honor, and bravery, were the three points of his creed. For Christianity, I fear, that, like too many of his countrymen, he considered it as an admirable method of imparting notions of order to the vulgar; and, though he would not openly scoff at it, yet, when alone with his friend Durnford, he would let fall such slight indications of a contemptuous toleration as almost justified the priests in calling him a Voltairean. Voltaire — or M. Arouet, as he preferred to call him — he always declared to be a man who had done an infinite amount of mischief; and he held all men of genius in equal dislike, from a persuasion that their mission in life was to prematurely popularize the ideas of the nobility. The Revolution, he would explain, was the work of men of genius. The ideas which they propagated had long been current among the more cultivated of the nobility. These, however, forbore to carry to their bitter end the logical consequences of their convictions. Nothing in social and political economy could be logical. All must be compromise. But what the Revolution took thirty years to achieve would, he maintained, have been accomplished by the liberality of the divinely appointed rulers of things in ten, without bloodshed.

"Obsairve," said Mr. MacIntyre, "Mirabeau was a gentleman."

To which M. de Villeroy replied, that Mirabeau's life was fatal to any kind of purity of action; and that, despite any alleged instances to the contrary, great things could only be done by men of pure life.

We must not, however, waste time on M. de Villeroy. He disappears directly out of the story. But he was one of the few influences brought to bear upon the boys' daily life. Mr. Durnford, with his high standard of duty and Christian honor; M. de Villeroy, with his standard of a gentleman's ideal; Mr. MacIntyre, alternately presenting the example of a scholar — various, if not profound — and the drunken, helpless helot; the ignorant, childish mass of Indians and blacks on the estate; and pretty little Madeleine, to keep them gentle, and give them that delicacy of feeling which only contact with the other sex can impart. Let us bear these things in mind, and remember, in the story to come, how ever so little an accident may mar the growth of the most promising tree.

The accident happened thus. Phil was now about fifteen, — a strong, handsome boy, whose dark, wavy hair, and slightly olive skin, were set off by a pair of bright black eyes and regular features, closely resembling those of Mr. Durnford. It was some little time, he could not himself say how it began, since the feeling had sprung up, that I have alluded to, of his own inferiority. As yet it was but an uneasy thought, sometimes dying away altogether, sometimes springing again full-grown into his brain. But it was there. He awoke this particular morning with it, and went out in the early dawn morose and sullen. Presently, when Arthur joined him, and they walked about with their arms round each other's necks in boyish fashion, the ghost vanished, and Phil became himself again. They got their ponies saddled, drank their coffee, and rode off to meet the tutor.

Presently they came upon him, plodding slowly up hill, on his broken-kneed Pegu pony, with his huge straw hat on, and his cigar in his mouth.

"Obsairve," observed the philosopher, as they turned to go back with him, "man's just the creature of habit."

He pronounced it "habbit."

"So he is," said Phil, who immediately guessed that his instructor had been more than usually drunk the night before. "Somebody else has made that remark before you, Mr. MacIntyre."

"Don't take the word out o' the mouth o' the prophet of the — I mean your tutor, young man," said Mr. MacIntyre. "Man as I said, is the creature of habit."

They rode on in silence for a while, waiting further light from the sage.

This presently came.

"Of all habits that flesh is heir to," he went on, "let me caution you against intemperance. Whiskey, in my country, may be taken in moderation; brandy, never. You will obsairve that it furs the tongue, confuses the brain, and prevents that orderly sequence of thought inseparable from metapheesical study. Take the advice of one who has seen the world, young men; and, when you go into it, be careful to stop at the fourth or fifth tumbler. What is taken after that gives headache."

"Have you a headache this morning, sir?"

"Philip, your question pains me. It is true that I have headache, the result of eating imperfectly cooked steak last night. But your question, in connection with my warning and advice, might seem — I only say seem — to imply suspicion that I had been drinking last night."

"Not at all, sir," said Phil. "Steak *is* indigestible. Let me bring you a bottle of soda when we get in."

"Ye're a good lad," answered MacIntyre, "and I think I'll take it."

He took it, and they presently fell to their studies till breakfast. The day passed as usual till the afternoon, when the clatter of hoofs told the approach of visitors. They were Madeleine and her father. The boys ran to help her off her pony, and they all three went off to the garden together.

Madeleine's favorite was Arthur; but Philip, as usual, wanted to appropriate her. Already the girl was conscious of herself. She took the usual feminine delight in being petted and caressed; and expected the homage of the boys with the air that seems to come naturally to beautiful women. She was born to be admired. Women who have that destiny accept it without any murmuring, and with no surprise.

Philip to-day, however, was cross-grained. He did not want her to talk to Arthur: he wanted to have her all to himself. Then they began to quarrel. It was a children's quarrel, that might have been ended directly but for a luckless remark of Philip's.

"Never mind, Madeleine," he said. "You can play with Arthur if you like; but when we grow up you'll marry me."

"Indeed I shall not," she said. "I am going to marry Arthur," and went and held up her face to be kissed by that blushing youth.

"Arthur!" said Philip with great contempt. "Why, I can turn him over as easy as — See."

He caught his cousin by the shoulder, and turned him round, throwing him off, so that he tripped and fell with his face to the ground. Arthur, however, rose to the occasion; and, springing up, struck him smartly in the face.

The battle lasted for a moment only, and Philip stood victorious. Madeleine ran to the rescue of her prostrate lover.

"Go away," she cried. "I believe what people say of you. I will never speak to you again."

"And, pray, what do people say?" asked Philip.

"They say that you are cruel and selfish: that you tease Arthur and vex him; and that you want to get every thing for yourself. Go away."

Philip went away. It was the first time the boys had struck each other. He was angry with himself, angry with Arthur, angry with Madeleine; and in this mood he strolled along till he found himself at the stables. Then he thought he would have a ride. Going into his own pony's box, he found the syce had not rubbed him down, or even touched him since the morning, and was now sitting — a tall, gaunt Indian of six feet — eating rice in perfect content. Phil's temper boiled over. He flew at the man in a fury of rage, kicking, striking, and cursing him. The poor groom was first appalled; and, standing up sideways to the wall, he lifted his leg, and covered his face with his arms, as some small protection against the blows. At last they became insupportable; and, in self-defence, he took the boy by the shoulders, and held him at arm's length.

Hindustani is gifted, above all languages, with a capacity of swearing. The power of insult is in no other language so great. Our own noble vernacular, when judiciously used, say, by the mate of an American sailing-ship, or an able seaman in our merchant service, can do a good deal; but its resources are miserable indeed compared with the strength and vivacity possessed by its sister branch of the Aryan family.

Phil had picked up this knowledge. He used it now, pouring out great volleys of insult — words which he had often heard, but never used before; terms which conveyed reproaches he did not understand — on the head of the offending groom. He, for his part, only looked scared; until, stung beyond all endurance, he pushed the boy back into the straw, seized the great wooden bar of the loose box, and brandished it over him, crying, —

"Bastard, I'll kill you!"

Phil looked at him, bewildered. Then, suddenly, he seemed to take in the whole force of the word; and instead of offering any resistance, or making any retort, he seemed to be suddenly crushed, and covered his face with his hands.

The groom put down the bar, and began to tremble. Then he furtively — something after the manner of a burglar on the stage — stole out of the stables. Between the stables and the nearest canes there was an open space, cleared for some purpose or other, of a quarter of a mile. Across this he sped, half doubled up, in long strides, and was lost in the canes.

Three weeks elapsed before he showed up again; then he was brought back, a monument of emaciation. He had been hiding in the forest, making predatory excursions at night to the nearest canes, and on these he had lived. The watchman apprehended him, and marched him in at daybreak, brandishing his long stick with an air of great importance and grandeur; the miserable prisoner, who was about two feet taller than his captor, slouching along after him. And when he came to the house, seeing Phil alone on the veranda, he fell, a mere mass of terror and despair, and grovelled before him. Phil kicked him up, and ordered loftily that he should be sent back to the stables.

But when he was left alone, he was, for the moment, stunned. Suddenly it all burst upon him. Without other evidence than the mere insult of the Hindoo, he knew it was true. The position he held in the house; the superior consideration in which Arthur was held; the silence of his uncle about his own father, — all were proofs to him. He rose and came into the open air, as miserable as boy could well be.

Suddenly, however, another thought struck him. Imagine that you have been brought up to believe — not by being taught in so many words, but by power of association — that there are two distinct races of mankind; that God has made one for mastery, and the other for subjection; that while it is your duty, as a sovereign, to rule wisely and mildly, you cannot but feel a certain amount of contempt — proportioned, of course, to your wisdom and mildness — for the governed race. Suppose you have gone on, being neither very wise nor very mild, till your contempt has become overweening, and your pride of race excessive. Then suppose, in the height of your arrogance, you hear suddenly that you are an impostor; that you belong to the race you despise; that you are nothing more nor less than one of the humblest of them. This was Phil's thought. Like the first, it was not a conjecture, but a certainty. Little as he knew of the wickedness of the world, he knew well enough that illegitimacy implied black blood: nothing else was possible in Palmiste. He thought, too, of his black wavy hair, his pale olive skin; and he moaned in his agony.

There was one more test. He looked at his nails. Beneath them was the blue stain that the African blood always leaves; and he gave up all hope.

Then he sat down and sobbed. It all seemed so cruel; it was so strange and so dreadful. The pride of life was gone. Nothing was left but shame and degradation. He crouched among the trees, and would have cried for death, had death occurred to him as even a remote possibility. He sat motionless, while the weight of his grief bent down his young shoulders.

As he sat there, the sun got lower. Presently it disappeared behind the hills. Long fingers of light came out, vibrating a sort of good-night to the world; and then it became dark. The darkness weighed upon him. He got up, and wandered out, thinking how he should go into the house, and found himself near the stables. There he saw some one with a lamp. It seemed as if the lamp was unsteady, shifting about like a light at a masthead.

After studying this phenomenon for a time, he went to discover its cause. I regret to say that he found his preceptor, Mr. MacIntyre, very drunk indeed, making shots at the stable door, with the view of getting out his pony and riding home to dinner.

He had been left alone all the afternoon, and finding a brandy bottle in the immediate neighborhood, had finished it, with these disastrous results.

Phil helped him to open the stable-door, and saddled his pony for him.

"Obsairve," said Mr. MacIntyre, "the mind of man, as you will find from a study of the Philosophy of the Condeetioncd, has a tendency to—to"—

Here he fell over the bar that the groom had left behind him.

"Mr. MacIntyre," said Philip, "you're drunk again."

"Young man, no—no, young man. The curry at breakfast was prawn cu—curry. It always makes me so."

A thought struck the boy.

"Mr. MacIntyre," he said, "did you know my father?"

"Your father?" repeated the drunken scamp. "Of course I know your father. Misther Durnford's your father, and Marie's your mother—pretty little Marie." Then he began maundering on—"Pretty little Marie, pretty little girl—wouldn't speak to me."

"Marie—what Marie?"

"Marie—never had 'nother name. Went away—went away to England—died."

Philip turned away and left him; and presently he heard the pony, who knew his way better than his master, go clattering down the road.

He went in, washed and brushed himself, and appeared at dinner, pale and quiet. Madeleine and Arthur had it all their own way for once, for he never even contradicted them.

CHAPTER V.

TIME passed on. Philip said nothing of his discovery, only he became quieter. The boy of fifteen in a year changed into a tall, resolute young man, who might have been taken for two and twenty. The light mustache on his upper lip proclaimed his manhood. Boyhood grows more rapidly into adolescence under the hot sun of Palmiste; and his firm step and upright carriage announced one who, at any rate, seemed ready to make a fight for it.

He never, but once, alluded to his conversation with Mr. MacIntyre. But one day, after a long silence, Arthur being out of the way, he reminded the tutor of what he had told him. Poor Mr. MacIntyre was thunderstruck. He remembered absolutely nothing of it.

"Tell me," he gasped, his face becoming fearfully red,—"tell me exactly what I said, Phil. Ah! Loard, what an evil spirit brandy is!"

Phil told him.

"I suppose it was true," he added carelessly.

Mr. MacIntyre rose, and went out on the veranda, looking round every corner to see if there were any listeners about. Then he opened every door,—there were seven in the room,—and looked in each chamber. No one was at hand, save in the dining-room. Here there were two of the Indian boys amusing themselves with a rude dramatic performance; for one had put on a pair of spectacles, and, with an empty bottle in his hand, was staggering up and down, like one who was well drunken, while the other looked on and applauded. Mr. MacIntyre himself wore glasses. He could not, of course, imagine that the representation was a description of himself; but, as a friend of discipline, he felt bound to inflict chastisement, and accordingly horsewhipped the one he caught, who had been doing nothing, and then he came back flushed with the exercise.

Sitting down again, and pouring out a glass of brandy and water, he sighed out,—

"Yes, Phil, it is true—more's the pity, my poor bairn! It's just awfu', the wickedness of the world. We fight against it, we philosophers; but we do awfu' little. It's quite true; but, Phil, no one knows it. I know it, because I brought you here, a wee bit thing of eighteen months, and told the folks you were Mr. Durnford's nephew; and Mrs. Durnford knew it, for her husband told her. Eh, she was good. There must be a heaven, boy, for some people,—if there's an after-life at all, which I vara much doot. We, who have had our backslidings, would not be comfortable in the same place with her and her life. They would have their own apartments. I sometimes think, Phil, I should be happier down below, near the bar."

"And no one suspects?"

"I sometimes think M. de Villeroy suspects. He's just a devil, that man. He finds out every thing. Last week he came to me, and told me that he'd found out how I had"—

"Well?" for the good man stopped.

"I think I'll take another glass, Phil. Yes, thank you. You were saying"—

"What became of my mother, then?"

"I don't know Phil. I can't tell you. She went away. Your father told me she went to England. Afterwards he said that she was dead. She was lady's maid, companion, humble friend, whatever you call it, to Mrs. Durnford before her marriage; and remember, Phil, that she was the handsomest woman in the island. Hardly a touch of"—

"Stop!" shouted Philip, crimson— "stop, I won't bear it!"

The tutor stopped, and presently went away, seeing no further opportunity for philosophy or drink.

And for good reasons of his own, he forebore to inform Mr. Durnford of what had passed between himself and Phil.

But, one evening, Philip had a little conversation with his uncle, as he still called him.

"If you can spare five minutes, sir," he said one evening when Mr. Durnford had smoked his cigar, and was showing the usual signs of departure to his own quarters.

"Certainly, Philip what is it?"

He sat down to listen. Then Philip began, with considerable trepidation, but with a certain dignity of manner, to explain himself.

"You know, sir, that I am past sixteen?" Mr. Durnford nodded. "And I think you will allow me to ask you if my father, of whom you have told me nothing, gave me at his death any means of entering life. I have seen, sir, for some time, that there are points connected with our family history that you do not wish known to me. I shall never ask for information. My father, as you have told me, was in the army. I ask for nothing more. He was a gentleman, because you are a gentleman. That he did nothing to disgrace himself in the eyes of the world, I am sure."

"In the eyes of the world? No," said Mr. Durnford.

"That is all I wanted to have from your lips. Now, sir, am I a beggar?—that is, am I wholly dependent on you?"

Mr. Durnford did not answer for a few moments.

"I am glad, Phil, that this talk has been held between us. It must have come sooner or later."

"Why should it not come, sir?"

"No reason at all—none; only family business is always disagreeable. Let me tell you, once for all, that your father's money was placed wholly and unreservedly in my hands, for your benefit. I have done for your benefit what I could for you. You will be, at the age of twenty-one, the master of four or five hundred pounds a year. It is not much; but, with a profession, it is plenty."

"It will do, sir," said Philip. "I am glad it is so much."

"But what profession will you take? You are not a bookworm. The law would do little for you. The church?"

"Impossible!"

"Quite so, as I was about to remark. Then, what are we to do with you?"

"I shall go into the army, sir. At least, I can carry a sword."

"And use it, too, Phil, I think. We will talk about this afterwards." But they never did.

Early that year, while the hot rains of January were still soaking into the steaming earth, and the sun was vertical at noonday, there was brought a rumor—vague at first, but too soon confirmed—that cholera had appeared in the principal town. Up to that day, cholera had been unknown. No scourge of pestilence had ever fallen on the island that insurance companies ranked rather higher than England, and on which they put a tropical percentage out of mere fun, and with the cheerfulness of men who are certain to make their money. Nobody ever died young, except from drink. Nobody read the lessons about the uncertainty of life as applying, even indirectly, to himself; and the very parsons had forgotten that life was ever any thing but threescore years and ten—fully told. So that, when men first heard that the cholera was come, they laughed.

There were various rumors as to its origin. One said that a captain of a coolie ship had put ashore, being then in quarantine, and, having spent the evening with four friends, had gone back at night to his ship: but the four friends died next day; and there was no one to tell whether the captain had left the ship or not, for all his sailors died.

Others said that it was produced by the shameful excesses of the Chinamen in pork. This was disproved by the fact that no Chinaman died of cholera at all. They went about in great glee, with mighty uplifting and pride of heart, rubbing their hands when they came upon some poor negro doubled up by the enemy that seized him so suddenly and killed him so easily.

Others, again, attributed it to the British Government. That malignant power—conscious for many years of the foe that threatened the island—deliberately, and with malice prepense, had left unguarded all the avenues by which it might enter. The editor of the most respectable paper, daring to say that the enforcement of the quarantine laws had been more rigid than usual of late years, was set upon, one starry evening, by a dozen public-spirited mulattoes, and horsewhipped. That is, they began to horsewhip him; but a soldier happening to come round the corner, slung his belt and dispersed them, devious, rapidly flying. An account of the affair appeared in both the straw-paper organs next day, in which the brave assailants were held up to public admiration as patriots of the deepest dye. They were compared to Timoleon, to Brutus, to Harmodius, to Mirabeau, to Soulouque, to Oliver Cromwell, to Wilberforce, and to Toussaint L'Ouverture. They were to have been brought before the magistrate for assault; but he and all the officials of his court died of cholera, and the affair dropped. And, as the pestilence grew worse, men's hearts failed them for fear. The town of St. Denys had a population of some sixty thousand. These were dying at the rate of three hundred a day. All day long, and all night, the prisoners were kept at work digging graves, — not single graves, but long common fosses, fifty feet long and eight feet deep. There was no time to make coffins. As fast as the bodies were brought, the upper part of the shell in which they were laid was slipped out, and the sand covered them up. The priests — is there any fearlessness like that of a Catholic priest? — stood all day by the grave, chanting the monotonous funeral service, burials going on all the time. Now and then one of the grave-diggers would be struck down, and carried off, shrieking and crying, to a hospital. For if a black is once taken to a hospital, he abandons hope; and, should he come out again, is received by his friends — not with the rejoicing that would await one risen from the dead, but rather with such disappointment as greeted Martin Chuzzlewit when he came back from Eden.

The shops were closed; the wharves deserted; the streets empty, save for the frequent bearers of the dead. Most mournful of all was the absence of mourners. You might see a little procession slowly moving down the street — one big coffin and three little ones. Following them, not some young and stalwart mourner, not one whose life was still before him, but a poor old down-bent black, the grandfather of the little coffins, the father of the big one, hobbling sideways after the dead. Or if it was one who had lived long and in high esteem, his coffin would be followed by two or three out of the hundreds who counted him friend, and who, in better times, would have followed him to the grave, and pronounced a funeral oration over him.

Sometimes the closed shops never opened again at all; and then, long after the cholera had gone, the police would go at dead of night, or in the early morning, and execute their dreadful task.

Englishmen got together — they always do in time of danger. I was once in a French ship with some half-dozen English passengers. One was the most foul-mouthed, blasphemous man I ever met abaft the fo'c'sle, that is. We had very bad weather for a week. For one whole day we thought we should go down. Involuntarily we of Great Britain found ourselves grouped together by the davits, holding on. Quoth the blasphemer, —

"Since we are to go down, we English will stick together, and let the damned Frenchmen drown by themselves. Is there any fellow here that can say a short prayer?"

It was a dreadful punishment to him for his evil life, that he couldn't remember even the shortest in the whole Church Service; and I am quite sure, so stanch an Anglican was he, that he would far rather have gone to the bottom with no prayer at all, than with any thing extemporaneous or irregular. Even the petition for rain would have comforted him.

However, in St. Denys, the English merchants sat together in each other's offices. They drank a good deal of brandy in those days, in little occasional nips, that touched up the liver if they did not keep off the cholera. No business was done of any kind, nor was there any pretence at it. No clerks came: these were mostly mulattoes, and kept themselves at home, with the shutters half-closed, sitting in a horrible circle in the dark, and with a fearsome fluttering at their hearts. If they perceived an internal rumbling, they took a dose of cholera mixture. If any one said he felt unwell, the rest sidled from him; and if one was actually seized, they generally ran away. The doctor in charge of the hospital — he was not a Frenchman, nor was he English, and it would be invidious to proclaim his race — ran away from his post. He had a struggle of some days between fear and honor. At last, as the sick were brought in more thickly, honor lost ground. He fled: "L'existence," he said, "avant tout." It was an honest confession, and proved a sort of martyr's creed; for when he came back, after the thing was all over, and the hospital swept up again, clean and neat, he was astonished to find that the Government — British, of course — was taking a harsh view of the matter, and that he was kicked out in disgrace. The straw-paper organs made capital out of the event. The writer of one crushing article crammed for it, like Mr. Pott's young man. John Huss, the early saints of the Church, Savonarola, Cranmer, Sir Thomas More, and Louis the Sixteenth furnished illustrations for this admirable treatise.

Nostrums came into great use. Men, at other times supposed to be of sound mind, went about peppering their noses with camphor powder. Some swathed their bodies with flannel, and some wore as little as they possibly could. Some would, at intervals, apply cold ice to the backbone; others, warm water. Others, again, would breakfast off bitter beer and boiled eggs, and dine on brandy and water and soup. One man wrote to the paper, calling attention to the fact that few Englishmen died of cholera; and that, as he had recently discovered, the English colonists always washed, every morning, all over. This he recommended to his own countrymen, as a thing not, indeed, suddenly to be adopted, but to receive that serious attention and thought which the gravity of the step demanded. For himself, he confessed he sometimes washed his feet, but rarely.

One poor Briton nearly came to terrible grief. He was a mariner; and one evening, finding himself some miles from St. Denys, overcome with liquor, he fell down by the wayside and slumbered. Native policemen, coming by with a cart, gathered him up as one dead; and a grave being already prepared, they laid him in it, fortunately removing the shell. The English clergyman read the service, with sorrow for the poor fellow cut off so suddenly, whose very name was unknown, and who lay there, perhaps, to be looked for, many a weary day, by wife and children. He had finished, and they began heaving in the earth. As soon as it fell upon his face, the shock awakened him. Starting up, still unsteady, he began to bawl out, " Ahoy there!—ahoy!" The aborigines fled, howling in terror; nor would they ever accept any other version of the story than that it was a veritable post-mortem appearance, a spectre, that greeted them. And the churchyard is haunted by it to this day.

As for the sailor, he was taken home by the clergyman, and took the pledge, which he kept till he got to the next port. But he always swore he would never get drunk again in Palmiste.

They were not all cowards. Brave deeds were done. Foremost of all, the brave deeds of the divine Sisters of Mercy. If I die poor and alone, forlorn and deserted, may one of these ministering angels come to me with her sweet, unlovely face, and passionless tenderness of heart! Then may she make me a Catholic, or a Ritualist, or any thing she like,—all for dear memory of the things I have known her sisters do. . For to them all duties are equally holy and equally divine. To them is nothing loathsome, nothing revolting; no form of disease or suffering too terrible to help; no accumulations of misery and poverty, no development of sickness, sufficient to keep them away.

Is it fair, without mentioning a living man's name, to mention his deeds? Perhaps he will never see it in print. This is what he did. In the height of the cholera, two coolie ships put into port, both with cholera raging on board. They were promptly sent off to quarantine off an islet —a mere rock, half a mile across—twenty miles away.

Thence, after some time, news came somehow to Palmiste that their apothecary was dead, and the captain, and all the English sailors but a few. And all the coolies were dying with cholera. Who would go there? One young army surgeon stepped out, so to speak, from the ranks. To go there was to go to certain death. It was a forlorn hope. There would be no one to help him, no one to talk to even; no one to attend *him* if he was seized. He went. For weeks he struggled with the pestilence, saving some from the jaws of death, and burying others. The place, which was a mere charnel-house, he turned into a hospital,—a Hôtel Dieu. The poor, terror-stricken Indians slowly regained hope, and therefore health; and, when the evil time died away, he was able to bring back half at least of his flock, rescued from death.

It is a heroism that is beyond the power of any Victoria Cross to reward; and when it fires the blood, and sets the heart aglow of him that reads it, the doer of the geste has his fittest crown of glory, though he never hear of it.

In the country, away down at Fontainebleau, they were comparatively safe. Few cases happened on the estate in the earlier stage; but when it began to leave town it broke out in the country. Mr. Durnford took no precautions. In these matters he thought it was like a battle-field. You could not, he said, devise any armor against a cannon-ball.

"Obsairve," said Mr. MacIntyre, taking a nip of brandy, " some men are killed by a bayonet thrust."

But one evening, when Phil and Arthur crme home from a stroll with their guns, they found MacIntyre in a state of wild alarm on the veranda. Mr. Durnford had been seized. No doctor had been sent for, because none was within twenty miles. They had no medicine, except brandy. Mr. MacIntyre had been giving him copious draughts. He had taken a bottle and a half without the smallest effect; and now Mr. MacIntyre, seeing the boys go into the bedroom, retreated to the other side of the house, and began to drink the rest of the bottle, glad to be relieved of his charge.

There was very little hope. They sent off a dozen messengers for as many doctors; but, with the utmost speed, no doctor could arrive before morning.

All night long they watched and tended him. Mr. MacIntyre by this time, what with terror and brandy, was helpless. They could do literally nothing. But in the morning came collapse, and comparative ease. The dying man lay stretched on his back, breathing painfully, but conscious. Philip bent over him, and whispered, with dry eyes and hard voice, while Arthur was sobbing on his knees, —

"Father, tell me of my mother."

Mr. Durnford turned his head and looked. He would have spoken; but a trembling seized his limbs, and his eyes closed in death.

He was buried the next morning. All the people on the estate went to the funeral. But Mr. MacIntyre was absent. For in the night a thought struck him. It was but a week since he had received, in hard cash, the half year's salary due to him. Now he saw his occupation gone. Without any chance of finding employment in the island, he would be left stranded. He was staggered at first. Then he reflected that no one knew of the payment except his late employer. How if he could get the receipt? So, when the funeral procession started, Mr. MacIntyre staid behind, — no one noticing his absence.

The house clear, he stole into the dead man's room. His desk was open, just as he had left it. Here was a chance which it was impossible to resist.

"It makes my heart bleed to wrong the lads," said MacIntyre, wiping his eyes; "but one must consider one's self."

Then he looked out the receipt from the file, and put it into his pocket. That done, he searched for the private account book, which also fell into his coat-tail pocket. Then it occurred to him that it would be an admirable thing to get a whole year's salary instead of a half, and he began to hunt for the previous receipt. This he could not find, though he searched everywhere. But he found something which interested him; and he wrapped it in brown paper, and took it also away with him. It was a big, fat book, with clasps and a small letter padlock, marked "Private." He went down to his cottage, and cutting open the clasps, he read it from end to end.

It was a sort of irregular journal, beginning sixteen years before. It opened with a confession of passion for Marie.

"If this girl were but a lady, — if only, even, she were not colored — I would take her away and marry her. Why should I not marry her? What difference does it make to me whether people approved of it or not?

. . . .

"I saw Marie to-day. She met me in the garden behind her mistress's house. How pretty the child looked, with a rose in her black hair! She will meet me again this evening."

And so on, all in the same strain.

In the leaves of the book were three short notes, kept for some unknown reason, addressed to his wife; but without date.

Mr. MacIntyre, in a fit of abstraction, took pen and ink, and added a date — that of Philip's birth. There was another paper in the journal: the certificate of marriage of George Durnford and Adrienne de Rosnay. He took this out; and, shutting up the journal, began to reflect.

In the afternoon, when the sun grew low, he went to the little Catholic church which lies hidden away among the trees, about three miles from Fontainbleau.

Just then it was shut up. For Father O'Leary, the jolly Irish priest, who held this easiest of benefices for so many years, had only lately succumbed to age; and, in the disturbed state of the colony, no priest had yet been sent down. The presbytère was closed, the shutters up, and the church door locked.

The tutor went to the back of the house; forced his way in with no difficulty, by the simple process of removing a rotten shutter from the hinges.

Hanging on the wall were the church keys. He took these, and stepped across the green to the vestry door, which he opened, and went in shutting it after him, whistling very softly to himself.

Then he opened the cupboard, and took down the two duplicate church registers of marriage. They were rarely used; because in that little place there were few people to get married except the Indians, who always went before the registrar. Turning over the leaves, which were sticking together with damp, — Father O'Leary was always the most careless of men, — he came to a place where one double page had been passed over. The marriage immediately before it was dated twenty years since; that after it sixteen. He looked at the duplicate register. No such omission of a page had occurred.

Whistling softly, he filled up the form between Marie — no other name — and George Durnford, gentleman, for a date about a year before Philip's birth. Then he attested it himself, — "Alexander MacIntyre," — in a fine bold, hand; forged the signatures of the others; and added, as a second witness, the mark of one Adolphe. Then he rubbed his hands, and began to consider further.

After this, he got the forms of marriage certificates, and filled one up in due form, again signing it with the name of the deceased Father O'Leary. Then he replaced that one of the two books in which he had written the forgery, put the forged certificate in his pocket, and the other register under his arm; then locked up the cupboard.

When he had finished his forgeries he looked into the church. The setting sun was shining through the west window full upon the altar, set about with its twopenny gewgaw ornaments. He shook his head.

"A blind superstition," he murmured. "We who live under the light of a fuller gospel have vara much to be thankful for."

He went back to the presbytère, replaced the keys, and walked home with his register in his hands.

He had no servant, and was accustomed, when he did not dine at Fontainebleau, to send an Indian boy to the nearest shop to buy some steak, which he curried himself. He went into the kitchen, — a little stone hut built at the back of the cottage, — lit a fire of sticks, and proceeded to burn the register and Mr. Durnford's private journal.

The book would not burn at all, being damp and mouldy.

"At this rate of progression," he remarked, "I shall be a twal'month getting through them. Let us bury them."

He dug a hole in a corner close to his house, buried his books, piled the earth over them, and cooked his dinner with a cheerful heart.

"A good day's work," he murmured. "Half a year's salary gained, and the prospect of a pretty haul, if good luck serves. Marie dead, O'Leary dead, one register gone, the certificates in my possession. Master Phil, my boy, the time will perhaps come when you will be glad to buy my papers of me."

Mr. Durnford's death showed that he had become a rich man. All his property went by will to "my son," while of Philip no notice whatever was taken. Only the lawyer wrote him a letter, stating that by a special deed of gift, dated some years back, a sum of money was made over to him, which had been accumulating at compound interest, and had now amounted to five thousand pounds. This, at Palmiste interest, was five hundred pounds a year. As his father had told him, it was his sole provision.

Philip's heart was stung with a sense of wrong. That no mention was made of him; that, through all his life, he had not received one word of acknowledgment or affection; that he had been evidently regarded as a mere encumbrance and a debt, — rankled in his bosom. He said nothing, not even to Mr. MacIntyre, who, now that he had no longer any further prospect of employment, began to turn his thoughts to other pastures: but he brooded over his wrongs; and now only one thought possessed him, — to escape from a place which was haunted by shame.

Arthur, too, wanted to go; and their lawyer and adviser took passages for the boys, and gave them proper letters to those who were to take care of them in England, till they were of age.

Mr. MacIntyre, the day before they started, came to say farewell. He had an interview with each of his pupils separately. To Arthur, by way of a parting gift, he propounded a set of maxims for future guidance, including a rule of conduct for morals, which he recommended on the ground of having always adhered to it himself; and he left his late pupil with a heavier purse, and consequently a lighter heart. Mr. MacIntyre, in all of his troubles, had never yet wanted money. As a Scotchman, he never spent when he could avoid spending.

His conversation with Philip was of greater importance. With much hesitation, and an amount of nervousness that one would hardly have expected of him, he hinted that he was possessed of certain information, but that the time was not yet arrived to make use of it. And then, biting his nails, he gave the young man to understand, that, if he ever did use it, he should expect to be paid.

"But what is your knowledge?" asked Philip; "and if you have any, why, in the Devil's name, don't you let it out at once? And how much money do you want?"

Mr. MacIntyre leaned forward, and whispered in his ear.

"Suppose my information proved your mother's marriage? Suppose that a man — I'm not for saying that I should be the man — brought all this to light?"

"Poor Arthur!" said Philip.

"That's not the point," urged the other. "To be plain. What would that information be worth?"

"I don't know."

"Should we say five thousand pounds?"

"You mean, that I am to give you five thousand pounds for giving information which you ought to give for nothing? MacIntyre you're a scoundrel?"

"Eh! mon," replied the moralist. "Can you give me these proofs?" cried Philip, his voice rising.

"No, I cannot — not yet. And perhaps I never shall be able to do so. Whether I do or not, depends upon yourself. And don't be violent, Mr. Philip Durnford. Remember," he added, with a touch of pathetic dignity, "that you are addressing your old tutor, and a Master of Arts of the Univairsity of Aberdeen."

"Go to the devil!" said Philip, "and get out of this. Go, I say!"

I am grieved to say that Arthur, who was sitting outside, was startled by the fearful spectacle of his reverend tutor emerging with Philip's hand in his collar, and Philip's right foot accelerating his movements.

It was all done in a moment. Mr. MacIntyre vanished round the corner, and his pony's hoofs were speedily heard clattering down the road.

Arthur looked up for explanation.

"Never mind, old boy," said Philip. "The man's a scoundrel. He's a liar, too, I believe. Arthur, give me your hand. I have been worried lately a good deal; but I won't wrong you; remember that. Whatever happens — you shall not be wronged."

The next night they were steaming gallantly away. The headlands of Palmiste lay low on the horizon as the sun set, and touched them with his magic painter's brush.

Arthur took off his cap, and waved it.

"When shall we see the dear old place again, Phil?" he said, with a sob in his throat.

"Never, I hope," said Philip. "It will be to me a memory of sickly sorrow and disappointment. Never. And now, old boy, hurrah for England and my commission! I am going to forget it all."

He stood there with the bright look of hope and fearlessness that so soon goes out of the eyes of youth, and the sea-breeze lifting his long black hair, a possible — nay, a certain hero. It is something in every man's life for once to have been at peace with God, — for once to have thrilled with the warm impulse of true nobility.

BOOK II. — AT HOME.

CHAPTER I.

HOME in England. It is ten years later on. We are in Gray's Inn, on a certain Saturday evening early in the year. The chambers where we are met, like most of those in that ancient hostelry, have the appearance of untidiness. Unlike most, they are clean and carefully dusted. The furniture is well worn, but comfortable, — easy chairs with bits of the padding sticking out here and there, and the leather gone in parts. The books are those of a man who regards binding less from an artistic than from a useful point of view, and is not careful to preserve their beauty, — in other words, the books are greatly battered. There is one table littered with papers: among them may be seen some in a girl's handwriting. One of the bookcases is filled altogether with books not often found in a bachelor's room, — children's books, books a little more grown up, and books of education. In the window-seat is a work-basket. On the mantle-shelf stands a glass full of violets. There are antimacassars on the worn old chairs and sofas; and amid the general air of bachelordom, pipes, and lazy ease, there is, one feels, a suspicion of some younger element, the handiwork of a girl, — the breath of youth and grace, — in these rooms whose walls are so dingy, whose ceilings are so black, whose furniture is so battered.

The tenant of this room is Mr. Hartley Venn, who is now standing on the hearthrug in the act of receiving his visitors. Of these, one is his old friend Lynn, of the Inner Temple, — a grave man, who seldom speaks and never laughs. He is sitting by the fire with a pipe in his hand, not yet lighted, stroking his heavy mustache. The other is our old friend Arthur Durnford, — a tall man now, of four or five and twenty, not long come up to town from Oxford: a man of slight proportions, and somewhat stooping shoulders. He wears his fair hair rather longer than most men, and a light fringe adorns his upper lip. A face of more sweetness than power; a face which may command love and respect, but scarcely fear; a face at which women glance twice in the street, because there are in it such vast possibilities of tenderness. He has not been a successful student, if you measure success by the schools. A second class rewarded his labors, it is true; and Arthur retired content, if not greatly pleased, at the result. Success he did not greatly care for; and he was too rich and too lazy to descend into the arena, and fight with other men. Poverty has its rights as well as its duties; and among these is a prescriptive law, — often enough violated, — that the rich should keep out of the battle. Remember this, if you please, Messieurs the Archbishops, Prime and other ministers, Deans and dignitaries; and next time you condescend to forward your invaluable, if prosy, contributions to current literature, reflect that they are taken — and would be taken, if they were bad enough to corrupt the taste of a whole generation — for the name that they bear. Then, be humble; or, better still, don't send the rubbish at all, — I mean the words of wisdom, — and let some poor penny-a-liner get the guineas. But Arthur Durnford's disposition led him rather to seclude himself, and to forget that, with all but a chosen few, life is a conflict. He was born for but one object, dilettante literature, — the investigation of the useless, the recovery of lost worthlessness, the archæological investigation of forgotten lumber; but of this, his high mission, he is yet all unaware, and is at present starting quite unconsciously in that road, which will eventually lead him to distinction. For the rest, a heart as innocent and a life as blameless as any girl's, and, like that of most girls, a life as devoid of any active interest or any benefit to other people. Some men are born for this kind of passive life. Their years float along in a kind of dream, or among occupations which interest without exciting, and occupy without wearying. Well for them if, as with Arthur, accident has given them the means to gratify their inclinations.

Venn is the son of his father's old tutor, and therefore, he explains, a kind of uncle to him. And to-night is the first time they have met. Venn found out Arthur himself, from some Oxford friend and "information received."

"Durnford," he explains, introducing him to Lynn, "is my educational nephew. I am his tutorial uncle. That is, his father was a private pupil at the rectory, when I was six years old. Your father afterwards went to Palmiste Island, I believe; yes, and made a fortune there — by — by — doing those things and practising those arts by which fortunes are made, did he not?"

Arthur laughed, and said such was the case.

"Palmiste Island is of a more simple nature than London, Lynn; that is the reason why you and I, in spite of our merit, have not got money. Now that you know Mr. Arthur Durnford, we will proceed to elect him, if you please, an honorary member of the Chorus."

The ceremony of election gone through, Arthur took an easy chair, and Venn proceeded to put bottles and glasses on the table. Then he took up a position on the hearth-rug, and, with his coat-tails under his arm, turned to Lynn.

"The preliminary oration, Lynn?"

"You make it," said Lynn, who had by this time lighted his pipe.

Venn bowed solemnly, and put on an air of great meditation, stroking his mustache. Presently he began, —

"It is customary, at the election of a new member into this society, to instruct him in the nature of the duties and responsibilities he is about to undertake. In the mysteries of the Cabeiri" —

"Pass two thousand years," growled Lynn.

Venn bowed gravely.

"In deference to the opinion of my learned brother, I pass to modern times. In the mysteries of Freemasonry, it is popularly supposed that the candidate for admission is put to bodily pain before receiving the terms of an oath so tremendous that the secrets of the craft have remained undisclosed from the time of Solomon, and Hiram, King of Tyre, to the present moment. The fraternity of the Chorus heats no poker, and administers no oath; and one penalty only awaits the offender, — we expel him."

"Was any one ever expelled?" asked Durnford.

"One, sir, was only last week expelled for levity. His name was Jones. Jones, at least, will never more be privileged to sit in the Chorus."

Here a loud knock was heard at the door. Lynn opened it. It was Jones.

The orator, no way disconcerted, shook hands with the new arrival with a greater show of delight than his words absolutely warranted, saying, as he pushed him into a chair, —

"Why do you come here, man void of shame? Did you not distinctly understand that you were never to appear again on Chorus nights?"

The new-comer, who was a smooth-faced, bright-eyed little man in glasses, sat down, and immediately began to twinkle.

"I come as a simple spectator," he said. "I cannot keep away.

'From sport to sport, concealment's guile
Preys on this heart of mine;
And, when the worm provokes a smile,
I drown the grief in wine.'"

"Why," said Venn, "he is positively doing it again! Miserable man! was it not for this we expelled you?"

"It was," said Jones with a groan. "It is chronic. I am truly wretched."

"Silence, then; and you, young candidate, listen. The Chorus was established ten years ago as a refuge for the unsuccessful. It was intended to answer the purposes, in a small degree, of a literary and artistic club, — admitting, however, only those professional unfortunates who can achieve no success. It is a club of the unfortunate.

When fortune comes to one of us, he shakes his wings, and goes. We who remain wrap ourselves in the cloak of poverty and neglect, and meet mischance with smiles. Of the original twelve who formed the first brotherhood, there remain but Lynn and myself. We do not care now greatly to enlarge the circle. Jones, here, was admitted five years ago. He is but a chicken in disappointment, and has only just begun to wait. I have already told you that he was expelled, and why."

"Not," said Jones solemnly —

"'Not for a crime he did, nor 'cause
He broke their own or nature's laws;
But for a simple trick he had
Of quoting what he learned and read.'"

Arthur began to feel as if he were standing on his head. The other two took no notice of the interruption.

"Society takes no heed of these unfortunates. They are legion. They occupy that middle ground which is above a small success, and cannot achieve a great one. Lynn, here, would scorn to be an Old Bailey barrister. Yet he could do it admirably. He goes in for Equity, sir, and gets no cases, nor ever will. Jones, I am sorry that you *must* be excluded. Jones, amongst other things, makes plays. No manager has yet put one on the stage."

"The manager of the Lyceum is reading my last play now," said Jones.

"He always is," said Venn. "I am, for my own part, a writer. I write a great deal. Some evening, when Jones is not here, I will read you a portion of my works."

"Pray," said Jones, "why not when I am here?"

"Because," said Venn, "the last time I read you an essay you fell fast asleep."

"I did," said Jones; "so did everybody."

"I have, at times, offered my productions to editors. They invariably refuse them. Under these circumstances, I retire into myself, and put together the Opuscula which will one day be eagerly bought by an admiring public. On that day Lynn will be made Lord Chancellor, Jones will get a play acted which will run for three hundred nights, and the Chorus will dissolve.

"You are to understand, then" — after a pause, during which Jones pulled out his handkerchief, and wiped his eyes in grief at the prospect of dissolution — "that we meet here weekly between the 1st of October and the 1st of April. During the week and in the summer vacation, we make observations which are afterwards communicated to the Chorus. Thus we form a running commentary on passing events, which will contain, when published, an admirable collection of maxims calculated both to inform and instruct. They are chiefly of a moral tendency. Excluded by our misfortunes from taking an active part in the drama of life, we stand by and remark. We are mostly resigned to our position. Some, however, aspire. Dolphin, for instance — you remember Dolphin, Lynn?"

He grunted.

"Observe the dissatisfied air with which Lynn receives that name. Dolphin aspired. He now edits 'The Daily Gazette,' and pays a fabulous income tax. Of all the excellent remarks that have been made in this room, Dolphin's were the poorest. Waterford, too, another instance. He now leads a circuit. Jones, what are you pursing up your lips about? If you have any thing to say, get rid of it."

"I was thinking of Tennyson's lines," said Jones, with great softness of manner.

"'Prate not of chance — the name of luck
Is blown the windy ways about;
And yet I hold, without a doubt,
He prospers most who has most pluck.'"

"Are those Tennyson's words?" asked Durnford, taken off his guard.

"You will find them in the two hundred and fortieth page of 'In Memoriam,'" said Jones readily. "The stanza begins with the well-known lines, —

'Balloon, that, through the fleecy rings
Of bosomed cloud and mottled sky,
Floatest athwart the wondering eye,
A wingèd eagle without wings.'"

"And this creature," said Venn, "aspires to be a dramatist. Let me finish. The one unfailing rule, which is alone incapable of being rescinded, is the rule of success. Any man who succeeds is turned out. *Ipso facto*, he ceases to be a member of the association. Success is of all kinds, and we admit of no excuse or palliation — the offender goes."

"How if he write a book which does not sell, but is yet praised?"

"He may, when his failure is quite established, remain with us. More — we allow him to be damned any number of times. Jones's works, for instance: his novel" —

Here Jones visibly blushed.

"It was really very bad, and no one took the least notice of it — not even the reviewers. Did any one buy a copy, Jones?"

"I believe," he said, "that there are still a few copies on the publishers' helves. These can be had now at a reduction. The published price was thirty-one shillings and sixpence."

"Your poems, Jones?"

"My poems," said the bard, "were not meant to be sold: I *give* them to my country."

"It is very liberal of you. I will presently detail my own experiences of failure. Suffice it now to remark that I have never succeeded in any thing. You will find in me, sir, as my friends have already found in me, a very Tupper in *posse*. I am the representative man of mediocrity — am I not, Lynn?"

The grave Lynn nodded.

"You say so."

"I will now give you — as Jones is not wholly acquainted with my fortunes, as Lynn is a good listener, as you ought to know something about me, and as it gives a sort of early Bulwer-Lytton, or even a Smollett-like air to the evening's talk — a brief sketch of the career of an unsuccessful man. Jones, will you kindly undertake the bottle and jug department? Lynn, be so good as to put the kettle on. Durnford, my dear boy, take tobacco, and help yourself to drink. Claret is there, which I do not recommend. That bottle of champagne is remarkable for its age. It is coeval with the Chorus. Ten years have passed since it left its native public. It is not to be opened, but stands there for respectability's sake. There is port, if you like: it is not good. Sherry is in the middle bottle. You can open it, if you please; but I should not advise you to do so. The bottled beer I can strongly recommend, and the Irish whiskey is undeniable. Jones, you rhyming wretch, what will you take? Lynn, I have your permission to talk tonight."

"Stop!" said Jones. "Have you got any thing to say before he begins, Lynn? Have you, Durnford? This is your only chance. For my own part, I can only say, with the poet Wordsworth, —

'Not the whole warbling grove in concert heard,
So gladdens me as this loquacious bird.'"

"Proceed, Venn," said Lynn, "and quickly; for Jones is bubbling with another quotation."

"I will try not to be tedious. I began life rather well, for I got into Eton as a colleger, and actually gained a considerable quantity of prizes. I also learned to wear my hat at the back of my head, to despise trade, to run bills, to make Latin verses, to regard science and mathematics with a proper and reasonable contempt, and to consider Eton as the apex of civilization, ancient and modern. So far, I resembled other boys. Occasionally I was flogged. And I very early formed the germ of that grand idea which I have since made the subject of an admirable essay."

Jones wagged his head solemnly; whether from admiration, envy, sympathy, approval, or some other emotion, was never known.

"It is that all the mischiefs of the world are due to the insufficient manner in which boys are flogged. Some, sir, I am ashamed to say, are never flogged at all. Jones, you were never flogged."

"I was not," said Jones. "If it is any extenuation of my master's crime, I may mention that he often caned me."

"I knew it," Venn returned, with an air of triumph. "There are subtle influences about the older and more classical instrument. It produces an effect which, in after life, is only to be detected by those who have made an early acquaintance with it. Caning is merely a brutal mode of inflicting fear and pain. The poetry of punishment is in the birch. The actual performance, I admit — the mere physical process, either active or passive — affords little food for reflection; but when I think of the effects upon the sufferer, I am carried away, gentlemen, efferor. There is the anticipation, so full of tumultuous fears and hopes, with its certainties as to the future fact, and its uncertainties as to vigor and duration; its bracing influence of the volition, its stimulating effect on the fortitude, its cultivation of patient endurance. All this, my friends, is truly poetical. Consider, next, the after-glow. The after-glow is, indeed, a magnificent combination of sensations. Nothing that I can remember to have experienced comes near it. It lingers like the twilight; and, like the summer twilight, it lasts all night. It warms like the memory of a good action, or the blush of conscious virtue. It is as soothing as the absolution of a bishop. It removes as many cares as a confession, and it wipes off sins like a pilgrimage."

He paused for a moment, and looked round. There was a murmur of applause, Jones rubbing his leg with a painful air of sympathetic abstraction.

"Let us go back to Eton. I was in the sixth, and stood well to get into King's. Unfortunately, the vacancy that should have been mine came too late by half an hour. I had till twelve on my last day, and a messenger bringing news of a vacancy arrived, having loitered on the way, at half-past twelve. The man, gentlemen, died young. I say nothing about Nemesis — I merely ask you to observe that he died young. So I went to St. Alphege. You, Lynn, were at the same time at Trinity. At St. Alphege's, which is not a large college, we passed our time in intellectual pursuits which were not among those encouraged by the Senate. This body, Durnford, which resembles a similar institution at Oxford, having, after long consideration, found out the most useless branch of science and the least useful method of studying classical literature, has fixed upon these as the only means of arriving at any of the University distinctions. I could not do mathematics, as I have said; and, as they would not let me take classical honors without knowing how to graduate the common steelyard, and such useful scraps of knowledge, I was fain to go out in the Poll. Sir, if it had not been for the invention of that infernal steelyard — an instrument which I have never seen, and never had the least necessity or desire to graduate, — I should this day have been a Fellow of St. Alphege's.

"Having failed here, I returned home. I found my family in some little confusion. My brother Bob, — you have met Bob, Lynn?"

Lynn nodded.

"An excellent fellow, Lynn, — most good-hearted man, though he had his faults," — here Venn rubbed his nose meditatively. "Bob had just taken a stand. He announced resolutely, and without any chance of misunderstanding, that he was never going to do any more work. The line he took was this. He said, 'I am not clever enough to get money. I am clever enough to look at other people getting money. Perhaps a life of contemplation, for which I am evidently intended, will lead to greater results than a life of work. I simply, therefore, say to the world in general, and my family in particular, Keep me. Give me a sufficiency to eat and drink.'"

"And how did the world receive this demand?"

"That very small portion of the external world that ever heard it declined to interfere. But out of my father — who, though quite unable to see Bob's logical position, could not let him starve, — he got a sufficiency to eat, and more than a sufficiency to drink. However, Bob having taken this unexpected line, I had to keep myself; and did, after a fashion, till Bob and my father died. Poor Bob! You remember him, Lynn, coming out of the Crown, with his elbows squared, quite drunk, and arguing with the policeman? Admirable traits of character were in that man. His wife allowed him a shilling a day, and his whole study latterly was how to make the most of the money. It went in six drinks; and each drink involved a pipe and an animated discussion in the tap-room. Bob, you see, miscalculated his forces. He had not the physique to stand up against a long course of leisure, and he succumbed. When he died, at the early age of thirty-five, he sent for me, and made over to me, with his usual kindness and thoughtfulness of heart, all he had to give me, — the care of his wife and boy.

"At this time, I was working for a living, — never mind how, — I got it, but only just got it. Every attempt that I made to do any thing better for myself failed. I had no energy, they said; or else no perseverance, or no luck, or no determination, and so on: you know the kind of talk. The fruits of life turned, when I touched them, to Dead-Sea apples. Then I complicated matters by falling in love."

"Did you?" said Lynn. "I never knew that before."

"Yes, I was in love. Oh, yes! for some months before I ventured to speak, and for some months after."

"What did she say?"

"She said, 'No,' in a very decided and resolute manner. I did not so much mind that, as I did the way in which she behaved afterwards. I made then the discovery that there is nothing in the world which more puffs out and inflates a woman with pride, than the fact, that she has had the heroism to refuse a man. For at least three months after my rejection, there was the mightiest feminine clucking ever heard about it. Her strength was overtasked, they said; and all the family went to Madeira with her. No one asked after my strength; and I staid in London, and was regarded as a sort of involuntary murderer."

"Did she die, then?" asked Lynn.

"Oh, no! — not at all. She came back, very fat. She is in London now; still unmarried, and likely to continue so. It may sound uncharitable; but, in the interests of husbands, I do hope that such a model of womanly heroic virtue may never be married."

"I also," said Jones, "have had my share of blighted affections."

"Have you, too, been in love?" asked Lynn.

"I have," sighed Jones. "A most unfortunate attachment, — an impossible attachment. Yet the dream was pleasant while it lasted."

He held his head down, blushing modestly, and went on, in a broken voice, —

"As a boy — slopes — Windsor — one of the princesses. Not my fault originally — mine to nurse the passion."

"Which was it?"

"The prettiest, sir."

"But how, when, where could *you* speak with the princess?"

"We never interchanged words; but the eye spoke — at seventy yards. Poor thing! she's married now. I hope she got over it. I did after a time."

Venn, bearing the interruption with an air of sufferance, resumed his history.

"Getting over my love difficulties, I resolved to fall into love no more, and went out of society. I have kept out ever since; and, on the whole, I prefer being out. Then I began to write; and the real story of my failure begins. You see, I was not absolutely obliged to do any thing when my father died, but I fondly hoped to make literature a staff. It has never been to me even a reed. I had, of course, faint glimmerings of success, gleams of hope. Every time Tantalus stoops to the water, he fancies that this time, at least, he will reach it; and I think that every now and then he gets a few drops — not enough to quench his thirst, but enough to revive hope. My gleams of success were like that poor convict's drops of water. They led to nothing more. I fancy every editor in London knows me now. They say, 'Oh! here's Hartley Venn again;' and I go into the rejected pigeon-holes. So complete is my failure, that even my own people have ceased to believe in me, — so complete, that I have ceased to believe in myself."

He paused; and, mixing a glass of whiskey and water, drank half of it off.

"You will remark — proceeding on the inductive method — those whom God destines to fail, he endows with excellent spirits. Jones is a case in point" —

"Why should sorrow o'er this forehead
Draw the veil of black despair?
Let her, if she will, on your head;
Mine, at least, she still will spare."

This was Jones's interruption.

"I am, also, myself a case in point. Lynn is not, which is one reason why I fear he will some day desert me. My own equable temper is not, however, wholly due to birth — partly to circumstances. You will understand me, Lynn, when I explain that when quite a little boy I used to sleep in the same bed with my brother Bob."

"Not the least in the world," observed Lynn.

"Dear me! The way was this. We had a wooden bed against the wall. Bob gave me the inside, and insisted on my lying quite straight on the edge, while he rolled up in the middle. By this arrangement, I got the wood to sleep on, and the wall to keep my back warm, with such small corners of blanket as I could wrest from Bob as soon as he went to sleep. If immediate effects led to open repining, I incurred punishment at once. I learned a lesson from Bob, for which I have never ceased to thank him, in resignation — cheerful, if possible — to the inevitable. Whenever, as happened to me this morning, I get a MS. sent back, I say to myself, 'For this were you prepared in early life by the wood and the wall.'"

Quoth Jones readily, —

"You remember, of course, those lines in Bunyan, quoted, I think, by Lord Willbewill? Observe the Bunyanesque turn of the second line, with its subtlety of thought: —

'He that is down may fear no fall;
The monk may wear his hood:
Give me, for moral warmth, the wall;
For moral bed, the wood.'

It was the answer to a riddle asked by the prince at the banquet given when Mansoul was taken, and Diabolus evicted. It follows the conundrum of the Red Cow, and is omitted in some editions."

"Thank you very much," said Venn, not smiling. "I have only one or two more observations to make. The curious in the matter of unsuccess may consult, if they think fit, my unpublished Opuscula. They will find there, clearly set forth, the true symptoms of an unsuccessful man. Thus, he may be known — not to be tedious — first, by his good spirits, as I have said; secondly, by his universal sympathy; thirdly, his extraordinary flow of ideas; fourthly, by a certain power of seeing analogies; and fifthly, by his constantly being in opposition. At all times he is a heretic. The mere fact of a thing being constituted by authority is sufficient to make him see, in more than their true force, the arguments on the opposite side."

"You remember," interrupted Jones, with a sweet smile, "the lines of" —

"Stop, Jones," cried Venn, "I will not endure it. Lynn, I have finished. We will now, gentlemen, talk of general topics."

They talked, as usual, till late in the night. It was past three o'clock when Venn said, —

"This reminds me of a passage in my essay on 'The Art of Success.' I will read it you. The night is yet young. Where are the Opuscula?"

They looked at each other in dismay. Venn searched for the essay everywhere; not finding it, he remembered that he had taken it to bed with him the night before, and went into the next room to get it. When he returned, with his precious paper in his hand, the room was empty, and there were sounds of rapidly retreating footsteps on the stairs; for all had fled. He shook his head in sorrow rather than in anger, and, looking at his watch, murmured, —

"A general exodus. They have left the

Desert of the Exodus. Past three o'clock! An hour's sleep before daybreak is worth three after it. Shall I have my beauty sleep? No: the cultivation of the intellect before all. Hartley Venn, my dear boy, had you always borne that in mind you would not now be the wreck you are."

He sat down and read, with an admiring air, the whole of his long paper from beginning to end. Then he gave a sigh of contentment and weariness, and went to bed as the first gray of the spring morning was lighting up the sky.

CHAPTER II.

HARTLEY VENN — whose account of himself to Arthur was, on the whole, correct — is at this time, a man of eight and thirty. In the course of his life he has tried a good many things, and failed in every one. He possesses a little income of between three and four hundred a year, comfortably housed in consols, where he allows his capital to lie undisturbed, being as free as any man in the world from the desire to get rich. He is by actual profession a barrister, having been called twelve years ago, at Lincoln's Inn. But as he has never opened a law-book in his life, or been inside a court of justice, it may safely be asserted that he would have great difficulties to encounter in the conduct of any case with which a too credulous solicitor might intrust him. Friends anxious to see him "get on," once persuaded him to buy a partnership in an army coaching establishment, the previous proprietor retiring with a large fortune. All went well for a year or two, when, owing to some of their pupils never passing, and both himself and his partner being hopelessly bad men of business, they found themselves, at the beginning of one term, with two pupils to teach. Naturally the affairs of the institution got wound up after this, Hartley being the loser of the fifteen hundred or so which he had invested for his share. Then it was that he retired to Gray's Inn, and took those chambers where we now find him. He then became, as he was fond of calling himself, a literary man, that is, he began that long series of Opuscula, of which mention has already been made. They were never published, because editors invariably declined to accept them: no doubt they were quite right. He was full of reading and scholarship, — full of ideas; but he never acquired that way of putting things which the British public desires.

He disliked revision, too, which bored him; and he had a habit of reading his own things over and over again till he got to know them all by heart, and their very faults appeared beauties. To some men a censor is absolutely necessary. I have often thought of setting myself up as a professed literary adviser, ready to read, correct, suggest, and cut down, at so much per page, — say ten pounds. He had a sort of uneasy consciousness that life would pass away with him without bringing any sort of kudos to him; and though, from force of habit, he still kept note-books, and covered acres of paper yearly, he had begun to look upon his works as precious private property, written for his own recreation and instruction, — a treasure-house of wisdom for those years of old age when his ideas would begin to fail him. There are hundreds of men like him. Reader, thou who hast never looked over a proof-sheet, are there not within thy desk collections of verses, sheets of essays, bundles of tales, which it is thy secret pleasure to read and read, and thy secret hope to publish? Deny it not. We, too, have had this time; and there is no such delight in reading the printed page — especially when the world has received it coldly — as in gloating over the glorious possibilities of the manuscript. What is the miser's joy, as he runs his fingers through the gold, to the young writer's, as he sits, door locked, pen in hand, as modest over the tender fancies of his brain as any young girl at her toilette over her charms?

Venn is a smooth-faced man, with a bright, fresh cheek, — in spite of late hours, — and a light mustache. His hair is perfectly straight; and he shows no signs of getting gray like Lynn, or bald like Jones. His face is long, with a somewhat retreating chin, — sign of weakness, — and a long drooping nose, — the melancholy and reflective nose. He is not a tall man, and his shoulders stoop somewhat. He has still an air of youth; which I think will never leave him, even when his hair is silvery white. And his expression is one of very great sweetness: for he is one who has sympathies for all. They talk of him still at the butteries of his old college, where, in his hot youth, he played many a harmless frolic in his cups, and where he endeared himself to all the servants. Indeed, it was no other than Hartley Venn who bearded the great Master of Trinity himself on that memorable night when, returning unsteadily from a wine, he accosted the doctor leaving the lodge, and there and then challenged him to a discussion on the nature of Jupiter's satellites. It was he, too, — but why recall the old stories? Are they not chronicled at the freshman's dinner-table, handed down to posterity like the legends of King Arthur? The waiters at his favorite places of resort regard him as a personal friend. They whisper secrets as to the best things up; hide away papers for him; tell him even of their family affairs; and sometimes consult him on matters of purely personal importance. It was through Hartley, indeed, that I first conceived the idea that waiters are human beings, with instincts, appetites, and ambitions like the rest of us. It is really the case. And at the British Museum, such was the esteem with which the attendants — he knew all their names, and would ask after their wives and families — regarded him, that he used never to have to wait more than an hour to get his books. And this, as every one who uses the reading-room knows, is the height of civility and attention.

An indolent, harmless, good-hearted man, who could not run in harness; who could do no work that was not self-imposed, and who did no work well except the self-imposed task at which he had been laboring for twelve years, — the education of his little girl.

Everybody in the inn — that is everybody connected with the administration of the place — knew Laura Collingwood. Everybody, too, felt that the production of so admirable a specimen of the English maiden reflected the greatest credit on all parties concerned, — on the benchers, the barristers, the students, the porters, and the laundresses; but especially on Mr. Venn.

It was about twelve years before this time, when Venn first took his chambers, and in the very week when Mrs. Peck, his laundress, began her long career of usefulness with him, that he found one morning, on returning from the Museum, a little child, with long light hair, and large blue eyes, sitting on the steps in the doorway of his staircase, crying with terror at an evil-eyed, solemn old Tom cat, who was gazing at her in a threatening manner behind the railings. Unwashed, dirty, badly dressed, this little rosy-cheeked damsel of six touched Venn's soft heart with pity, and he proposed at first to purchase apples, a proposition which he carried into effect; and leaving her with a handful of good things, proceeded up stairs with a view to commit to paper some of those invaluable thoughts which were seething in his brain. Presently, to his astonishment, the child followed him up like a little terrier, and, sitting down gravely upon the hearth-rug, began to talk to him with perfect confidence. Thereupon he perceived that here was a new friend for him.

"What is your name, absurd little animal?" he asked.

"Lollie Collingwood."

"And who are your amiable parents, Miss Lollie Collingwood, and what may be their rank in life? Where's your mother, little one?"

"Mother's dead."

"Father too?"

"Got no father. Grandmother told me to sit still on the steps. Only the cat came. Here's grandmother."

Grandmother was no other than Mrs. Peck herself. Later on, she explained to Venn that her daughter, who had left her to go into service, and was a "likely sort o' gal" to look at, had come back to her the year before with the child.

"Said her name was Mrs. Collingwood. Said her husband was dead. Oh! dear-a-dear-a-me! Said he was a gentleman. And here was the baby, — great girl already. And then she pined away and died. And never a word about her husband's relations; and the child for me to keep, and all. And bread's rose awful."

Hartley took the child on his knees, and looked at it more closely. As he looked, thinking what a sad lot hers would be, the little girl turned up her face to him, and laughed, putting up her lips to be kissed with such a winning grace that Hartley's eyes ran over.

"I'll help you with the child, Mrs. Peck," he said; "don't be afraid about it. Will you be my little girl, Lollie?"

"I'se your little girl now," said the child. And they gave each other the first of many thousand kisses.

"Now, wait here with grandmother, while I go to get some things for you."

He set her down, and went to the establishment of a young lady, with whom he had a nodding acquaintance, devoted to the dressmaking mystery. The lady, by great good luck, had a complete set of clothes for sale, — property of somebody else's little girl, deceased, and, by invitation of Venn, went round to his chambers, where, first by the aid of warm water and soap, Dame Nature's handiwork was made to look clean and white; and then, with needle and thread and scissors, the child was arrayed in what to her was unspeakable grandeur.

"That's my little girl, Miss Nobbs," said Hartley looking at the result with beaming eyes.

"Well, I'm sure, Mr. Venn! You might have the good taste not to throw your child in my teeth, I do think."

"My good soul, I didn't. Are your teeth broken. Let me look at them."

Venn, you see, was younger then.

"Ha' done now, Mr. Venn. You and your little girls, indeed!"

"My dear Miss Nobbs, you and I, I am sure, have the greatest possible respect for each other. Do not let me be lowered in your eyes. The child is the granddaughter of my laundress, the aged but still industrious Mrs. Peck."

"Snuffy old woman she is! I can't think how you can have her about you. And that is her grand-daughter?"

"This is her grand-daughter — Miss Laura Collingwood. . I propose, Miss Nobbs, to devote a portion of my leisure moments to the cultivation in this child of those mental accomplishments and graces which have made you the admiration of the quarter."

"Good gracious, Mr. Venn! — you'd talk a donkey's hind leg off. Don't be ridiculous!"

"And, secondly, Miss Nobbs, I propose to ask your assistance in providing her with a set of suitable clothes."

"Now you talk sense. Let's see — she'll want six pr' of socks, two pr' of boots, three new pettikuts, four pr' of — yes, four pr' of" —

"Let us not go into all the details," said Venn. "I need hardly say, Miss Nobbs, that in selecting you out of the many talented and tasteful costumières in our aristocratic and select neighborhood, I rely entirely on that professional skill which" —

"Lord, lord!" said Miss Nobbs, "if all the gentlemen talked like you, where should we all be, I wonder? You let the child come to me to-morrow, and then I'll do all I can for her. You're a good man, I do believe, Mr. Venn, though you are so full of talk."

"Take a glass of wine, Miss Nobbs, and drink the health of Lollie."

This was the beginning of it all. Next day the child was brought round, solemnly arrayed in her new splendor, to be looked at. Hartley kept her with him all the afternoon, and gave her the first glimpse of the alphabet. This he found so amusing, that he repeated it every day until he had taught the child, who was wonderfully quick and intelligent, to read. Then he laid in an immense stock of picture-books, and gave them to his little girl as fast as she could read them; and then he taught her to write.

Three or four years passed on in this way. The afternoon lessons had never been interrupted, save when Venn went away for a fortnight or so in the autumn. They had gradually lengthened out, so as to take up nearly the whole day. Lollie came now between eleven and twelve, and did not go home till six, arrangements being made with a neighboring purveyor to send up luncheon to Mr. Venn every day at two, which was Lollie's dinner. She was then ten or eleven years old, — a child with long fair curls hanging down her back, knuckly elbows, and long legs, such as most young ladies of her age may show. Only her face is much the same as when Venn picked her up on the doorstep, with a soft, confiding expression. She promises well — little Lollie — to grow up into a beautiful woman.

CHAPTER III.

THE most perfect love and confidence existed between Hartley and the child. They were a strangely assorted pair. He told Lollie, almost as soon as she could understand any thing, all his projects, all his disappointments. She learned to know him with that perfect knowledge which comes of always reading one mind. She knew what he would think, what he would say, what he liked. Her whole life was in him, and all her thoughts borrowed from his; for him, the girl had become a necessary part of his existence. Her education was his pleasure; talking to her the only society he had; she the only person in the world who seemed to care about what he did and how he did it.

When she was ten or eleven, the child had a fever. Then Hartley kept her in his own chambers till she was well again. Her grandmother came, too, — deeply resentful at being put out, but afraid to murmur. When she hovered between life and death, and prattled, when delirious, of green fields, it was Hartley who sat up night after night, watching her with anxious eyes, while the old woman slumbered in the easy-chair; and when she got better, — for it was bright spring weather, — he took her away up the river for a fortnight, where they rowed, and walked, and talked, and the roses came back to little Lollie's cheeks.

There was no question of affection between them, because there was no doubt. Do you think Adam was always bothering to know whether Eve loved him? Rubbish! He knew she did. As for Hartley, what had he to think about but the girl? What had the girl to think about but Hartley? Whom had she to love except him? What grace of life, what sweetness, what joy, what hope, but in him, — her guardian, her teacher, her protector?

The fortnight up the river was the first break Lollie had known from her town life. Henceforth it was her dream, her ideal of all that constitutes real and solid pleasure. She had, before the story begins, one more break in a month by the sea; but this was not the same thing, because there was a third person with them. This was how it came about.

It was autumn, and Hartley was meditating his usual brief flight to the seaside. The girl was sitting in her usual place in the window-seat, with her feet up, a book in her lap, and in her hands some little work.

"Lollie," said Hartley, "how should you like to go to the seaside with me?"

She jumped off the seat with a cry of delight.

"I am not quite certain whether I can manage it; but I am going to try. I shall ask my sister to take you."

Her face fell.

"But that won't be going with you."

"I shall go too. Listen, Lollie. I want you, as you grow up, to grow up a lady. I am teaching you the things that ladies are supposed to learn at schools; but there are some things which I cannot teach you. These you can only learn from a lady. I refer, my child, not to those little dialectic peculiarities, if I may call them so, of our neighborhood"—

"O Mr. Venn! don't say I talk like a little street-girl."

"Not to those idioms," he went on, as if obliged to get rid of one sentence before he could frame another—"invaluable as they are to the philologist, but to the minor details of deportment."

She sat pouting.

"I'm sure you always said I behaved very well."

"So you do, Lollie, my child; and you have always been the best of little girls. That is the reason why you are going to be on your best behavior now. Put on your hat, and walk part of the way with me to Woburn Place, where Sukey lives."

Sukey was Miss Venn. Her real name was Lavinia; but her brothers—Hartley and the unfortunate Bob already mentioned—agreed early in life that so ridiculous a name should be suppressed, and changed it, without her consent, to the homely name by which she was ever after known. She, too, inherited a little money, with a house, from her father, on which she lived in considerable comfort, with the old family servant Anne, and a subordinate maid. She was a fat, comfortable sort of person, now approaching perilously near to forty. She had given up all ideas of matrimony, and chiefly occupied herself with her different curates,—because she never could quite make up her mind between Low and High Church,—and with the little things to eat.

Hartley used to go and see her once in three months or so, every now and then asking her to come and breakfast with him. On these occasions he would provide kidneys,—"to keep up the family tie," he used to say.

Sukey received him with her usual cordiality, and rang the bell for Anne to come up and shake hands with him.

"I am going to the seaside for three weeks, Sukey," said he; "and I want you to come with me."

It was the very first time in his life that Hartley had expressed any desire whatever for his sister's company; and she was, for the moment, taken all aback. It took a considerable time to get her to make up her mind that it would do her good; and it was not till Anne herself interfered despotically that she gave way.

"Very well," said Hartley; "then that's settled. We'll go the day after to-morrow. Oh! I forgot to say that I am taking my little girl with me."

His sister changed color.

"It is for your sake, my dear Sukey," he said persuasively,—"for your sake entirely. Far away from Anne, from your—your pill-box and your little comforts, suppose you were taken ill? So Lollie is to go with us to look after you, and be your companion in hours of solitude."

Sukey fairly burst out laughing.

"My hours of solitude, indeed! Hartley, you are the greatest humbug I ever knew. I am to go with you because you want the child taught to be a lady. Oh, don't tell me! A lady, indeed—the daughter of a laundress!"

"Pardon me, dear Sukey. Her grandmamma occupies that position. Her father was a gentleman. Our grandfather, my sister"—

"Was a bishop, Hartley. Don't forget that, if you please."

"We had two, dear. It may be uncommon; but such is the fact. In our family we had two grandfathers. One of them was, if I may remind you, not wholly unconnected with the wholesale glue and"—

"Don't be provoking! Well, Hartley, though I must say your taking up with the child at all is the most ridiculous thing; and what you are going to do with her I don't know. Yet"—

"Yet you'll go the day after to-morrow, my dear Sukey. Come and breakfast to-morrow at ten. That will not be too late for you. At this season, sister, kidneys attain to a size and flavor unknown as the year advances."

And this was the way in which Lollie got her education.

Time passes on his way; and, as is his wont, takes from one to give to another. Little Lollie grew from a rosy-faced child to a woman, — not so rosy, not so brimful of mirth and glee; but bright, happy, intelligent, and beautiful. Do you know the time — it may be a year, it may be a month, it may be a day or an hour, according to circumstances — which separates the child from the woman? It is a curious time. Watch the young maiden of seventeen. You will find her fitful, fanciful, inclined to long reveries; sometimes impatient and petulant. The old habits of thought are passing away from her, and the new ones are as yet strange and awkward. It is a time of transition. It lasts but a little while; for soon the sweet spring breezes blow, the buds of thought and fancy open into blossom, and your child is a maiden, *tempestiva viro*, — fit for love.

It is at this time that Venn's little girl has arrived. Hartley is conscious, dimly conscious, of a change in her. At times an uneasy feeling crosses him that the old, childish customs must be, some time or other, modified. Then he puts the thought from him, glad to get rid of an unpleasant subject; and things go on the same as before. Not that Lollie thinks any change will ever come. To her, life means reading, playing, working, in the old chambers; and pleasure means going up the river in the summer, or to the theatre in the winter, with her guardian.

It is a Sunday in early spring; one of those which come in April, as warm as a July day, and make the foolish blossoms open out wide in a credulous confidence, which no experience can shake, that the east wind is dead, and has been comfortably buried. "Courage," they say, like Charles Reade's Burgundian soldier, "courage, camarades! le diable est mort." Taking advantage of the weather, Mr. Venn has brought his little girl to Richmond; and they are floating on the river, basking in the sun, — Lollie holding the strings, Venn occasionally dipping his sculls in the water to keep a little way on the boat.

"I've been thinking, Lollie," he begins, after half an hour's silence.

"Don't let us think now. Look at the flecks of sunlight on the water," she replies, "and how the trees are green already. Can you not write a poem on the river, Mr. Venn?"

"What are we to do with each other?" he went on, without noticing her interruption. "We can't go on forever like this, child."

"Don't, Mr. Venn. Let us be happy while we can. Listen! there are the church bells! the church bells!" she went on. "Why have you never taken me to church, Mr. Venn? Why do we not go like other people?"

"There are various reasons why *they* go, none of which seem applicable to us, Lollie. They go because it is respectable: we are not respectable. Poor, we are, it is true, and scrupulously clean, but persons of no occupation, and certainly not respectable. Then a good many worthy people go because it is the custom: it is not our custom. Because they want to wear their best clothes: we, my dear, have no best clothes at all. Because they want a little variety and excitement: you and I take our pleasure less sadly. And some go out of religion and devotion, which we do not feel at present."

She was silent. Somehow, perhaps, she felt that there was a sort of separation between her and that respectable world of which she could only know the outside.

"But when we do feel religious, we shall go, shall we not?" she asked.

Venn nodded. He was full of thought on this new question of the girl's future.

"Here is a water-lily for you, Lollie, — sit steady, — the first of the season.... Let us number up your accomplishments, child. You can play the piano; that is something. You can sing a little, — not much, it is true; your voice being, as Sukey would say, what Providence made it. Very odd that they put all the failures on to Providence! You can read, and talk, and write, French. You know Latin; though why I taught you Latin, I don't know."

"If it was only to read Horace with you," said the girl, half pouting, "I really think you might have taught me something else. With his wine, and his lyre, and his eternal egotism!"

"He should have been here to-day, lying at your feet, Lollie, crowned with myrtle, playing on his lyre, and singing, as he floated down the sunny river, to the spring, —

'Diffugere nives, redeunt jam gramina campis,
   Arboribusque comæ.'"

"Which you translated, the other day, when we read it, —

'The year, for her reasons, keeps changing her seasons.
Now the leaves to the terrace return, and the crocus to Kew.
Earth puts off her seal-skin; and, clad in her real skin,
Smiles bright through her blossoms at spring with its sunshine and dew.'"

Venn laughed.

"Yes, child; that is, I believe, how Horace might have written had he lived in these latter days. You know how to touch the tender place in my heart. If we have any pride, it is in certain portions, unpublished, of the Opuscula, where an imitation touches — we only say touches — the original. But we were talking about Horace. I introduced him to you, you know. Surely you would like him — the fat little man, melancholy because he is getting older — to be with us now?"

"Yes, pretty well; only I suppose he would have tired of us very soon. We are not grand enough for him, you know. Ovid would have been better. He would have told us stories, like those we read together in the 'Metamorphoses,' about Cephalus and Procris, for instance. But no: I think I don't care much for your old poets. I tell you what we will do when the summer comes, Mr. Venn: we will come here with Alfred de Musset, and read 'La Nuit de Décembre,' for contrast, while the sun is high over our heads, in the shade of a willow, — sometimes what? I sometimes think" — here she stopped.

"What do you think, Lollie?"

A child, you see, can tell you all; but, in the transition state, the thoughts grow confused; for then the mind is like a gallery of pictures lit up with cross lights, so that none can be properly seen. She half blushed.

"Go on with my accomplishments, Mr. Venn."

"Well, we left off at the Latin. As for Greek" —

"No, I will not learn Greek. You may translate things to me, if you like."

"At the new College for Ladies, I believe they make the damsels learn Greek. That shows your prejudice to be unfounded."

"Never mind: I won't learn Greek."

"Well, then, I believe you have come to the length of your knowledge. Stay! it is not every girl of eighteen who has read Hallam, or who knows the literature of her country half so well as you. Upon my word, Lollie, I begin to think that our system of education is a success. You are a very learned little person: a few ologies and we should be perfect. Unfortunately, I don't know any, not one — not even the ology of describing nasty things in ponds. How long is it since the education began? Twelve years. You are eighteen, child: we must think about" — he stopped for a moment — "about sending you to the new college, to carry off the prizes," he went on.

She shook her head, and he rowed on, Lollie thoughtfully dipping her gloveless finger in the bright water, as the boat floated along under the bank.

"Could we not come always and live in the country, Mr. Venn? Why do people choose to spend their lives in a great town? See, now: we could have a cottage, my grandmother and I; and you should have a house like that one, only smaller, with willows over the river, and a sloping lawn. We would sit out in the air all day, and read and talk."

"And never get tired, — never want a change?"

"No, never. Why should we? I have such a lot of things, sometimes, coming into my head, — questions, thoughts. I should like to put them all down as they come to me; and then bring them to you."

"Why don't you put them down, my little girl?" said Hartley, looking in her face with his kindly eyes. "Why not come to me? And if I can't answer them, we will try to find somebody who can. Tell me some of them."

"I hardly remember. Only the contrast of the quiet and beauty out here with London makes me sad sometimes, when I ought to be happy. Do you think I am grateful, Mr. Venn?"

"It is I who am not grateful, Lollie. Do you know all you have done for me?"

"No. I am selfish. I am always thinking of what you have done for me. What have I done?"

"I can hardly tell you all, Lollie. I will tell you something. It is about twelve years now since I made out, quite clearly and unmistakably, what fate had in store for me. The prophetic voice said to me, 'Hartley Venn, you are no good. You are a person without common-sense, without energy, without courage. You must therefore make up your mind to obscurity. You will not be able to marry — you must not fall in love. You had better resign yourself to live in your chambers until you require a nurse.' I said, 'Very well, my venerable sisters of the fatal spinning-machine. I would have asked a few questions; but perhaps, as it is easier to ask than get an answer, I had better hold my tongue. I accept the position, ladies, with a general protest against the inequality of things. I accept the position. Perhaps,' I went on to say, with withering irony, 'I may not be so proud of your handiwork as to wish for a continuance of my kind. You may break up my mould, if you please, and as soon as you please. It won't be wanted again.' They hadn't a word to say in reply."

"I don't understand," said Lollie; "that is, I only half understand. You mean, that you had not enough money for marriage?"

"Exactly so; and that I did not see my way to getting any. The prospect was not alluring. But then, you see, that compensating power in nature, whom, I think, the Romans should have made a goddess, one who would go about administering compensatory gifts, gave me — you, child; and I have been happy ever since, watching you grow, and become wiser and better; trying to show me what a lady ought to be, and getting younger myself in catching the enthusiasm of your youth. My little girl, you have been the sunshine of my life!"

The tears came into Lollie's eyes.

"You are too good to me, Mr. Venn. I will try and remember what you have said to-day. But don't say it again. Never say it again, please."

"Why not, my child?"

"I don't know. When you said that I was your sunshine — ah! what, then, is my sunshine? A cloud crossed the river, and it seemed as if your sunshine was suddenly taken away. It is foolish — foolish — foolish!" she repeated, laughing; "but please don't say it again."

Venn was resting on his sculls, and looking in her eyes with a vague sort of anxiety. Her cheeks were flushed, and her lips trembled. She held out her hand to him, and smiled.

"Forgive me. I am your little girl — your daughter — your ward — and you are my" —

"Not your father, child," returned Venn hastily. "Here is Teddington, Lollie. Let us have no more confessions. Tell me some of your thoughts while we go back, and keep a look-out. Remember that day when you ran me into a tree at Clieveden Woods."

"Oh, what fun it was!" she laughed; "and it took us half an hour to get the boat out again. Now, then, we shall be back in a quarter of an hour. What shall I tell you — some of my old thoughts? I used to think that if I was rich — very rich, you know — what a different world I would make it. Every poor man's house should be clean, every poor man should be taught not to drink, there should be no cruel want in the winter, bread and coals should never 'go up,' and the world should not know what was meant by the word hunger. Those were doll's thoughts, you know. Then I used to think, when I got a little older, how that one person — tolerably rich — might make a little street his own, and by force of example show people how they ought to live. Then I got older still; and now I think what one person could do, if he had the strength and the will, without any money at all."

"How would he do it, and what would he do?"

"He might live among poor people, and find out the way to help them without making them dependent. A man could do it, if he was not always trying to make people go to church. A clergyman might do it, if he was not like those I see about. But nobody will do it; and the people are getting worse and worse."

"Don't think too much of the people, Lollie."

"But I must think of them, Mr. Venn. Do I not belong to them? Do I not live among them? They are all good to me; and it goes to my heart that I have been taught so many things, and can do so little. Well, then, you see, I think about other things, — myself and my lessons, and you, and the dear old chambers, with the chairs dropping to pieces. If I were rich, I should cover the chairs, and get a new carpet, and buy you a new dressing-gown, and have the walls painted over again, and make them so fine that we should hardly know each other again."

"They do for us, Lollie."

"Ah, yes — they are delightful old chambers. Do you know, Mr. Venn," she went on with a sigh, "I should like to know some young ladies. I don't mean like Miss Venn, but quite young girls like myself. I see them walking in the squares with each other and their governesses. I wonder what they talk about. Do you know?"

"I knew a young lady once," answered Venn meditatively. "She used to ask everybody if they liked 'In Memoriam,' and she used to talk about dress a good deal."

"I suppose in those houses about Tavistock and Russell Squares, they have every thing they want. Plenty of amusement, with all nice people, — ladies and gentlemen. They make all their interest in study, don't you think? With their opportunities, you know, they ought to. They are always trying to do good to each other. They never have bad tempers, or say unkind words to each other, like poor people. They don't talk scandal, like poor people; and they are not always talking of finery, like poor girls — not always craving for excitement, like my class. It must be a delicious thing to be a young lady. 'Manners makyth ye man,' as I read the other day. Isn't it a funny thing to say? But I should like to see how manners makyth ye woman. I imagine the life of one of these young ladies. When I see one walking along, looking so quiet and thoughtful and proud, I say, 'My dear, you are very happy; you have no frivolous or foolish tastes, because you are so well educated. You have read all the best books, you know how to dress tastefully, you do not spend more than half an hour a day over your things, you are full of schemes for doing good, you are not always thinking about sweethearts, but some time or other your lover will come to you, and take you away.' Every woman must think of love a little, you know. We are happy so, — isn't that the reason, Mr. Venn? Then, I see them going to church. It must be a beautiful thing going to church, — all kneeling together, without a thought except of goodness and religion. You can teach me, Mr. Venn, and educate me to all sorts of things; but you can never make me like one of the young ladies I see as I walk about."

"I don't want to, Lollie. I like you best as you are. Let me pull her in. Now, then, child, take care how you step."

They went back by train and dined together at seven; then up to Venn's chambers, where Lollie, who was very quiet and thoughtful, made tea. After tea, she played for him one or two of his favorite "Lieder ohne Worte," while he smoked a pipe by the fireside, and looked at his little girl.

She was a tall girl now, — not little at all. Her light hair had darkened into brown, her blue eyes were of a deeper color. She had a perfectly oval face; her mouth was small, and her lips perhaps a little too thin, tremulous; her nose straight and clear cut, her chin slightly, very slightly, projecting — just enough to show possible strength of will. Her wealth of hair wanted no artificial pads to set it up and throw it off as it lay, like an Apocalyptic crown of virtue, upon her head. She was dressed in a blue alpaca, simple and tasteful. She had thrown off the jacket and hat she had worn all day; and her little fingers rambled up and down the keys of the old piano as if they knew, without any telling, where the music lay. As she played, by the upturned eye, by the trembling lip, by the fixed gaze, you knew that her soul was in the music, far away.

Venn looked at her long and earnestly. What was he to do with this treasure, — this pearl of maidens, that he had picked out of the very gutter, and made a princess? Did you ever mark, in some rough, squalid field, rank with coarse grass, foul with potsherds and rubbish, some sweet wild flower, blossoming all by itself, — the one single pretty thing in the compound? Nature is always providing such wild flowers. Over the ruinous wall she trains the ivy, on the broken-down ramparts she plants the wall-flower: she will not that any thing should go on without some touch of beauty to redeem the rest. On the seas are the loveliest sunsets, in the desert the Children of Israel had their mirage. So you have seen, in some coarse, rough place in London, in some reeking manufacturing town, among faces blotched, faces smirched, faces besotted, faces sharp with the gold hunger, faces heavy with the remembrance of crime, faces vulgarized by common and stupid vices, faces low, bad, base, some one face in a crowd so bright, so pure, so beautiful, so *lofty*, that it seemed to redeem the ugliness of all the rest, — and such was the face of Lollie.

Venn put down his pipe, and stood behind her as she played. She looked up in his face without stopping.

"You are happy, child?" he asked, taking her face in his hands, and kissing her forehead in his paternal way.

"As if I am not always happy here!"

A cold chill passed through Venn's heart; for he then, for the first time, perceived that there was another side to this picture.

CHAPTER IV.

ANOTHER side to the picture! Yes: for twelve long years the girl had been growing at his feet, coming to him daily, sitting beside him as he unfolded the treasures of knowledge to her, and taught her, within the bounds of innocence, all he knew himself. She came in the morning; she left him about six: for eight hours or so she was his constant companion. Then she went away, out of his thoughts, according to his habit; and he went to his club, to his restaurant, to his half-dozen friends, talked, smoked, drank brandy and water, and came home again.

And what did she do?

She went home — what she called home — to Puddock's Row.

There was once, in the old times, an unfortunate young person whose fate it was to be half her life an animal, — I believe a cat if my memory, a treacherous one at best, does not play me false; the other half she might spend in the ordinary delightful figure of the girl of the period. So, too, Melusine, daughter of Pressine of Avalon, and wife of the Knight Raimondin, who was obliged to forbid her husband ever to look upon her on Saturdays, when she put on, from waist downwards, the scales and skin of a serpent. Little Lollie, very early in life, realized that her life was to be something like one of these ladies, — of whom, however, she had never heard. From ten to six, or thereabouts, — Sundays as well as week days, — civilization, light, ease, cleanliness, comfort, culture; all the pleasures that can be had in talking, learning, writing, and music; a life of affection, thoughtfulness, and care; a time spent with a man so much older than herself, that even now that she was grown up she looked upon him as almost her father, and loved him as much as any father could be loved. From ten to six, a sweet innocence of trust, the growth of twelve years' intercourse, of the outpouring of confidence which she could give to no other person in the world. From ten to six the modest pride that the girl had in being the object of all this grace and tenderness in her Bohemian protector.

But from six to ten, Puddock's Row.

To know Puddock's Row aright, you must visit it at least every night in the week, at each successive season. As the progress of my story might be hindered in the description of eight and twenty nights, let us only give a few general details. Lollie's grandmamma occupied a first floor, — four and sixpence the two rooms, — in the row, and was considered a rich and fortunate woman. She had only one set of rooms to attend, and Venn only gave her six and sixpence a week for all her motherly care; and Lollie did not know that her own pension money, weekly administered, in addition to this, by Venn, was all they had to live upon. The inhabitants of the row looked upon the girl with respectful admiration. Of her virtue there could be but one opinion, and but one of her beauty. She was the pattern of the court; and moralizing mothers, when they were sober enough to point the moral and improve the tale, were apt to fix her success as a theme, and narrate her story to envying daughters as that of one who had risen by her own merits.

They were a kindly, dissolute, improvident race, —always sinning, always repentant, always sick and sorry. There was the old lady at the end of the court, who worked hard all the week, and got drunk every Saturday night, and was wont to come out at twelve, with her hand to her head, crying aloud unto the four winds, "O Lord, how bad I be!" There were the family of five brothers at No. 2, who fought most nights in pairs, the other three looking on. There were two or three laundresses of the Inn, who were even worse, as regards personal habits and appearance, than poor old Mrs. Peck, and envious of her superior fortune. There was a swarming population all day and all night; there was no peace, no quietness, no chance for any thing but endurance.

And, in the midst of all this, the poor girl had to spend her evenings and her nights. Sometimes she would cry aloud for shame and misery. Sometimes, when she was left alone, the squalor of her surrounding circumstances would appear so dreadful, so intolerable, so miserable, that she would resolve to beg and implore Mr. Venn to take her out of them. Sometimes she would shut out the world around her by building castles in the air, and so forget things. Only, as time went on, and things did not change but for the worse, she found it becoming daily more difficult to keep up the illusions of hope, and persuade herself that all this would have an end.

The poor grandmother was a trial. I am afraid the wicked old woman purloined half the money that Venn gave her for his ward, and put it into a stocking. She was not a nice old woman to look at. She had disagreeable habits. She was not reticent of speech. She was interested mainly in the price of the commoner kinds of provisions, such as the bloater of Leather Lane. And when she was in a bad temper, which was often, she was a nagster. From habit, Lollie always let her go on till it was bed-time. Then, at least, she was free; for the little room at the back belonged to her. She could have comparative quiet there, at any rate. The old woman preferred sleeping among her pots and pans, as she had been brought up to do, in the front room. Besides, she was afraid of her grand-daughter, and yet proud and fond of her. She felt more comfortable when the child was gone to bed, and she could nag all to herself, — audibly, it is true, and with the assistance of a little bottle containing some of Mr. Venn's brandy. On the whole, she was well pleased that she had but little of the girl's society. For like will to like; and many were the cheerful gatherings, not unenlivened with gin, which took place on that first floor, what time Lollie was gone to the theatre with Mr. Venn, with ancient contemporaries of this dear old woman.

I think I see her now. "Tout ce qu'il y a du plus affreux." An antique "front," always twisted awry over a brow, — marbled, indeed, but not with thought. A countenance in which deep lines were marked with a deeper black than covered the rest. Small, cunning eyes: if you lead a small, cunning life, your eyes do most inevitably become small and cunning of aspect. Fat lips, such as might come from always eating roast pork, — the greatest luxury with which Mrs. Peck was acquainted. A bonnet never removed day or night. A dress, — but, no, let us stop. Is there not a sort of sacrilege in describing, only to mock at her, a poor old creature who was what the conditions of life made her? Let us bring honor and reverence to old age. For Mrs. Peck no more shall be said. To her virtues very kind, Hartley Venn was to all her faults very blind. She cribbed every thing. She never cleaned any thing. She smashed every thing. She cheated. But she was Lollie's grandmother.

Lollie's education we have sufficiently described. It had, as we have hinted, one capital defect. There was not one word of religion about it. Venn — not because he was an infidel, which he was not; nor because he wished to make an experiment, which was not the case; but simply out of pure carelessness and indifference, and because he never went to church himself — taught his little girl no religion whatever. She knew, from reading, something, — the something being the most curious medley possible, from a mixture of every kind of Latin, French, and English authors. Venn respected maidenly innocence so far as to keep harmful books, as he thought them, — that is, directly harmful, — out of her way; but he gave the child, first a literary taste, and then access to writers whose ideas of religion were more "mixed," than would have been good for the most masculine intellect. The Bible she had never seen; for the only copy in Venn's possession had, many years before, tumbled behind the bookcase, and was thus lost to view. And of ladies she knew but one, Miss Venn, who still asked her to tea once or twice a year, treated her with exemplary politeness, and sent her away with a frigid kiss. Miss Venn, you see, was suspicious. She always fancied her brother was going to marry the girl; and therefore made it her business to try and make her understand the great gulf which comparative rank establishes between people, — grandchildren of bishops for instance, and grandchildren of laundresses. She had two lovers, — past and rejected, *bien entendu*. One was a gallant young lawyer's clerk in the Inn, about her own age, who accosted her one morning with a letter, which she handed, unopened, to Venn. It contained honorable proposals. Venn descended to the court, where the aspirant was waiting for an answer, and there and then administered a light chastisement with a walking-cane; the policeman, — he of the big beard and the twinkling eyes, not the thin one, looking on with a grim but decided approval.

Then there was Sims the baker. A quite genteel young man of a Sunday, if you see him got up in his best blue tie and flower in his button-hole, with a cane. He attacked the fortress through the grandmother, and persuaded her to accept the first offerings of love, in the shape of certain fancy ones, which greatly pleased the old lady. To her astonishment, the child threw the gifts out of the window; and Mr. Venn went round the next day, and had a serious talk with the young man. He put on mourning the next Sunday, and walked up and down the Gray's Inn road all day in the disguise of a mute. But Lollie never saw him; so his silent sorrow was thrown away, and he returned to his Sally Lunns.

And this is all her story up to the point when we left her in Venn's chamber, playing to him.

It was between nine and ten o'clock that she left Gray's Inn for home, — not five minutes' walk, and one she always took alone. Here she had a little adventure; for, as she was striding fast along the pavement of Holborn, she became aware of a "gentleman" walking beside her, and gazing into her face. It was one of those moral cobras, common enough in London streets, — venomous but cowardly, and certain to recoil harmless before a little exhibition of daring. He coughed twice. Lollie looked straight before her. Then he took off his hat, and spoke something to her. Then, finding she took no notice of him, he took her hand, and tried to pass it under his arm.

"We are old friends, my dear," he said, with an engaging smile.

She shook him off with terror, crying out.

There were a few people passing at the time who were astonished to see one gentleman take another gentleman by the coat-collar, and kick that gentleman into the gutter.

"Insulted a lady," said the champion to the by-standers, and going back to Lollie.

"Yah!" cried the mob, closing round him, *for he was down*; and, when Lothario emerged from that circle, his hat was battered in, and probably a whole quarter's salary of mischief done to his wardrobe. The moral of this shows how prudent it is not to be taken at a disadvantage; also that it is best to get up at once, if you are kicked into the gutter, and to cross the road; and thirdly, that, as the mob is sure to join the winning side, it is best to be the victor in all street encounters. Some historians give no moral at all to their incidents; for my part, my morals are my strong point. When I do not give one, it is only because the moral may be read in so many ways that even three volumes cannot stretch so far.

"Permit me to see you safely part of your way at least," said Lollie's knight.

He was a gentleman, though apparently of a different kind to Mr. Venn, being very carefully and elaborately dressed. His face she hardly noticed, except that he had a small and very black mustache; but she was so frightened that she was not thinking of faces.

"I live close by," she said. "Permit me to

thank you, sir, for your brave interference: I have never been insulted before. You have done me a great service. Good-night."

She held out her hand, with a pretty grace. He took it lightly, raised his hat, saying, —

"I am very happy. Perhaps we may meet again under more fortunate circumstances. Au revoir, mademoiselle; sans dire adieu."

She smiled, and turned into Gray's-inn Road. She looked round once. No: her champion was a gentleman; he was not following her. Why did he speak in French?—"Au revoir, sans dire adieu." She found herself saying the words over and over again. Nonsense!—of course she would never see him again; and, if she should, he was only a stranger to her.

She told Venn in the morning, who flew into a great rage, and promised always to take her home himself when she left his rooms later than six. In the course of the day he calmed down, and delivered an oration, — I am sorry I have no space for it here, — on the nature and properties of the common or street snob.

CHAPTER V.

PYTHAGORAS once compared life to the letter Y. This letter, starting with a trunk, presently diverges into two branches, which represent respectively the two lines of life: the good and consequently happy, — that is the thin line to the right; and the bad and consequently miserable, — the thick black one to the left. It is an elementary comparison, and hardly shows the sage at his best. For as to happiness and misery, they seem to me somehow dependent on public opinion and the length of a man's purse. A man with a hundred thousand a year may really do any thing; not only without incurring ignominy, but even with a certain amount of applause. He will not, of course, practise murder as one of the fine arts, nor will he cheat at whist; and he will have little difficulty in resisting the ordinary temptation to commit burglary. But, for the poor man, public opinion is a mighty engine of repression. Virtue is his stern, and often bitter, portion. Public opinion exacts from him a life strictly moral and rigidly virtuous. In all places except London, it forces him to go to church: in a manner, it drives him heavenwards with a thick stick. The rich man, in whose favor any good point — even the most rudimentary — is scored, may be as bad as he pleases; the poor man, against whom we score all we can, is just as bad as he dares to be. This is one objection to the Pythagorean comparison. Another is, that young men never set off deliberately down the thick line. It is, I admit, a more crowded line than the other; but then there are constant passings and re-passings to and fro, and I have seen many an honest fellow, once a roysterer, trudging painfully, in after years, along the narrow and prickly path, dragged on by wife and children — though casting, may be, longing looks at the gallant and careless men he has left.

"I knew that fellow, Philip Durnford," an old friend of his told me, "when first he joined. He was shy at first, and seemed to be feeling his way. We found out after a while that he could do things rather better than most men, and more of them. If you cared about music, Durnford had a piano, and could play and sing, after a fashion. He could fence pretty well too; played billiards, and made a little pot at pool: altogether, an accomplished man. He was free-handed with his money; never seemed to care what he spent, or how he spent it. Queer thing about him, that he was a smart officer, and knew his drill. I think he liked the routine of the regimental work. Somehow, though, he wasn't popular. Something grated. He was not quite like other men; and I don't suppose that, during the whole six years he was in the regiment, he made a single good friend in it. Perhaps he was always trying to be better than anybody else, and he used to flourish his confounded reading in your face; so that some of the fellows were afraid to open their lips. We didn't seem to care — eh? about John Stuart Mill. Then, he wouldn't take a line. The fast man we can understand, and the man who preaches on a tub and distributes tracts, and the army prig we know, and the reading man; but hang me if we could make out a man who wanted to be every thing all at once, and the best man in every line. I can assure you we were all glad when we heard that Durnford was sending in his papers."

That was the state of the case. Phil Durnford started heroically down the thin line. When we meet him again, he is in the thick, the left-handed one, with the mob. This is very sad; because we shall have to see more than enough of him. You see, he wanted patience. He would gladly have won the Victoria Cross, but there was nothing in that way going just then. He would have liked to climb quickly up the tree of honor; but this is a tree which can be only attempted under certain conditions. Had he been a drummer in the French army, about the year 1790, he might have died Marshal of the

French Empire. But he fell not upon the piping times of war. So he went in for being a dashing young officer : rode — only he did not ride so well as some others ; gambled — only not with the recklessness that brought glory to others; and was a fast man, but without high spirits. In personal appearance he was handsome, particularly in uniform. His cheek showed — what is common enough in men of the mixed breed — no signs of that black blood which always filled his heart with rage whenever he thought of it. His hair was black and curling, his features clear and regular. Perhaps he might have been an inch or two taller with advantage ; while his chin was weak, and his forehead too receding.

Always weak of will, his heroic element has now, though he is only six and twenty, almost gone out of him. He looks for little beyond physical enjoyment of life : he has no high aims, no purposes, no hopes. Worse than all, he has no friends or belongings. So his heart is covered with an incrustation, growing daily harder and deeper, of selfishness, cynicism, and unbelief. When the Devil wanted to tempt him to do something worse than usual, it was his wont to show him his finger-nails, where lay that fatal spot of blue which never leaves the man of African descent, though his blood be crossed with ours for a dozen generations. Then he waxed fierce and reckless, and was ready for any thing. If the consciousness of descent from a long line, which has sometimes done well and never done disgracefully, be an incentive to a noble life, surely the descent from a lower and inferior race must be a hinderance.

He thought nobody knew it, and trembled lest the secret should be discovered. Everybody knew it. The colonel and the major had been in Palmiste, and knew more. They knew that George Durnford, late of the 10th Hussars, had only one son by his marriage, and never had any brothers at all. Then they put things together, and formed a conclusion, and said nothing about it, being gentlemen and good fellows.

No brandishing of the sword in front of a wavering line of red ; no leading of forlorn hopes, — nothing but garrison life and camp life: what should a young man do ? Here my former informant comes again to my assistance.

"Durnford," he said, "used to be always trying to out-pace some other fellow. Don't you know that a hunchback always makes himself out a devil of a lady-killer ; and a parvenu is always the most exclusive ; and a fellow with a nose like a door-knocker always thinks himself the handsomest dog in the regiment ? Well, you see, Durnford was a mulatto, an octoroon, or a sixteenth-oroon, or something. He'd read in a book, I suppose, that mulattoes were an inferior race ; so nothing would do for him but showing himself an exception to the rule by proving himself our superior, — all the same as making himself out a bird by trying to fly. He muddled away his money ; but, bless you ! he couldn't really chuck. Chucking is a grand gift of nature, cultivated by a course of public school, army coach, and garrison life. Durnford did not understand the art. Now, young Blythe of ours, when he heard of the step vacant, wrote to his governor about it. Well, the governor actually sent him the money, instead of paying it into Cox's. The young beggar screamed with delight. 'O Lord !' he said, 'look what the governor's done !' And chucked it all in a fortnight, without purchasing the step at all. Durnford could never come up to that, you know. He didn't drink much ; but there was one thing men liked in him. If loo was on, Durnford never played sober against men screwed. Always reputed the soul of honor in that respect. But he wanted too much. He would have liked to be popular among all classes, and he was popular among none."

My friend, upon this, took to philosophizing upon the nature and basis of popularity.

"I believe," he said, with some plausibility, "that a fellow is popular if he is believed to be better than he seems. One man, A., is a frightful villain, but he loves and respects B., another tremendous scoundrel and ruffian, because he thinks him possessed of some noble and elevating qualities wanting in himself. He once saw B. toss a halfpenny to a beggar, and say, 'Poor devil.' Now, that showed a fine vein of native generosity. You don't like a man you think to be worse than yourself, because he must belong to such a devilish bad lot ; and the formula of A., the big rascal, is always that he 'may not be a religious man, by gad !' but there are some things which he would not do. . . . Well, you see, that poor beggar Durnford was believed to be *worse* than he really was. He did it himself. Used to scoff at religion : which is bad form, in my opinion, — religion being the business of the chaplain ; and I'd just as soon scoff at the adjutant or the sergeant-major. That did him harm ; and in spite of his riding and fencing, and all the rest, he really had very little strength in his body. Fellows said he padded."

When we pick up Philip, which is on the evening when he — for it was he — gallantly came to the rescue, he has not yet sold out, but is enjoying the beginning of a long furlough from Malta. His affairs are not yet desperate, though he has got through a considerable portion of his fortune; having less than half of it left, and a good pile of debts, whenever it shall suit him to pay them. I fear that the account his old brother officer gave of him was, on the whole, correct. Certainly Philip Durnford, having had a six years' run of "pleasure" and dissipation, knew most things that are to be learned in that time, and was almost beginning to think that the years had been purchased by too great an expenditure of youth, health, and capital.

When the girl left him, he staid for a moment looking after her, as she tripped up the street with her light and buoyant step, and, turning on his heel with a sigh, strode off westward. He went to Arthur's club. Not finding him there, he went to his lodgings, and caught him reading in his usual purposeless, studious way.

"What are you going to do, Arthur," asked Philip, lighting a cigar, and taking the best easy-chair, "with all your reading?"

"Spare me," said Arthur. "I am one of the men who are always *going* to do every thing. Frankly, it *is* useless. I want some one to pull me out of my own habits; but you, Phil, have got energy for all the family."

"I've used some of it to-night," said Phil, laughing, and telling his story. "Such a pretty girl, Arthur! Oh! such a beautiful girl, — tall, sir, and as straight as an arrow! I should like to meet her again. I don't believe too much in the sex; but I do believe in the possibility of my making a fool of myself over one, at least; and, by Jove! it would be this one."

"Take care, Phil."

"Were you never in love, Arthur? Come, now, gentle hermit, confess. Was there not some barmaid in Oxford? Was there never a neat-handed Phillis — ne sit ancillæ tibi amor pudori — at the college buttery?"

"I have not been in love, Phil," said Arthur, lifting his fair, serious face, "since we left Palmiste; and then I was in love with Madeleine."

"Poor little Madeleine! So was I, I believe. And where is she now?"

"She was sent to Switzerland, after her father's death, to be educated."

"The education ought to be finished by this time. Why don't you go, old fellow, and search about the playground of Europe? You might meet on the summit of the Matterhorn. 'Amanda' he, and 'Amandus' she; and all would be gas and fireworks."

Then they began to talk about old times and boyish freaks; and Philip's better nature came back to him, for a time at least. He saw little of Arthur. They had not much in common. When they did meet, it was in great friendship and kindliness; but they were almost strangers; and it was only now — Philip being home on furlough, and Arthur just come up to London — that they had come together at all since the old days in Palmiste.

I forgot to mention one curious thing in Philip's life. On the first day of the year, some unknown person always paid into his account at Cox's the sum of two hundred pounds. This came with a recurrence so regular that Phil looked for it, and counted on it. He put it down to a freak of Arthur's. Certainly Arthur had a good deal more of his own than he at all knew what to do with; but it was not Arthur, — who, living so simply himself, did not understand that his cousin might sometimes be in want of money. Philip took the money, spent it, and wished it had been more; and he said nothing about it to Arthur. The fountain of benevolence, you see, is a source which may possibly be muddled and spoiled by the uncalled-for tears of gratitude.

CHAPTER VI.

So, about this time, Hartley Venn began to be seriously troubled about the future of his *protégée*. He realized, for the first time, that she was now a woman; and yet he was loth to change any of the little customs which had gone on so long. For instance, that kiss at arrival and departure. A man of thirty-eight is certainly old enough to be the papa of a girl of eighteen. On the other hand, many men of thirty-eight are not too old to be the lovers of girls of eighteen. He could not put a stop to that tender little caress. And yet, of late days, he caught himself blushing, and his pulse quickened, when his lips touched her forehead, and her lips touched his cheek. Only quite lately this feeling of constraint had sprung up. Not on her part: the last thing the girl thought of was love on the part of her guardian. There was no constraint with her, — only that hesitation and doubt which came from the birth of new ideas within her. The germ of many a thought and aspiration is sown in childhood, lying concealed in the brain till the time of adolescence makes it appear, and brighten into life.

Then Hartley, putting the question of love out of sight, resolutely refusing to admit it at all into his mind, set himself to work out, as he called it, a practical problem. As he was the most unpractical of men, the result did not appear likely of "come out."

He appealed, in his distress, to his sister Sukey.

"You've educated that child," said his sister, " till she can laugh at young ladies. You've put your notions into her head, till she is as full of queer thoughts as you are yourself. She talks about nothing but philanthropy and history and what not. She is like no other girl under the sun. And then you come and ask me what you are to do with her. Do you want to get rid of her?"

"Get rid of her! Why, Sukey, you must be mad to think of such a thing. No. I want to put her in some way" —

"Of earning a livelihood. Quite proper. And time she did it. By rights she should be a kitchen-maid. Not that I am unkind to her, dear Hartley," she added, as her brother flashed a warning look at her—"not at all. And she is, as I believe, a very good girl — spoiled, of course. What do you say, now, to the bonnet-making?"

Hartley shook his head.

"She shall not work for her bread, Sukey. I have taken a decisive step. I've made my will, Sukey. You don't want any more money. Bob's boy is looked after by his mother's people. And, besides, you can leave him your money, you know."

"I always intended to," said his sister. "You needn't go on. You have left all yours to Laura. Well, of course it's a shame, and all that. But you can do as you like with your own, What do you want my advice about?"

"That is just the difficulty. I want, somehow, to do something for her that will take her into a brighter atmosphere, out of the dingy surroundings of her life."

"She lives with her grandmother, does she not? At least, I have always understood that this was the very proper arrangement."

"Yes: where her grandmother lives I have never thought about till the other day. Sukey, my dear, I am a selfish animal. It was all to please myself that I made a toy of the child. To please myself, I watched her intelligence grow under my hands; only to please myself, I put into her head ideas and knowledge. In my own selfish gratification, I have made her ten times as well taught as young ladyhood is apt to be. I have never thought about what was to come of it — or of me. And now — now — she is a woman — and I" —

Sukey laughed.

"My poor dear Hartley, and you?— you are in love with her! I knew it was coming, all along. Of course it is a blow. After all your brilliant prospects, and the grandson of a bishop, and a Master of Arts, and a barrister-at-law, and a scholar, and all — and — oh ! dear, dear ! But I always expected it, and always said it. If you will kindly ring the bell and call Anne, she will tell you that I have prophesied it any time this last six years."

When the misfortune comes upon you, it is, at least, a consolation to your friends to have foretold it; but Hartley was walking up and down the room, not listening.

" In love with her ? I in love with Lollie? I have loved her ever since she looked up in my face, the very first day I saw her, and put up her lips to be kissed. In love with her ? I have never thought of it. Upon my word, Sukey, I have never even thought of it till the last few days. It is nonsense — it is absurd. I am twenty years older than Lollie. She looks on me as her father: told me so last Sunday. Love! Am I to think of love, at my age? I thought it was all put away and done with. Sukey, forget what you have said. Don't raise up before me the vision of a life with such love as that. Let me go on having the child's childish affection and trust. It is all I am fit for. It is more than I deserve."

Hartley was not a demonstrative man. It was rare, indeed, that the outer crust of a good-natured cynicism was broken, and the inner possibilities laid open.

"Ask her, Hartley, if she can love you."

"No, no; and lose all that I have!"

"Shall I ask her, then?"

"You, my dear sister?" he replied, laughing. "He that cannot woo for himself is not worth being woed for. No. Let things be as they are. Only I should like to see a way " —

"At any rate, there is no such great hurry."

"If she had any creative power, it might be worth while to make her a novelist. But she hasn't. She only imitates, like most of her sex — imitative animals. Man, you see, originates. Woman receives, assimilates, and imparts. In a higher state of civilization, women will be teachers in all the schools, from Eton downwards. Flogging, I suppose, will then "—

"Hartley, do be consecutive."

"I've tried her at writing, and she really makes very creditable English verses. Her Latin verses are a failure, principally because she will not study the accuracies of language."

"You don't mean to say you have taught her Latin?"

"Why not? Of course I have. We read together portions of Horace, Ovid, Virgil, and other poets. Lollie is a very fair Latin scholar, I assure you. Well, I suggested that she should write a novel; and, after a great deal of trouble, we concocted a plot. That was last year. We went up the river, and elaborated it all one summer's afternoon. It was a capital plot. Three murders which all turned out to be no murders, a bigamy, and the discovery of a will in a bandbox, formed the main incidents. Unfortunately we couldn't string it together. The result was not satisfactory; and we took it out one day, tied a great stone to it, and buried it solemnly above Teddington Lock. It lies there still, in a waterproof oilskin; so that when the river is dredged for treasure in a thousand years' time it may be found, and published as a rare and precious relic of antiquity. There we are, you see. We can't be literary or musical; our gifts and graces are so wholly receptive, that we cannot even become a strong-minded woman. What are we to do?"

"I'm sure I don't know. I only half understand what it all means."

"It means, Sukey, plainly, that the time is staring me in the face when I must do something for the child which will bring her into the world, and — and — away from my old chambers, where the atmosphere, very good for children, may prove deleterious for a young woman."

"If she could be honorably married," said Sukey.

"I suppose," murmured her brother, "that would be the best thing." Then he shook himself together, and brightened up. "My dear sister, I never come here — it is wonderful to me why I come so seldom — without getting the solution of some of those problems which, as I am not a mathematical man, do sometimes so sorely worry me. Married, of course! She shall be married next week."

"But to whom, Hartley? Do not laugh at every thing."

"Eh?" His face fell. "To be sure. I never thought of that. There is Jones — but he has no money; and, besides, I should certainly not let her marry Jones. And Lynn — but he is poorer than Jones, and I should not let *him* have my little girl. Then there is — Sukey, you have floored one problem only to raise another and a worse one. To whom shall I marry her?"

He put on his hat, shook his head mournfully, and went away. Next day he propounded some of his difficulties to Lollie.

"And so, after a long talk with my sister, the most sensible woman that at present adorns the earth, she gave me, Lollie, the answer to the question I have been troubling myself with for so long. She says, my child, that there is only one way: you must be comfortably and honorably married. Her very words."

"I, Mr. Venn?" The girl looked up and laughed in his face, with those merry blue eyes of hers. "What have I done, that I must be married?"

"Don't raise difficulties, Lollie," he said, in a feeble way. "After all the trouble we had in getting Sukey to give us the right answer too."

She laughed again.

"I suppose I am not to be married unless I like?"

"Why, no — I suppose not. No. Oh, certainly not! but you will like, won't you?"

"And who am I to marry?"

"Why, you see, Lollie" — He grew confidential. "The fact is, I don't know. Jones won't do."

"Oh, dear, no! He is too — too — undignified."

"Mr. Lynn?"

"Certainly not. Is there any one else?"

"Not at present, my child; but we shall see. Let us look around us. London is a great place. If London won't do, there is all England; besides the rest of Great Britain, Berwick-upon-Tweed, and the colonies."

"What does it all mean, Mr. Venn?" she asked, sitting at his feet on the footstool. "Last Sunday you were talking in the same strain. You are not going away, or any thing, are you?"

He shook his head.

"I have not offended you, have I?"

He patted her cheek, and shook his head again.

"And you love me as much as always, don't you?"

"More, Lollie, more," he said, in a queer, constrained voice. But she understood nothing.

"Then, what is it? Do you think I am not grateful to you?"

"Don't, child — don't talk of gratitude."

"Do you think I do not love you enough? O Mr. Venn! you know I do."

Perhaps it would have been well if he had spoken, then, the words which rose to his lips, —

"It is that I think you can never love me as I love you — no longer as your guardian, but your lover; no longer as a child, but with the hungry passion of a man who has never known a woman's love, and yearns for your love."

But he was silent, only patting her cheek in a grave and silent way.

"Would you really like me to be married, Mr. Venn?"

He left her, and began walking about; for the spectre which he had deliberately refused to see stood before him now, face to face,—the spectre of another feeling, newer, sweeter, altogether lovely; but he faced it still.

"Can there be a better thing for a girl than to be married, Lollie? I wish what is best for you."

"Would it be best for me to give up coming here every day?"

"No, child, no," he replied passionately.

"Then why want me to?"

"It would break my heart not to see you here every day," he went on, not daring to look her in the face. "But — but — there are other things. Lollie, I want you to be happy during those long hours when you are not with me."

She turned red, and the tears came into her eyes.

"I have been, as usual, a selfish beast," he said. "I have only, since Sunday, realized in a small degree what a difference there is, of my making, between you, and the people in whose midst you live. Lollie, you are a lady. Believe me, there is no girl in all England better educated than yourself. I think, too, there is no girl so beautiful."

She looked at him with surprise. He had never before even hinted at the possibility of her being beautiful.

"Am I pretty? O Mr. Venn! I am so glad."

"Mind," he went on, careful to guard against possible error, "I only *think* so. I've got no experience in these things, you know."

"Ah!" she replied, "and very likely you are mistaken. I suppose all girls like to be beautiful, do they not? And you are not in such a very great hurry to see me away, married, or any thing else, are you?"

He smiled in his queer way. Hartley Venn's smile was peculiar to himself; at least, I never met anybody else with it. There was always a sort of sadness in the curve of his sensitive lips. He smiled with his eyes first, too, like the damsel in Chaucer.

"Hir eyen greye and glad also,
That laugheden ay in hire semblaunt,
First or the mouth by covenaunt."

"Not in a hurry at all, Lollie — only I thought we would talk things over some day. Now let us do something. It is six o'clock. We will dine together, and go to the theatre. Shall we? Enough of sentiment, and of confidences enough. We will rejoice. What does Horace say?—

'Hic dies vere mihi festus'"—

"That is delightful," said Lollie, clapping her hands. "When you begin to quote, I know you are happy again. Let us have no more talk of marrying, Mr. Venn. One thing, you know," she said, placing her hand on his arm —, "I could never marry anybody but a gentleman; and as no gentleman will ever love me, why I shall never marry anybody at all; and we shall go on being happy together, you and I,—

'Il n'y a que moi qui ai ses idées la.
Gai la riette — gai, lira, lire.'"

And so, singing and dancing, she put on her hat and gloves, and taking Hartley's arm, went out to the restaurant which knew them well. As she passed through the portals of the dingy old Inn, with her springing step and the laughing light of her happy face, the old porter rubbed his eyes, the policeman assumed an attitude of respectful attention, and the cads who loafed about for odd jobs became conscious of something in the world superior to beer and a dry skittle-ground. Whenever I meet a maiden happy in her beauty, methinks, in my mind's eye, I see again Aphroditê springing up anew from the ocean. Happy Aphroditê! She reigns by no virtue of her own; she is not wise, or strong, or prescient; she does not hold the thread of destiny; she is unconnected with the electric department; she has no control over the weather; she is not consulted in the distribution of wealth or honors; and yet she is Queen among goddesses, Empress over gods — Regina Cæli.

CHAPTER VII.

THE days passed on, and Lollie thought no more of her champion; but Philip thought of her; and, when he took his walks abroad, more often than not bent his steps down Oxford Street and Holborn, praying silently that he might chance upon her again. He might have walked up and down Holborn forever on the chance of seeing her again, and yet missed her altogether. But one day, thinking of something else, he was walking round a square in Bloomsbury, when, raising his eyes from the ground, — I believe he was thinking of his bets, — he saw the maiden of his exploit tripping along a few yards before him. There was no mistaking her. She came along, with a light, elastic step, full of youth and health, with her frank, sweet face, her deep blue eyes, and her tall, lithe figure: only by day she looked ten times as well as by night.

She, too, saw him, and blushed. Philip took off his hat. She hesitated a moment, and held out her hand.

"I ought to thank you properly," she said. "I was very much frightened."

Philip took her hand, and turned. The girl went on, and he went with her. You see, it was one of the radical defects of her education that she positively did not know the dreadful "wrongness" of letting a man, not properly introduced, speak to her, and walk with her.

"I shall tell Mr. Venn I met you," she said. "He will be glad. Come and see him yourself, for him to thank you."

"May I ask — excuse me, but I do not know Mr. Venn."

"He is my guardian. I am going to him now. He lives in Gray's Inn."

It seemed strange to the girl that all the world did not know Mr. Venn.

Philip did not know what to say. As he walked along by her side, he turned furtive glances at her, drinking in the lines of beauty of her face and form.

"Do you live near here?"

"No, I am here by accident. I am living in St. James Street, in lodgings. I am on leave from my regiment.

"I don't think," said Lollie, "that I should much like to be an officer." She always took the male point of view, from habit. "I should like best to be a writer, a dramatist, or perhaps a barrister. But I should like to wear the uniform. Once I saw a splendid review at Windsor, when the Viceroy of Egypt was here. Are you in the cavalry?"

"No. I am in the line."

"Why do you not go into the cavalry? It must be delightful to charge, with all the horses thundering over the ground. Do you like your profession?"

"Yes, I suppose so — as well as any thing."

"You know," said the girl, "it is absurd for a man to take up with a thing, and then take no interest in it. I should like something I could throw my whole heart into."

"I could only throw my whole heart away upon one thing," Philip replied softly, and with a half-blush; for he was afraid he was making a foolish observation.

"What is that? If I were you, I should take it up at once."

"I could only throw my whole heart away — upon a woman."

Laura received the remark as one of profound philosophical importance.

"That is a very curious thing. Not a right thing at all, I should think it would be so much better to put your heart into work."

"Tell me," said Philip, in a half-whisper, "Do you not think love a worthy object of a man's life?"

"I really do not think any thing about it," said the girl. "And now I must leave you, because I am going down here, and so to the Inn. Won't you come in and be thanked by Mr. Venn?"

"No, it is enough to be thanked by you. May I — am I impertinent in asking you — will you tell me your name?"

"I am called Laura Collingwood," she answered freely and frankly. "What is yours?"

"Philip Durnford."

"Philip Durnford — I like the name. Mr. Venn has a friend of your name, but I have not met him yet. Good-by, Mr. Durnford."

"One moment. Shall we never meet again?"

He looked so sentimental that Laura burst out laughing.

"You look as if you were going to cry. I think we shall very likely never meet again."

Phil grew desperate. His hot Southern blood rose at once.

"I must speak — laugh at me if you like. I have been hanging about Oxford Street in hopes of meeting you, and for no other reason. I think you are the sweetest-looking girl I ever saw, and — and — I am a fool to say it, when I have only spoken twice — I love you."

She looked at him without a blush on her face — quite coldly, quite openly, as if it were the most natural thing in the world for a man to tell her this at the second meeting.

"Do you mean, you want to marry me?"

The question, so abruptly and boldly stated, took Philip by surprise.

"Of course I do," he cried hastily — "of course I do."

"Oh!" she replied slowly, "I don't know. You see, I've no experience in marriage matters. I must ask Mr. Venn what he thinks about it. He told me the other day he should like to see me married. I shall see what he says about it first. We must never do serious things in a hurry, you know."

Surely the quaintest answer that ever man had to a proposal. Philip felt as if he were in a dream.

"Won't you come and see him yourself?" she asked.

He hesitated.

"I have been too hasty," he said. "Pardon me. I am rude and uncouth. Miss Collingwood, I ask your forgiveness."

"I wonder what for?" thought Lollie; but she said nothing.

"Let us wait," he said. "Marriage is a very serious thing, as you say. I am worse than a fool. Believe only that I love you, as I said; and meet me again. Let me learn to love you more, and try and teach you to love me."

"I will ask Mr. Venn."

"No," said Philip, with a sharp pang of conscience, "do not ask him. Wait. Meet me once more first, and let me speak to you again. Then you shall tell him. Will you promise me so much? Meet me to-morrow."

"I promise," said Laura. "But"—

"Thanks—a thousand thanks. You will meet me to-morrow, and you will keep the secret."

He took off his hat, lightly touched her fingers, and walked away.

Lollie went in to Mr. Venn. It was four in the afternoon, and the sage was hard at work on his last essay.

"I thought you would never come, child. What did Sukey say?"

"Miss Venn is better, and much obliged for the papers; and, O Mr. Venn! I've had an adventure, and I've got a secret!"

"What is the adventure, Lollie?"

"That is the secret. I will tell it you as soon as I can. Tell me, Mr. Venn, is it wrong to have a secret?"

"That is a wide question, involving a profound study of all casuistry and debated points from Thales to Mill. I would rather refer you to their works generally."

"Well, then, may I have a secret?"

"Fifty, my dear, if you will. You look a great deal better to-day, Lollie; and, if this east wind would be good enough to go away,—where would it go to, and what becomes of all the other winds when they are off duty?"

"Eurus keeps them in a bag, you know."

"So he does—so he does. Well, in spite of the east wind, let us go and look at the shops, Lollie."

They did; and at ten, after a little music and talk, the girl went home as usual, but feeling strangely excited.

Let us follow her newly-found lover, and tell how his evening was spent.

Just now this part of the day was usually devoted to the billiard-room of the very respectable club to which he had been elected on his arrival in England. He was an indifferently good player,—nowhere in good company, but could hold his own in bad. He had no scientific knowledge of the angles of the table; he handled his cue clumsily; and was not within thirty-five points in a hundred of the best players at his club. Besides, he was not really fond of the game: it was the money element that made him play at all; and he never cared to play without having from a half a crown to a sovereign on his game. Philip was that very common animal, a born gambler. Now, pool always presented the attraction of chance; so Mr. Phil played much more at this than he did at billiards. He generally got put out of the game among the first. Still, there is always a large element of luck about it; and, though you are knocked out, there is a chance of a bet or two on the lives left in. It was a mild enough affair,—three-shilling pool and shilling lives, just enough to keep the spark of gambling alive. At the pool-table, as a matter of course, Philip picked up a few friends—Capts. Shairp and Smythe, late of the —th, in which regiment they had lost all their money, and perhaps a little of their honor; living now, it is whispered, largely on their wits. Gentlemen such as these play well at most games, whether of chance or skill. They have a habit of making friends with new members of the club, though it is observed that these friendships seldom last long; and yet Smythe and Shairp were two of the most agreeable, polite, open-hearted fellows it is possible to conceive. No men corrected the marker's mistakes so softly: no men called to the waiters for a drink in so jolly and affable a tone. Yet nobody cared for their society. Perhaps the captains were to blame for this. Who knows. On the other hand, people might be wrong in whispering away their fair fame. The fact is indisputable,—they had the misfortune to be disliked.

Philip Durnford knew nothing of all this when he joined his club; and so, in two days' time, he nodded to the captains as they chalked their cues for business, chatted in a week, and was a friend in a fortnight. Perhaps, if Smythe and Shairp had known the exact amount of Mr. Philip's balance at his agent's, they might not have been so free and open-handed in the matter of cigars.

It was on the evening of this, his second meeting with Laura, that Philip dined at his club, and went quietly into the billiard-room after dinner: intending to play till nine, and then go the French play, where he had a stall—centre of the second row. The evening proved a sort of turning-point in his career; for, unluckily, he never went to the French play at all. His two friends had also two friends with them,—very young fellows, with the air of wealth about them. In a word, pigeons being plucked. Two or three other men were playing in the pool with them: among these was young Mylles, cornet in the Hussars, the most amiable and the silliest young gander in the club, a little looked down upon, because his father had been connected with the soap-boiling interest. Said Shairp, when Phil proposed to put down his cue and go, —

"If you would stay, we could make up two rubbers. Pray don't go, — that is, if you can stay."

It poured in torrents. Phil looked out into the wet street, hesitated, and was lost.

The card-room was cosey enough, bright and warm; though the rain pelted hard against the windows, and came spitting down the chimney into the fire. Over the fireplace hung the usual rules against heavy bets and games of chance, — a fact which did not restrain the astute Shairp. He said, after a rubber, —

"By Jove! Whist is a very fine game, and a very noble game, and all that; but at the risk of being thought an ass, I must say it is not exciting enough to please me."

Capt. Smythe concurred.

So did Phil. He hated whist with all his heart. He was a bad player.

"I really think, now, if you will excuse me, I shall go to the play. It is past ten already, and I want to see Mdlle. Dufont."

"But you can't go out in this rain, you know. It's absurd to have a cab to cross the street in. Wait a bit."

Phil waited. Another rubber was played through. Smythe walked to the window, threw up his arms over his head, and yawned loudly.

"Smythe's tired," said Shairp.

"So am I," said Phil.

"We might have a little something else for a change, eh?"

"Ah," said Smythe, "we might. Confound it, though, we can't play here, and" — pulling out his watch — "I've got a most particular appointment at eleven."

"I haven't had a hand at loo for — let me see — six months, I know, if it's a day," said Shairp.

His friend had ten objections — overruled in ten seconds.

One of the party never played at loo, and left them. The younger pigeon, who had just got into newly furnished chambers, said, —

"It paws so with wain, or we might go to my diggings. What a baw it is! One's boots would be sopped thrwough before one could get into a hansom."

So they played at the club.

"Just ten minutes, you know," said Shairp and Smythe.

The ten minutes grew into an hour and a half. The strikes were doubled twice, and the game was "guinea unlimited," when the pigeons were so thirsty that they risked ringing the bell.

"Brandy and soda, waiter."

The drinks arrived, and with them a hint that they were breaking the rules of the club.

Phil was the heaviest loser, and with his money he lost what is of much more value at games of chance, — his temper. He answered the polite message of the servant with an oath. Two minutes afterwards the steward came. Civilly he pointed to the rules hanging over the fireplace, and asked the gentlemen to desist.

Shairp and Smythe said he was quite right, and mentally calculated what they had won by handling the money in their pockets.

But Philip acted differently. He said, —

"It's an infernal silly rule, that's all I've got to say."

"It is the rule, sir," said the nettled servant.

"Then d — n the rule, and you too." And he tore the cardboard from the nail it hung on, and tore it into a dozen pieces. Some fell in the fender, some in the fire.

"I say, Durnford," said Shairp, "I think that's rather strong."

Phil laughed. The man said he must report the act to the secretary, and left the room.

They played till there was a single. Then everybody but Philip and one of the two pigeons had had enough. They were either winners on the night, or had not lost. So the pigeon, backed by Phil, insisted that they could not leave off yet; and the party of seven adjourned in two four-wheeler's to the pigeon's chambers.

Here, when the fire was lighted, and they had tried the quality of their host's liquors, the game went on. A fresh place, new cards.

"My luck will change, you'll see," said Phil. But it did not; and, as all his ready money was gone, he put in I O Us, written on scraps of paper, and signed P. D., with an apology.

"A man can't carry the Bank of England about with him," he said.

"I suppose he is good," whispered Shairp.

"Right as the mail," replied Smythe.

So they went on, and the two friends took Phil's paper as readily as their young pigeon's notes.

The game waxed warm. The stakes

got high. Their host emptied two gold-topped scent bottles filled with sovereigns out of his dressing-case on to the claret cloth of his card-table, and they were gone in three rounds. The bottles held fifty a-piece too.

"My usual luck," growled Philip. "Looed again."

"I never saw any thing like it," said Smythe. "It must turn, though, and we need not hurry."

"Oh, no — play forever, if you like, heah," said their host. He was getting rather tipsy.

But Shairp and Smythe, who had earned their money, got fidgety, and began to feel very sleepy.

Shairp nodded in his chair. Smythe looked at his watch every few minutes, although there were three French clocks in the rooms, chiming the quarters, and his own watch had stopped at half-past three.

Phil's luck had not turned, and he was very much excited. His head ached, his eyes ached, the brandy he had drunk had made his legs feel queer, and his temper was what a gentleman's is when luck has been against him all night.

There were frequent squabbles as to the amount of the pool, the division of it into tricks, as to who was looed and who was not; but oftenest about who had not put his money in.

Little silly, honest Mylles was now the soberest of the party — always excepting the two confederates — and he was only kept out of his bed in his father's house in Eaton Square by the feeling that he ought not to be the first to run away, as he had not lost much.

Phil was inaccurate, and Mylles corrected him more than once. The others supported Mylles's view, and this riled Phil. At last, when Phil exclaimed, —

"Somebody has not put in again," he looked pointedly across the table.

"I put in," said Shairp, wide awake. "I know nine. It was a two half sovs and a shilling."

"I saw you," said Smythe, quite careless whether the assertion possessed the merit of truth or not.

"—— parcit
Cognatis maculis similis fera."

"I know I put in," said Shairp and everybody.

"Then it's put on to me again," said Phil snappishly.

"You did not put in, I know," said Mylles quietly. "I saw who put in."

"That be d——d," said Philip, his features swelling, and his lips twitching.

The cornet turned a little pale.

"If you mean those words, I must leave the room."

"Consider them repeated," said Philip, in a fury.

"I must go," said Mylles, rising.

"Go, then; and be d——d to you."

To two persons present it did not matter. Their end was served — for the night. The three gentlemen who heard it were shocked, and ran after Mylles; but he could not be prevailed on to come back.

When they returned without him, Phil was laughing immoderately, with laughter half real, half affected.

"I'll tell you what I'm laughing at," he said. "I was thinking what a scene Thackeray would have made out of all this."

"Thackeray, at least, would never have behaved so to anybody," said the soberest of the men.

Phil laughed, feeling a good deal ashamed, and the party separated. Phil, with a note of the amount of the I O Us, — a good deal heavier than he at all expected, and a promise to send checks the next morning, — went home to bed.

It was broad daylight, and therefore tolerably late.

As he felt for the latch-key, he found the ticket for the stall in his pocket.

"Wish I'd gone there," he sighed.

Morning brought repentance. He sent his checks; he sent in his resignation to the club; he sought out Mylles and apologized; and then — most fatal act — he met Smythe, and accepted a proposal of that gallant officer to put his name down at the Burleigh Club.

CHAPTER VIII.

IF you want to see Marguerite waiting for Faust, as likely a spot as any to find her is the left-hand walk, below the bridge, in St. James's Park, — that part of the walk which is opposite to the Foreign Office, and has an umbrageous protection of leaves and branches. I am told that the British Museum is another likely place. Certainly it has never yet been satisfactorily explained why so many pretty girls go there. South Kensington is greatly frequented by young ladies who delight in those innocent dalliances with a serious passion which we call a flirtation. According to some authorities, the Crystal Palace is the most likely place of all; but my own experience leads me to select St. James's Park. There, between the hours of ten and one, or between three and five — because Marguerite dines with her family at one — you may always see some pretty rosy-cheeked damsel strolling, apparently with no purpose except that of gentle exercise, up and down the shady walks. Sometimes she stops at the water's edge, and contemplates the ducks which adorn the lake, or impatiently pushes the gravel into the water with the point of her parasol. Sometimes she makes great play with her book; but always she is there first; for very fear, poor child, that she may miss him. And he always comes late.

On this particular morning, — a fresh, bright morning in May, — the east winds having gone away earlier than usual, and the leaves really beginning to feel tolerably safe in coming out, a young girl of eighteen is loitering up and down, with an anxious and rather careworn look. Big Ben chimes the quarters, and people come and go; but she remains, twisting her glove, and biting her lips with vexation. The appointed time was half-past ten. She was there at a quarter before ten. It is now eleven.

"And he said he would be there punctually," she murmurs.

Presently she leaves off tapping the ground impatiently. Her cheek flushes. Her eyes begin to soften. She hesitates. She turns into the shadiest part of the walk, while a manly heel comes crunching the gravel behind her. There is no one in the walk but a policeman. He — good, easy man — as one used to the ways of young people, and as experienced as the moon herself, turns away, and slowly leaves them alone.

"Laura," whispers the new-comer, taking both her hands.

She makes a pretence of being angry.

"Philip! And you promised to be here at half-past ten."

"I could not help it, child. Regimental duties detained me."

"But your regiment is at Malta."

"That is it. Correspondence. Letters which had to be answered."

Lovelace himself never told a greater fib.

And presently they sit down and talk.

"See what I have brought for you, Laura," says the lover, lugging out a pair of earrings, in the child's eyes worthy to be worn by a duchess. "Will you wear them, and will you think of me every time you put them on?"

Laura takes the earrings, and looks up at him in a grave and serious way. She has none of the little coquettish ways of girls who want to play and sport with their lovers, like an angler with a fish. That was because she had never associated with girls of her own age at all. Straightforward, and perfectly truthful, she answered him now with another question.

"Will you tell me again what you told me when we met last, — the second time we ever met?"

"I told you that I loved you, and I asked you to marry me. Tell me in return that you love me a very little. If you give me back a tenth part of my love for you, Laura, I should be rich, indeed, in love."

"I don't know," she answered, looking him full in the face. "I like you. You are a gentleman, and — and handsome, and you are pleasant. Then you fall in love with me, which, I am sure, must be a silly thing to do. That's against you, you know; but how am I to know that I love you?"

"Do you want to see me?"

"Yes," she answered frankly; "else I should not be here now."

"Do you love anybody else?"

"Oh, no!"

"Do you think of me?"

"Why, of course. I've been thinking of nothing else. It is all so strange. I've been dreaming of you, even," she added, laughing.

"And you have said nothing to Mr. — what is his name, your guardian?"

"Mr. Venn? No — nothing. I only told him I had a secret and wanted to keep it for the present."

"Good child."

"Then I told him yesterday that I was coming here — all part of my secret — at half-past ten."

"You told him you were coming here?" said Philip, starting up. "Then he is quite sure to come too."

"Mr. Venn is a gentleman, Mr. Durnford," said Laura, with great dignity. "He trusts people altogether, or not at all."

"By Jove!" murmured Phil, "he must be a very remarkable man."

"Mr. Venn told me to keep my secret as long as ever I pleased. So that is all right. And now I must tell you two or three things about myself; and we will talk about love and all that afterwards, if you like."

"No: let us talk about love now. Never mind the two or three things."

"But we must, you know. Now, listen. Who do you think I am? Tell me honestly, because I want to know. Quite honestly, mind. Don't think you will offend me."

"Well, honestly, I do not know and cannot guess. You dress like all young ladies, but you are somehow different."

"Ah," replied Laura, "I never shall be like them."

"But, child, you are a great deal better. You don't pretend to blush, and put on all sorts of little affectations; and you haven't learned all their tricks."

"What affectations, — what tricks?"

"And I like you all the better for it. Now tell me who you are, and all about yourself."

"My mother was a poor girl. My father was a gentleman — I am glad to know that. He died before I was born. My grandmother is a poor old woman, who gets her living by being a laundress in Gray's Inn. And if it had not been for Mr. Venn, I should have been — I don't know — any thing. He took me when I was five years old, and has been educating me ever since. I never spoke to any lady in my life, except Miss Venn, his sister. I never go anywhere, except with Mr. Venn; and I never spoke to any gentleman, except Mr. Venn's most intimate friends, until I met you. I have no relations, no friends, no connections. I belong to the very lowest stratum of London life. Now, Mr. Durnford, you have all my story. What do you think of it?"

His face wore a puzzled expression.

"Tell me more. Have you no brothers?"

"No, none."

"That's a good thing. I mean, of course, it is always best to be without brothers and cousins. Don't you think so?"

"I don't know. It must be nice to have one brother all to yourself, you know. There's a large family of brothers, grown-up brothers, living next door to my grandmother's. They get tipsy every Saturday evening, and fight. I should not like brothers like them. To be sure, they are stone-masons."

"And now tell me more about your guardian, Mr. Venn. I suppose he is a fidgety old gentleman, — likes to have you about him to nurse him, and all that?"

Lollie burst out laughing.

"Mr. Venn is not an old gentleman at all. Older than you, of course, ever so much. He must be thirty-seven, at least."

"Oh!" Philip's face lengthened. "And does Mr. Venn never — never make love to you on his own account?"

She laughed the louder.

"Oh, what nonsense!" she cried: "Mr. Venn making love to me! He has told me twice that he wants me to marry a gentleman. That is why I agreed to meet you again."

"So there was no love for me at all," said Philip.

"I wish you wouldn't talk like that," replied the girl. "I've told you already. What more can I say? You asked me if I loved anybody else. Of course I do not. Then you asked me if I liked you. Of course I do. And if I have been thinking about you. Of course I have. Now, sir, what more do you want?"

"Laura, if you loved me, you would long to see me again; your pulse would beat, and your face would flush, when you met me; but you are cold and passionless. You know" — his own face flushing — "that I think of no one but you. You know that — that there is nothing in the world I would not give to win you. And yet you play with me as if I were a statue of marble."

She looked at him in a kind of surprise.

"I don't understand you at all. What am I to say? You tell me you love me. That makes me very proud, because it is a great thing to be loved by a gentleman. I am grateful. What more do you want? My pulse doesn't beat any faster when I see you coming along the walk — not a bit. If it did I would tell you. Tell me what it is you want me to do, and I will do it. But of course you would not like me to tell you any thing but the truth."

She looked at him with her full, earnest eyes. His fell before them. They were so reproachful in their innocence and purity.

"I want nothing, Laura," he said, in a husky voice — "nothing. Only I love you, child, and you must be mine."

"Oh!" she replied, clapping her hands. "Then I will tell Mr. Venn at once. He will be glad. And you shall come up with me to see him."

"I am afraid that will hardly do," said her lover feebly. "No. Listen, Laura, dear. Mr. Venn knows you have a secret, and has given you permission to keep it, hasn't he?"

"Yes."

"Then we will keep it. We will keep it till the day we are married; and then we will go together to his chambers, you and I, and you shall say, —

"'Mr. Venn, I have done what you wanted me to do. I have married a man who loves me — who is a gentleman; and I have done it, first, because you will be pleased, and, secondly, because I love him too.'"

She pondered a little.

"I wonder if that is right. Don't you think I ought to tell him at once?"

"Oh, no! certainly not yet. Not till we are actually married. Think how gratified Mr. Venn will be."

She was not yet satisfied.

"I will think it over," she said. "Mr. Venn always says that going to bed is the best thing for bringing your opinion right. Whenever he is troubled with any thing, he goes to bed early; and, in the morning, he is always as happy as ever. I am quite sure he would be very glad to be told all about it at once. Some day, how proud and happy we shall all be to have known him."

"Very likely; and meanwhile, Laura, nothing will be said to him."

"No: I will go on keeping the secret. But, Philip, it will be so delightful when we can all three go together up the river. Do you know the Bells of Ouseley? We often go there in the summer, row down the river, you know, have dinner, and row back again in the evening for the last train. There is nothing in the world so delightful."

"But, if we are married, you may not be able to be so much with Mr. Venn."

Her face fell.

"Tell me," she said. "Marriage does not mean that I am to be separated from Mr. Venn, does it? Because, if it does, I would never marry any one. No, not if he loved me — as much as you say you do."

"Marriage, my little innocent pet," said Philip, laughing, "means, sometimes, that two people are so fond of each other that they never want anybody else's society at all; but with you and me, it will mean that we shall be so proud of each other, so pleased with each other's society, that we shall be glad to get Mr. Venn, whom you are so fond of, to share it with us. He shall be with us all day if you like, as many hours in the day as you spend with him now; but all the rest of the day you will spend with me, and my life will be given up to make you happy."

She looked at him again with wondering eyes, softened in expression.

"That sounds very pleasant and sweet. I think you must be a good man. Are you as good as Mr. Venn?"

"I don't know how good Mr. Venn is."

"I could tell you lots of things about Mr. Venn's goodness. There was poor Mary. That is four years ago now, and I was a very little girl. I don't know what she did; but her father turned her away from his doors, and she was starving. I told Mr. Venn, and he helped her to get a place in a theatre, where she works now. Poor Mary! I met her the other day; and, when she asked after Mr. Venn, she burst out crying. Then once, when old Mrs. Weeks's son Joe fell off the ladder, — it was a terrible thing for them, you know, because he broke his leg, and was laid up for weeks, and nothing for his mother while he was in the hospital, — Mr. Venn heard of it, and kept the old woman till Joe came out of the hospital again. I saw him, one Sunday, carrying a leg of mutton himself, wrapped up in 'The Observer,' to Mrs. Weeks's lodging. And I think Joe would cut off his head to do good to Mr. Venn."

Big Ben struck twelve.

"There's twelve o'clock; and he will be waiting for me. Good-by, Philip. I must make haste back."

"Keep our secret, Laura."

"Yes: he said I might. Good-by."

"Meet me here next Monday. To-day is Friday. I will be here at ten. Will you?"

She took his hand in her frank and honest way, and tripped away. Presently, she came running back.

"Please, Mr. Durnford," she said, "give me some money for a cab. I cannot bear that he should wait for me."

"He." Always Mr. Venn first in her thoughts.

She took a florin from the silver Philip held out to her, and ran out of the park.

He lit a cigar, and, strolling round the ornamental water, began to think.

What did he mean to do about the girl?

At this point he hardly knew himself, except that he was madly in love with her. It was but the third time they had met. He loved her. The passion in his heart was born a full flower, almost at first sight. He seemed now no longer master of himself, so great and overwhelming was his desire to get this girl for himself; but how? He knew very well that there was little enough left of the original five thousand. How could he marry on a subaltern's pay? How could he take this young lady, with her very remarkable education and history, her quaint and unconventional ideas, and her ignorance of the world, into his regiment? And lastly, how about Mr. Venn? There was another thing. When she accepted him — which she did, as we know, after a fashion quite unknown to fiction and little practised in real life — when she listened to his tale of love, it was all in reference to Mr. Venn. The very frankness with which the innocent girl had received his suit was galling to a man's pride, especially if it happen to be a man with a strong sense of personal superiority. Had he been a hunchback, had his legs been bowed and his back double, had he been an idiot and a crétin, she could not well have been colder or less encouraging. She did not love him, that was clear; but was he sure that all this innocence was real? Could a London girl be so brought up as to have no sense of the realities of life? Would it be possible that a girl would accept a man, promise to marry him on the very first offer, solely because her guardian wanted her to marry a gentleman?

Some men's passions are like a furnace,

not only because they are so hot and burning, but also because they are only fanned by cold air. Had Laura met her lover's fond vows by any corresponding affection, he would have tired of her in a week; but she did not, as we have seen. Met him with a cold look of astonishment. "Love you? Oh, dear, no! I cannot even tell what you mean by love. Yes, I love Mr. Venn." Amaryllis, pursued by Corydon, laughs in his face, and tells him that she will marry him because she loves Alexis, and Alexis wants her to marry somebody. And yet poor Corydon loves her still.

Corydon, meditating these things, and trying — to do him justice — to repel and silence certain wicked voices of suspicion and evil prompting which were buzzing in his ears, slowly walked round the ornamental water, and emerged into Pall Mall. On either shoulder was seated a little devil, one of the kind chiefly employed for West-end work — young, but highly promising, and well-informed.

"You love her," said one. "She is young and innocent, unsuspecting and credulous."

"She does not love you," said the other; "she only wants to please the man she really loves."

And so on, amusing themselves as such little imps are wont, while he sauntered along the "sweet shady side," a prey to all kinds of imaginings and doubts. Perhaps, after all, the imaginings came from the depths of his own brain, and not from any little imps at all; and, certainly, the existence of these animals does present enormous difficulties to the speculative philosopher, and since the times of the Rev. Mr. Barham they have not been prominently before the public. If they have any functions to perform in this generation, I should think they are used chiefly to influence men like our poor Philip — whose strength of will has been corrupted by evil habit, by vanity, by false shame — to draw a veil over what is good, to represent the bad as fatal, inevitable, and not really so bad as has been made out.

Now, as he turned the corner of Waterloo Place, a thing befell him which must really have been the special work of the chief of the Metropolitan Secret Iniquity Force. I may seem harsh in my judgment, but the event will perhaps justify me.

There came beating across the street, from the corner of Cockspur Street to the far corner of Waterloo Place, with intent to go down Pall Mall, a team of animated sandwiches. With that keen sense of the fitness of things which always distinguishes the profession, they had selected this as the fittest place to advertise a spectacle at the Victoria Theatre. The ways of this curious and little-studied folk afford, sometimes, food for profound reflection. I have seen the bearer of a sandwich, on one side of which was inscribed the legend, "Silence, tremble!" and, on the other, words more sacred than may here be lightly written, heavily drunk outside a public, while a friend, engaged in making known the Coal Hole and the Poses Plastiques, was expostulating with him on his immorality. The perfunctory preacher had not taken his own text to heart. The principle is exactly the same as that by which the Cambridge undergraduate from far Cathay, who confesses that there is but one God, and Mohammed is his prophet, passes that barrier to distinction called the Little Go, wherein he has to master Paley's "Evidences of Christianity," and goes back to his native land and to Islam.

This particular procession consisted of thirteen men. On the proud shield which each bore in front and behind was blazoned a scene of almost impossible splendor and magnificence, while a single letter on each enabled the whole to be read by the curious, as the pageant streamed past, as "Titania's Haunt." "Streaming past" is poetical, but scarcely correct. It rather shuffled past. Most of the knights, or esquires, — scutiferi, — were lined with men well-stricken in years, their faces lined with thought, or it may have been experience. After some five or six had passed along, one experienced a feeling as of red noses. Their dress was shabby and dirty; their looks were hopeless and blank; some of them seemed to have once been gentlemen; and the spectator, looking at the men who carried rather than the thing they bore, was touched with a sense of pity and fear.

Poor helots of our great London. You are paraded, I suspect, by the philanthropists, — perhaps it is the great, secret, unsuspected work of the Society for the Suppression of Vice, — who make you carry a shield to hide their intentions and spare you unnecessary shame. They spend their money upon you, — not too much, it is true, — that we may have before our eyes a constant example of the effects of drink. March! Bands of Hope, with colors flying, and music playing, sing "Sursum, corda," and strengthen resolution by speeches and hymns; but, on your way home, look at this poor creature of sixty, who was once delicately nurtured and carefully brought up, — a scholar and a gentleman, — and tremble lest you give way; for the sandwich men mean drink, drink, drink. Better to have these woe-begone faces before us as we walk down the street than the Lacedæmonian helot staggering foolishly in front.

Phil stood and watched them dodging the cabs. One by one they got across that difficult and dangerous corner where there ought to be an island every three yards to protect us. Presently the bearer of the letter I arrived on the curb, and fell into line. Philip dropped his cigar, and started. The man was looking straight before him. His face was perfectly white and pale, and without hair. His locks were of a silvery white, although he could hardly have been much more than fifty. His nose — a fat, prominent organ — was deeply tinged with red; his mouth was tremulous; crow's-feet lay under his eyes, which were small, bright, and cunning, set beneath light brown or reddish eyebrows. The aspect of the man, with his white hair, smooth face, and bushy eyebrows, was so remarkable that many people turned to look at him as they passed.

Philip walked with the procession, keeping behind him.

A tall hat, well battered by the storms of life, a thick pea-jacket, and a thin pair of Tweed trousers, seemed to make all his dress.

Presently Philip touched him on the shoulder.

The man turned upon him with a glare of terror, which, to a policeman, would have spoken volumes.

Philip looked at him still, but said nothing. He shuffled along with the rest, trembling in every limb. Then Philip touched him on the shoulder again, and said in a low voice, —

"Obsairve, Mr. Alexander MacIntyre."

The ex-tutor looked at him in a stupid way.

"I know you, man," said Philip. "Come out of this, and talk."

They were at the corner of Jermyn Street. To the surprise of his fellows, letter I suddenly left the line, and dived down Jermyn Street. They waited a little. He was joined by a gentleman; and, after a few moments, he slipped his head through the boards, and, leaving them on the pavement, hurried away.

This was what passed.

"You will remember me presently," said Philip. "I am Philip Durnford. There is my card. Get food, clothes, not too much drink, and come to my lodgings at eight o'clock this evening. Here is a sovereign for you."

Mr. MacIntyre spoke not a word, but took the coin, and watched his patron go striding away. Then he bit the sovereign to see if it was good, a dreadful proof of his late misfortunes. Then he laughed in a queer way, and looked back at his boards. After that of course, he went round the corner; gentlemen down in the world always do. There was a public-house round the corner. He felt in his pocket, where jingled three-pence, his little all, and dived into the hostelry. A moment after he came out, his eyes bright, his mouth firm, his head erect, and walked briskly away.

CHAPTER IX.

IN the evening, about nine o'clock, Mr. MacIntyre presented himself at Philip's lodgings. He was greatly changed for the better. With much prudence he had spent the whole of the sovereign in effecting an alteration in his outward appearance, calculating that his old pupil would be at least good for two three more golden tokens of esteem. He was now, looked at from behind, a gentleman of reduced means; everything, from his black coat to his boots, having a second-hand and "reach-me-down" look, and nothing attaining to what might be called a perfect fit. The coat was obtained by exchange or barter, the old pea-jacket having been accepted in lieu of payment; while the other articles were the result of long haggling and beating down. He looked, however, complacently on his new garb, as indicating a partial return to respectability.

Philip greeted him with a friendly shake of the hand.

"Why, man, do you mean to say that a sovereign has done all that?"

"All," said his tutor. "I'll just tell you how I did it. First, the trousers. Saxpence the man allowed for the old ones, which I left with him. They're just dropping to pieces with fatigue. Eh, they've had a hard time of it for many years. Then I got a second-hand flannel shirt. He wouldn't give me any thing for the old one. Then I got the coat for my pea-jacket, which, though a most comfortable garment, was hardly, you'll obsairve, the coat for a Master of Arts of an old and respectable univairsity."

"Well — well. Did you get any thing to eat?"

"Dinner, ten-pence. I'm no saying that I'm not hungry."

Philip rang the bell, and ordered some supper, which his guest devoured ravenously.

"Short commons of late, I am afraid?"

"Vera short, vera short! I'll trouble you for two, three, more slices of that beef. Ah, Phil, what an animal is the common ox!

You feel it when you come to be a stranger to him. And bottled stout. When — eh, man?"

He took a pull which finished the bottle, and proceeded to eat; talking, at intervals, quite in his old style.

"Obsairve. The development of the grateful feeling, commonly supposed to be wanting, — thank ye, Phil, one more slice, with some of the fat and a bit of the brown — wanting to the savage races, must be mainly due to the practice of a higher order of eating. My supper has lately been the penny bloater, with a baked potato. No, I really cannot eat any more. The spirit is willing, for I am still hungry, Phil; but the capacity of the stomach is limited. I fear I have already injudiciously crowded the space. Is that brandy, Phil, on the sideboard?"

Philip rose, and brought the bottle, with a tumbler and cold water, and placed it before him.

"Brandy," he murmured. "It has been my dream for four long months. I have managed, sometimes, a glass of gin; but brandy! — oh, blessed consoler of human suffering! Brandy!" He was clutching the bottle, and standing over it with greedy eyes. "Brandy! — water of life! — no, water that droons the sense of life — that brings us forgetfulness of every thing, and restores the fire of youth — stays the gnawings of hunger. Brandy! And they say we musn't drink! Oh, Phil, my favorite pupil, for those who have memories, brandy is your only medicine."

He filled a tumbler half full of spirit, added a little water, and drank it off at a draught. Then he looked round, sighed, sat down, and, to Philip's astonishment, burst into violent sobbing. This phenomenon was quite unprecedented in the history, so far as Philip knew, of his late tutor.

"Nay," he said kindly, "we shall manage to mend matters somehow. Cheer up, man. Have another glass."

Mr. MacIntyre gave a profound sniff, and looked up through his tears.

"Give me a pocket-handkerchief first, Phil. I want to blow my nose. I pawned my last — it was a silk one — for ten-pence ha'penny."

Philip brought him one from his bedroom, and he began to mop up.

Then he took another glass of brandy and water.

"Tears, — it is indeed a relief to have an old friend to talk to, — tears are produced from many causes. There are tears of gratitude, of joy, of sorrow, even of repentance, if you think you are going to be found out. Mine are none of these. They rise from that revulsion o' feeling projuiced by a sudden and strong contrast. Obsairve. The man unexpectedly or violently removed from a state of hopeless destitution to the prospect of affluence must either cry or laugh; and not even a philosopher can always choose which. I have got decent clothes, an old friend; and my brains — a little damaged by a hard life perhaps — are still greatly superior to the average."

"And you have been really destitute?"

"For four months I have been a walking advertisement. Part of the time I was getting eighteen-pence a day as one of the Associated Boardmen. Eh, Philip Durnford, think of your old tutor becoming an Associated Boardman! Then I got dru— I mean I took too much one day; and they turned me out in the cold. I starved a day or two, and then got employment at one and threepence, which I have had, off and on, ever since. It is not a difficult employment. There is little responsibility. No sense of dignity or self-respect is required. On the Sunday, there is no work to be done; consequently, for four months I have cursed the sawbath, — the Lord forgive me! Don't ask me too much, Philip: it has been a sad time — a terrible time. I am half-starved. I have had to associate with men of no education and disagreeable habits. A bad time, — a bad time." He passed his hand across his forehead, and paused a moment. "A time of bad dreams. I shall never forget it, never. It will haunt me to my grave, — poison my nights, and take the pleasure out of my days. Don't ask me about it. Let me forget it."

"Tell me only what you like," said Philip.

"The passions, I have discovered, the follies, and the ambitions, of man depend a'togither on the stomach. The hungry man, who has been hungry for three months, can only hope for a good meal. That is the boundary of his thoughts. He envies none but the fat. He has no eyes for beauty. Helen would pass unnoticed by a sandwich man, only for plumpness. He has no perception of the beauties of nature, save in the streakiness of beef; none for those of art, save in the cookshops. He has no hatred in his heart, nor any love. And of course he has no conscience. Obsairve, my pupil, that religion is a matter for those who are assured of this world's goods. It vanishes at the first appearance of want. Hence a clause in the Lord's Prayer."

"You — I mean your companions between the boards — are honest, I suppose?"

"Ah, well — that's as it may be. It is one of the advantages of the profession that you must be honest, because you can't run if you do steal any thing. No line of life presents fewer opportunities for turning a dishonest penny. Otherwise — you see — stomach is king at all times; and if not satisfied, my young friend, stomach becomes God."

" Tell me, if you can, how you came to fall into these straits.'

" Infandum jubes renovare dolorem. Eh! — the Latin tags and commonplaces, how they stick. It is a kind of consolation to quote them. When you saw me last was on that unfortunate occasion when you treated your old tutor with unwarrantable harshness. I have long lamented the misconception which led you to that line of conduct. Verbal reproach alone would have been ill-fitting to your lips; but actual personal violence ! Ah, Phil ! But all is forgiven and forgotten. You went away. I applied to M. de Villeroy for a testimonial. I still preserve the document he was good enough to send me. It is here."

He produced a paper from a bundle which he carried in an old battered pocket-book.

" There are papers here, Phil, that will interest you some day, when you have learned to trust me. Now listen. This is what your poor father's old friend said of your old tutor."

He shook his head in sorrow, and read, —

" I have been asked to speak of Mr. MacIntyre's fitness for the post of an instructor of youth. I can assert with truth that I have on several occasions seen him sober; that Mr. Durnford, his late employer, never detected him in any dishonesty; that his morality, in this neighborhood, has been believed in by no one; and that, in his temperate intervals, he is sometimes industrious."

" There, Philip. Think of that."
" You do not show that testimonial much, I suppose?" said Philip.
" No," replied the philosopher. " I keep it as a proof of the judeecial blindness which sometimes afflicts men of good sense. M. de Villeroy is dead, and so it matters little now. Do you know where Miss Madeleine is?"
" No. In Palmiste, I suppose."
" There ye're wrong. She's in London. I saw her yesterday with an old lady in Regent Street, and followed her home. She's bonny, vera bonny, with her black hair and big eyes. Oh, she's bonny, but uplifted with pride, I misdoubt. Why don't you marry her, Philip? She's got plenty of money. Arthur will marry her if you don't. Give me Arthur's address."
" You want to borrow money of him, I suppose?"
" No. I want just to ask him to *give* me money. Ye're not over-rich, I'm afraid, Philip, yourself, my laddie."

Philip laughed.
" My father gave me five thousand pounds. All that is left of it is in our old agent's hands in Palmiste. I get ten per cent for it. As I only got a hundred and fifty last February, a good lot of it must be gone; and I've had another little dig into the pile since then."
" Ah, ay? — that's bad; that's vera bad. But perhaps a time will come for you as well as the rest of the world."
" Arthur can help you, and I dare say will; but you must not tell him too much."
" I do not intend to tell him any thing," said the man of experience loftily, " except lies."
" Tell me something, however," said Philip. " Tell me how you got into such a hole."
" I went to Australia from Palmiste. Spent all my money in Melbourne, trying to get something to do, and at last I got put into the school of a little township up country, where my chief work was to cane the brats. Such an awfu' set of devils! That lasted a year. Then there came a terrible day."

He stopped and sighed.

" I shall never forget that day. It was a Saturday, I remember. The boys were more mutinous than usual, and I caned them all — there were thirty-five. And when one was caned, the others all shouted and laughed. At twelve, I read the prayers prescribed by the authorities, with my usual warmth and unction. Then I dismissed the boys. Nobody moved. There was a dead silence, and I confess I felt alarmed. Presently the five biggest boys got up, and approached my desk with determined faces. I had a presentiment of what would happen, and I turned to flee. It was too late."
" What did they do to you?"
" They tied me up, sir. They tied me up to my own desk, and then they laid on. They gave their reverend dominie the most awful flogging that ever schoolboy had. None too small, sir, to have a cut in. None so forgiving as to shirk his turn. Not one, Philip, relented at the last moment, and spared some of his biceps. Pairfect silence reigned; and when it was over, they placed me back in my chair, with my cane in my hand; and then the school dispersed. What I felt, Philip, more than the ignominy, was the intense pain. A red-hot iron might projuice a similar, but not a greater, agony, if applied repeatedly on every square inch over a certain area of the body. A thirty-handed Briareus, if he turned schoolmaster, could alone rival the magnitude of that prodeejious cowhiding.
" Next day I left the town. It was dur-

ing church-time; but the boys were waiting for me; and, as I stole out with my bundle in my hand, they ran me down the street on a rail, singing 'Drunken Sawnie!' That was a very bad time I had then.

"I tried Sydney after that, and got on pretty well in business — till I failed; and then the judge wanted to refuse my certificate, because, he said, the books were fraudulently kept. That wasn't true, for they were not kept at all. So I came away, and got to the Cape. A poor place, Phil — very poor, and dull; but the drink is good, and the food is cheap. I learned to speak Dutch, and was very near marrying the daughter of a Dutch farmer, well to do, only for an unlucky accident. Just before the wedding, my cruel fate caused me to be arrested on a ridiculous charge of embezzlement. Of course I was acquitted; but the judge — who ought to be prosecuted for defamation of character — ruined me by stating that I only got off by the skin of my teeth, because the jury understood English imperfectly. I came back to England, and went down to see my relations. My cousin, only four times removed — the baillie of Auchnatoddy — ordered me out of his house, and wadna give me bite nor sup. Then I came up to town, and here I am ever since. Ye won't do me an ill turn by telling Arthur my story, will you, Philip?"

"Not I; particularly as you have only told me half of it."

"May be — may be. The other half I keep to myself."

It was as well he did, for among the second half were one or two experiences of prison life, which might not have added to his old pupil's respect for him. These other adventures he omitted, partly, perhaps, out of modesty, and partly out of a fear that their importance might be exaggerated.

The astonishing thing was, the way in which he emerged from all his troubles. They seemed to be without any effect upon his energies or spirits. Utterly careless about loss of character, perfectly devoid of moral principle, he came up, after each disaster, seemingly refreshed by the fall. Mother Earth revived him; and he started anew, generally with a few pounds in his pocket, and always some new scheme in his head, to prey upon the credulity of good and simple men. That he had 'not yet succeeded argued, he considered, want of luck rather than absence of merit.

His projects were not of very extraordinary cleverness. But he was unscrupulous enough to succeed. Cleverness and freedom from scruples do somehow seem the two main requisites to produce the success of wealth. The cleverest rogue becomes the richest man, often the most revered. He has been known, for instance, to get into the House of Lords. Mr. Gladstone will always, if he spends £20,000 on the cause, make him a baronet. But quite lately a new feeling had come over Mr. MacIntyre. He was beginning to doubt himself. For four months he had lived on about three half-crowns a week; and as the days went on, and he saw no chance of escape, he grew more and more despondent. It was a new sensation, this, of privation. He suffered, for the first time in his life. And also, for the first time, he saw no way to better things, — no single spot of blue in all the horizon. Rheumatic twinges pinched him in the shoulders. He was fifty-three years of age. He had not a penny saved, nor a friend to give him one. In the evening he crept back to his miserable lodging, brooding over his fate; and in the morning he crept out again to his miserable work, brooding still.

But now a change, unexpected and sudden. Hinc illæ lacrimæ. Hence those tears of the tutor, wrung from a heart whose power of philosophy was undermined by a long-continued emptiness of stomach. That night he slept on Philip's sofa; and the next day, after taking a few necessities, — such as a shirt, a waistcoat, collar, and so on — from his benefactor's wardrobe, making philosophical reflections all the while, he devoured a breakfast of enormous dimensions, and proceeded to call upon Arthur.

"Ye'll remember, Mr. Philip Durnford," he said, putting on his hat; "by the way, lend me two or three pounds, which I shall repay from what I get from Arthur: I must have a better hat — ye'll remember to forget the little confidential narrative I imparted to you last night. It is not always possible to preserve the prudence of a philosopher, and to know what things should be said and what concealed, — quæ dicenda, que celanda sint. I told you more than I should; but I trust to your promise."

He found Arthur at work in his usual purposeless way. That is, he was surrounded by a great pile of books, and had a pen in his hand. Arthur was not happy unless he was following up some theory or investigating some "point," and had a Sybaritish way of study which led to no results, and seemed to promise nothing: a kind of work which very often lands the student among the antiquarians and archæologists; but there was a tone about Arthur which impressed Mr. MacIntyre with a sense of constraint and awkwardness. Philip he somehow felt to belong to his own stratum of humanity. With Philip he was at ease, and could talk familiarly. Arthur belonged to that higher and colder level where self-respect was essential, and any confidences of the criminal Christian would be out of place. Philip, for instance, had insisted upon his fortifying his stomach against the rawness of the morning air with a glass of brandy before going out. Arthur, on the other hand, offered him nothing: but, giving him a chair, stood leaning against the mantle-shelf, and contemplating his visitor from his height of six feet.

"I hope you are doing well, Mr. MacIntyre," he began.

"I am not doing well," replied the Scotchman. "I'm doing very badly."

"I do not ask your history since I saw you last."

"Mr. Arthur Durnford, you are my old pupil, — I may add, my favorite pupil, — and you are privileged to say what you please. My life is open to any question you may like to ask. The failure of a school in Australia, through my — my firmness in maintaining discipline; that of a prosperous place of business in Sydney, through an unexpected rise in the bank-rate; and the breakdown of my plans in Cape Town, brought me home in a condition of extreme penury. From this I was rescued by the generosity of Lieut. Philip Durnford, who has most liberally assisted me out of his very slender means, — his very slender means. Ask me any questions you like, Mr. Durnford; but do not, if you please, insinuate that I have any thing to conceal."

He smote his chest, and assumed an air of Spartan virtue.

"Well, well. Only, the fact is, Mr. MacIntyre, I remember that the last time I saw you, you were receiving punishment from Philip's hands for some disgraceful proposals."

"Pardon me — Mr. Philip was under a mistake. This, I believe, he will now acknowledge. I have forgiven him."

"I hope he was mistaken. Anyhow, my opinion of you, formed as a boy, could not possibly be favorable."

"At the time you speak of, I was suffering from deepsomania. I am now recovered, thanks to having taken the pledge for a term of years, now expired."

"What are you doing now?"

"Nothing."

"What have you been doing?"

"Starving."

"What do you want to do?"

"I want you to find me some money. I cannot promise to pay it back, because I am too poor to promise any thing; but if you will advance me fifty pounds, I think I can do something with it."

Arthur took his check-book, and sat down thoughtfully.

"I will do this for you. I will lend you fifty pounds, which, as you are a thrifty man, ought to last you six months. You will spend that time in looking about you, and trying to get work. At the end of six months, if you want it, I will lend you another fifty; but that is all I will do for you. And I shall specially ask Philip not to give you money."

Mr. MacIntyre was not profuse in his thanks. He took the check, examined it carefully, folded it, and put it in his pocket.

"I knew you'd help me," he said. "I told Philip so this morning. Can I forward you in your studies now? The pheelosophical system of Hamilton, for instance."

"Yes; never mind my studies, if you please. Is there any thing else I can do for you?"

"I do not ca' to mind that there is. I'll look in again when there is. Have you seen Miss Madeleine, Mr. Durnford, since she came to London?"

"Madeleine? No. Is she in London? What is her address? — how long has she been here?"

"I dare say I could find out her address; but it might cost money."

He looked so cunning as he said this, that Arthur burst out laughing.

"You are a cool hand, Mr. MacIntyre. How much would it cost? — five pounds?"

"Now, really, Mr. Arthur, to suppose that a man can run all over London for five pounds! And that to find the address of your oldest friend."

"Well, twenty pounds? — thirty pounds? Hang it, man, I must know."

"I should think," said the philosopher, meditating, "it might be found for forty pounds, if the money was paid at once."

Arthur wrote another check, which MacIntyre put into his pocket-book as before.

"This does not prejudice the fifty pounds in six months' time?" he said. "Very well. I remember now that I have her address in my pocket. I followed her home, and asked a servant. Here it is, — No. 31 Hatherley Street, Eaton Square."

"Did you speak to her?"

"Is it likely?" replied Mr. MacIntyre, thinking of his boards.

"Confess that you have done a good stroke of business this morning," said Arthur. "Ninety pounds is not bad. You can't always sell an address for forty pounds."

"Sell an address? My dear sir, you mistake me altogether. Do not, if you please, imagine that I am one of those who sell such little information as I possess.

Remember, if you please, that you are addressing a Master of Arts of an ancient "—

"You are quite yourself again, Mr. MacIntyre," said Arthur. "Good-morning, now. Keep away from drink, and "—

"Sir, I have already reminded you that "—

"Good-morning, Mr. MacIntyre."

He went away, cashed both his checks, and, taking lodgings, proceeded to buy such small belongings as the simplest civilization demands, such as a hair-brush, linen, and a two-gallon cask of whiskey. Then he ordered the servant to keep a kettle always on the hob; sat down, rubbed his hands, lit a pipe, and began to meditate.

CHAPTER X.

It was quite true. Madeleine was in England.

Eight years since, Madeleine, before leaving her native island, had ridden over to Fontainebleau to take farewell of a place where she had spent so many happy days. The house was uninhabited and shut up; but the manager of the estates was careful to keep it in repair. It all looked as it used to. The canes, clean and well kept, waving in the sunlight, in green and yellow and gray; the mill busier than ever, with its whir of grinding wheels; the sweet, rich smell of the sugar; the huge vats of seething, foaming juice, and the whirling turbines. But the old veranda was no longer strewn with its cane mats and chairs; and, when the doors were opened for her, the house felt chill and damp. She lifted the piano-lid, and touched the keys, shrinking back with a cry of fright. It was like a voice from the dead, — so cracked and thin and strident was the sound. In the boys' study were their old school-books lying about, just as they had left them; in a drawer which she opened, some paper scribbled with boyish sketches. One of these represented a gentleman, whose features were of an exaggerated Scotch type, endeavoring to mount his pony. The animal was turning upon him with an air of reproach, as one saying, "Sir, you are drunk again." This was inscribed at the back, "Philippus fecit." Then there was another and more finished effort, signed Arthur, of a girl's head in chalk. Perhaps the merit of this picture was slender; but Madeleine blushed when she looked at it, and took both pictures away with her.

There was no other souvenir that she cared to have; and, leaving the house, she paid a visit to the garden. Oh, the garden! Where once had been pine-apples were pumpkins; where had been strawberries were pumpkins; where there had once been flower-beds, vegetables, or shrubs, were pumpkins. Pumpkin was king. He lay there — green, black, or golden — basking in the sun. He had devoured all, and spread himself over all.

So Madeleine came away; and, under the maternal wing of the Bishopess, — whose right reverend husband, as happens once in two years to all colonial bishops, had business connected with his diocese which brought him to England, — was duly shipped to Southampton, and presently forwarded to Switzerland.

Education. Her guardian was a Frenchman by descent, a Swiss by choice. He had enlarged views, and brought up the girl as a liberal Protestant. He had her taught the proper amount of accomplishments. He made her talk English, though with a slight foreign accent, as well as French; and, what was much more important, gave her ideas as to independence and unconventionality which sank deep, and moulded her whole character. Insomuch that one day she announced her intention of going away and setting up for herself.

"I am of age," she said. "I want to see the world a little. I want to make up my mind what to do with myself."

Old M. Lajardie chuckled.

"See what it is," he observed, "to bring up a girl as she ought to be brought up. My dear, if it had not been for me, you would at this moment be wanting to go into a convent."

She shook her head.

"I know the sex, child. You belong to the class which takes to religion like a duck to water. This being denied you, you will take to philanthropy, usefulness, all sorts of things. That is why I taught you English, because England is the only country possible for a full exercise of these virtues. Then you are of a temperament which would have induced blind submission in a man, and makes a delightful obstinacy in a free woman."

"Upon my word, my dear guardian "—

"And then, my child, there is another quality in you, which would have made you the most rapturous of sisters, which will make you the best and most devoted of wives. You will marry, Madeleine."

"It is possible," she said. "It may come in my way, as it does in most people's lives; but I do not count upon marriage as a part of my life."

"You are rich, Madeleine. You have — well, more than your fair share of beauty. Black hair and black eyes are common;

but not such splendid hair as yours, or eyes as bright. There are girls as tall as you, but few with so good a figure."

"Don't, guardian," said Madeleine, with a little *moue* and a half-blush. "I would rather you told me of my faults."

"I know the sex, I tell you," repeated the old man. "When I was young — ah, what a thing it is to be young! — I made a profound study of the sex. It is quite true, Madeleine, though I am only an old man who says it, that even Madame Récamier herself, in her best days, had not a more finished style than yours. You will succeed, my child : you will be able to marry any one — any one you please."

"You do not imagine, I suppose, that I am to fall in love with the first rich young man who tells me that he loves me? As if there was nothing in the world for woman to think of but love."

"Most women," went on her critic, "like to be married to a lord and master. I prophecy for you, Madeleine, that your husband will be content to obey rather than to command. So, child, you shall see the world. Let me only just write to our friend, Mrs. Longworthy, who will act as your chaperon. You will find yourself richer than you think perhaps. All your money is in the English funds, and the interest has been used to buy fresh stock. Go now, my ward — I will think over what is best to be done."

The old man attended her to the door, and, shutting it after her, went through a little pantomime of satisfaction. That done, he took down a volume of Voltaire's "Philosophical Dictionary," and wagged his head over the wisdom that he found therein.

"Independent," he murmured ; "rich, self-reliant, able to think, not superstitious, not infected with insular prejudices, philanthropic, beautiful. She will do. Elle ira loin, mon ami," he said, tapping his own forehead. "You have done well. When revolutions come, and lines of thought are changed, it is good to have such women at hand, to steady the men. France rules the world, and the women rule France. Hein? it sounds epigrammatic. Has it been said before?"

So to England Madeleine came. A chaperon was found for her in the widow of an old friend of M. Lajardie, — a certain Mrs. Longworthy, who was willing — and more than that, able — to take her into society. They took one of those extremely comfortable little houses — the rent of which is so absurdly out of proportion to their size — close to Eaton Square : a house with its two little drawing-rooms and greenhouse at the back, — a little narrow as regards dining-room accommodation, but broad enough, as Mrs. Longworthy put it, for two lone women.

Madeleine's chaperon was only remarkable for her extraordinary cosyness and love of comfort. A cushiony old lady, — one who sat by the fireside and purred ; and, when things went badly with her, went to bed, and staid there till they came round again. An old lady who went to church every Sunday, and, like the late lamented Duke of Sussex, murmured after each commandment, "Never did that : never did that." So that the rules of prohibition did not affect her own conscience. For all the rest, she entirely trusted and admired Madeleine, and never even ventured on a remonstrance with her.

Madeleine was what her guardian described her. In her presence most men felt themselves above their own stratum. There was a sort of gulf; and yet, with all the men's experience, the clear light of her eyes seemed to read so far beyond their actual ken. If she liked you, and talked to you, you came away from her strengthened and braced up. Beautiful she certainly was, in a way of her own : striking, the women called her, — a word which the sex generally employ when they feel envious of power and physique beyond their own. Rolls of black hair ; a pale and colorless cheek ; a small and firm mouth; clear and sharply-defined nostrils ; eyes that were habitually limpid and soft, which yet might flash to sudden outbreaks of storm; and a figure beyond all expression *gracieuse*. A woman who could talk ; one whom young warriors, having to take her in to dinner, speedily felt beyond them altogether ; one who lifted a man up, and made him breathe a purer air. This is, I take it, the highest function of woman. We cannot, as a rule, run comfortably in signal harness, but are bound by the laws of our being to have a mate of some kind. It is surely best for us to find one whose sense of duty is stronger than our own, and whose standard is higher. We may have to do all the work ; but we want a fellow in the harness to show us that the work is good, and that it behooves us to do well.

Madeleine was not, it is certain, one of the girls whom a certain class of small poets love to style "darling," "Pet Amoret," "sweet little lily." Not for any man's toy ; no animated doll to please for a while, and then drop out of life ; nor yet that dreadful creature, a "woman's rights," woman. Perhaps she was not clever enough.

Arthur Durnford called upon her the same day on which he got the address. He was a little prepared to gush, remembering the little sylph with whom he used to play twelve years ago; but there was no opportunity for gushing. The stately damsel who rose, and greeted him with almost as much coldness as if they had parted the day before, silenced, if she did not disconcert him.

"I knew that we should meet again some time," she said; "and I had already written to Palmiste for your address. Mrs. Longworthy, this is my old friend, Arthur Durnford, of whom I have so often told you."

He saw a little, fat old lady, with a face like a winter apple, crinkled and ruddy, sitting muffled up by the fireside.

"Come and shake hands with me, Arthur Durnford," she cried, in the pleasantest voice he had ever heard. "I knew your father when he was a wild young fellow in the Hussars. Let me look at you. Yes, you are like him; but he had black hair, and yours is brown. And you stoop, — I suppose because you read books all day. Fie upon the young men of the present! They all read. In my time there was not so much reading, I can tell you, but a great deal more love-making and merriment. Now, sit down, and talk to Madeleine."

She lay back on her cushions, and presently fell fast asleep, while the two talked.

They talked of Palmiste and the old days; and then a sort of constraint came upon them, because the new days of either were unknown.

"Tell me about yourself, Arthur," said Madeleine. "I am going to call you Arthur, and you shall call me Madeleine, just as we used to. Mrs. Longworthy, — oh! she is asleep."

"No, my dear, — only dozing. Wake me up by telling me something pleasant."

"I was going to tell Arthur that I am sure you would like him to come here a great deal, — I should."

"That ought to be enough, Mr. Durnford. But I should too. We are a pair of women; and we sometimes sit, and nag at each other. Don't look at me so, Maddy! — if we don't actually do it, we sometimes want to. Come a great deal, Mr. Durnford. Come as nearly every day as you can manage. It is very good for young men to have ladies' society. We shall civilize you."

"You are very kind," Arthur began.

"But I must say one thing. Do not come early in the morning. I consider that the day ought to be a grand processional triumph of temper. That is why I always take my breakfast in bed. Handle me delicately in the morning, and a child may lead me all day. Come, if you want to see me, in time for luncheon, at two; if you want to see Madeleine, at any time she tells you."

"And how is Philip?" asked Madeleine.

"Who is Philip?" said Mrs. Longworthy.

"My cousin, the son of my father's brother."

"Your father, my dear boy, never had any brothers."

"Pardon me, Mrs. Longworthy."

She shook her head, and lay back again.

"And what is your profession, Arthur?"

"I have none."

"What do you do with yourself?"

"I waste time in the best way I can. I read, write a little, make plans; and the days slip by."

"That seems very bad. Come and help me in my profession."

"What is your profession?"

"Come some morning at ten, and I will tell you. Send Philip to call upon me."

As Arthur went out of the room, he heard Mrs. Longworthy saying, —

"I am not wrong: I am quite right. George Durnford was an only son; and so was his father. The De Melhuyns, quite new people, told me all about it."

A sudden light flashed upon Arthur's mind. He *knew*, in that way in which knowledge of this sort sometimes comes, that Philip was his half-brother. He was certain of it. He reasoned with himself; set up all the objections; proved to himself that the preponderance of chances was against it; marshalled all the opposite evidence; and remained absolutely certain of the truth of his conviction.

CHAPTER XI.

BUT Arthur went round, the same evening, to Philip's lodgings.

"How much did MacIntyre charge you for Madeleine's address?" asked the man of larger experience.

Arthur colored, —

"Well, we did drive a bargain. Why did you not send it to me?"

"First, because I did not possess it; secondly, because, if I had, MacIntyre was so entirely frank with me as to what he intended, that it would have gone to my heart to spoil his little game. Tell me how Madeleine is looking."

"Here is the address. Go and see her yourself."

"Is she milk and water? But of course" —

"Go and see her yourself."

"I don't know that I shall, Arthur. We are different, you and I. You are an eligible *parti*: I am only a detrimental."

"But, my dear fellow, there is no question of that sort of thing. Madeleine is not like the ordinary girls you meet."

"Oh!" said Philip, "is she not? I don't go into society much myself, because I feel out of my element in that rank of life in which my fortunes allow me to circulate. The domestic business, with the conventional young woman, lacquered with accomplishments which get rubbed off when the babies come; the piano for the last new piece, and the song for the dear creature who breathes hard, and thinks she sings; the mind without an idea outside the narrow circle in which it has been trained — I do not think, Arthur, that my idea of happiness is quite this."

"Well, well; but all women are not so. Madeleine is not."

"Give me," he went on, — "give me some girl brought up out of ladies' circles and women's ways, brought up by a man; full of ideas, thoughts, and quaint fancies; pretty, in a way that the Tyburnian misses are not pretty; able to talk, able to amuse you, able to please you, when the little stock of accomplishments is all run through."

He was thinking of Lollie.

"A lady, and not brought up by ladies?" said Arthur.

"I was in 'society' the other day: five and twenty young ladies, whispering bitter things of each other, bursting with envy and malice. I want a girl who does not look on all other girls as rivals and enemies. I talked to one of them."

"You did not expect the poor girl to pour out her soul at the first interview."

"She had very little to pour. That little was poured. I came away early."

"That is not society. Come with me to see Madeleine."

The other, who was in his bitterest mood, sneered in reply, —

"They are all alike. Every woman wants to be admired more than other women in the room. That is the first thing. Without that, there is no real happiness. Then they want to be rich: not because they may live well, for they do not understand eating and drinking; not for the sake of art, because they only know the art chatter. If they felt art, do you think they would dress as they do? No, sir: they want money in order to make their acquaintance envious. For themselves, what a woman desires and likes most in the world is to be kept warm. Give the squaw her blanket, or the lady her cushion, and she is happy. Warmth, wealth, admiration: those are the three things she desires. What can we expect? Read the literature about women, from Anacreon to the comic against the sex. We have agreed to ke them foolish and vain, — to limit their a pirations to dress; and deuced well have succeeded."

Arthur laughed.

"Take the Newgate Calendar, Phil, represent manhood, if you like. Just well exaggerate the faults of women, a make them represent womanhood. Wom love admiration because it is an instin Their influence is through their beauty. is a net spread by nature to entrap a catch men, in order that they may be l heavenwards. Wild beasts, like you, w prefer the woods, full of pitfalls and snar to the soft green glades " —

"Rubbish," said Philip.

"Not rubbish at all. Don't despi women, — don't cry them down. Go for marrying, and try the domestic hap ness you declaim against."

"All which means that you are ép with Madeleine yourself, I suppose. It perhaps, the best thing you can do. B look at the other side of the picture. Su pose that what we call the highest kind life — by which you mean, I take it, t calm cultivation of all that is artistic, u biassed by passion and undisturbed by r grets — is out of your reach, because yo can't afford it, don't you think it prude to say, 'Young man, you are not intende to marry. Do not be an accomplice in t production of a generation of paupe On the other hand, get as much as you ca out of life with the resources at your di posal.'"

"Every man may lead the higher life.'

"Perhaps, if he remains unmarrie What kind of higher life is that in whic one trembles at the butcher's bill, and ea out his heart thinking of the children future? And, besides, your higher life, what is it? Bah! Wine, love, song Get what you can, and leave the gods t rest. It is their care, I suppose, — th 'rest,' whatever it is."

But he did call on Madeleine. Went see her the very next day. Madeleine w: alone, as it was one of Mrs. Longworthy sick days, or, as she put it, one of tho days when temper got the better of her.

Madeleine was not so unconstrained wi him as with Arthur. Perhaps it w something in his look, — perhaps the mer ory of old childish quarrels. People ver seldom take kindly in after-life to tho who have teased them as children. Sh was colder than to Arthur, — asked but fe questions of him, and turned the convers tion on things general. Philip, in h unhappy way, chafed at his receptio welcomed, — putting it down as due to that fatal taint of blood.

"Do you like the army as a profession?" asked Madeleine.

"There is not much to like or dislike in it," he replied carelessly. "It does to carry one along."

"To carry one along, — yes, but not as the highest object of one's life, I suppose you mean?"

"I certainly did not mean that," replied Philip. "I know nothing about highest objects in life. My life consists in getting as much enjoyment as my income will admit. Very low aims, indeed, are they not?"

"Yes."

"At the same time, suppose I was to go in for the higher kind, — very odd thing, Arthur is always talking about the higher life, — I suppose I should do it because I enjoyed it best. Do you not think so?"

"Yes. But one ought not to be thinking about enjoyment."

"Pardon me, — I only said that one *does* think about enjoyment."

"There is duty, at least," said Madeleine.

"Yes, — my duties are light and easily fulfilled. When I have got through those, there is nothing left but to fill up the time, as I said, with as much amusement, enjoyment, frivolity, whatever you like, as my money will cover. As we are old acquaintances, Madeleine, it is just as well that I should not pretend to any thing but what I am. Now, tell me, if I may be impertinent, what you think I ought to do?"

"I don't know," she said. "Life is so terrible a thing at best, so full of responsibilities, of evils that must be faced, and dreadful things that cannot be suppressed, that I don't know what to say. It seems to me as if the whole duty of the rich man " —

"I am not a rich man."

"The man of leisure, the man of culture, were to throw himself among the people, and try to raise them " —

"You would make us all philanthropists, then?"

"I hardly know. If only — without societies and organizations — people would go among the poor and teach them, — help, without money, you know. But one can only do one's self what one feels right."

Here, at least, was a woman different from the type he had set up the preceding night, — different, too, from Laura.

"You are talking to a mere man of the world," said Philip, rising. "We have no ideas of duty, you know, only a few elementary rules of right and wrong, which we call the laws of honor. My friends, for instance, always pay up after each event. On the other hand, it is dangerous to have to do with them in the matter of horses; and they will take any advantage that fairly offers in the way of a bet. We like gathering in club smoking-rooms, drinking good wine, smoking good cigars. We like to be well dressed, to do certain things well, such as riding, billiard-playing, and so forth " —

"But, Philip, does not this life tire you?"

"I assure you, not in the least. Greatly as I must fall in your eyes by the confession, I declare that I do not care one straw for my fellow-man. You tell me the people are starving. I say, there are poor-rates, rich men, and our luxurious staff of parsons, beadles, and relieving officers, to help them. You say they are badly taught. Where, then, are the schools? I meet with the poor man in the street, and read of him in the paper. He has, it appears to me, two phases in his character. He either fawns or bullies. He begs or tries to rob. I am told that he gets large wages in the summer, which he spends in drink, and has nothing left for the winter. If I were a poor man, and knew that I should be pitied by charitable people directly I was hard up, I should do just the same thing. What is the poor man to me? I owe him' nothing. I do not employ him. I do not get rich by his labor. Therefore, you see, I am quite indifferent to his sufferings, quite awake to his vices, and quite careless about his virtues."

Madeleine looked at him with astonishment.

"You are frank, indeed," she said; "but believe me, you are quite wrong. I must teach you that the poor, whom you despise, are not worse than ourselves, — better than your friends, if I may say so, because they help each other, and have sympathy. Why are you so frank? Why have you told me so much about yourself?"

"Because I am anxious that you should know me as I am," replied Philip.

"But I am sorry you told me what you are. After all, you have exaggerated. I shall wait for a woman's love to soften you."

A wondrously softened look did pass over Philip's eyes. He was thinking of the girl whom he was to meet the next day.

"Love," he said, "the old story. If I am to be reformed, I would rather meet my fate that way than any other. Forgive my bluntness, Madeleine. You see, I do not belong to your world."

"But do belong to my world. It really is a better one than yours. Of course, we have our little faults; and we may be slow for you, and sometimes — what is it, that quality for which the French have no word, because they never understand it ? — what is it that people are when they not only do their duty but overdo it ? "

"You mean your world is sometimes priggish."

"That is the word, — not a lady's word, I know; but Mrs. Longworthy tells me when I make mistakes. And this word does so beautifully fit its meaning. Yes, priggish. Only English and Germans are that, I cannot tell why. But come into my world."

Philip shook his head.

"You are on one side of the stream, and I am on the other; and the stream is widening. Arthur is on your side too. We can still talk. The time may come when the river will be so wide that we cannot even do that."

"I think I know what you mean," she replied. "Cross at once, and stay with us — with those who — who love you, in memory of old days."

"You cannot cross a river," he said, smiling, "without a bridge or a boat. Just at present I see none. The bridges are all higher up, behind me; and so are the boats. And the two paths are getting farther and farther apart. Good-by, Madeleine."

He left her with these words. Very oddly, they recall my illustration from the works of Pythagoras a few chapters back. That must be because "les esprits forts se rencontrent."

"Tell me," said Mrs. Longworthy, at dinner, "what kind of man is this Mr. Philip Durnford."

"He is not so tall as Arthur, has black hair, a black mustache, and large, soft eyes, — almond-shaped eyes."

"Oh! Did you ever see eyes like his anywhere else?"

"Yes: they are like the eyes of the mulattoes in Palmiste."

"Humph!" said Mrs. Longworthy.

"He dresses very well, and he talks very well. Only, my dear Mrs. Longworthy, you know what I told you about the garden at Fontainebleau, when I saw it last."

"Yes."

"Well, Philip Durnford's mind is like that garden, — all overgrown with pumpkins."

CHAPTER XII.

"LET us have," said Venn, trimming the lamps on Chorus night, "a cheerful evening. What fresh disappointment has any one to communicate?"

"A lawyer," said Lynn, "who would have sent me some cases, has absconded with other people's money. That is all that has happened to me."

"He may possibly come back," said Jones. "My manager, who had accepted my play, is a bankrupt. Perhaps Setebos, who troubles every thing, ruined him to prevent the play coming out. I mourn for him.

'He was not fair to outward view;
He was not nice to see;
His loveliness I never knew
Until he smiled on me.'"

"As an honorary member of the Chorus," said Arthur, "I can hardly be expected to have any misfortunes, — consequently, I have none."

"This," said Venn, with a beaming face, "is quite like old times. I, too, have had my disappointment. I had spent the last twelve months in revising and polishing the Opuscula. They are now as complete as a Greek statue. I proposed them to a publisher. He kept my letter for a month, and then sent me a refusal. It is his loss pecuniarily, the world's loss intellectually."

"It is very sad," sympathized Jones. "And yet, I dare say, you would not exchange your literary fame for my dramatic glory?"

"One great compensation of affliction," Venn observed, "is the law of self-esteem. No man, whatever his drawbacks, would change with any other man. We admire ourselves for our very afflictions. We lie on our bed of torture till even the red-hot gridiron becomes a sort of spring mattress; and then we pity the poor devils grilling next to us. Following out this idea, as I intend to do, I shall write a life of that Jew whose teeth King John pulled out day by day. I shall show that he rather enjoyed it as he got on, and looked for it every morning, till the teeth were all gone. Then he talked about it for the rest of his life. So, too, the old woman, who hugs her rheumatism to her heart."

"Ourselves are too much with us: late and soon,
Still at the mirror do we waste our powers;
Little we see in Nature that is ours.
We give ourselves our praise, — a sordid boon."

Jones made the above remark, which fell unnoticed.

"Another compensation," says Lynn, "may be got from the magnitude of misfortunes. To have had more funerals than anybody else confers a distinction on any woman. To have had more MSS. rejected than anybody else confers a distinction upon you, my dear Venn."

"Let us change the subject," Venn replied, with a blush, showing that he felt the delicacy of the compliment. "I have now to submit to the Chorus a scheme by which all our fortunes may be made."

He drew forth a bulky manuscript, tied with tape. They all rose, and began to look for their hats, with one accord.

Venn replaced the roll in the drawer with a sigh.

"You may sit down again," he said. "You will be sorry, some time, not to have heard the prolegomena to the scheme. But I will only read the prospectus. You are aware, perhaps, that a million a year is collected for the conversion of the blacks."

"It is a fact over which, in penniless moments, I have often brooded," said Jones.

"Then," said Venn triumphantly, "let us raise the same sum for converting the whites."

"What are we to covert them to?"

"I shall give nothing for converting anybody," Lynn growled.

"Don't talk like an atheist, Lynn; because this is a philanthropic scheme, and, besides, one out of which money may be made. We shall Christianize the world. We shall teach the people that their religion needs not consist in going to church every Sunday, and sometimes reading a 'chapter.' We shall begin with the House of Lords. There is a great field open among the peers and their families. The House of Commons,—which comes next upon my list—will, after a few years' labor among them, be so changed that the constituents won't know their own members again. No more putting into office because a man makes himself disagreeable out of it; no more bolstering a measure because it is brought forward by a minister; no more legislating for class interests; no more putting off for a better day. And, above all, a stern sense of Christian duty which will limit every speaker to ten minutes, like a Wesleyan preacher at a field-meeting. Next to the House of Commons, we shall take the Inns of Court. Oh, my readers!"—

"You are quite sure that you are not quoting from the prolegomena?" said Jones.

"Pardon me,—I was about to delight you with perhaps as fine a piece of declamation as you have ever heard. Now you shall not have it. The Inns of Court will be taken by a series of door-to-door visitations; and the missionaries, who will not be highly paid, will receive special allowances for repairs to that part of their dress most likely to be injured. If one converts a barrister, he shall be promoted to the conversion of the bench. If one converts a judge, he shall be still further promoted to the conversion of certain ex-Lord Chancellors. In the army, after a few months of our work, you will find so great a change that the officer will actually work at his profession; the same rules will be maintained for officers as for men,—those about getting drunk, and so forth. And in the navy, similar good effects will be produced. The best results will be obtained in the trading-classes. For then the grocer will no more sand his sugar and mix his tea; the publican will sell honest drink; and all shall be contented with a modest profit."

"Of course," said Lynn, "the missionaries will behave in exactly the same way as if they were at Jubbulpore or Timbuctoo,— go in and out, uninvited; and, like district visitors, they will make any impertinent observations they please?"

"Of course; and the consequences will be part of the day's work."

"I quite approve of the scheme," said Jones. "Only, I don't see my own share in it."

"You are to be secretary, Jones. It is your name that we shall put forward."

"Then I retire."

"Do not, Jones, let a promising scheme be ruined at the very outset by an obstinate selfishness. What matters it if the world does scoff?"

But Jones was obdurate.

"Then, Jones, you shall have nothing, while Lynn and I will divide all the profits. I go on to a second theme. This will not be so lucrative, but still safe. It is nothing less, gentlemen, than the establishment of a Royal Literary College,—a college devoted to the art and mystery of writing,— not, understand, for the old and worn-out purposes of conveying thought, but for the modern purpose of conveying amusement."

"It sounds well," said Jones. "Of course, as it is the project of the Chorus, it will fail.

'Fair pledges of a fruitful tree,
Why do ye fall so fast?'"

"And now listen to the prospectus, which you will find to be drawn up with great care.

"'ROYAL LITERARY COLLEGE.

"'The promoters of this institution, bearing in mind the enormous increase in the population, the consequent increase in the number of readers, and the necessity of providing for their daily, weekly, and monthly requirements, propose to establish a college expressly for the training of popular mediocrity. They have observed with pain, that, in spite of the efforts of able editors, a great deal of time is still spent in providing papers containing thought. And though a large number of these leaders of popular amusement care nothing for the merits of a paper, provided it be written by a well-known man, there are yet a few who study to present their readers with what they require least, — food for reflection. Among other objects, it is proposed to prevent this lamentable waste of time and energy; and, in doing so, to anticipate the tastes of the age and the wants of the reading public. Literature, in fact, is to be reduced to a science. The increased demand for literary men by no means represents an increased supply of genius. On the contrary, the promoters are of serious opinion that genius was never at so low an ebb as at present; and the art of writing upon nothing, although it has not yet been systematically taught, never at so high a pitch. In order to convince themselves of this, the promoters, by means of a sub-committee, have carefully studied the whole popular literature of the last twelve months. They are happy in being able to report that there has not been, so far as their labors have permitted them to discover, a single new truth introduced to the British public, not a single good thing said, nothing old newly set, and not one good poem by a new man. This they consider highly satisfactory and gratifying. And it is in the hope of perpetuating, improving, and extending this state of things, that they desire to found the Royal Literary College.

"'In the ordinary course of events, it cannot be but that an occasional genius will arise. Should such appear by any accident among the students of the college, he will be promptly and firmly expelled. But the college will gladly welcome any one, of either sex, who, having a quick memory and a facile pen, is quite justified in considering himself a genius; and every allowance will be made for the weaknesses of humanity, should any student give himself, or herself, the airs of genius.

"'As students of both sexes will be admitted within the college, the promoters, considering how great a stimulus poverty is to work, will encourage, by every means in their power, early marriages. In case of husband and wife being both students, arrangements will be made to enable them to starve together, with their innocent progeny, outside the college walls. No chaplain will be appointed, as the promoters desire to consider the college quite undenominational. In deference, however, to popular opinion, a chapel will be built, in which service will be held on Sundays, in as many Christian denominations as time permits. The hall will be set apart for the more advanced thinkers, who will not, however, be allowed to smoke during the delivery of orations.

"'The great festivals of the college will be Commemoration Day, Old Dramatist Day, Old Chronicle Day, Scandalous Chronicle and Memoirs Day, Horace Walpole Day, Boswell Day, and French Play Day. On these days will be celebrated the names of those great men who, by their writings, have furnished models for copying, or provided storehouses for plagiarists. Every student will be expected to produce a panegyric in his own line. Those which, in the opinion of the examiners, have most merit — from the Literary College point of view — will be printed and kept for one month. The successful students will read them out in the college hall; but no one will be compelled to listen.

"'There will be no holidays or vacations. Every student will absent himself as often as he pleases. On Sundays, conveyances will be provided for intending excursionists.

"'The college library will not, on any account, receive the works of the college students.

"'In the examinations for scholarships and degrees, if any composition, in the eyes of the examiners, should be found to partake of the nature of philosophy, research, or erudition; or should the reading of any composition demand the exercise of thought; or should any reflect on the glory and dignity of light literature, the offender shall be publicly reprimanded, and, on a repetition of the offence, shall be disgracefully expelled. No objection will be made to the offering up of prayers for any erring student.

"'The college will be divided into several sections. These, which are not yet quite settled, will be somewhat as follows: —

"'I. POETRY. — Students will be recommended to take a year's course at this, after the regular three years at any of the other branches. Several gentlemen will be invited to lecture from time to time. Mr. Browning on the Art of Obscurity and Apparent Depth; also on the Art of going on Forever. Mr. Swinburne on the Attractiveness of the Forbidden, and on the Melody of the English Language. Mr. Tupper on Catching a Weasel Asleep, applied to the British public. Mr. Buchanan on the Art of Self-laudation. Mr. Rossetti on the Mystery of Mediæval Mummeries; also on the Fleshly School and on the Art of Poetical Pretension. Mr. Tennyson on quite a new subject: The Yawning of Arthur; or, Guinevere Played Out.

"'The students will be required to read the mortal and perishable works of some of these poets. They will also be examined in the poems of Southey, Cowper, the imitations of Pope, and the magazine poetry of the day, particularly that which decorates the monthlies.

"'II. The second branch will be the writing of essays. It is, of course, superfluous to say that A. K. H. B. will be invited to undertake the department of Commonplace and Glorified Twaddle. He will be assisted, provided their services can be secured, by the authors of the monthly magazine essays. A large number of clergymen, including the Master of the Temple and several of the bench of bishops, will be asked to instruct in reeling off 'goody' talk by the foot or yard, as required, for religious papers.

"'Certain essay writers will be excluded altogether,—among them will be Emerson and Oliver Wendell Holmes; while but a sparing use will be allowed of Sir Arthur Helps.'

"'The authors from whom cribbing will be recommended are Steele, Addison, Goldsmith, and Johnson. Montaigne will also be largely used.

"'III. HISTORICAL ARTICLES.—This department is exceedingly difficult to arrange. It is hoped that Canon Kingsley may be induced to give a lecture on the Historical Forgiveness of Sins, based on that celebrated essay of his where he has shown that Raleigh's sins were forgiven because a baby was born unto him. He may also be asked to give over again his Cambridge course. The gentleman who writes the weekly articles in "The Saturday," abusing Mr. Froude, will be invited to illustrate the method of establishing a raw, and always pegging at it. He will also be asked to give a lecture on Mr. Freeman, called "Moi et Moimême." But the arrangements for the historical course are not yet completed, and the promoters beg for further time.

"'IV. We come next to leading articles. On this head it will only be observed here that the paper which has the largest circulation, whatever that may be, will be chosen as the model. "The Saturday," "The Spectator," "The Examiner," and a few other papers which occasionally address the intellect, will be excluded from consideration.

"'V. The department of novels will receive the most careful attention and the most profound study. All the students, without any exception, will be required to pass through it; and no student shall receive a degree, a diploma, or any certificate of honor, until he has produced a three-volume novel, complete, finished, and ready for the publisher. The professor of the branch should be, if he will undertake the duties, Mr. Anthony Trollope. There will be lecturers to point out the secrets of manufacture in all the sub-divisions: the principal of these will be the religious novel, in which the works of Miss Yonge and Miss Wetherell will, of course, form the most useful guides to the student. Lord Lytton will serve for the student of the sentimental, the political, and the highly-colored unreal. There will be several forms of the muscular novel, including the rollicking, the Christian hero, the sentimental, the pint-pewter crushing, and the remorseful. Ouida, Miss Broughton, Charles and Henry Kingsley, and Mr. Lawrence, will be the chosen models for this sub-division.

"'For the sensational, there can be but one model.

"'For the plain work of the department, the mere story-telling, with puppets for characters, of course Mr. Wilkie Collins will be the guide.

"'If there *should* be any student who would rashly propose to make a picture of real life, he will be set to study Charles Reade; but not in the college, from which Mr. Reade's works will be excluded.

"'The promoters will have great pleasure in receiving tenders and designs for a building. Names of candidates will be received at once by the secretary, Mr. Hartley Venn, M.A.'"

"There!" said Venn, "what do you think of that?" He sat down, and wiped his forehead. "I have thought of you both. You, Lynn, shall be the standing counsel, with a large retaining fee. You, Jones, shall be professor of the dramatic art. You will observe, that, out of regard to your feelings, I abstained from mentioning this department. I myself shall be the first warden, with a salary of £2,000 a year."

CHAPTER XIII.

MADELEINE'S world and the two worlds of the "boys," as she called them, were all three wide enough apart. Woman-like, she tried to bring them into her own groove, and began by asking them to dinner. Arthur went with a sort of enthusiasm. The queenly beauty and the imperiousness of the young lady—so great a contrast to his own shrinking indecision—fired his imagination. In her he saw something of what he himself might have been but for his fatal shyness. Philip went too, at first unwillingly, but presently with a pleasure which astonished him. His pastime seemed to be to rouse the spirit of antagonism in Madeleine; and he delighted to rouse her to wrath by opposing to her enthusiasm the cold barrier of cynical selfishness.

"If it were not," she said one night, — "if it were not that I know you exaggerate your opinions, I should hate you."

"Do not hate me," Philip answered; "because hatred is an active passion. I dislike a lot of people; but I never take the trouble to hate anybody, — not even a bore."

"Then, do not talk as if self was the only thing in the world."

"I must, Madeleine, if I talk at all. You would not have silence at your table, would you? And Arthur never says any thing. Arthur has made a wonderful discovery, which is going to cover him with glory. Has he told you?"

"No. What is it, Arthur?"

Arthur blushed vividly.

"It is only a point of archæological interest," he said. "There has been a dispute in the Archæological Institute for years about the number of buttons that went to the shirt of mail, and I have at last been enabled to settle the question."

"There," said Philip triumphantly, "what did I tell you?"

Madeleine sighed. It seemed to her so sad that one of the boys should openly worship self, and the other should fritter away his time in the pursuit of useless knowledge.

In the course of the evening she delivered an animated oration on the subject, while Mrs. Longworthy slumbered by the fire. The boys stood before her, each in his turn receiving punishment; Philip enjoying it above all things, and Arthur, because he saw that she was in earnest, with blushes and shame.

"It is all true, Madeleine, every word," he said.

"So it is," said Philip. "We are a disgraceful pair."

"You are the worse, Philip, by far," went on the fair preacher, "when I look at you, and think what you might be doing"—

"See, now, Madeleine," Philip said: "tell us exactly what we can do, and we will have a try at it. The care of other people may possibly have a charm in it which is unknown to us at present. Who knows? I may yet be preaching on a tub, while Arthur collects half-pence in his hat. I fancy I see him now."

"You turn every thing serious into ridicule."

"Seriously," Arthur said, "my life is wasted. I suppose antiquarian research *is* useless to the world. I am afraid, however, I shall never quite give it up. What can I do? Do you want any money for your objects, Madeleine?"

"No — no — no," she replied impatiently. "How often am I to tell you that the real work of charity is done without money? Now, listen, and I will tell you what a man of leisure should do. It is the interest of everybody that the condition of the poor should be raised, — by schools, by giving them instruction in the arts of life, by giving them sufficient wages for good work, by maintaining their self-respect."

Philip began to groan softly.

"I will come to what I mean most." She blushed a little, and went on: "I have got a friend, a middle-aged woman, who gives all her life to the care of a certain house, where she receives and finds work for women. We give them as much work as they can do, at a fair price. We ask no questions, — we form no society. Some of them live in the house, others in the neighborhood. We do not let them work all day, and we give them instruction in housework, in medicine, and all sorts of things that may be useful to them when they marry, as most of them do."

"I suppose," said Philip the irrepressible, "they are driven to church three times every Sunday."

"Not at all. We never interfere with their religion. Some of them are pious; some, I suppose, are not. We have one broad principle, — that our work shall not be mixed up with religion in any way."

"Good."

"And what do you do with their work?"

"It goes to a shop which belongs to us. We can sell as cheaply as any other, in spite of our high wages; because, you see, there is no middle-man."

"Madeleine, you are a radical."

"I know nothing about that. I am determined to do what I can to have women properly paid. All that come to me shall get work, even if we lose, — though I think we shall not lose by it, — so long as I have any money left. Now, you two can help me."

"I have never learned to sew," said Philip, looking at his fingers.

"The girls and women have got brothers and sons. We cannot find work for them, too, but we want to get up a night-school. Will you come down and teach?"

They looked at each other with alarm.

"Of course we will," said Arthur, "if you wish it."

"Then come to-morrow."

They went.

It was in Westminster that Madeleine's "house" stood; properly speaking, three or four small houses knocked into one.

They went with her at seven o'clock, both feeling horribly ill at ease.

She took them up stairs into a room made out of two, by taking down the wall between, where a dozen boys were assembled, under the care of a young man whose pale cheeks and thin figure concealed a vast amount of courage and enthusiasm. With him, — a young martyr to the cause which yearly kills its soldiers, — we have here nothing to do.

"This is our school," said Madeleine. "Mr. Hughes, these two gentlemen will try to do something for us, if you will put them in the way."

Mr. Hughes bowed, but looked suspiciously at his two new assistants.

"Come, gentlemen," he said, "there are your pupils, — the more advanced boys. Mine are down below."

He divided the boys into two sets, one at either end; giving Philip care of one, and Arthur that of the other.

"You will be firm, gentlemen," he whispered. "Don't let any single step be taken to destroy discipline. We have to be very careful here. Here are books for you."

He gave Philip a geography, and Arthur a little book containing hints of lectures on all sorts of elementary subjects, chiefly connected with laws of health, rules of life, and of simple chemical laws. Arthur sat down mechanically, and turned pale when he opened the book; for of science he was as ignorant as the pope himself. In a few moments Philip came over to him.

"What have you got, Arthur?"

"Here's science, — what am I to do with it?"

"I don't know. I've got geography. What am I to do with that?"

"Draw a map on a board, and tell them something about a country. Any thing will do."

Philip went back and faced his class. They were a sturdy, dirty-faced lot of young gamins, all whispering together, and evidently intent on as much mischief as could be got out of the new teacher. Behind him was a blackboard and a piece of chalk.

"What country shall we take, boys?" he asked, with an air of confidence, as if all were alike to him.

"Please, sir, yesterday we had Central Africa, and Mr. Hughes told us a lot about travellers there. Let's have some more about Livingstone."

Philip was not posted up in Livingstone. He shook his head, and tried to think of a country he knew something about. Suddenly a bright thought struck him.

"Did you ever hear of Palmiste Island, boys?"

They never had.

"By Jove," thought Philip, "I shall get on splendidly now."

As he was drawing his map of the island, he heard Arthur, in a hesitating voice, beginning to describe the glory of the heavens; and nearly choked, because he was certain that five minutes would bring him to grief.

He began to talk as he drew his map, describing the discovery of the island, the first settlers, and their hardships; and then, warming to his subject, he told all about sugar-making and coffee-planting. From time to time Arthur's voice fell upon his ear; but he was too busy drawing his map, and decorating the corners of the board with fancy sketches, illustrating the appearance of the people, niggers' heads, Chinese carrying pigs, — for Phil sketched very fairly, — and he did not look up. Presently he turned round. All Arthur's boys had deserted their instructor, and come over to him, while their unhappy lecturer, in silence, sat helpless in his chair, book in hand. As for his own boys, they were all on the broad grin, enjoying the lesson highly.

Philip stopped.

"I say," he said, "this won't do, you know. Go back, you boys, to your own end."

"He ain't no good, that teacher," said one of the boys, with a derisive grin.

Arthur shook his head mournfully. There was something touching in his attitude, sitting all alone, with his book in his hand. Perhaps Arthur had never felt so humiliated in his life before. It was perfectly true: he was no good. In the brief five minutes during which he lectured, he made more mistakes in astronomical science than generally falls to the lot of man to make in a lifetime. Some of the boys, who had been to national schools, found him out in a moment, and openly expressed their contempt before seceding to the other end of the room.

"He ain't no good, that teacher," said the boy. "You go on with your patter. We're a-listenin' to you. Draw us some more pictures. Make a white man latherin' a nigger."

"Obsairve," as a friend of ours would say, the instinctive superiority of race.

"Boys," said another, rising solemnly, "this one ain't no good neither. He's a-gammonin' of us. There ain't no such place. I sha'n't stay here to be gammoned on."

He was about four feet nothing in his boots, this young Hampden. Phil, cut to the heart by the ignominy of the thing, caught him a box of the ears that laid him sprawling. The urchin raised a howl, and, falling back upon his friends, pulled the form over with him, so that the whole row of a dozen fell together. The yells were terrific for a moment; and then, seized by a common impulse, the boys grasped their caps, and fled down the stairs like one boy.

"Arthur!" said Philip.

"Philip!" said Arthur.

"You never experienced any thing like this before, I suppose?"

"Never."

Just then Madeleine herself appeared, followed by Mr. Hughes. All the forms lay on the floor; for, in the brief moment of tumult, every boy had seized the opportunity of contributing something to the noise; and at either end of the room stood one of her new allies. Arthur, with his arms helplessly dangling, holding the unlucky book of science, Philip trying with his pocket-handkerchief to rub out some of the pictures.

Madeleine looked from one to the other.

"Take this wretched book, somebody," said Arthur, as if the volume chained him to the spot. "Do take the book."

Mr. Hughes took the book, and Arthur turned to Madeleine.

"It's a failure, Madeleine," he said, with a sad sigh. "They only laughed at me."

"And what have you been doing, Philip?"

"I've been getting on capitally," he said, trying to efface the pig and the Chinaman. "I've been giving a lesson on geography."

"Illustrated," said Mr. Hughes quietly, pointing to the pig.

"Yes, illustrated. I've been telling the boys about Palmiste, Madeleine; and they actually refused to believe there is any such place."

"Is much mischief done, Mr. Hughes?" asked Madeleine.

The question was like a box on the ear to both. They looked at each other, and Philip began to laugh.

"Honestly, Madeleine," he said, "I am very sorry. We have done our best. I thought we should have to give a lesson, and was not prepared to give a lecture."

"Never mind, sir," said Mr. Hughes. "I dare say we shall soon mend matters; and perhaps your pictures amused the children."

"You may take me home, both of you," said Madeleine.

She said no more, though she was greatly disappointed at the failure of her scheme.

"Madeleine," said Philip in the carriage, "I am inclined to think, that, on the whole, I can serve my fellow-creatures best by not teaching them."

"Try me again, Madeleine," Arthur whispered.

CHAPTER XIV.

SETTLING down in most respectable lodgings, in Keppel Street, Russell Square, with a clear six months before him of no anxiety for the next day's dinner, Mr. MacIntyre felt at first more elation than becomes a philosopher. We must excuse him. When a man has had seven years of shifts, hardly knowing one day what the next would be like, racking his brain for contrivances to keep the wolf from the door, busy with never-ending combinations for the transference of cash from other people's pockets to his own, a clear holiday of six months seems almost like an eternity.

After a few days of seclusion and whiskey toddy, Mr. MacIntyre awoke to the conclusion that something would have to be done. Reason once more asserted her sway. His first idea was to take pupils; and accordingly he invested a small sum in second-hand books, another in reports and examinations, and another sum in advertisements. No pupils came at all. Another thing he did was to go to a lawyer, and instruct him to write a certain letter to a firm of lawyers in Palmiste. They were directed to search the register of marriages at the Church of St. Joseph for that of George Durnford with Marie; to make a formal and attested copy of it, and to send it to London, — the whole being strictly secret and confidential.

And then, this being fairly put into hand, as he found he had a good deal of time upon his hands, he began to spend it chiefly in the society of Philip, watching him closely, getting his secrets out of him, communicating his opinions, trying to get a real influence over him.

"Obsairve," said the philosopher one night to Philip himself, "there are some kinds of men who go uphill or downhill, according as they are shoved. They have no deliberate choice in the matter; because, if they had, they would prefer the better path. While they are hesitating, some one comes and gives them a gentle shove downwards."

"What is the meaning of all this, MacIntyre?" asked Philip, ignorant of the application.

"Ay, ay — the wise man talks in parables, and is understood not. Ye've heard of Mr. Baxter, and his 'Shove to Heavy Christians,' Phil? He was a sagacious man. There may as well be shovers up as shovers down. I do what I can, but it's vera little, — vera little, indeed. In me, my pupil, you behold an up-shover; in yourself, — one who is shoved upwards."

In his easy way, having very few friends

and long leave, Philip fell back a good deal on MacIntyre. First, the man amused him; then he took pleasure in his company, because he flattered him; thirdly, he fell into the snares of a will stronger than his own, and confided every thing to him. MacIntyre, not by any means a deep, designing villain, had yet a game of his own to play. He read the character of his ex-pupil, and began to consider his own plan almost as good as carried out.

"See," he seemed to say, while he and Philip sat opposite each other in the evening, smoking and talking,—"see how goodly are the fruits in the neighborhood of the Dead Sea. Let me give you a friendly shove in that direction. Obsairve, how sickly is the perfume—how faint the odor of the Jericho rose. Truly, the apples of the plain are better than the grapes of Eshcol. I have been myself, all my life, in search of these fruits; unsuccessfully, I admit, through no fault of mine; for I had no scruples. I fought for my own hand. I was a beggar born; and, because circumstances were too strong for me, I am a beggar now, at fifty-three. But mine is the true road, and your philosopher knows no scruples."

Phil's secrets were simple. The young fellow was in debt, of course, but not badly. More than half of his little fortune was gone. He always had a heavy balance against him in his speculative transactions. Worse than this, he was in love.

All these things considered together, Mr. MacIntyre was, perhaps, justified in rubbing his hands at night. What did he do, though, with those two or three bits of yellow paper which he was always reading, holding to the light and examining, before he put them up again in the dirty old pocket-book which he carried inside his waistcoat?

"I think," he murmurs, "that in three months, or six at most, it may be done. It shall be done. The pear will be ripe. Bah! it must drop into my hands."

He talked over the love matter. That was the most pressing business.

"Ye cannot do it, Phil," he said: "it's beneath yourself."

"Nonsense," said Philip, coloring. "I can make no mésalliance."

"Pardon me, you can. And if you knew all— Obsairve, young man, he who"—

"I know, I know. Do not philosophize. I suppose you cannot imagine such a thing as love, MacIntyre?"

"No, I think not. I've been married, though; so I know very well what is *not* love."

"I believe you have been every thing," said Philip.

"Most things I certainly have; and most things I have made notes of. As, for instance, that the British officer, does not, as a rule, marry the girl of inferior position whom"—

"MacIntyre, stop!" cried Philip. "Do not try me too far. I have been a gambler, if you like—a profligate—any thing you like to call me; but I swear that I never had that sin laid to my conscience."

"Aweel, aweel," said MacIntyre. "Was I tempting you? You apply a general proposition to a particular case. A most illogical race the English always were."

He changed the subject, but kept on recurring to it, night after night; while Philip, meeting Laura but once a week or so, was daily growing more and more passionately in love with the girl.

"A marriage beneath your station, Philip," he said one night enigmatically, "would be madness to you, just now."

"And why just now?"

"Because you will have to take your proper place; give up the soldiering, and become a country gentleman; that is, as soon as you like to hold out your hand and ask."

"What is the man talking about?"

"Never mind—we can wait. Mind, I say nothing about the young leddy."

"She is too good for me."

"Na doot, na doot. They always are. She's all that you imagine, of course, and more behind it; but after a month, ye'd wish ye hadn't done it. Eh, what a pity that there is nothing short of marriage! Hand-fasting would be something."

It was the second time he had thrown out this hint. This time Philip did not spring from his chair. He only looked at him thoughtfully, and shook his head.

"I must have her, MacIntyre—I must have her. Only this morning I saw her. See, here is a lock of her pretty hair. How soft it is, the dear little lock that I cut off with her own scissors! and here is her face in my locket. Look at it,—you, with your fifty years of cold philosophy,—and warm your blood for a moment. Think of what you would have been, if you had met her when you were young, when you were five and twenty! Eh, Mephistopheles? Did you ever have any youth?"

"I'll tell you about my youth some other day," returned the preceptor,—"not now. Well, it's a bonny face, a bonny face; and a good face too."

"By Heaven, sir," Philip went on, "there's no woman like her,—not one.

'There is none like her, none,
Nor shall be till our summers have deceased.'

You know, you know —

'Her sweet voice ringing up to the sunny sky,
Till I well could weep for myself, so wretched
    and mean,
And a lover so sordid and base.'

It isn't quite right: but never mind. I feel the touch of her fingers in mine this moment, man of the icy veins. I tell you that I feel the warm blush on her cheek when I kissed her; I hear the sweet tones of her voice, — the loveliest and sweetest you ever heard. And she trusts me," he went on, with a sort of sob, — "she trusts me, and thinks I am good. Good! She is not happy with the secret, poor child. She longs to tell Mr. Venn, who is a friend of Arthur's, all about it."

"And has she told Mr. Venn?" cried MacIntyre, greatly excited.

"Why, no. I tell her not to."

"Don't let her, Phil. Keep it secret. Whatever you do, don't let Mr. Venn know."

Phil was in a hot fit that night, and MacIntyre let him down with his simple remonstrance.

Next day he was despondent, because things looked badly for a horse he had backed. He began again. Philip answered surily, —

"I am going to marry her, pillar of Presbyterian scrupulosity. My mind is made up."

"I knew a man once," said MacIntyre, filling his tumbler with brandy and water, "much in your predicament. He was in love with a girl beneath him."

"Now you are going to invent some lies of your own," said Philip.

MacIntyre half rose.

"Sir, do not insult your own guest. If it was not for — for this full glass of grog, I'd go at once."

"No, no, — I beg your pardon. Go on with your parable."

"It is no parable. Truth, sir, — plain, unvarnished truth, will always be found better than parable. This, sir," tapping his breast, "is a wholesale dépôt of truth. I knew the man of whom I am telling you well. A friend of his had been once an ordained Presbyterian minister. He said to him, 'I will marry you privately. The marriage is pairfectly good north of the Tweed. What it is south, I do not know. It will be time to raise the question after the ceremony is completed.' Well, Philip, they were married. My friend performed the service in his own house. The question has never been raised, and never will be raised, because the marriage turned out happily — in consequence of the demise of the leddy."

"Is that true?" Philip asked.

"Quite true. I was the man who married them."

Mr. MacIntyre's powers of fiction are already too well known for me to waste any time in comment upon this speech. No tear, I have reason to believe, blotted that falsehood from the paper where it was taken down.

"I was the man," said Alexander the Great without a blush.

"Were you ever in orders, — you?" asked Phil.

"I, — why not? I was ordained, called, set aside, whatever you call it. It is true that I was young and inexperienced."

"Good Lord, what a man it is!"

"I began by preaching in Edinburgh; but I failed in my very first appearance. They said I wanted unction. I don't know what I wanted. I had learned my discourse by heart the day before. Unfortunately, I took too much on the Saturday night; and in the morning, what with the whiskey and what with the position, and the sermon half forgotten, I fear I made but a poor appearance in the pulpit, a sort o' stickit minister. I never preached there again."

"What did you do next?"

"They wanted a missionary for the Jews in Constantinople. I went there. I staid seven years. I converted three Jews, who, as I afterwards found, had been converted by all my predecessors in turn. They did not cost much; and, as their names were always changed, they helped to make up the quarterly report. However, I had to give that work up; and I believe my three converts all relapsed. Eh! the hundreds of pounds those three rascals cost our country. I say nothing, Phil; but you will think over my parable, as you please to call it. Mind, I believe the marriage was pairfectly legal. You may find out afterwards, whatever you please. Remember, the Church of Scotland is not yet disestablished. It is as respectable as your own church."

"Truly," said Philip, saluting him.

"I say, sir," repeated the reverend divine, "it is as respectable as yours. Otherwise, I should not be in it."

"Quite so," said Philip, — "quite so."

"My friend, you see," he went on, "argued thus, by my advice: 'If I choose, I can at any time investigate the question of legality. On the other hand, my wife will always believe herself married. There will be no question of a very ugly word, because the Church will have done her part. A blessed thing it is, Philip, that there is a church to protect the world."

He stopped for a moment, and took a

sip of half a pint or so of brandy and water. Then his speech became suddenly thick.

"A real-a-tooll-a 'lessed 'spensation of Providence. What that friend of mine, in love and all with most beautiful creech', would have done withou' th' Church, impossible to say." He steadied himself with an effort. "Phil, my dear boy, brandy always makes me ill. Gi' me a ma' hat, ye blettherin' deevil, telling your stories, and keeping your old tutor out of bed, Gi' me ma hat, and le' me go. I'll tell ye the rest to-morrow."

Philip, left alone, began to meditate. The evil suggestion of his tempter lay at his heart like a seedling waiting to put forth its leaves. There was, over and above the other difficulties of the position, that of living if he were to marry. A very considerable slice of the five thousand was gone, that was quite clear. About the rest he was not quite clear, but there could not be much.

"What matters?" he murmured. "I will sell out, and we will do something,— love like the birds, by gad. But I must and will have the girl."

He took out the locket again, and looked at the face which lay in it, with its bright, innocent smile. As he looked, his face softened.

"It is a shame," he said, "a shame! That scoundrel, MacIntyre. No, child, no, I will never wrong you."

CHAPTER XV.

PHIL, you see, was born for better things. His heart was open to all noble impulses, as his eye and his ear were attuned to all harmonies of color and sound. He had a quick appreciation, could take a broad view of things. He knew his own powers; for men no more really deceive themselves on the score of intellect than women on that of beauty. If a man has brains, he knows it. I reserve the rights of those that are not clever and know it, and pretend to be, and are proud of their pretensions. These are the men who go about the world with all the letters of the alphabet after their names, imposing more upon themselves than on the credulous public. There is yet another difference to be made. Some few men are proud of the ἐνέργεια, and many men are proud of the δύναμις. The pride of potentiality lingers long after the power of real work has altogether gone, long after the regret that tinges the first twenty years of an idle man's life. You may see, at Oxford and Cambridge, old men who walk erect and proud, still flushed with the triumphs they achieved as boys, and proud still as men; though their strength has been measured against no other competitors, and in no larger battle-field, and though the men they once defeated have long since conquered in far greater struggles, while they have grown rusty over the combination port.

Philip was now at the age when regret is strongest. At no time do the possibilities of life appear so splendid as at twenty-five, or is the conscience quicker to reproach us for wasted opportunities. But, after all, what was he to do? Life is but a vague thing to a young subaltern of distinct ambitions, not clearly seeing what glorious path to take up. Often enough it becomes a merely ignoble thing, meaning billiards, betting, brandy and soda, et talia. In Phil's case, the life he led was telling on his face, broadening his features, giving them a coarse expression. Our lives are stamped upon our faces. Does there not come a time in every good man's life when the hardest and unloveliest of faces softens into beauty by reason of the victory within? Do not buy a "nose machine," unlovely reader. Have patience, and aim at the highest things; and one day your face, too, shall be beautiful. As for Adonis, if he had lived the life of men about town, his face would have been coarse as theirs before the age of thirty.

The colored blood had something to do with it. It helped to make Philip at once sensitive, eager of distinction, and vain. But not every thing. Fain would I put it all down to color. Mighty comforting thing as it is to us white men to reflect on our superiority, we must be careful about the theory. We may be the aristocracy of Nature. To be sure, the creature who walks about in the similitude of man, with the leg in the middle of the foot; whose calf is in front, and shin behind; whose lips are thick; whose hair is woolly; whose nose is flat; whose brain is small in front and big behind; who has had every chance, and has clearly shown that he can do nothing so well as the white man,— the full-blooded negro, I say, must be regarded as a distant cousin, a poor relation of humanity, and not a "brudder" at all. But as for the mulatto class, I don't know. Take a good quadroon mother, and a good white father, and I really cannot see why the resulting octoroon is a whit inferior to our noble selves,— the aristocrats by color.

But the influence of color is always bad. It helped to make Philip inferior to himself. Let it be remembered about our Phil, the backslider, that, till he was twelve years old and more, he had been accustomed to look on color as the outward mark of a degraded race.

It is all part of the same question. Take the heir of all the Talbots — I mean nothing personal to the heir of this distinguished house. Rear him in pride of birth, in contempt for low-born people, in ideas of the responsibilities and dignities of rank, you will turn out a creature whom the whole world cannot match for pride, self-respect, self-reliance, and the virtues of courage pluck, and endurance, which depend on these.

But take the little *Echo* boy. Suppose he had been subjected from infancy to the same teaching and treatment, would there have been any difference?

Mr. MacIntyre would have replied, "I, vera much doot it."

"The future of a boy, sir," Venn said one evening, "may be entirely prophesied from an observation of his early habits and prejudices. I have gathered, for instance, a few particulars from the boyhood of great men, which throw a wonderful light upon their after-career. When I tell you, for example, that Mr. John Stuart Mill, early in life, had to submit his nails to a disfiguring course of bitter almonds to cure him of biting them, you feel at once that you understand the whole of the philosopher's works."

"I do not, for one," said Jones.

"I have also heard," he went on, "that Mr. Gladstone was birched more than once for cutting Sunday chapel at Eton. Remark that the years pass over his head, and presently he disestablishes the Irish Church. And I believe it is a fact that Mr. Disraeli, as a boy, was wont to sit on a rail, and suck sweets. The analogies between these small circumstances and the after-lives of these men are subtle perhaps, but, once pointed out, ought to be clear even to Jones."

It was on another occasion that Venn showed how an apology might be made for a criminal on higher ground than that reached by the evidence. He delivered his "Oratio pro Peccatore" one night in wig and gown. The following is a portion : —

"Circumstances, my lud, have been against my unhappy client. Brought up under the contempt, or fancied contempt, of society, he early manifested his superiority to the ordinary trammels imposed on the thick-headed by becoming a prig. I do not mean assistant masters of Rugby or Marlborough, who are all prigs, but the common prig of the London streets. From a prig of Holborn, the transition was easy to being a prig on a larger scale and in a more extended sphere. Step by step, my lud, and gentlemen of the jury, you may trace every thing back, not to the want of education, because my client was taught in a National School, and possesses even now a knowledge of the Kings of Israel, but to the fact, that, in the circles wherein he should have moved, his parentage was despised, — his father, gentlemen of the jury, having been a barrister at law, and his mother at one time a lady of the ballet."

And with this as a preface, he would go on to defend his client.

You may leave out the preceding, if you like; but I would rather you read it.

Meantime, it is the month of May, —

" Ce fut en très doux tenz de Mai,
Que di cuer gai,
Vont cis oiseillon chantant,"

as the old French song has it. Laura has met Philip in all about six or seven times — always with another promise of secrecy. She is to marry Philip. That is agreed upon between them. It will please Mr. Venn. Meantime, she is trying to understand her lover. He is kind to her, but not with the tenderness of her guardian to whom she compares him. He is not gentle with her; but passionate, fitful, uncertain of temper, being, indeed, in constant conflict with himself. Then he was suspicious and jealous. Worse than all, he was always asking her if she loved him more, if she loved him at all, if she ever could love him. It wearied and teased her, — this talk of love. "What did it mean?" she asked herself over and over again, but could find no answer.

"I don't know, Philip," she said. "What is the use of always asking?"

"You must know if you love me, Laura."

"How am I to know?"

"Do you love Mr. Venn?"

"Oh, yes!" — her face lit up at once; " but I don't feel at all like that — oh, not in the least bit! If that is love, why I suppose I do not love you."

Philip ground his teeth.

"Always Mr. Venn," he growled. "Tell me, Laura, do you like to be with me?"

"Yes, it is pleasant — so long as you are in a good temper — to talk to you. I like you a great deal better than when I saw you first. I don't think you are such a good man as you ought to be, because I have heard you swear, which is vulgar."

"You shall make me good, when we are married."

"And when will that be?" she asked suddenly. "Because, you see, I will not go on having secrets from Mr. Venn; and I must tell him soon."

"Then, you will give me up," said Philip gloomily.

"Very well," she returned calmly; "that will be better than deceiving Mr. Venn. To be sure, I am only deceiving him with the idea of pleasing him. Of course he will be pleased." She sighed. "If only I felt *quite* sure! But be told me so distinctly that I was to marry a gentleman. Oh, he will be pleased! and I am sure he will like you."

"Only wait a little longer, my dear."

"No, Philip, I will not wait any longer. We must be married at once, or I will tell Mr. Venn all about it. I cannot bear to have secrets from him. I believe, after all, you are only laughing at me, because I am not a lady."

The tears of vexation came into her eyes.

Philip's face was very gloomy. It was in his moments of anger that the cloud fell upon his face which altered his expression, and changed him almost to a negro. It was then that his nostrils seemed to broaden, his lips to project, his cheeks to darken.

"Tell him, then," he returned; "and good-by."

He turned on his heel: it was under the trees in Kensington Gardens. She sat down, and looked at him. There was no anger in her breast for the *spretæ injuria formæ*: none at the loss of a love, none at the destruction of an idol; for she had no love. Philip Durnford had never touched her heart. To please Mr. Venn — let us say it again and again — to please Mr. Venn, who wanted to see her married to a gentleman, and because she was wholly, utterly ignorant of the world and innocent of its ways, she listened to Philip's pleading, and almost offered herself to him in marriage. What did marriage mean? She knew nothing. How was she to know? She spoke to no one but Hartley Venn. She never read novels or love-poetry. Her life was as secluded as that of any nun.

Her lover was three or four yards off, when his expression changed as suddenly to his old one. He wavered, and half turned.

"Philip," cried Laura, "come here."

He turned, and stood before her.

"I think I have made a great mistake. Perhaps Mr. Venn would not be pleased. Let us say good-by, and go away from each other forever. You will soon forget me; and, before I listen to any one again, I will take Mr. Venn's advice."

She spoke in a businesslike tone, as if the whole thing was a mere matter of expediency; and shook her head with an air of the most owl-like wisdom, and looked more beautiful than ever. It was one of the characteristics of this young lady that she had as many different faces as there are thoughts in the brain; for she changed with each. I think her best was when she was playing in the evening — far away, in imagination, in some paradise of her own — alone with Mr. Venn.

Philip's blood leaped up in his veins. All the love and desire he had ever entertained for her seemed multiplied tenfold. He seized her hand, and held it fast.

"My Laura!" he cried, "my little bird, my pet! Do you think I will let you go? At least, not till I have had another chance. It is all finished, — all the waiting and hoping. I am ready to marry you whenever you like. You shall name your own day, and you shall tell Mr. Venn after we are married. Only keep the secret till then."

"How long am I to wait?" asked the girl.

"A week, — ten days, not more. We must make our preparations. I must get you all sorts of things, darling. I love you too well to let you go in a fit of passion. If I have been ill-tempered at times, it is because I am sometimes troubled with many things of which you know nothing. Make a little allowance for me. You, at least, shall never be troubled, Laura, my pet. My happiness is in your hands. Give it back to me; and, in return, all my life shall be spent in trying to please you."

"You frighten me," she said. "You are so passionate. Why do you hold my hand so hard? Look here, Philip — I will do this. To-day is Wednesday. I will meet you and marry you next Wednesday, if you like. If you do not marry me then, you shall not marry me at all. And now, good-by till Wednesday morning."

She tripped away, without her heart beating a single pulsation faster; while he was left trembling in every limb.

"Wednesday!" He began to reflect how people were married. "Wednesday. A week. And there is every thing to be got ready."

He went to the city, to his agent's, and drew five hundred pounds.

"It is my duty, Mr. Durnford," said the agent, "to remind you that you have only a thousand pounds left. Although it is invested at ten per cent, a hundred a year is not a large income."

"You are quite right," said Philip. "It is not, indeed, — too small to be considered, almost. But I must have the five hundred."

He lodged it at Cox's; and then went to a milliner's shop, and ordered a complete trousseau, to be ready packed in a few days. They wanted to try things on;

but he picked out a young lady in the shop of about Laura's dimensions, and told them to try the things on her.

After that, he began to investigate the great marriage question, being as yet little conversant with legal procedure of any kind. He knew that you might go to church, or that you might go to a registrar's office; so he found out the office of a registrar, and asked what he had to do.

It appeared to be very simple. You must reside for a space of three weeks in a parish, — that had already been done; but, which made it impossible, he must have the names posted up in the office for a fortnight. And so he went and bought a special license.

He went home radiant with hope and happiness, and spent a quiet evening alone communing with the future.

The next day he went to see how the trousseau was getting on, and bought a wedding-ring. Then he ordered several new suits of clothes to be made at once, and a large stock of linen, with an undefined feeling that married life meant every thing new.

That was Thursday's work.

Then came Friday, and, with Friday, a visit from Mr. MacIntyre.

"You will not spend many more evenings with me," said Phil; "so sit down, and make yourself comfortable."

"And wherefore not?" asked his tutor.

"Because I'm going to be married next Wednesday."

"Gude guide us!" The good man turned quite pale. "Next Wednesday? Is all settled? It is Laura, of course — I mean Miss Collingwood."

"Of course it is Laura."

"And how are you to be married?"

"By special license."

Mr. MacIntyre looked as if he would ask another question, but refrained; and presently went his way.

On Tuesday evening, Mr. MacIntyre looked up quietly, and asked, —

"What church are you going to be married in?"

Phil turned pale.

"Idiot that I am! I never thought about the church at all."

CHAPTER XVI.

"UNDER ordinary circumstances, Lollie," said Venn, on Tuesday morning, when the child came round, — "under ordinary circumstances, the middle-aged man awakes in the morning with the weary feeling of a day's work before him." He always spoke as if he was oppressed with the duties of labor. "By some unlucky accident, I feel this morning as if the innocent mirth of childhood was back again. I fear nothing. I hope every thing. Two courses are therefore open to us."

"What two courses?" asked the girl, always watchful of Venn's words, and never quite able to follow the conclusions to which they led him.

"I ought, I suppose, to take advantage of this unusual flow of spirits, and write something with the real glow of joy upon it. My works are, perhaps, too uniformly meditative. I dare say you have remarked it."

"I think they are beautiful, all of them," replied the flatterer.

"Ah, Lollie, I ought to be a happy man. I have an audience — limited at present, to be sure — which appreciates me. Mohammed had his Cadijah. But there is another course open to us. See the sun upon the leaves of the two trees in the court. Listen to the sparrows chirping with renewed vigor. They know that the hilarious worm will be tempted forth to enjoy the sun. The purring of the basking cat is almost audible if you open the window. The paper-boy whistles across the square. The policeman moves on with a lighter step. The postman bounds as he walks. The laundresses put off their shawls. Lollie, what do these things mean?"

"They mean going into the country, do they not?" she replied, catching his meaning.

"They do, child. They mean Epping Forest. We will take the train to Loughton, and walk to Epping. They mean a little dinner at the Cock, and a pint of Moselle. They mean strolling through the wood to Theydon Bois, and coming home in the evening with roses in our cheeks."

Another time, Lollie would have jumped for joy. Now she only looked up, and smiled.

"What is the matter, my little girl?" asked Hartley, taking her face in his hands. "For a fortnight past you have not been in your usual spirits. To-day you are pale and worn. Are you ill, Lollie?"

"No," she cried, bursting into tears, "I am not ill; only — only — you are so good to me."

His own eyes filled as he stooped and kissed her forehead.

"You are nervous this morning, little one: you must go to Epping, that is clear."

"It is not only that: it is something else."

"What else, Lollie? You can tell me."

"It is my secret, Mr. Venn."

"Well, then, Lollie, if that is all, I can [w]ait for this precious secret. So be happy [ag]ain."

"It is a secret that concerns you. I [th]ink it will make you happier — you said [on]ce that it would. Oh! I wish I might [te]ll you — I wish you would let me."

"Little Impatience! And what sort of secret would that be which I know al[re]ady? Do you remember the man who [w]hispered his to the winds? Never tell a [se]cret, child; because the birds of the air [m]ay carry it about."

"I have been so unhappy about it," the [gi]rl went on, through her tears. "I can't [sl]eep for thinking of it. Oh, you will be [displ]eased. I know you will! But I wish I [co]uld tell you. I will — I don't care who [is] offended. Mr. Venn, I am going"—

"Stop, Lollie," he replied, putting his [fin]ger to her lips — "Don't tell me. See, [I] give you perfect control over your secret [til]l to-morrow. I refuse to listen — I am [d]eaf. If you try to tell me I shall begin [a]sing, and then the nearest cows will fall [ill], and the calves will lie down and ex[pi]re."

She sighed, and was silent. Alas! if [on]ly she had spoken. Fate was against [h]er.

They went to Loughton, and took that [w]alk through the forest which only the [e]ast-end cockneys love. In the long [gl]ades which stretch right and left the [ha]wthorn was in full blossom; the tender [gr]een of the new leaves, freshly colored, [an]d all of different hues, the soft breath of [th]e young summer, the silence and repose, [a]ll on the girl's spirit, and soothed her. [F]or the moment she forgot the secret, and [al]most felt happy. And yet it lay at her [he]art. Her life — she knew so much — [w]as going to be changed; how much she [co]uld not tell. The life of two would be, [sh]e thought, a life of three. It was what [M]r. Venn had wished for her; and yet — [an]d yet — there was the shade of a danger [up]on her, a foreboding of calamity, which [sh]e tried in vain to throw off. Venn pour[ed] out his treasures of fancy, — those half-[th]ought-out ideas and half-seen analogies [w]hich filled his brain, and evaded him when [h]e tried to put them on paper. But they [fe]ll, for once, on unfruitful ground. She [ca]ught some of them or only half caught [th]em; and then talk grew languid.

"My spirits of this morning seem to have [fa]iled me," he cried impatiently: —

'Not seldom, clad in radiant hue,
Deceitfully goes forth the morn.'

[A] spiritual shower has fallen, and we have [no] umbrella. What is it, child?" he asked impatiently. "Why are we so silent and sad to-day? Let us be happy. Are we drenched with the shower?"

Lollie half laughed, and they walked on. Presently they came upon a woman, toiling along with a baby in her arms, and two children toddling after them. As they came up to her, the woman turned, and struck one of them sharply, for lagging.

"Don't do that, my good creature," said Venn. "Perhaps the little one is tired."

"He's tired and hungry too, sir," she replied; "but I've got to get him to Epping, for all that, and walk he must."

"Poor little man!" said Venn. "Say, are you very tired?"

The child was evidently worn out.

"We are going the same way," he said. "I will carry him for you."

"You, sir? — and a gentleman, and all!"

"Why not? Come, my boy."

He lifted the little one in his arms.

"Lollie, I am not going to let you carry the other. He is big enough to walk."

"Ah, yes, miss, — don't ee now," said the woman. "He's strong enough — ain't you, Jackey?"

Then they all walked away together, — Venn talking to the woman, and she telling her little story; how her husband had got work at Epping, and she was walking all the way from town with her babies.

"I had a comfortable place, sir," she said, "six years ago; and little I thought then of the hardships I should have to undergo. God knows we've been half starving sometimes."

"And are you sorry you married?" asked Lollie.

"Nay, miss, a woman is never sorry she married," replied the poor wife. "My man is a real good sort, unless now and then when it's the drink tempts him. And then I've the children, you see. Ah! well, sir, — God gives us the good and the bad together. But never you think, miss, that a woman is sorry she married."

"Truly," said Venn, "marriage is a continual sacrament."

"Are you married yourself, sir?"

"I am not," he replied gravely. "So far I am only half a man; and now I shall never marry, I fear."

Lollie looked up in his face, over which lay that light cloud of melancholy which alternated in Venn with the sweet smile of his mobile lips. She walked on, pondering. "No woman ever sorry for being married." There was comfort!

"You are happy when you are with your husband?" she asked presently.

The woman turned sharply upon her.

"Of course I am happy with my Ben," she said. "Happiness with us is not made of the same sort of stuff as with you rich folks."

"I am not a rich folk," said the girl, smiling.

"Well, well,—never mind my sharpness, miss. You're one of the kind folks, and that's all I care about."

She trudged on, talking to herself, as such women do, between her lips. Venn was behind them now, talking to the boy in his arms; and so they reached Epping. At the outskirts of the long town, where the cottages begin, the woman insisted on the boy being put down, and began to thank them. Venn gave her a little present of a few shillings, and left her trudging along with the children.

"There goes our Moselle, Lollie," he said with a sigh. "Always some fresh disappointment. I had set my heart on that Moselle for you."

"Mr. Venn! As if I should be so selfish."

"All the same," he grumbled. "It was a stroke of my usual bad luck, meeting that woman."

The bottle of Moselle made its appearance in spite of her; but even the sparkle of the wine failed to raise Lollie's spirits to their usual level. The girl was profoundly dejected. Venn tried the wildest talk, told her the wildest stories; but in vain. It grew close to the hour of the last train,— the Great Eastern, with its usual liberality, having fixed the last train at eight, so as to prevent everybody from enjoying the evening in the Forest. They walked together to the station,—silent, dejected, and unhappy.

"I wish—oh, I wish to-morrow was over!" the girl sighed, when they were alone in the railway carriage.

"Does that secret worry you, Lollie? Is that the wretched cause of your depression? Forget it,—put it out of your mind."

"Let me tell it you."

"Nonsense, child," he laughed: "as if I wanted to know. Think of Midas, as I told you this morning. You shall not tell me now."

"Tell me once more," she said, "what you would like me most of all to do."

He hesitated. Had he followed the promptings of his own heart, he would have said,—

"To marry me, Lollie: to go away with me from London; to live together, never to get tired, in some country place,—the world forgetting, by the world forgot."

If he had but said so!—for it was not yet too late, and the girl was yearning to tell him all.

"I think, child," he said slowly, after a pause, "there is but one thing I really want you to do. I should like, before all else, to see you married happily. Sukey settled that for us, you know. I haven't seen Sukey now for two months. Let us go there to-morrow."

"Not to-morrow," said Lollie. "Do you really mean,—really and truly mean what you say? You would like to see me married?"

Heavens, how blind the man is! He does not see that the girl's whole heart is his; that after all those years her nature is responsive to his own; that she has but one thought, one affection, one passion,— though she knows it not,—the love of Hartley Venn.

"Mean it?" he says, with his tender smile. "Of course I mean it. Recollect what the woman said to-day. You have seen how love may survive poverty, hunger, misery, and rise triumphant over all. Think what love may be when there is no misery to beat it down."

"Love—yes, love. They are always talking about love. I mean marriage."

"They go together, Lollie."

"Does," —she checked the name that rose to her lips—"do people, when they talk of marriage, always mean love."

"They are supposed to do so, Lollie. On the other hand, when they talk of love, they do not always—Ah, here is Fenchurch Street."

No more was said that night. The girl went up to his room, and made him tea; and at half-past nine, she put on her hat.

"To-morrow, Mr. Venn—ah! to-morrow—I shall tell you my secret."

"Sleep soundly, little bird, and forget your secret. What time am I to know it?"

"I don't quite know. I should think, in the afternoon."

"Very well, then; I shall stay in from one till four, and if you do not come then I shall suppose the secret is not ready. Will that do? Good-night, Lollie dear."

He stooped to kiss her forehead; but she took his face in her hands, and kissed his lips almost passionately.

"Always believe," she said, "even if you are not pleased, that I love you, and am so grateful to you that nothing can tell it. Always believe I love you, and hope to please you."

And so slipped away, and was gone.

Did Hartley have no suspicion?—None —none—none. He was not, you see, a man "about town." He did not think or suspect evil. Least of all could he suspect evil in the case of his little girl. And that she should take his words so literally as to marry a man in order to please him would have struck him as beyond all belief.

And yet it was exactly what she was going to do.

CHAPTER XVII.

It is the morning of Lollie's wedding-day. As the girl dresses in her little room, she is crying silently; for a great fear has fallen upon her,—the fear that what she is going to do will not meet with that approval and praise which she at first anticipated. It had been growing in her brain; and when, only yesterday, she first gave it expression, it assumed a clear and definite form. She dressed quickly, trying to soothe her own excitement, drank a cup of tea, and slipped out at ten o'clock to meet her lover. No thought, you will remark, of her grandmother. On the whole, I hardly see how any could be expected. The girl did not belong to the old woman. She owed nothing to her, she had not a thought in common with her, she hardly ever spoke to her; and, save that they slept under one roof, they had nothing to do with each other. Certainly, the idea that the old woman might be made unhappy by conduct of hers never occurred to her. It was a lovely morning in June, one of those days when London puts on its brightest aspect, and looks — as it always would, were Heaven pleased to improve our climate — the empress of cities. Through the crowded streets, down Oxford Street and Regent Street, without stopping to look at the gratuitous exhibitions in the shop-windows, Lollie tripped along, with heightened color and quick-beating pulse.

Going to be married, — going to marry a gentleman! What would be Mr Venn's surprise and delight when she went to him in the evening!

For once, Philip was first at their trysting-place in the park.

Going to be married, going to plight her troth, — for better for worse too. A girl, who, in the absolute innocence of her heart, gives herself to him for no love that she bears him, but only to please, as she thinks, another man. Going to be a bridegroom? He does not look it, as he paces up and down the gravel, driving down his heels, with a pale face and a troubled look. Surely a bridegroom should look in better spirits; and when he sees the girl approaching, his own betrothed, soon to be his bride, why do his knees tremble beneath him, so that he must fain sit down on a bench?

Then she holds out her hand, and he takes it undauntedly.

"Remember what I said, Philip," she began directly. "Unless you marry me to-day I shall not marry you at all; and I shall tell Mr. Venn every thing."

"Is that the only love-vow you have to give me?" asked the bridegroom.

"O Philip! do not talk like that. Always of love, and love-vows! I tell you again, I do not understand it. What should I say, if not the truth?"

Philip sighed. There was yet time to save himself. The girl did not love him; but, then, he loved the girl. He had that passionate longing for this sweet, fair-haired maiden, — so bright, so clever, so new, — which, I think, can never come to a man more than once in his life. God has made us so that not more than one woman can be an angel to us. Her excepted, — we know the sex. We grovel to her; we stand upright before the rest, conscious of the head and a half difference between the man and the woman. Lollie was Philip's angel. And — alas! the pity of it — there are so many men who cannot hold their one woman an angel for longer than the honeymoon; and must needs cry shame and folly to themselves for the sweet infatuation which alone makes life tolerable to us.

"Come, Laura," said Philip, "I have the license in my pocket, — a special license. See here." He pulled out the document. "The Archbishop of Canterbury has given his consent, you see; so that is all right. I thought you would best like a private marriage."

"Oh, yes!" cried Lollie, — "much best."

"And as we shall have no wedding-breakfast, no carriage, and nothing but our own two selves, I have arranged with a very excellent clergyman — a Scotch clergyman — to perform the ceremony for us which will make you my wife. Will that do for you?"

He had fallen, then, into the pit digged for him.

"Surely, Philip," she said, "it shall all be as you think best for us; and then I shall tell Mr. Venn."

He had been out of the park into the Strand, and took a Hansom cab to Keppel Street.

Mr. MacIntyre was himself standing at the window in the ground-floor front, and came to open the door. Then he led them in, and shut the door carefully. That done, he stared hard at the bride.

"Come into the other room a moment," said Philip in a hoarse voice. "I want to say a word."

The other room was Mr. MacIntyre's bedroom, opening from the first by folding-doors. Lollie, left alone, looked out of the window and waited. As she looked, a funeral procession came from an opposite house, and the dismal *cortège* passed down the street. Then, too, the sky was clouded over, and big drops of rain were falling. Her heart sank within her. Truly, an omen of the worst. She turned from the window, and looked round the room. A curious fragrance, unknown to her, was lingering about the corners. It was due to toddy. A small fire was burning in the grate, though the morning was warm; and a kettle was singing on the hob. Two or three pipes lay on the mantle-shelf; and a few books, chiefly of the Latin grammar class, bought when Mr. MacIntyre meditated taking pupils, stood upon the shelves. The furniture was hard and uncomfortable. And her spirits fell lower and lower.

In the other room she heard voices. If she had heard what was said, she might even then have escaped; but she only heard the murmur.

Philip, when the door was shut, turned upon his companion, with lips and cheeks perfectly white, and, seizing Mr. MacIntyre by the shoulders, shook the little man backwards and forwards as if he had been a reed.

"Villain!" he groaned, — " black-hearted, calculating scoundrel."

"When you've done shaking your best friend," returned his tutor, " and calling bad names, perhaps you will listen for a few moments to the voice of reason."

"Go on, then."

Philip sat down on the edge of the bed.

"I can't do it, MacIntyre, I can't do it," he murmured. "It is the blackest villany. Poor Laura! poor darling! Oh what scoundrels we are! And I, who was once an honorable man!"

"Hoots, toots," said the philosopher.

But Philip was lying with his face in his hands, shaking with emotion.

MacIntyre contemplated his old pupil for a few moments with a puzzled expression; then — for he felt unequal to the ordeal without support — he went to the cupboard, and very silently poured out just half a glass of raw spirit, which he swallowed hastily. Then he addressed himself to business, and tried, but with small effect, to assume a sympathetic air.

"Ma puir laddie," he said " You surely never thought that I, Alexander MacIntyre, the releegious guide of your infancy, was going to counsel you to take a dishonorable step. Phil, ye'll be as legally tied up as if the archbishop did it. Believe me, a regularly ordained minister of the established kirk o' Scotland. If a prince was going to be married, this would be the right shop to come to. And you, with a license, special and most expensive, and all."

Philip sat up again.

"Is it true, MacIntyre? Is it really true, what you say?"

"True, my Phil, every word true. Shall I swear to it? Now brush your hair, and look bright, and let us go back to the lassie. Hech! man — there's a thunder-clap. Come along, or she will be frightened."

He pushed him back, and, sitting down at the table, laid open a Bible, borrowed for the occasion from the unsuspecting landlady.

"Sit down, both of you," he began imperiously.

They sat down opposite him.

"Have ye got a license, Mr. Durnford?" he asked. "Good. A special license, granting you permission to be married in any parish? Good. At any time? Good. In any place of worship? Vera good. And by any clergyman? Vera good indeed. Young leddy, your name, if you please. You may write it here."

He had prepared two slips of paper to imitate a marriage certificate. And Philip noticed now, for the first time, that he was "dressed" for the character, in complete black, with a white neckcloth that would not have disgraced a banjo man, and which, with his red nose, gave him quite the appearance of a superior mute. And, the signatures obtained, when he turned over the leaves of the Bible a cheerful piety became diffused over his face, quite new to his friends, and very remarkable to witness. Lollie looked at the clergyman who was marrying her with an instinctive feeling of aversion. The ill-fitting black clothes, the voluminous necktie, the red nose and pale cheeks, the shaking hand, all told her, as plain as words could speak, that the man was one of the great Stiggins's tribe of whom Hartley Venn had told her. Nevertheless, she was in Philip's hands; and, like the birds on the solitary's island, she had not yet learned to distrust mankind, because she only knew one man.

It does not befit this page to describe with greater detail the mockery of marriage which Mr. MacIntyre solemnly went through. Suffice it to say, that, after reading a chapter of the Bible, he prayed. And, after his prayer, making the two stand up, he joined their hands, pronounced them man and wife, and concluded by an exhortation mainly made up of what he still recollected of the Shorter Catechism. What it wanted in unction it gained in doctrine; and, though there was little in the discourse calculated to assist the bride in her duties of married life, there was plenty which might have been used as a rod and staff by the Calvinistic Christian. Lollie stood frightened and bewildered; for all through the "service," the thunder had been rolling and crashing, and the lightning seemed to play over the very house where this great wickedness was being committed. Even Mr. MacIntyre was moved by it. It was one of those great thunderstorms which sometimes break over London, striking terror to all hearts, such as those which fell upon us last year — I mean the year of grace 1872, — a fierce, roaring, angry, thunderstorm. And as the lightning flashed across his eyes, and the thunder pealed in his ears, the minister fairly stopped in his discourse, and murmuring, "Hech! sirs, this is awfu'!" waited for the anger of the elements to subside.

But he ended at last, and, congratulating the bride, offered Philip one of the slips of paper, keeping the other for himself. Then he rubbed his hands and laughed, — a joyless cackle. And then he produced a black bottle and a small cake, and poured out three glasses of wine. He drank off his own at a gulp, refilled it, and sat down rubbing his hands again.

This was Lollie's wedding-breakfast.

Outside, the hail pattered against the windows, the thunder rolled, and the warm spring air seemed chilled again to winter.

Philip said nothing. A look was in his face such as neither MacIntyre nor Lollie had ever seen before, — a sort of wild, terrified look; such a look as might be imagined in the face of a man who, after long planning, has at last committed a great and terrible crime; such a look as one would have if he heard the voice of God accusing him, — the voice Philip heard in the storm. Men are so. That unlucky Jew whom the thunder-storm rebuked for eating pork was not the first, nor will he be the last, to connect natural phenomena with his own misdoings. In the storm outside, Philip, with the superstition of a Creole, heard the anger of Heaven. It only echoed the remorse in his own heart. A second time he seized MacIntyre by the arm, and led him to the bedroom.

"Once again," he said, "I *must* speak to you. Tell me whether it is true — is it true — are we married? Speak the truth, or I will kill you!"

"You are married, Phil," returned the other. "No question can ever arise on the legality of the marriage until — until ". —

"Until when?"

"Until you come into your property. And now, listen. There is, *perhaps*, — I only say perhaps, — a little irregularity. If you want to remove that, remember to take your wife into Scotland, whenever you please, and live with her as your wife openly. Then you need fear nothing. I say this to make you quite certain; but I do not believe there can be any legal doubt."

Philip looked at him with a surprised air. Then, with great relief, he walked into the other room, where Lollie was standing, waiting and puzzled.

"Laura, my darling," he cried, kissing her passionately. "My wife, my bride! we are married at last. If ever I desert you, may God desert me!"

She drew herself from his arms, not blushing, not coy, not ashamed; but only cold.

"We are really married?" she cried, clapping her hands. "I wasn't certain. And now we will go straight to Mr. Venn, and tell him."

The two men looked at each other.

"My child," said Philip, changing color, "we must be married like everybody else, must we not?"

"But we are, Philip, are we not?"

"Yes, dear; but married people always go away for a journey together. You and I are going to France for a month. When we come back, we shall call at Mr. Venn's chambers."

She stamped her foot.

"I shall go to-day. You said I was to tell him to-day. I *will* tell him. Philip, if you do not go with me, I will go by myself."

"Make her write," whispered the man of experience.

"You certainly cannot go, Laura," said her husband. "That is impossible; but I tell you what you shall do. You shall write him a letter, telling him all. Mr. MacIntyre shall take it, and tell him the particulars. We have but a quarter of an hour to spare, for our train starts at once. Now, dear" — taking pen and paper — "sit down and write. It is best so — it is indeed."

She burst into tears. She declared that she had been deceived. She insisted on going at once to Gray's Inn. If Philip had not held her, she would have gone.

Mr. MacIntyre said nothing; only, when he caught Philip's eye, he pointed to the pens and paper. Meantime, it was a critical moment; and his nose, which he constantly rubbed, seemed bigger and redder than ever.

"Laura, you must not go to Mr. Venn to-day. It is absurd," pleaded Philip. "Sit down now. Write: no one shall read what you say. And it shall be sent at once; but you cannot go to Gray's Inn."

Lollie sat down, and tried to write; but she burst into fresh tears, and was fain to bury her face in her hands.

"Women are so," whispered the Scotchman. "Obsairve. In ten minutes she will be laughing again."

In less than ten minutes she recovered, and tried to write. Philip waited patiently, watching her.

She began three or four sheets of notepaper, and tore them up. At last she wrote hurriedly, —

"Dearest Mr. Venn, — My secret may now be told. I have done what you wished me so much to do. I have married a gentleman. I have married Mr. Philip Durnford; and I am always, and ever and ever, your own most grateful and most loving little girl —

Lollie."

She folded it up, addressed it, and gave it to her husband.

"MacIntyre," said Philip, "take the note round, will you, this very day? Tell Mr. Venn that my wife and I are gone to France — probably to Normandy — for a month; that we shall call upon him directly we return; that my greatest wish is to gain his friendship. Will that do for you, Laura?"

"Philip," she said, taking his hand, — "now you are really kind."

"That is my own Laura; but now we must make haste. I have got your boxes at the station."

"My boxes?"

"Yes. You did not think you were going to France with nothing but what you have on, did you?"

"I never thought about going to France at all."

"The tickets are taken. There will be nothing to do but to make ourselves happy. Now, MacIntyre, get me a cab, will you?"

It seemed strange that so reverend a gentleman should be ordered in this peremptory way to fetch a cab; but Lollie was too much surprised with every thing to feel perplexed at this. The cab came.

"Now, my darling! MacIntyre, goodby. Jump in, Laura."

"Don't forget my letter, Mr. MacIntyre," cried the girl. "Mind you take it to-day."

And so they drove off.

Mr. MacIntyre returned to his room. "About this letter, now," he said. "Let me read it."

By the help of the kettle he steamed the envelope, opened, and read the poor little epistle.

He put it down and meditated.

"Suppose I take it round," he said. "Why should I? Poor bonny little lassie! Loves him more than her husband — that is clear. If I take it, difficulties, dangers, all sorts of things, may happen. If I do not take it, this Mr. Venn will never forgive the girl. Well, which is it, — my happiness, or hers? A man, or a woman? Myself, or another?"

He meditated a long time. Cruelly selfish and wicked as the man was, he had been touched by the girl's beauty and innocence, and would willingly have spared himself this additional wickedness; but then there rose up before him the vision of a court of justice. He saw himself tried by a jury for mock marriage. He knew that the law had been broken. What he did not know was, how far the offence was criminal, or if it was criminal at all. Then a cold perspiration broke out upon him.

"Let us hide it," he said, — "let us hide it. Perhaps we can devise some means of preventing this man Venn from knowing it — at all events, just yet."

And so saying, he pushed the letter into the fireplace, and watched it burning into ashes.

"And as for Master Phil," he murmured, "why, I'll give him just two months to cure him of this fancy, and bring him to the end of his money. Then, we shall see — we shall see. The great card has to be played."

CHAPTER XVIII.

"I am ill at ease to-night," said Hartley, on the Wednesday evening when Jones and Lynn found him at the "Rainbow." "I am low-spirited. Forebodings, like the screech-owl's mew, oppress me. Laura was to have told me some grand piece of news to-day, and has not come. Then there was the thunder. I am afraid of thunder. Engineers ought to turn their attention to it. Bring me some bitter beer, George — unless the thunder has turned it sour."

"I like this place," he went on. "It is quiet. The mutton is good, the beer is good, and there is an ecclesiastical air about it. The head-waiter resembles an elderly verger without his gown. The manager might pass for a canon; and as for the carver, I have never known any one beneath the dignity of a prebendary grow bald in that singular manner."

"Life, Jones," he continued, in the course of his dinner, "may be compared to a banquet. You have, perhaps, often anticipated this comparison."

"Not I," said Jones — "not I, myself; but Longfellow has."

'Life is but an endless banquet,
 Where we still expectant sit;
Be not thou a cold, wet blanket,
 Damping all thy neighbor's wit.

Chops for one; and for another,
 Turkey stuffed with truffles gay:
Only bread for me. My brother,
 Turn the carver's eye this way.

> Let us all be up and eating,
> With a heart for any slice;
> Beef grows cold, and life is fleeting;
> Pass the champagne and the ice.'"

Venn repeated his first words, and resumed the topic.

"When it comes to my turn to be served, the noble host, addressing me with a countenance full of benevolence and friendship, says, 'Hartley, my dear boy, take another disappointment.' It would be bad manners, you know, to refuse. Besides, I am not quite certain how a refusal would be received. So I bow and smile: 'Thank you, my Lord. One more, if you please. A very little one, with gravy.'"

"Gravy! Is gravy the alleviator?"

"Gravy, Jones, is the compensator. So I get helped again, and sigh when the plate comes back to me. In the distribution of good things, no one is consulted; but, by tacit agreement, we show our good breeding by pretending to have chosen. So, too, I believe, when convicts at Portland converse, it is considered manners to take no notice of each other's chains. I might prefer, perhaps, pudding and port, such as my neighbor gets; but I am resigned."

He sighed heavily, and went on eating his dinner with a tremendous appetite.

"Let us have," he said, when they had finished, "a Chorus night. Arthur Durnford is coming. Not a regular Chorus, but a Chorus of emergency. I hope it will not thunder any more."

"I have been making observations lately," he began, "on a class of women hitherto little studied. Speak up, Jones."

"Nay," said the dramatist, "I was but thinking of the old lines — I forget the author — about women, —

> 'Virtue and vice the same bait have:
> On either's hook the same enticements are.
> Woman lures both the base and brave,
> And beauty draws us with a single hair.'"

"There is method in his madness," said Venn. "It is to be regretted only that Virtue does not always choose the bait with the same discrimination as Vice. This, however, is a wide subject. I was about to call the attention of the Chorus to the woman who sniffs. About a week ago, having nothing to do, I got into a favorite omnibus for an hour or two of quiet thought. The rattle of the omnibus glasses, when the wind is westerly, I find conducive to meditation; and as the Favorite line runs from Victoria to the extreme verge of civilization at Highgate, there is ample time. Several women got in, and I noticed — perhaps it was partly due to the time of year — several sniffs as each sat down and spread her petticoats. Your regular female omnibus passenger always takes up as much room as she can, and begins by staring defiantly round. I was at the far end, whither I had retired to avoid an accusation of assault; for they kick your shins across the narrow passage, and then give you in charge, these ladies. So delicate, my friends, is the virtue of the class to which I allude, that even the suspicion of an attack is resented with this celestial wrath. Presently, however, I being the only male, there came in a young person, quiet, modest, and retiring. She made her way to the far end, and sat down next to me. Instantly there was fired a volley — a hostile salute — from seven noses: a simultaneous sniff of profound meaning. Versed in this weapon of feminine warfare, and therefore understanding the nature of the attack, the newcomer blushed deeply, and dropped her veil. It was like the lowering of a flag. I took the earliest opportunity of tendering her respectfully the compliments of the season; and, in spite of a second and even a fiercer attack, we held our own, and conversed all the way to Highgate. Coming back by the same omnibus, I insensibly glided into a vision."

"Good," said Jones, "let us have the vision."

"Methought I stood on an eminence, and looked down, myself unseen, upon an island where men and women wandered about, of uncouth form and strange proportions. Some with venomous tongues, which lolled out in perpetual motion, yet saying nothing; some with trumpet-like noses; some with curiously deformed fingers; some with large and goggle eyes; and some with heads of enormous dimensions. This, my guide — I had an angel with me, of course — told me, was one of the lesser islands of Purgatory. It appears that Dante was quite wrong in his account of that place, which consists really of a group of contiguous islands, like the Bermudas. I dare say I shall see some more of them before I die. The one I was standing over was appropriated to sinners in small things, — backbiters, envious, malicious, mean, grasping, selfish (these last had enormous stomachs, like barrels of port wine), and attributors of unworthy and base motives (who were gifted with a corresponding prominence behind). I requested permission to inspect the company more closely, and was taken down into their very midst. I was astonished to find that a very large majority of them were women: their dress and behavior showed them to belong to our own middle class. They were all English; because, by reason of the great babble of conversation that goes on among this sort of criminals, it is found advisable to separate the nationalities.

"Looking more closely, I observed that the men chiefly carried the protuberances, fore and aft, of which I have spoken; while the women, nearly one and all, had the trumpet-shaped nose. The peculiarity of its shape was that the mouth of the trumpet was outward. Its musical effect could therefore only be produced by drawing the air towards the head, much in the same way as by a sniff. This struck me as a very singular arrangement. I was also informed that most of them, on their first arrival, had but very small trumpet noses; but that these, by dint of practice, increased daily and gradually, until they arrived at the gigantic proportions which I saw around me. They began by being proud of this growth; but by degrees grew alarmed, and were seriously inconvenienced by its great size. They then began to reduce its dimensions, by allowing it to remain, so to speak, unexercised; and if, as sometimes happened, they arrived at a perception of its manifest ugliness, they discontinued its use altogether, when it totally vanished. Others had the great tongues of which I have spoken. They were too big to use for speech; but, as their owners were always wanting to communicate some fresh piece of malicious gossip, they were perpetually wagging and bobbing, though no articulate sound came forth. The possessors of the tongues were more melancholy of aspect than the trumpet-nosed sisters, because they were debarred from the use of their instruments altogether. The tongue followed the same laws as the nose, and there were even women provided with both tongue and nose. While I was contemplating these unhappy victims of vice, my attention was directed by my guide to a young lady of about twenty-five, whose nose had at its extremity the merest rudimentary mouthpiece, — so small as to be almost a beauty spot, — suggestive only of where a trumpet had formerly been. My guide accosted her, and requested her to give a history of herself. She smiled and complied.

"'I was the daughter of a professional man, living in the neighborhood of Russell Square. We were not rich, but we were well off. I was sent to a boarding-school at Brighton, where the principal things we were taught were to dress well, to aspire to a wealthy husband, to despise people of lower rank, to aim at getting as much amusement out of life as possible, to consider the admiration of men as the glory of a woman's life, and to regard the labor of men as performed only with one aim, — to provide dress and a good establishment for their wives. This was the kind of education in our fashionable boarding-school; and when my sister and I came back to Russell Square, we were fully provided with all the weapons for that warfare which constitutes the life of most women. I found, wherever I went, nearly all girls the same as ourselves. We were good, inasmuch as we all went to church regularly, and would have done nothing wrong. But we filled up our time with frivolity and gossiping. We were petty in our vices, and, therefore, you see, our punishment is petty.' She pointed to her nose, whereon the least tip of a kind of button marked the place where the mouth-piece had been only five minutes before. 'The evil we did was not very great, and so our punishment is light. Even this is generally removed, if we repent.'

"'Do you repent?' I asked.

"'Oh, yes!' she said; 'the lives of women, which might be so smooth, so happy, and full of love, are eaten into and poisoned by these habits of malice and envy. You men think us angels; and when you marry us, and find out that we are full of faults, you begin to decry the whole sex. When will some one teach us that largeness of heart and nobleness that so many men have?'"

"A most sensible young woman," Jones interrupted.

"At this moment the button at the end of her nose entirely disappeared, and she vanished.

"'Where is she gone?' I asked my guide.

"'There was that in his face which betokened temper. I fancy he must have been paid a percentage on the inhabitants of his island, or taken them on board by contract, according to number; for he refused to answer me, and was on the point of ordering me to move on, when I awoke."

"The young woman, you say, is in the Bermudas," said Jones. "I would she were in the arms of one who would rightly appreciate her.

'Where the remote Bermudas ride,
A trumpet-nosed maid I espied;
And, as I looked her through and through,
Her imperfections thus she blew, —
"In Purgatory still I sniff,
And I will gladly furnish, if
You wish it, such a dismal tale,
As well may frighten maidens all."'

I leave out a good many lines, which I have forgotten, —

'So sang she with the trumpet nose;
My own with sorrow at her woes,
I loudly blew; and as she spoke,
The neighboring sniffs the echoes woke.'

I believe the lines were originally Andrew Marvell's."

It was Jones's hard fate in the Chorus, that whatever he quoted nobody seemed to take any notice. Venn's face betrayed no signs of having heard what he said; while Lynn, as usual, smoked in his chair, saying nothing at all. For Lynn was one of those men who seldom speak at all; and when they do, speak with more earnestness and energy than is generally heard.

Arthur, however, laughed; and the spectacles of Jones beamed gratefully on him.

"My Cousin Philip," said Arthur, "started an infamous theory some little time ago, that women prefer warmth to any thing else in the world."

"Well," said Venn, "there may be something to be said for it. I believe that he is partly right. Women live in the house. Their ideas of life are those of the domestic circle. To have every thing pleasant, comfortable, and elegant round them is quite a natural thing to desire. It is perhaps a brutal way of putting it, to say that they like to be warm. In the Chorus, we prefer a more indirect way of approaching a subject."

"Poor Phil takes direct views," said Arthur.

"Bring him here, and we will cure him," said Jones. "On the subject of women, there is nothing so elevated as the views of the Chorus, — the Sophoclean Chorus. We are, if we are nothing else, Sophoclean in our views of love.

'Love, the unconquered, thou whose throne
　Is on youth's fair and rounded cheek,
　Whom neither strong nor brave nor weak
Can e'er escape, — thee, thee we own.

Thou by thy master magic's aid
　Cheatest keen eyes that else see well;
And o'er the loudest-sniffing maid
　Pourest the glamor of thy spell.

The nymph whose deepest, fondest prayer
　Is for a sheltered nook and warm,
Glows with a thousand fancies rare,
　Lit with thy pyrotechnic charm.'

"I suppose you will say that Sophocles wrote that?" growled Lynn.

"A free imitation only. It may, perhaps, in some points excel the original. I say nothing."

"They talk a great deal," said Lynn, breaking his usual silence, "of educating women, and making them less frivolous. Of course, the immediate result is to send them to the opposite extreme. Now, of all the odious women you can meet, give me the strong-minded."

"Do not give her to me," said Jones.

"But it's all nonsense. They have made a college for them, and have Cambridge men there to teach them. In other words, they are going to make them second-rate scholars and third-rate mathematicians. What on earth is the use of that?"

"Is it," asked Venn, "the function of the Chorus to discuss female education?"

"Why not?" returned Lynn. "By Jove! I've a good mind to have a vision too."

"Do," said Jones. "Two visions in the same evening are at least more than we could have expected."

Lynn smoked meditatively for a few moments.

"I dreamed a dream," he began. "I thought that I stood in the world of the future, — the future of a hundred years. Woman was emancipated, as they said. Every woman did, like all men do now, what was right in her own eyes. They could preach, teach, heal, practise law, live alone, and be as free as any man can be now."

"Well?" asked Jones, for Lynn stopped.

"Well, I can't be as graphic as Venn was, because I have not the art of telling a story. I walked about the streets of London. I went into the houses, into the clubs, into the theatres, — everywhere. The first thing that struck me was the entire mixture of the sexes. Women were everywhere. They drove cabs, they were markers at billiard-tables, they kept shops, they plied trades, they were in the public offices — for every thing was open to public competition. I talked to some of them. I found they were very much changed from what I remembered them. Not only were they coarse in appearance and manners, but they seemed to have lost the delicacy of woman's nature. The bloom was off the youngest of them. Men, too, had lost all their old deference and respect. There were none of the courtesies of life left; for the women had long since revolted against being considered the weaker sex. A new proverb had arisen, — 'The six-shooter makes all equal.' Every woman carried one ostentatiously ; not, I fancied, so much for self-protection as for purposes of attack. Their talk seemed loud and coarse, their jokes were club-jokes, their stories were like those we hear on circuit and in mess-rooms. Their dress was altered too. The old robes were discarded; and short kilts, with a tight-fitting jacket, seemed to be all the fashion. I asked my guide, — did I say I had a guide?"

"You did not," said Jones. "Was he an angel?"

"Of course I had an angel. I asked him — or her — if they were all married women? Marriage, she told me, had been abolished by a large majority of women, as contrary to the true spirit of liberty. This was directly against the wish of the men, who, it seemed, desired to retain the custom. As, however, the ceremony is one which requires the consent of two, it was abolished. Then the men turned sulky, and formed a kind of union or guild for the protection of the marriage-laws. For a time it appeared as if the world would be depopulated: the statistics of the Registrar showed a falling-off in the number of births, which excited the gravest apprehensions. This league, however, fell to the ground from want of strength in the weaker brethren. After that, all went well. The laws of property were altered, and an old law, belonging to an obscure Indian tribe in the Neilgherry Hills, was introduced. By virtue of this, property descended only through the mother. The interests of freedom were served, it is true; but it seemed to me as if there were some losses on the other hand, for all the men seemed dejected and lonely. There were no longer any high aims; no one looked for any thing more than worldly advantage; no one dreamed of an impossible future, as we do now; there were no enthusiasts, no reformers, no religious thinkers, no great men. All was a dead level. I asked my guide if there were any exceptions, if what I saw really represented the actual world. She confessed it did; but she boasted, with pride, that the world was now reduced to a uniform mediocrity. No one looked for any thing better, therefore no one tried for any thing better; no one praised any thing good, therefore no one tried to do any thing good; there were no prizes for excellence, therefore no one was excellent. But it all seemed dreary, stupid, and immoral as a modern music hall; and I awoke, glad to find that it was, after all, only a dream. I forgot to tell you that there were no homes, — there were no families. Children were sent out to be nursed, and the necessity of labor on the part of the women necessitated the abolition of the maternal instinct."

"Is that all?" said Jones.

"It is," said Lynn; "and, before you make a rhyme about it, — I can see you are meditating one, — I just wish to state my moral. Women are only what their circle of men make them. If they are frivolous, it is because the men are frivolous; if they are vain, it is because the men teach them vanity. But men have always to fall back upon their one great quality, — their purity. Deference to a quality which they so seldom possess seems to me the truest safeguard for women, and the thing most likely to be a restraint upon men. Education, emancipation, suffrage, — it is all infernal humbug. We confuse words We call that education which is only instruction; we call emancipation what is a departure from the natural order; we take woman from her own sphere, and put her into ours, and then deplore the old subjection of the sex. Good God! sir, — man is the nobler as well as the stronger. His function is to work, — to do; to drag the world along, to fight against and keep down the great surging sea of sin and misery that grows with our civilization and keeps pace with our progress. But woman's function is to stand by and help; to train the children, to comfort the defeated, and succor the wounded. Why, in the name of all the — all the saints, should she want to leave her own work and take ours?"

CHAPTER XIX.

ON that Wednesday night, when Hartley Venn went to bed, it was late, even for him; and when, at six in the morning, a fierce knocking came to his bedroom-door, it was some fifteen minutes or so before he could quite make up his mind that he was not dreaming. At last, however, he roused himself sufficiently to be certain that somebody was actually knocking. Mrs. Peck was, in fact, the disturber of his rest. She was beating on the panel with a hammer, in despair of being able to awaken him in any other way. He half opened the door cautiously, and peered through to discover the cause of this phenomenon.

"Mrs. Peck," he said, "we have known each other now for a great many years, and I never before remember you doing so ridiculous a thing as to call me at six, the very hour when civilized life is on the point of recovering its strength. Pray, Mrs. Peck, do you take me for the early worm?"

The old woman pushed the door open, and came into his bedroom, looking curiously round. She was not, taking her at the best, a pleasant specimen of womanhood to look upon; but this morning she looked even less attractive than usual. For her false front was slipping off sideways; her black stuff dress was covered with mud; her wrinkled old face was begrimed with dirt, and puckered up with trouble; and Venn, rubbing his eyes, gradually awoke to the consciousness that she was staring at him with frightened eyes, and that something had happened.

Realizing this, he stepped back and got into bed, disposing the pillows so that he could give audience with an air of preparedness. Nothing, he used to say, speaking after the manner of Charles the Second's period, makes a man look more ridiculous in the eyes of his mistress than an appearance of haste; and, whatever happens, it may as well be received with dignity, which only costs a little time for reflection. Now, there was no possibility, short of genius for dignity, of preserving a dignified appearance while shivering on a mat with but one garment on, and that of the thinnest and lightest kind. Therefore he retreated to the bed, and, propped up by the pillows, prepared to receive Mrs. Peck with self-respect. Not one thought of danger to himself: not one gleam of suspicion about the girl.

The old woman came in, confused and trembling. She looked about in a dazed sort of way, and then sank into a chair, crying,—

"O Mr. Venn! what have you done with her? What have you done with her?"

All Venn's dignity vanished. He fell half back on the pillow for a moment, and then started up, and caught the old woman by the arm.

"Done with her? Done with her? Done with her? Speak, Mrs. Peck. Tell me what you mean."

"You know, sir," she said. "You know who I mean. What have you done with her, I say? What have you done with the girl as you petted and made so much of, till she wasn't fit company for her grandmother? Oh, I ain't afraid to speak! Where is she, I say? Where have you gone and hid her away? But I'll find her,—if I search all London through, I'll find her. Oh, my fine grand-daughter, that was why he wanted you up here every day, and nothing too good for you; and lessons every day, and grand clothes. And what am I to say now to the people that cried out how good she was? And where, oh! where is my 'lowance for her?"

Venn stared at her, speechless.

"Give her back to me, Mr. Venn. Nobody knows nothing. It shall all be as it used to be. Only let her come back, and we can make up a story and stop their mouths. Nobody knows."

"Woman!" cried the man, not knowing what he said, "woman! you are mad,— where is Lollie?"

"And you, too, that I thought the best of men. You made her a little lady, so that all the people envied her. And one pound ten a week gone! You made her so good that not a creature could find a word to say against her. But you are all wicked alike. And now it's you. And after all these years. And I'm to lose my 'lowance, and go into the workus."

Her voice changed into a sort of wail, for her feelings were divided between the loss of her grand-daughter and the probable loss of her allowance.

"Give her back to me, Mr. Venn. It isn't only the loss of the one pound ten a week, paid regular, though the Lord knows it's the parish I must come on. Give her back to me, and I'll go on my bended knees to you. Say she's good, and I'll pray for you all the days of my life; and go to St. Alban's, though I can't abide their ways, a purpose. Oh, give her back to me! Tell me where you've put her."

She sat down exhausted, in the chair by the bedside.

"It isn't the 'lowance I mind so much; nor it isn't the girl, because we never had much to say to each other, her and me; but it is the people. And they will talk. And one pound ten a week's an awful sum to lose. And see, Mr. Venn,—I know that gentlemen will be gentlemen; and though the pore men curse, the pretty ones always goes to the gentlemen. That's right, I suppose! though why it's right, God only knows. But give her back to me; for I am an old woman, and respected, by reason of my grand-daughter. Give her back to me, Mr. Venn. I mind an old story about a man and a ewe lamb, and let me look the folk in the face again, for the love of God!"

He was standing before her in his night shirt all the time, not knowing what to say, feeling dizzy and confused.

Now he took her by the arm, and led her to the door.

"One moment, Mrs. Peck. Sit down and wait while I dress. I shall not be long. Don't say another word till I come."

He dressed with feverish haste, though his fingers were trembling, and he could not find the buttons. Then, after ten minutes or so, he came into the sitting-room, and, pouring out a glass of spirits, made the poor old creature drink it down.

"Now, Mrs. Peck, let us try and get all our courage. I have not seen her—believe me, my poor woman—since Tuesday evening."

"She came home on Tuesday evening at ten o'clock."

"Yes; she was to have come and told me something yesterday."

"She went out at half-past nine yesterday morning, and she never came back. I waited for her till ten last night; and, thinking she was with you, I went sound asleep, and didn't wake till this morning at six. And then I looked in her room, for the door was open, and she wasn't there. And the workus is all I've got to look to."

Venn's hands were trembling now, and his face white.

"She cried when she left me on Tuesday.

She had her secret then. Mrs. Peck, remember, my little girl is good. She has done no harm,—she can do nothing wrong. Fool that I was when she wanted to tell me her secret, and I would not hear it. Where is she? But she is a good girl. Only wait—wait—wait—we shall see."

He spoke hopefully, but his heart fell. Nothing wrong? Whence, then, those tears? Why had she been so sad for two or three weeks? Why had she harped upon her secret? And yet, what could she do? Always with him,—whose acquaintance could she make?

"You're telling me gospel truth, sir?" cried his laundress. "Swear it—swear it on the Bible."

"I don't know where my Bible is,—the Lord forgive me!" he answered. "Do not let us be miserable," he went on, with an attempt at cheerfulness. "I expect she is stopping out with some friends."

"She has no friends. Never a soul has she ever spoken to, for twelve years, but you and me, and Miss Venn."

"Perhaps she is up there. I will go and see."

He tried to cheer up the old woman; invented a thousand different ways in which the girl might have been obliged to pass the night away from home; and then, because his own heart was racked and tortured, he hurried off to his sister's.

Sukey he met on her way to early service,—that at half-past seven. It was one of the peculiarities of that young lady to find a considerable amount of enjoyment in these extra-parochial, so to speak, and extraordinary forms of religion.

"Hartley!—you, of all men in the world, at half-past seven!"

"Sukey, have you got Lollie with you?"

"Laura? I haven't seen her for six weeks,—not since she had tea with me. But, Hartley, what is the matter?"

He caught hold of the railing which ran round the garden of the square, and almost fell. For it was his one hope; and his head swam.

"God help us all!" he murmured,—"my little girl is lost."

What could she say?

"She left me on Tuesday evening. She told me that yesterday I should learn a secret which would please me more than any thing,—she even offered to tell me. She was excited and nervous when she said good-night to me; and yesterday evening she never went home at all. Sukey, don't speak to me—don't say any thing, because I cannot bear it. Come and ask in a day or two. Sukey, you believe in prayer. Go into church, and pray as you never prayed before. Throw all your heart into your prayers for the child. Pray for her purity,—pray for her restoration,—pray for my forgiveness; or—no—why do men always want to push themselves to the front?—pray, Sukey, that my ill-training may bear no ill-fruit. And yet, God knows, I meant it all for the best."

He turned away and left her. She, poor woman, with the tears in her eyes, went back to her own room; and there, not in the artificial church, with the cold and perfunctory service, but by her own bedside, knelt and prayed for her brother and his darling, while sobs choked her utterance, and the tears coursed down her cheeks.

Hartley returned to his chamber, and found Mrs. Peck still there. The effect of the excitement upon her was that she was actually cleaning things. He tried to cheer her up, and then went to the police-station, where they heard what he had to say, made notes, looked wise, and promised great things, after he had given an exact description of her dress and appearance.

"What next?"

"Had she any friends?"

"None," Mrs. Peck had replied.

He knew of an acquaintance, at least; though Mrs. Peck had never heard of her. There was a certain Miss Blanche Elmsley, third-rate actress, *figurante*, any thing attached to the fortunes of Drury Lane Theatre. Her papa, who rejoiced in the name of Crump, was the proprietor of a second-hand furniture shop in Gray's Inn Road. He had not much furniture, but he sold any thing, bought any thing; and was not too proud to do odd jobs at the rate of a shilling an hour. Moreover, Mr. George Augustus Frederick Crump, christened after one of the late lamented royal princes, was a most respectable man, and highly esteemed in his quartier. He was the worshipful master of a lodge of Ancient Druids, and accustomed to take the vice-chair at a weekly harmonic meeting. His daughter Mary was a child to whom Venn, who knew everybody, had been accustomed to make little presents, years before. She was about five or six years older than Laura. When she grew up to woman's estate she obtained—chiefly through Venn's interest—a post as assistant in the refreshment department of one of the leading railway stations. Then he lost sight of her altogether till a twelvemonth or so later, when Lollie came to him one night with a piteous tale: how that poor Mary, for some reason unknown to her, had been turned from her father's door, and was penniless and houseless. Then Hartley Venn—a Samaritan by legitimate descent, as much as the present Sheikh, Yakoob Shellaby—went to the rescue; the end being that he saw the poor girl through a good deal of trouble, and, by dint of wonderful self-sacrifice, living on herbs and cold water for a quarter or so, managed to put things straight for her.

The Samaritan, you know very well, not only bound up the wounds which the wicked robbers had made, but poured in oil. Not content with that, he lifted the poor man, all bleeding as he was, upon his own beast, doubtless covered with a new and highly respectable saddle-cloth, trudging alongside, — and those roads of Palestine, unless it was the Roman road, were none of the best, mind you, — until he came to the nearest Khan, where he bargained with the landlord for a small sum. The priest and the Levite, I make no doubt, would have done exactly the same, but for the look of the thing. It would seem too disreputable for persons of their respectability to be seen tramping along the road with a bleeding man upon their private ass, bedabbling their saddle-cloth. Yet make no doubt that their hearts were deeply touched; and I think I can fancy the priest making a very fine point of it, in his way, next sabbath day's discourse. It would turn on the duty of being prepared.

Mary's father was the priest. So, with a pang at his heart and an oath on his lips, he told the girl to go, and never again to darken his doors.

She went. His respectability was saved. Close by, she met little Lollie on her way home. She knew her by sight, and told her some of the story. The rest we know.

Venn was her Samaritan.

Mary was sitting in her second-floor back, making a dress for the baby, and crooning a tune in as simple freshness of heart as if she had never sinned at all. The blessed prerogative of maternity is to heal, at least for the time, all wounds. Besides, we can't be always crying over past sins. When the sun shines, the birds will sing. In her child, Mary had forgotten her troubles. Man leaves father and mother, and cleaves to his wife. Woman leaves father and mother, husband and lover, and forgets them all, and cleaves to her little ones.

Venn came in, hurried and excited.

"Where is Lollie?" he asked. "Have you seen Lollie?"

"Your little girl, Mr. Venn? Oh, what has come to her?"

Hartley's last slender reed of hope was broken. He sat down, and dropped his face in his hands. Then he looked round, blankly.

"If I could find him!" he groaned — "if I could find him! By G—d! if I should but for once come across him somewhere!"

Polly understood in a moment.

"Don't say that, Mr. Venn. Don't tell me that Lollie, of all girls in the world" —

"Hush! Perhaps — perhaps — Mary, you know nothing of it?"

"God forgive me!" sobbed Mary. "Mr. Venn, I'd rather my little boy died in my arms; and then, Heaven knows, I'd lie down, and die myself. Lollie! Oh, it was she who brought me to you in all my trouble. What should I have been without her? Where should I be now?"

"I must go," said Venn, rising abruptly. "Think of her, my girl. If you can devise any plan for looking after her, tell me. If you can think of anybody or any thing, — remember that every penny I have in the world I will spend to bring her back. Where can I look for her — where?"

He spread out his hands in his distress, and walked backwards and forwards in the little room.

"Don't be angry with me, Mr. Venn, at what I'm going to say. She must have gone off with some one. No doubt he promised to marry her: they all do. And if he does it, you will have her back in a day or two, with her husband, asking for your forgiveness; and if he doesn't, why, then, — why then, Mr. Venn, don't let us think of it. But if she comes back, all wretched and tearful, will you forgive her, Mr. Venn? will you forgive her?"

"Forgive her? Is there any thing my child could do that I would not forgive? You don't understand, Mary. She is my life. I have no thought but for her. In all these years, while she has been growing up beside me, every hour in my day seemed to belong to the child. What could I not do for her? Let her come back, and all shall be as it was before; but, no! that, at least, cannot be. The fruit of the tree of knowledge, of good and evil, prevents that. Eden is shut out from us. But let her come back; and we may be but as another Adam and Eve, making aprons to hide the memories of our souls."

"Perhaps they were happy," said Mary the mother, "because they had children."

"I don't know," said Venn. "History says very little about it. Perhaps they were. Let us hope so. Good-by, girl."

She took his hand, and, out of her gratitude and sympathy, raised it to her lips. The action had all the grace of a duchess, though it was but in a poorly furnished lodging, — bedroom, sitting-room, and all in one, — and the performer was only a ballet-girl.

From her, Venn went to Lynn's rooms. These were at the top of an endless staircase in the Temple.

"You, Venn!" said Lynn, opening the door. "I thought it was the long-expected case. What has brought you here at this time of day?"

Venn sat down, and answered nothing. After a minute or so, which his thoughts turned into half an hour, he got up again.

"I must go," he said. "I've staid here too long."

He put on his hat, and made for the door, with staggering step. Then Lynn caught him by the arm, and forced him into an armchair.

"For God's sake, Venn, what is the matter?"

Hartley looked at him in a dazed way. Then he fairly fainted, falling forwards. It was two o'clock, and he had eaten nothing all day. Lynn lifted him, and laid him on the sofa, pouring water on his forehead, which was burning. Presently he recovered a little, and sat up.

"Do you remember our idle talk last night, Lynn?"

"Perfectly. What about it?"

"Do you remember what we said about women?"

"What about it?"

Venn was silent again. Then he went on, with a deep, harsh voice,—

"I found a little child. In my loneliness, and the despair that followed all my ruined hopes, I made her the one joy and comfort of my life."

"Laura?"

"I brought her up myself, and taught her all that I thought the child should know. I forgot one thing."

"Venn, what has happened?"

"I forgot religion. All the rules of right and wrong do not come by observation. The habit of fearing God comes by teaching. But I loved her, Lynn—I loved her. She looked to me as a kind of elder brother; but I—I loved her not as a little sister. I looked for a time when she should be old enough to hear the love story of a man nearly twenty years her senior. I thought to win her heart, and not her gratitude. So I was content to wait. Her only joy in life was to come to me. But I forgot that there are wolves abroad. If ever I meet the man. But it is idle threatening. Old friend of twenty years, if I thought you had done this thing, I would strangle you as you stand there."

"But, Venn — Venn, what is it?"

"I was reading a story in a novel the other day,—a French novel. There was a Laura in it, and a man: a foolish sort of story. She left him one evening, hanging upon his neck, vowing a thousand loves, showering kisses upon him. She said she was going to the seaside—to Dieppe—somewhere for a fortnight. She wrote to him a fortnight later, when he expected her back,—told him in three lines that she had left him forever, that she could never see him again, that she was to be married to some one else. Not a word, you see, of regret. Nothing left, no memory at all of the days they had spent together. A foolish story. I laughed when I read it.

"He who was only a poor sort of loving fool, and believed that women could be true sat down in his lonely room, and cried. Then he wrote to a post-office where she might possibly go and ask for letters, and told her to be happy; that he forgave her; that if any thing happened to her—any poverty, any distress — he was still her friend. I thought what an ass he was. Her name was Laura too. That must have been why I read the story. Laura— Laura — a lover's name."

"In Heaven's name! Venn, what has happened?"

"Women, you see," Venn went on, in a hard, unnatural voice, "require positive teaching. You must say to them, do this, do that, and avoid something else. I forgot this. I treated the girl as if she had been a boy.

"Life, you will observe, is a series of unexpected retributions. For every mistake you make, down comes the avenger. No quarter is given, and no warning. It seems hard when you first begin to understand it, doesn't it?

"We have been accustomed to look at the disappointments of life as so much capital,—the occasion for saying clever things. Why, Jones makes fifty rhymes every time he fails, and I say fifty remarkable things. And you utter fifty oaths. Here is only another disappointment. We will have another brilliant Chorus next week. Life's disappointments are so many of a small kind, that when a big one comes — the biggest that can come — we really ought to be prepared.

"I loved her, Lynn, I loved her."

All the time he had been sitting on the sofa, talking in this incoherent way, with his eyes strained and his lips cracked. Then Lynn took him by the arm.

"Come back to Gray's Inn," he said. "We will take a cab."

He led him down the stairs, and took him back to his own chambers. When they got there, the old woman, still waiting for them, rushed forward.

"Have you found her, sir? Have you found her?"

And then Venn sat down in his old easy chair, and cried like a child.

"I think," he said, presently, recovering a little, "that I will go to bed. The kings of Israel, whenever they experienced any little disappointment, used to do it, and turned their faces to the wall. Ahab, you remember, in that affair of his about the vineyard. I shall turn my face to the wall. When I was ill as a child I used, directly I got into bed, to fancy myself in a coach and four; and the relief was wonderful. Good-by, Lynn, it's very kind of you; but — but — well, you can go away now."

"I shall stay," said Lynn, not liking the way in which he talked. "I shall stay all night, and sleep on the sofa."

Venn went to bed; and his friend, getting a steak sent up at six, sat quietly waiting and watching. At midnight he stole into the bedroom. Venn was sleeping soundly, with his fair, smooth cheeks high up on the pillow. As Lynn bent over him, the lips of the sleeper parted; and, with that sweet, sad smile which was his greatest charm, he murmured, softly and tenderly

"My little girl — kiss me again."

CHAPTER XX.

Do you know the coast of Normandy? It is a country that everybody thinks he knows well. We have all been to Dieppe, some even to Havre. Dear friends, that is really not enough. What you do not know is the existence of a dozen little watering-places between Havre and Boulogne, all charming, all quiet, all entirely French. These secluded retreats are like the triangles in the sixth book of Euclid's immortal work, — they are all similar and similarly situated. Where the sea runs in and makes a bay, where a river runs down and mingles the fresh with the salt, where the cliffs on either side stoop to the earth and disappear in space, there lies the little fishing-town. What it must be like in winter, imagination vainly endeavors to realize; but in summer, between June and October, there are no pleasanter places for quiet folk to stay in. Right and left, the cliffs rise to a height of some hundreds of feet. You climb them in the morning after your coffee and brioche, and stride away in the fresh upland air, with the grass under your feet and the woods behind. As you go along, you see the girls milking the sleepy-eyed Norman cows, you salute the women going to market with their baskets, you listen to the lark, you watch the blue sea far away beyond, with perhaps a little fleet of fishing-boats. Presently you turn back, for the sun is getting hot. Then you go down to the shore and bathe. Augustine, the fat, the bunchy, the smiling, the rosy-fingered, brings you a *maillot*. Clad in this comfortable garb, and throwing a sheet about you, you trip down the boards which lead to the sea, and enjoy a feeling of superiority when you feel all eyes turned to behold you swimming out to sea. Family groups are bathing together beside you, — father of family and circle of children, bobbing, with shrieks, up and down; next to them some ancient dame, of high Norman lineage and wondrous aspect, gravely bobbing, held by both hands by the Amphibious One, who spends his days in the water, and never catches rheumatism. Everybody bobbing. Then you go back to breakfast. The *table d'hôte* might be better, but it is wholesome. Here you become acquainted with strange fish, — conger eel, for instance; and you learn the taste of mussels. The claret might be a more generous wine, but it is light and sound. After your walk, you may drink a bottle for breakfast.

Presently you stroll into the town, and look around. Here is a fisherman's church. In the little chapel, as you go in, are the *ex voto* pictures, — they mean countless tears and anxiety. Here is the ship tossed by the storm; here the ship entering the port; here are the rags of a flag, the bits of an oar, — all the little memorials of an escape from danger, aided by Our Lady of the Sea, influenced by the prayers of the faithful. Are we in the nineteenth century? So, too, the Roman sailor offered his *ex voto* to Venus Marina; while yonder priest, in stole, alb, and dalmatic, may stand for his predecessor of Brindisium two thousand years ago, who chanted the service to his goddess in the self-same dress, and very likely in the self-same Gregorian. Verily, my readers, we take a long time to change.

There is a quay. Lazy sailors lie about and talk. There is a smell of soup in the air, curiously blending with the tar. Over the cobbled roads thunder the country carts with their bells. The diligence is preparing, with a tremendous clatter and bustle, to get under way; and where, in an English country town, would be dismal silence and sluggishness, are life, animation, activity.

At six you may dine; in fact, you must, if you want to dine at all. The dinner is the same as the breakfast. And after that you may go to the casino. Ah, the casino! It is the home of all dazzling pleasures. There is the theatre, with a stage the size of a dining-room table; then the ball-room, with a piano and violin for music, — no better music can be found; and there are the young bloods of the place, panting for the fray, with waxed mustache, and patent leather boots, the Don Juans of a thousand harmless amourettes; for here, mark you, we have not the morals of Paris. And the young ladies. They are not pretty, the Norman girls, after our notions of beauty. Some of them are too big in the nose, some of them are flat-faced, some of them are inclined to be "hatchety;" but they are *gracieuses*. Say any thing you will of the Frenchwomen, but tell me not that they are clumsy. Always graceful, always at ease, always artistic. I believe, speaking as a bachelor, and therefore as a fool, that a Frenchwoman is, above all, the woman one would emphatically never get tired of. Pretty faces pall, pretty little accomplishments are soon known by heart. A loving heart may be no prevention against that satiety which cometh at the end of sweet things. In love, as in cookery, one wants a little — eh? a very little — sauce piquante. Now, the Frenchwoman can give it you.

And at eleven o'clock you may go to bed; because, if you sit up, you will be the only soul awake in all the town. They are all alike, as I said before. I have seen them all. The prettiest of them is Etretat, the sweetest of watering-places, with its little châlets perched on the hillsides, its perforated rocks, its sharp cliffs, and its gardens; but it is also the dearest. Reader of the middle class, sensible reader, who, like me, does not pretend to be a milord, go not to Etretat to stay. Go rather to little Yport, close by, where the *établissement* is no bigger than a family pew, and where in a day you will be the friend of all the good people — chiefly connected with the cotton, or perhaps the cider, interests — who are staying there for the benefit of the sea-breezes.

It was to Vieuxcamp that Philip took his bride. They arrived there the day after their marriage. Laura was too confused with the novelty of every thing to be able to think. She was wild with excitement. This, then, was the world. How big it was! These were the people who spoke French. Why, the little children talked it better than she did, after all her lessons! Then, the Norman caps, and the cookery, and the strangeness of it all. I don't believe there is any thing in the world — not even love's young dream, or love's first kiss, or the first taste of canvas-back, or the first oyster of the season, or the forbidden port, or a glass of real draught bitter after years abroad; or the sight of those you love, when you come home again; or the news that your play is accepted, or the first proof-sheet, or a legacy when you are sick with disappointment, or praise when you are dying with fatigue, or a laudatory review: there is not one of these delights —

I forgot to mention twins, but not even that — which comes up to the first joy of seeing a foreign land, and that land France.

Lollie saw some English children at Dieppe the morning after they came.

"O Philip!" she cried, "what a shame to bring those children here! Think of the happiness they will miss when they grow up."

That, as the Yankees say, is so.

He brought her by diligence from Dieppe to Vieuxcamp, and they began the usual life of the place. He had taken the best rooms in the hotel, where they could sit and look at the sea. Laura had not seen it since she went with Sukey to Deal, eight years ago. In the morning they bathed together in the pleasant French fashion. In the hot daytime they staid indoors, and read novels. In the evening, they went to the Casino.

At the *table d'hôte*, Philip's wife was quite silent for three days. Then, to his utter amazement, she turned to her neighbor, a lively little Frenchwoman, who had addressed some remark to her, and answered her quite fluently, and in perfect French.

"Where did you learn it, my darling?"

"I learned it at home. Mr. Venn and I used to talk; but, somehow, I could not say a word at first. Now I begin."

And then the French ladies all made much of her, admiring the sweet innocence of her beauty, and that fair wealth of hair, which she wore loose and dishevelled at breakfast, and neatly bound up for dinner.

On the very first morning after their arrival, Philip found her, on coming in from a walk, writing a letter to Venn.

"That is right," he said. "Tell Mr. Venn where we are. He will want to know more than your little note told him. Write all you can, darling; but tell him you are happy. Are you happy, my own?"

She smiled contentedly, and went on writing. It was a long letter, and took a good half-hour to write, though her facile pen seemed to run glibly enough over the paper. When it was finished, she folded and placed it in an envelope.

"Now, let us go and post it," she cried, looking for her hat.

Phil looked at his watch. It was a quarter to eleven.

"Better let me go, dear," he said: "it only wants a quarter of an hour to breakfast. I shall be ten minutes, and you will be ready to go down then."

She gave him the letter, and he went out.

On the way, the landlady of the hotel gave him a letter from England, which he opened and read. It was from MacIntyre.

"I thought it best not to take that note Mr. V. It has been burnt instead. If [we]re you, all things considered, I would [no]t let her write to him. Questions will [be] asked. Things perfectly legal in Scot[lan]d may not be so in England. From [wh]at I have learned of Arthur, who is his [fri]end, Mr. V. is a man capable of making [hi]mself very disagreeable. *Don't let her [wr]ite.*

Philip read it with a sinking heart. This [m]an seemed to stand between himself and [ev]ery effort at well-doing. He had firmly [ste]eled himself to letting Venn know what [he] had done, and taking any consequences [th]at might befall him. The last orders he [ha]d given were that the note was to be ta[ke]n to Gray's Inn; and now the letter was [retu]rned, and the poor girl's guardian would [be]lieve that she had run away from him. [A]t the first shock, Philip felt sick with dis[m]ay and remorse. Then he began to think [to] himself. Should the new letter be sent. [H]e strolled along the esplanade by the sea[sh]ore, sat down, and looked at it. The [en]velope was not yet dry. He opened it and [to]ok out the letter. Then he committed [th]e first crime — unless the marriage was [on]e — in his life. I mean the first thing [wh]ich destroyed his own self-respect, and [ga]ve him a stronger shove downhill — see [th]e philosophical remarks in a previous [ch]apter — than any thing he had yet expe[ri]enced. For he read the letter.

"MY DEAR MR. VENN, — I do not know [ho]w to begin my letter. You have heard [m]y secret now, because Philip sent on my [le]tter. I was so sorry not to be able to [co]me with it myself. When I saw you on [T]uesday, I came determined to tell you all, [in] spite of Philip's prohibition; but you [wo]uld not hear it. And now I wish you [ha]d, because then you would have come [yo]urself, and been present at my marriage. [Y]es, I am really and truly married. I can[no]t understand it at all. I keep turning my [we]dding-ring round and round my finger, [an]d saying that I have done the very thing [yo]u wanted me to do. And then I feel that [it] was wrong in not telling you of it. Direct[ly] after the marriage we came over here, — [P]hilip and I, — and are going to stay for [an]other fortnight. I will tell you all about [th]e place and the people when I see you; [bu]t it is all so strange to me, that I feel giddy [th]inking about it. And you will like Philip, [I] know you will; if only because he is so [ki]nd to me and loves me. It is all through [yo]ur kindness. I can never say or write [wh]at I feel towards you for it all. You will [al]ways be first in my thoughts. We are [no]t very rich, I believe; but we have [en]ough to live upon, and we are going to be happy. The old life has passed away, and all our pleasant days; but the new ones will be better, only you will have to come and see me now. I think I shall be very happy as soon as I hear that you are satisfied and pleased with what I have done. Write at once, and tell me that you are, dear Mr. Venn; and then I shall dance and sing. Let me always be your little girl. I had to keep the secret for Philip's sake; but he always promised that as soon as we were married you should know every thing.

"He is too good for me, too handsome, and too clever. Of course he is not so clever as you are: nobody is; and I do not think he has ever written any thing, — at least, he has never told me of any thing.

"Write to me at once, dear Mr. Venn, by the very next post that comes back. To-day is Saturday: I shall get your letter on Tuesday. Give my love to my grandmother: she will not miss me. And always believe me, dear Mr. Venn, your own affectionate and grateful little girl, —

"LOLLIE DURNFORD."

Philip's handsome face grew ugly as he read the letter, — ugly with the cloud of his negro blood. What business had his wife to write a letter so affectionate to another man? Jealousy sprang up, a full-blown weed, in his brain. What right had she to love another man? His nostrils dilated, his forehead contracted, his lips projected. These were symptoms that accompanied the awakening of his lower nature.

Two men passed him as he sat on the beach. Quoth one to another, as they both looked in his face, —

"C'est probablement un Anglais?"

And the other made reply, —

"Je crois que c'est un mulâtre. Peut-être de Martinique."

He heard them, and his blood boiled within him. The lower nature was in command now. He tore the letter into a thousand fragments, and threw them into the air.

Then he resolved to go back, and tell a lie. At any cost — at the cost of honor, of self-respect — he would break off all connection with this man. His wife should not know him any longer, should not write to him a second time.

He strolled back, angry and ashamed, but resolved.

Lollie was waiting for him, dressed for breakfast. He kissed her cheek, and tried to persuade himself that he was acting for the best.

"And what did you say to Mr. Venn, darling?"

"I said that I was married, and happy,

and eager to get his letter to tell me he is pleased."

"Why did you not write to your grandmother, my dear?"

"Oh!" she replied lightly, "she will hear from Mr. Venn; and, besides, as she cannot read, what does it matter.? You know, she never liked me at all; and only kept me with her, I believe, on account of Mr. Venn. I must have been a great trouble to her."

Caresses and kisses; and Philip, with the ease of his facile nature, put behind him his deceit and treachery to be thought of another day.

After all, letters do miscarry sometimes.

The honeymoon, married men of some standing declare, is wont to be a dreary season, involving so much of self-sacrifice and concession that it is hardly worth the trouble of going through it. It has some compensations. Among these, to Philip, was the real pleasure of reading all the thoughts of a pure and simple-minded girl. When he was under the influence of this maidenly mind, his mind — Augean stable though it was — seemed cleansed and purified. The prompting of evil ceased. The innocence of his youth renewed itself, and seemed to take once more, with a brighter plumage, a heavenward flight, — only while he was in her presence; and, as we have seen, a few words from his evil genius had power enough to make him worse than he was before. For the stream of Lollie's influence was a shallow one: it had depth enough to hide the accumulations of mud, but not enough to clear them away. Like the transformation scene in a theatre, for a brief five minutes all is bright, roseate, and brilliant: before and after, the yellow splendor of the gaslight. With a lie hot upon his lips, with a new sin fresh upon his conscience, Philip yet felt happy with his wife. It is not impossible. The poor habitual criminals of the thieves' kitchen are happy in their way, boozing and smoking, though the policemen are gathering in pursuit, and they know their days of freedom are numbered.

"Tell me," said Philip, "did Mr. Venn never make love?"

"What a question!" she replied, laughing. "Mr. Venn, indeed! Why, he is as old — as old — No one ever made love to me except yourself. But take me down to breakfast. Philip, when we go back to London, will your own relations be ashamed of me?"

"I have no relations, dear, except a cousin. If he is ashamed of you, I shall wring his neck. But he will be proud of you, as I am proud of my pretty wife. But for the present you must be content with your stupid husband. Can you?"

"Don't, Philip," said his wife. "And the bell has gone ten minutes."

And on the Sunday — next day — Lollie got a new experience of life.

It was after breakfast. They were strolling through the town. The bells were ringing in the great old church, so vast and splendid that it might have been a cathedral. And in one of the little streets, where there was a convent school, there was assembling a procession — all of girls, dressed in white, and of all ages and sizes, from the little toddler who had to be led, to the girl of twenty, gorgeous in her white muslins and her lace veil. As they stopped to look, the procession formed. At its head marched the toddler, supported by two a little taller than herself; and then, wedge fashion, the rest followed, the nuns with their submissive, passionless faces, like the sheep of sacrifice, following after. And as they defiled into the street, they began to sing some simple French ditty, — not more out of tune than could be expected from a choir of French country girls, — and went on to the church. Philip and Laura followed. The girls passed into the church. As the darkness of the long nave seemed to swallow them up, a strange yearning came over the girl.

"Philip, I should like to go into the church."

"Do, my dear, if you like. I shall go and stroll along the beach. You can go in and see the ceremony, whatever it is, and then come back to the hotel."

She walked hesitatingly into the church. A man with a cocked hat and a pike in his hand beckoned her, and gave her a seat. She sat down, and looked on. A tall altar, garnished with flowers and lights, men with colored robes, boys with incense, and an organ pealing. In all her life of eighteen years, she had never been inside a church: in all her education, there had been no word of religion. Now, like another sense, the religious principle awakened in her; and she knew that she was, for the first time, worshipping God.

When the people knelt, she knelt, wondering. Always, the organ pealed and rolled among the rafters in the roof, and the voices of the singers echoed in her ears, and the deep bass of the priest sounded like some mysterious incantation. It was so grand, so sweet, this gathering of the folk with one common object. Her heart went up with the prayers of the Church, though she knew nothing of what they meant. Lines from poetry crossed her brain: words from some authors she had read. The Madonna and the Child looked on her smiling: the effigy of our Saviour seemed to have its eyes, full of tenderness and pity, fixed upon her. When next she knelt, the tears poured through her fingers.

The service ended. All went away except Laura. She alone sat silent and thinking.

"Madame would like to see the church?" asked the beadle.

She shook her head.

"Let me sit a little longer," she said, putting a franc into that too sensitive palm.

"Madame is right. It is cool in here." And left her.

She was trying to work it all out. She had discovered it at last, the secret which Venn's carelessness had kept from her. She knew the grave defect of her education: she had found the religious sense.

She rose at last, refreshed as one who, suffering from some unknown disease, suddenly feels the vigor of his manhood return. And when she rejoined her husband, there shone upon her face a radiance as of one who has had a great and splendid vision.

For the child had wandered by accident into the fold.

CHAPTER XXI.

An answer was to be expected from Venn in three or four days. Laura passed these in suspense and anxiety. Every morning she went to the church and heard the service, daily gaining from her artistic instincts a deeper insight into the mystery of religion. After the service, she would go back to her husband, and pour into his wondering ears the new thoughts that filled her heart. He, for his part, sat like a Solomon, and shook his head, only half understanding what she meant. Nor did she quite know herself. The instinct of adoration, of submission; the sense of a protecting power; the sweetness of church music; the gorgeous ceremonial to which it was wedded,—all these things coming freshly on the girl's brain confused and saddened her, even while they made her happier. For in these early days, when every thing was new and bright, she was happy,—save for that gnawing anxiety about Venn.

Tuesday came, and Wednesday, but no letter; and her heart fell.

"I shall write again, Philip. He must be ill. He would never else have left my letter unanswered."

Philip changed color; for in the early days of dishonor men can still feel ashamed.

"If you like," he said, with an effort.

"Yes, write again, dear. We will try one more letter before we go back to London. Sit down, and write it now."

The second letter was harder to write than the first; but she got over the beginning at last, and went on. After repeating all she had said in the first, she began to talk of the church:—

"I have been to church. O Mr. Venn! why did we not go together? There is no place where I am so happy. It seems as if I were protected — I don't know from what — when I am within the walls, and listening to the grand organ. When we go back to England, you will have to come with me. Do not, dear Mr. Venn, keep me any longer in suspense. Write to me, and tell me you forgive me. I seem to see, now, more clearly than I did. I see how wrong I was, how ungrateful, how unkind to you; but only tell me you forgive me, and ease my heart."

This time, with less compunction, her husband quietly took the letter to a secluded spot under the cliffs, and tore it up. For, having begun, he was obliged to go on. Laura, he was determined, should have nothing whatever more to do with Mr. Venn. She should be his, his own, his only. Some men make angels of their wives. These are the highest natures: perhaps on that account the greatest fools in the eyes of the world. Philip did not commit this noble fault. He knew his wife was a woman, and not an angel at all. Even in those moments when she tried to pour out all her thoughts to him, — when, like Eve, she bared her soul before his eyes, and was not ashamed, — he only saw the passing fancies of an inexperienced girl; played with them, the toys of a moment, and put them by. Of the depths of her nature he knew nothing, and expected nothing: only he was more and more passionately fond of her. For it seemed as if the change had made her more lovely. Bright and beautiful as she was before, she was more beautiful now. Some of Philip's five hundred went to accomplish this change; for she was now well-dressed, as well as tastefully dressed, — a thing she had never known before, — and was woman enough to appreciate accordingly. She was animated, bright, and happy, except for the anxiety about the letter; for no answer came to the second.

"We will not try again," said Philip. "Promise me faithfully, my dear, that you will not write again without my knowledge."

"I promise, Philip. Of course I will not."

"When we go back to England, perhaps, we may think proper to make another attempt; but we have our own dignity to keep up," said her husband grandly.

Laura only sighed. If Mr. Venn would but write!

Sunday came round, and there was still no letter. Laura grew very sad. Could it be possible that Mr. Venn was angry with her? Was it possible that he would not forgive her? She sat in the church with a sinking heart. For one thing she had already found out, — a bitter thing for a young wife, though yet it was but an uneasy thought, — a sort of pin-pricking, whose importance she did not yet know, that her husband would never be to her what Hartley Venn had been.

Presently the service was finished. She sat on, while the people all went out of the church. As she sat, she watched the women, one after the other, going to the confessional. They had, then, some one in whom they could confide, some one to advise, some one who would listen patiently to their little tales of sorrow and anxiety.

She felt desolate; because, now there was no longer Mr. Venn, there was nobody. Had Philip touched her heart but a little, had she been able to love him, she would not have had the thought; but she did not love him. There was between the pair the barrier which only love can destroy between two human beings.

The women went away. It was getting late. The confessor — an old priest with white hair — came out, stretching himself, and suppressing a little yawn. The confidence of the wives and mothers had been more than usually wearisome to the good man. As he came out, Laura stood before him.

"Hear me too," she whispered in French.

He looked at her in astonishment.

"Madame is English — and Catholic?"

"I am English. I am not a Catholic. Hear my confession too, and advise me. Do not send me away."

"Let us sit here — not in the confessional, my child. That is only for the faithful. Tell me — you have doubts; you would return to the ancient faith?"

"I want advice. You have given it to all those women. Give some to me."

"Tell me how I can help you."

She told him all her little story.

"I did not know that by marrying him I should separate myself from Mr. Venn. I thought to please him — I did, indeed. Oh! what shall I do — what shall I do?"

"My poor child, you talk to an old priest. I know nothing of love."

"Love! it is always love. What is love? I love Mr. Venn because I am his ward, his daughter — because he is my life," she said simply.

The priest was puzzled.

"I think you must go to see him directly you get back to England. Consult your husband, and obey him. Your — your guardian never took you to church, then?"

"No, I never came to church till I entered this one. It has made me happier."

"It always does, — it always does. Come to see me again. Come to-morrow. When you go to England, my dear young lady, search for some good and faithful priest who will teach you the doctrines of the Faith. But obey your husband in all things; that is the first rule."

She rose and left him, a little comforted.

This Sunday was a great day for Vieuxcamp, the day of the annual races. These were not, as might be expected, conducted on the turf as is our English practice — perhaps because there was no turf, except on the mountain side. The Vieuxcamp races are held on the road behind the long promenade, which stretches from the two piers to the Casino, about a quarter of a mile. The course is hard, as may be imagined; but, as the horses are used to it, I suppose it matters little.

Philip was as excited as a boy over the prospect of a little sport, and was engaged all the morning in discussing events at the Casino. The preparations were on a magnificent scale. Flags were placed at intervals. *Gardes champêtres*, if that is their name, were stationed to keep the course. There were stewards, who began to ride about in great splendor, very early in the morning; the ladies drove in from the country, dressed in their very best; the fisherwomen had on their cleanest caps; and the day was clear and bright.

"Come out, Laura," said her husband, bounding into the room. "I've got a splendid place for you to see the fun."

"I don't want to, Philip. I think I would rather sit here, and read."

"Oh, nonsense!" he urged; "it will do you good. Come."

But she refused; and he went by himself, leaving her to solitude and her reflections.

The races began at two. First came a velocipedists' race, which was fairly run and gallantly won, though not by the ladies' favorite, — a tall, good-looking young fellow, with a splendid velocipede and an elaborate get-up. A ragged little urchin from the town, on a ramshackle old two-wheel, beat him by a couple of yards. Then there came a running race, — four times up and down the course, which made a mile. The competitors were chiefly the fisher-boys of the place. The poor lads, good enough in their boats, are weak in such unaccustomed sports as running. Philip looked at them for a little while, and then turned to his neighbor, and offered to bet twenty francs on the boy who was last, though they all kept pretty close together. The bet was taken. Philip's favorite was a man, older than the others, who were mere boys. He was a little fat fellow, close upon forty, with a funny look on his face, as if every step was taking out the last bit left. But he kept up; and, just at the middle of the last course, he opened his mouth quite wide, gave a sort of suppressed groan, and put on the most comical, quaint, and unwieldy spurt ever seen; but it landed him first, and Philip pocketed his Napoleon.

Then they had a walking race, with some of the school lads and others. It was severe upon the sailors. From time to time one would burst into a run, and be turned out of the race by a steward who rode behind. And just at the finish — there being only three boys left, and all close together — the middle one slipped and fell. With the greatest presence of mind he kicked out hard, and brought the other two down upon him. Then they all laid hold of each other, trying to be up first, and, forgetting the terms of the contest, ran in together, amid inextinguishable laughter. That prize was not adjudged.

Then pony races; and then the grand trotting-match, of which the Normans are so fond. It was not like the American institutions, inasmuch as the horses were simply harnessed to the heavy carriages of every-day life, and the pace was a good deal under a mile in two minutes. Still, the interest and delight of the people were immense. Philip made his selection out of the animals, and offered his neighbor to take the odds against him. It was his neighbor's own horse. He was delighted.

"Come," he said, dragging Philip away by the arm, — "come, we will get the odds."

And so Philip found himself in the centre of a gesticulating crowd, making a little book on the trotting-match.

Philip had his faults, as we have seen; but an ignorance of horseflesh was not one of them. That day he went to his wife with a flushed face, having come out of the *mêlée* thirty Napoleons the richer. He might as well have tried to communicate his enthusiasm to a Carmelite nun, because the girl had no more power of understanding the excitement of betting. There was, therefore, one point, at least, in which there would be no community of interests. After dinner Philip went to the Casino, and played billiards with his new friends, while his wife sat at home, and read and meditated. It was the first evening she had been left by herself; but she was not lonely. She had some pretty French novel of a religious tone, — there are not too many of them; and she was happily passing over the bridge that leads from ignorance and indifference to faith. In what creed? She knew not: it mattered not. Faith is above dogma. So while she read, pondered, and prayed, her husband smoked, drank, and gambled.

He had not come back at ten, so she put on her hat, and went to look at the sea. No one was on the beach. The waves came swelling gently in with their soft, sad murmur, as the Sysyphean stones rolled up the beach and back again. The hoarse voices of the sailors on the quay, a quarter of a mile away, sounded even musical in the distance. The air was warm and sweet. The moonless sky was set with stars, like diamonds, seeming to fall back into illimitable depths. Sitting there, the girl gave herself up to the thoughts newly born within her, — thoughts that could produce no echo in the heart of her husband, — thoughts without words, too deep, too precious, too sweet, for words.

When the clock struck eleven she was roused by the carillon from her meditations, and went slowly back to the hotel. As she passed through the hall to the staircase she heard her husband's voice, loudly talking in the little room on the right, where lay the papers and journals. There was the *cliquetis* of glasses and the popping of soda.

A cold feeling stole over her, she knew not why; and she went up to bed alone, saddened and melancholy. It was the first real glimpse of the great gulf between herself and the man with whom her fate was linked.

A week after this, no letter having come from Mr. Venn, they went back to London; for Phil's five hundred had walked away, — thanks to the *écarté* of the last few days, — and he had barely enough left to pay his hotel-bill.

There was still another five hundred which he might draw from his agent, and he had his commission.

And after that?

CHAPTER XXII.

PHILIP took his wife to a little cottage near Notting Hill. She was pleased with the place and the furniture, and the little garden, but more pleased still with the prospect of seeing Mr. Venn again. She talked about it all the evening; wondered what she should say; and made her husband silently furious with jealousy and foolish rage. But he said nothing. Only in the morning, when, after breakfast, she came down to him dressed, and announced her intention of going to Gray's Inn at once, he took a line, and sternly forbade her to go at all.

"But you promised, Philip."

"I did," he answered. "But your letters, Laura: where is his answer to them? Listen to me,—one word will be enough. You shall not go and see this man until he answers your letters, or till I give you leave."

She sat down, and burst into tears. Philip, not unkindly, took off her hat, and laid it on the table.

"It is hard, Laura," he said,—"I know it is hard for you; but it is best. He has given you up."

"He has *not* given me up," said the girl. "He would never give me up—never —never. He loved me better than you can ever dream of loving me. I am his— altogether his. You made me promise not to tell him,—you made me leave him."

"Why does he not answer your letters?"

"Something has happened. O Philip! let me go."

"I will not let you go," returned her husband. "You, in this new religious light that you have got, know at least, that you are to obey your husband. Obey me now."

She sat still and silent. It was what the priest had told her. Yes, she must obey him.

"For how long?" she said. "O Philip! for how long?"

"For two or three months, my dear. Forgive me: I am harsh,—I am unkind; but it is best. Besides, other things have happened. You must not go. Promise me again."

She promised.

He took his hat. His hands were trembling, and his cheeks red.

"I am going to my club on business," he said. "I shall not be back till late this evening. Kiss me, Laura."

She kissed him mechanically,—obedient in every thing; and he went away.

A bad omen for their wedded life. It is the first day at home; and her husband, unable to endure the torture of his conscience about the letters, and the sorrow of his wife, flies to the club—his club of gamblers and sharpers—for relief.

It is late when he returns,—a heavy loser at play,—his cheek flushed with wine, not with shame.

O Philip!

"Tu tibi supplicium, tibi tu rota, tu tibi tortor."

Among the earliest callers on Mrs. Durnford—in fact, her only visitor—was Mr. Alexander MacIntyre. He came dressed in a sober suit of pepper and salt; and, sitting with his hat on the floor and his hand supporting one knee, he began to discourse to Laura—for her husband was not at home —on the topics of the day.

"Did you take my note to Mr. Venn?" asked the girl, interrupting him.

"That note? Oh, yes, I remember! Yes: I had not the pleasure of seeing the gentleman, because he was out. I dropped it into the letter-box."

Laura sighed. There was, then, no doubt. He had received all her letters, and would write to her no more.

"Has there been no answer, Mrs. Durnford?"

"None," she replied. "And I have written to him twice since then; but he will not take any notice of my letters."

The tears stood in her eyes.

"I have promised Philip not to write again without his consent. He says we have done as much as we can. I don't know,—I wish I could go round myself and see Mr. Venn."

"Oh! you must not think of doing that," interposed Mr. MacIntyre hastily.

"So Philip says; but I shall think about it."

Presently she began to ask him questions about himself. It was a new thing for the philosopher to have anybody taking an interest in his movements; and he perhaps "expanded" more than was absolutely prudent.

"What am I to do?" he said. "I am getting old: my hair is gray. People want to know all sorts of things that it is not always easy to tell."

"But the simple truth can always be told, and that ought to satisfy them."

"There," said the man of experience, with a curious look, "is exactly the point. It is just the simple truth that will not satisfy these sharks. I might write a book, but what about? People only buy books written on the side of morality; and, the moral ranks are so crowded that there seems little chance of getting in with new lights."

"But you would not write on any other side, surely?"

"Obsairve, my dear young leddy; if there ever were such a thing as a clever scoundrel, who had the moral strength to take his stand as such, and write an autobiography without the usual sacrifice to supposed popular opinion, he might make a fortune. A general case—a heepothetical case only; but one which occurred to me. I mean, of course, an unscrupulous man, without religion of any kind, — such a man as, to secure his own safety, would ruin any one else who stood in his way, and do it without a pang."

"I should hope no such persons exist. Why are we talking about such creatures!"

"They do exist. I have met them, — in the colonies. Mrs. Durnford, if ever you should come across such a man, remember my words. They would rather do a good turn than a bad one; but if the bad turn has to be done for their own good, why — then it must."

"But go on about yourself.'

"About myself, then. I have a small sum of money, the fruits of many years of careful living and economy."

O Mr. MacIntyre! was not this a superfluous evasion of truth?

"This small amount is rapidly decreasing; what I shall do when it is gone I do not know. It is my rule through life, Mrs. Durnford, and I recommend it to your careful consideration, never to decline the proffers of fate. Very often, behind the drudgery of a position which fortune puts into your hands, may be found, by one who knows how to take an opportunity, the road to wealth, if not to fame; now I think nothing of it. What does it matter? You do great things; at least, popular things. You get money, — you are asked to make speeches at dinners. When you die, your friends write your life and distort your character. Bah! The only thing worth living for is money. Get money — get money. Be comfortable; eat, drink, enjoy all the senses of nature, and care for nothing else. That is what the city people do, in spite of their snug respectability."

"Mr. MacIntyre, is this the faith that Scotch clergymen teach?"

He began to think that perhaps Laura was not sufficiently advanced to accept all his views.

"Is your religion nothing?" she asked. "Is it nothing to lead a life of sacrifice and self-denial like the nuns I have seen in France? Is there no sacred duty of life but to make money? Surely, Mr. MacIntyre, — surely these are not the things you preach in your church?"

"You are right," he replied: "they are not the things I preach in my church. Forgive my inconsiderate speech. I say sometimes more than I mean."

But the conversation left a bad impression on Laura, and she began to regard the man with something like suspicion.

As the weeks went on, she found herself, too, left a good deal alone. Philip was growing tired of her. Her sadness, her coldness, were silent reproaches to him; and he neglected her more and more.

One night he entertained a party of friends. On that occasion he insisted on her keeping up stairs all the evening, without explaining why. They staid till three. She could not sleep till they went away, being kept awake by their noisy laughter and talk. Philip came up when the last was gone.

"I'm an unlucky Devil," he murmured, pacing to and fro.

"What is it, Philip?" asked his wife.

"Nothing you understand, my dear; unless you can understand what dropping three ponies means."

"No, Philip, not in the least."

He put out the light, and was asleep in five minutes.

The clouds grew thick in Laura's sky. She could not understand horse-racing and betting. She took not the smallest interest in events and favorites. On the other hand, Philip took no interest in what she did: never asked her how she spent the day, never took her out with him, never gave her his confidence. At least, however, he was kind; never spoke harshly to her, never ill-treated her, only neglected her. This was not what the girl pined and sickened for. Philip occupied her thoughts very little. She longed for the old life. She longed for the freedom of her talks with the only man she could talk to. She was solitary in spirit. She was beginning to feel the misery of mating with low aims. She stood on a higher level than her husband, and she did not have that perfect love for him which sometimes enables a woman to stoop and raise him with her.

The new and congenial society of gentlemen more or less interested in the noble and exciting sports of our country, to which Philip's friends had introduced him when he retired from his old club, was banded together under the title of the Burleigh Club. To the name of Burleigh the most captious can take no exception. To such members as the name suggested any thing, its associations were stately and dignified. To the majority, for whom it meant nothing beyond being the patronymic of a noble house and the name of their club, it did as well as any other. It looked well, embossed in colors on the club-note paper. By any other name, the Burleigh could not have smelt more sweet. And another name, by which it was not uncommonly called, had been bestowed on it by a body of gentlemen who, though not members themselves, had heavy claims upon many who were. The ring men dubbed it, before it had existed a twelve month, The Welshers' Retreat. The members, recognizing the happiness of the sobriquet, jocularly took the new title into favor; and Philip's club had thus two names, — interchangeable at pleasure, — always understood, and the latter for choice.

This was Philip's club. A tall, narrow-fronted house in the centre of club-land; what an auctioneer would describe as "most eligibly situate." Outside, the quietest and most respectable club in London, — Quakerlike in the sober sadness of its looks. Inside, a gambler's paradise. Day at the Burleigh begins at three o'clock in the afternoon. The blinking waiters would prophecy the speedy ruin of anybody who required their services before that hour. It is the custom of the club for members to leave it at any time, but never to enter it till two or three hours after noon.

Breakfasts are served till five, P.M., suppers till six, A.M. Between these hours a smart Hansom can always be had opposite the door. Business begins in the poolroom at half-past three; the chat is animated at five, and very lively between six and seven. Then the men go away to dinner, to return any time after ten to whist, loo, hazard, blind-hookey, — anything that can be gambled at. Rules? The code is short. It is summed up in this one regulation, — betting debts must be paid on the usual settling days; card debts not later than the next day after they have been incurred. "Complaints of the infraction of this rule, on being referred to the committee, will render the defaulting member liable to expulsion." And they do expel. Oh, honorable men, how admirable, how necessary, is your rule! In this way the honor of the Burleigh is kept sweet. For the rest, you may do as you like : every member is a law unto himself; their club is Liberty Hall. What manner of men, it may be asked, is it that people this little paradise?

The members of the Burleigh are young and old. Postobit has just heard of his election at twenty. Leatherflapper, one of the fathers of the society, is seventy-three. They are rich and poor. Four-in-hand, with the string of forty thoroughbreds in training at Newmarket, and the rents of twenty thousand acres to keep them and himself upon; and Philip Durnford, with five hundred pounds at his agents, and his shovel in his hand to dig it out with, both belong. They number in their ranks the richest and the poorest, the kindest and cruelest, the most unimpeachably respectable and the most undeniably shady gentlemen, in these kingdoms. In some clubs the elders are unsociable, crusty old hunkers. Not so here. They are so communicative, so ready to teach all they have learnt, and to tell all they know, that it is quite beauti-ful to see. Every man disposed to turn misanthrope should witness it. It always goes straight to my heart to see old Leatherflapper taking young Postobit in hand, and putting him up to every wrinkle on the board. True, there is a price to be paid — understood, never expressed: a fee for experience. But what that is worth having on earth is to be had for nothing? You would like to be introduced to this company of wise and benevolent men? You know their faces well. They are to be studied at every race-meeting, seen in the Park on sunny days, at German spas, at Hurlingham, — everywhere where excitement can be bought. And the bond that makes them such friends and such enemies, — you guess it : Gambling. The universal passion. The passion of all times of life, from earliest youth to latest age; of all places, from Christian London to Buddhist Yeddo; of all periods, from the first recorded tradition of savage life till the Archangel shall sound the last trump; of men and women, from the tramp card-seller, who bets his sister two pennies to one against a favorite for a race, to the nobleman who stakes a fortune on a cast of the dice; the miser, the spendthrift, the stock-jobber, the prince, — gambling has joys for all.

So the Burleigh was founded for play that might run to any height, for games prohibited at other places; as a rendezvous for every gentleman who wanted a little excitement, a place where there should always be "something doing." You must know the members by certain characteristic habits and ways they have. They breakfast late; they are fond of a devil early in the day; they take "pick-me-ups." In the daytime they are busy with their books. Notes addressed in female hands lie waiting for their arrival in the morning, the writing being generally of such a kind as to suggest a late acquisition of the art of penmanship. They have a keen, cold look about the eyes, where the crow's-feet gather early. For the most part they dress very carefully; though sometimes, just a day in advance of the fashion, they affect drab or brown gaiters and cloth-topped boots; carry, in this year of grace, their walking-canes by the ferule; and smoke eternally. From these gentlemen Philip's companions were chosen.

This was his club; this the place where he spent his days and nights, a short month after his marriage, while his wife staid at home, or, if she went out at all, was afraid to go far for fear of meeting Mr. Venn. In this company, starting in July with his five hundred pounds and the proceeds of his commission, — for he sold out, — he was trying to make hay while the sun did not shine, and melting it all away.

He kept no accounts; but kept on digging at the little heap, ignorant and careless of how much was left. His great hope lay in his pluck and skill in playing cards, and betting on horse-races. He was often advised by Mr. MacIntyre, who had the useful talent of clear-headedness, and used to come to Notting Hill about Philip's breakfast-time; and then the two would sit and go through the "Calendar" and "Ruff's Guide," while the neglected girl looked on, and wondered what it was they talked about. It was one of her great sorrows at this time that she had no books to read, — none of her old books; none of those old poets, which she and Mr. Venn used to pore over in the summer evenings, while the shadows fell upon the dingy old court of the Inn. Philip, who seemed to have given up his old reading tastes, had only a few novels. She had never read any novels at all until she went to France. Phil's did not please her. They were barrack novels, stories of camp-life, sporting stories, — books to her without interest. She could not read them, and put them down one after another, — falling back upon the piano, for which she had no educated lady, how far superior to the music, and could only play the things she knew.

MacIntyre saw what was coming. Philip was plunging; and his method, infallible on paper, as the experience of twenty seasons proved, did not work quite perfectly in practice.

Mr. MacIntyre had seen this from the first. In the multitude of his experiences he had tried the martingale, new to Philip, even before that young gentleman was born. Like his pupil, he had been fascinated by it. The lever that was to raise him to wealth and power, so beautifully simple, so utterly impracticable.

He remonstrated with Philip, pointing out the rocks ahead. But he spoke to a deaf man.

"I know better. It's my cursed luck. I'm sure to warm the ring at ——." Philip urged. Then, with a shrug of the shoulders, he added, " And if my luck sticks to me, why — at the worst I shall pay up; and then Laura and I will go away somewhere, borrow money of Arthur, and become farmers in New Zealand, or keep a shop in Ballarat, or mock the hairy-faced baboon somewhere. We shall do. The world is wide."

"It is, Phil. I have found it so. The world is wide — and hungry."

Mr. MacIntyre took the book again, and totted up the amount that Philip had lost at his last meeting. Then he made a little note of it on a slip of paper, and put it into his pocket.

"Phil," he said, with an insinuating air, "I hope you have not lost much since you came home."

He changed color.

"I've dropped more than four hundred at the club, and a hundred and fifty one night here. when I had those fellows to play loo: besides that pill at the last meeting."

Mr. MacIntyre shook his head. When he went home, he made a little sum in arithmetic.

"When I consider," he said to himself, "that in $a-b$, b is greater than a, I'm afraid that Phil is likely to be up a tree, and my great card may very likely be played to advantage."

He went up to dine a few nights after this talk. Laura was charming, in a fresh, bright dress and in better spirits than usual. Philip, in one thing, had been disappointed in his wife. He had promised himself the trouble of teaching her the little courtesies of life, — the ordinary accomplishments, perhaps her mother tongue. He never made a greater mistake. She came to him a lady ready to his hand : in all points an accomplished, refined, well-educated lady, how far superior to the ordinary run of young ladyhood he hardly knew.

The little dinner went off pleasantly; and, when Laura left them in the little dining-room, both men were pleased. She sat down in the drawing-room, and played while they talked over their wine. She played on till the clock struck ten; then she waited till eleven ; then she opened the door timidly, and looked in. Philip, flushed in the face, was making calculations on paper. Mr. MacIntyre, with face very much more flushed, had a long clay pipe in his mouth, not lighted, at which he was solemnly sucking.

"By Jove!" said Phil. "I thought I was a bachelor again. Come in, Laura, come in."

MacIntyre rose solemnly, holding by the table-cover.

"The shoshiety of leddies is — what'sh wanted — ceevileeze the world. Ye will obsairve — at the 'yershety of which I am — member — Master of Arts, — they always obsairved that the shoshiety of leddies — Phil, ye drunken deevil, whaur's my tumbler?"

Laura looked at him with amazement. The reverend gentleman was hopelessly drunk, — as drunk as any stouemason in Puddock's Row. Port, followed by whiskey toddy, had produced this lamentable effect.

"All right," said Phil. He was not drunk himself; but, as policemen say, he had been drinking. "All right, darling. Here, old bag of evil devices, put on your hat, and try to tie your legs in as many knots as you can on your way home."

"Shir," said the MacIntyre, putting the bowl of the pipe into his mouth, "apologeeze. This is — this is — eh? — pershnal."

"To-morrow," said Phil. "Don't be frightened, Laura."

For his reverence made a sudden lurch in her direction, inspired neither by animosity, nor yet by friendship, nor by any amorous inclination, but solely by the toddy.

"I was shtudying" —

"Yes — yes — we know. Don't trouble yourself to say good-night."

Philip pushed him down-stairs, and out of the door, and returned.

"O Phil! how could you?"

"Well, dear, he did it himself. I always let the MacIntyre have the full run of the bottle : so did my father."

"But he is a clergyman."

"My dear wife," her husband exclaimed, "*they all do it* in private life."

CHAPTER XXIII.

ABOUT the same time that Philip Dormer, Lord Chesterfield, was bringing the powers of his great mind to the alteration of Old Style into New Style by making our English year begin on the first of January instead of the twenty-fifth of March, and cheating the common people of eleven good days of the year of grace 1752, his right trusty and well-beloved friend, my Lord Bath, after spending ten days at Newmarket, delivered himself of a sentiment. His lordship was pleased to remark of his favorite sport, that " it is delightful to see two, or sometimes more of the most beautiful animals of creation struggling for superiority, stretching every muscle and sinew to obtain the prize and reach the goal ; to observe the skill and address of the riders, who are all distinguished by different colors of white, blue, green, red, or yellow, sometimes spurring or whipping, sometimes checking or pulling to give fresh breath and courage. And it is often observed that the race is won as much by the dexterity of the rider as the vigor and fleetness of the animal." The flourishing era of the English turf dates from the time of this memorable saying of Lord Bath's ; and it is doubtful if the change in the calendar introduced by Lord Chesterfield has had one tithe of the effect upon manners and society that this new fashion set by Lord Bath of patronizing horse-races all over the country has been the means of bringing about.

It is still as delightful as it was in the days of the second Charles or the second George to stand on that magnificent expanse, Newmarket Heath, and watch, from the rising ground at the top of the town, or from the A.F. winning post, the struggles " of two or sometimes more of the most beautiful animals of creation," though the " skill and address of the riders " are not always turned to the account of making the " beautiful animals," they bestride stretch " every muscle and sinew to obtain the prize," as seems to have been the custom in the innocent days Lord Bath knew. Probably, in his lordship's time, roping, as an art based on scientific deductions, had not been invented, though his description mentions " checking and pulling," but it is for the now obsolete custom of giving ." fresh breath and courage." What the noble author would say if he saw a field of thirty horses facing the starter for a fifty pound Maiden Plate, T. Y. C. (A. F.), and his distinguishing colors " of white, blue, green, red, or yellow" complicated and modernized into " French gray, scarlet hoops and chevrons," or " black, white sleeves, death's head, and crossbones," we do not care to speculate upon. In his time, honest races were run over four and six mile courses ; a match was the favorite description of race ; betting was not a profession ; and the scum did not invade the sacred precincts of the Duke of Rutland's heath. A noble sport was in the hands of noble men.

Now —

Well, this is hardly my business.

" Obsairve," said Mr. MacIntyre, speaking to his pupil, Philip Durnford, above a hundred years later, " the fascination of this noble sport. You never knew a man in your life who had once tasted the delights of the turf who did not return to them again as soon as he had the means. There is something about it that no man can resist, break him as often as you like. If he has got the money to go racing, and bet, he goes racing, and bets. I knew a man who had three several fortunes, and lost them all gambling on the turf," Mr. MacIntyre proceeded to say ; " and Phil, ye'll obsairve that when he came into a fourth, he went and did likewise with that one also."

Like every idle young man with the command of cash, and the slightest possible amount of egging on, Philip Durnford was inclined to fiddle a bit at long odds. He had, on some score or so of occasions, taken a long shot, backed a tip or a fancy, before he had become the instrument in the hands of Providence of rescuing Mr. MacIntyre from his advertising agency. But he was not sweet upon the practice, for he had hardly ever won. It is notorious that, at all other sorts of gambling, a man invariably wins at first. This is not so in wagering upon horses; and Philip, with the common inclination to bet, and his full share of love for the sport, felt a little soured by his experience. Now, part of the universal scholarship of Mr. MacIntyre was an interest in horse-flesh, a knowledge of betting, and an experience of races. Added to this, he was an infatuated believer in the well-known doubling martingale. Practising on the credulity and ignorance of Philip, he unfolded the secrets of this wonderful system of winning fabulous sums, as his — the MacIntyre's — whole and sole discovery and property. And he represented to that willing ear that, if he only had the means of working it out, the Fuggers in the past, and the Rothschilds in the present, might be regarded as poor men compared with the *cidevant* pedagogue.

"Eh, my dear young friend, it's just the mighty lever that can make us meellionaires, an ye'll only believe it."

And there was evidence forthcoming to support the assertion. Racing calendars for twenty years were referred to; piles of paper scribbled over, and two or three lead-pencils consumed over these calculations. The system stood the test of all these years; generations of horses passed away as Phil and his mentor tested the lever's strength, and no run of luck was ill enough to break it. Philip believed in it, — as, after such an array of evidence, who would not? — but he doubted MacIntyre.

"And do you mean to say you found this out yourself?" he often asked.

And without either blush or smile, the old vagabond declared that he was the great discoverer, and accordingly rolled a Newtonian and Copernican eye on Philip, and gave himself the airs of the Spaniard holding in his hand the key of the Incas' gold, or of Raleigh with El Dorado in full view.

1, 2, 4, 8, 16, 32, 64, 128, 256, 512.

These figures were MacIntyre's ladder of fortune; and he offered boundless wealth to needy Philip Durnford, on the modest condition of "standing in." He had confided his great secret to him, and he trusted to his honor.

His pupil was convinced and fascinated. Could the favorite lose ten times in succession? MacIntyre said no. Could a tipster be out ten times running? MacIntyre said no. Could Philip's own selection be wrong ten times? MacIntyre said no. Could any mortal thing happen ten times? Mr. MacIntyre's calculations were there to give it the lie.

So they worked away at the books, going carefully through the results of thousands of races. They applied their lever to betting on billiards, boats, guns, cards, dice, — any thing that a wager can be made about; and nothing could happen in the ordinary course of things to beat them.

Philip rejoiced; for he held power and houses and wealth in his hand. He was the lucky possessor of the certain method of making a colossal fortune. He could break the ring, the banks, the world of gamblers. He did not envy his richer brother now, nor any man. He only pined at the little delay that kept him from beginning. His brother was the slowest fellow in the world.

"The mighty lever that can make us millionnaires" — he held it in his hand; and the fulcrum was the Newmarket July Meeting, two weeks hence. He began to spend his great wealth. He dreamed long day dreams. He was rich, famous, generous, too, to poor Arthur, with only three or four thousands to spend in good years. He made up the deficit in bad ones. Arthur was a brother, after all, and could draw on him for what he liked. Laura, his wife, — no princess of Russia had such jewels. His four-in-hand was the admiration of the park. His horses were always first. If they cost their weight in gold, what did it matter? He could pay it. He won the Derby. The most splendid prince in Europe came into his box to drink champagne-cup with him, and congratulate him on his success. He bought vast estates, — the envy of the envied, — Mr. Durnford the millionnaire! He had his troubles too. He distressed himself when he had bought all the land in the market, — in parcels large enough to be worth having. He had no devise schemes for keeping his secret from the ring, or betting would be over. He could not get on all the money he wanted. His friends quarrelled about his wealth. People watched him in the ring, — followed his lead, — mobbed him.

Châteaux in Spain, and castles in the air beyond all power of description, he built on MacIntyre's ingenious multiplication-table.

But in all his unbounded belief in the doubling martingale there lurked a doubt. He never could credit Mr. MacIntyre's statement that he was the inventor, though that canny gentleman stuck to his lie with characteristic hardihood. If he had been disposed to tell the truth, he might have mentioned that he got it from a groom at Melbourne, who in turn had got it from a little shilling " Guide to the Winning Post," which had been read no doubt by hundreds of people who had a shilling to lay out. The author of the pamphlet, again, was indebted to somebody before him; and so on, *ad infinitum*. But the curious part of it was that all these persons claimed the invention of the system of doubling, and imparted their information as something of a very secret and confidential nature. In this way Philip Durnford received it from Mr. MacIntyre. He gave a solemn promise not to tell it to anybody, but to go to work as speedily as possible to make his own and his mentor's fortune.

MacIntyre had received the precious talisman as a secret. He believed that few people knew of it; that those who did must grow rich by working this most productive vein. He honestly believed in his system, and gave it to Philip as a chart to guide him over the shoals and quicksands in the sea of turf enterprise to the land of gold on the other side. He had carefully worked out — always on paper, though — every known method of winning money by gambling, he had seen generations of backers and betters go, from a late noble marquis with a capital of a quarter of a million to "Ready-money Riley" and his lucky five-pound note. Before Mr. MacIntyre's eyes, all had gone the same way. It was only a question of time. Their ruin the philosopher attributed to want of system; and, among all the systems, his own was the best. He had waded through all the "Racing Calendars" from 1773 to date, had applied his system to every race for a period of ninety odd years, and on paper he had never broken down, and was the winner of many millions. He showed his figures to Philip, and completely satisfied him. But Philip, being a genius, went to work to improve it; and he tried, on paper, all sorts of little modifications of his secret method of breaking the ring. Not to go into petty details, he broke the ring in half a dozen different ways, and became Crœsus six times over. The leaves of his pocket-books were scribbled over with a thousand repetitions and combinations of the same series of figures; and he argued with himself that he was not going to gamble, — it was merely speculation.

"The mathemateecian, Dr. Morgan," said Mr. MacIntyre, "remarks that a gambler ceases to be such when he makes his stakes bear a proportion to his capital, and takes no hazards that are unduly against him."

And Philip Durnford's capital left him a large reserve, over and above his working money, for contingencies that might arise. So he started with a light heart on his course of speculation. For a few days all went well. A fortnight brought a change, and showed him that paper and practice are two mightily different things, and that his system could not be worked out, if he had had the pluck to do it. Half his money was gone in following his system. The other half was punted away in indiscriminate wagering on any tip that might turn up trumps.

CHAPTER XXIV.

CHACUN à son secret. Philip had his, and he kept it well. Every young fool who airs his inexperience on the turf — and, for that matter, every old one — has his own way of breaking the ring. How many of these ingenious devices are the same, fate knows, and bookmakers may guess perhaps. The infatuated themselves guard their secrets more closely than their honor; and the system, method, modus, martingale, — call the thing by what name you will, — is never spoken of by the lucky possessors. They are careful over each operation, for fear some inkling of their royal road to fortune should be discovered; jealous, lest, on turning over the leaves of their books, some eye, looking over their shoulder, should see their game. Once out, they think, the mischief is done. Everybody will do as they do; winning will be a certainty; and in a trice there will be no ring for them to break. The motive is selfish, but easily understood: for is not the world we live in selfish, and the least disinterested corner of it a betting-ring? Granted a system that makes winning certain, and that it is generally known, and there is the end of betting; and with it your own particular chance of becoming richer than the Rothschilds. No wonder, then, that when you have the magic talisman in your pocket, you keep it there, jealously buttoned up. That thousands of men have carried such a talisman for turning all they touched to gold, that thousands of men have reduced winning on the turf to a certainty, — on paper, — are matters of common knowledge. That theory is one thing, and practice another, — in a word, that the systems do not work to the satisfaction of the owners, it is sufficient to call attention to the fact that there are as few Rothschilds among us as of old; or to the pockets of the greasy ring-men, still stuffed as full as ever with Bank of England notes. The common fate of methods based on paper calculations had befallen the martingale which Mr. Philip Durnford had hugged to his heart for half a season. Owing its existence, as Philip believed, to the original intellect of Mr. MacIntyre, modified and perfected by his own hand, he felt as certain of the great results to be obtained from working it out as he did that the bank would change its notes for gold on demand. With his hat jauntily set on his head, a flower in his coat, and the blue satin notecase Laura had quilted for him with her fair fingers, in his pocket, crammed with bank-notes, he had paid his guinea, and plunged proudly and defiantly into the babel of the ring at the Newmarket July.

Here he was, at the beginning of November, driving down to Kingdon races in a Hansom: alone with his thoughts, which were far from pleasant, with his bettingbook to remind him of past mistakes and misfortunes, and all the money he had in the world in the inside pocket of his waistcoat, — that pocket which was to be found in all his waistcoats, secret and secure, in which he had meant to carry away the spoils he wrested from the ring.

Down on his luck, and as nearly desperate as a gambler can be who has one throw left, there was this chance for him still, — the two hundred pounds he had about him — one month of racing. In that month, with luck, he might turn the two hundred into thousands. Without luck, — well, it hardly mattered.

The method had long since been cast aside. He made his bets now without reference to it. He had followed the phantom chance through seven losing weeks. They had ruined him. There is nothing demoralizes the gambler like a long tide of ill-luck. His judgment leaves him. He can no longer thread the mazes of public form, or make clever guesses at the effect of weight in handicaps. He makes this wager and that, for no reason but that a feather turns the scale. In his mind, the strongest reason why a horse should lose is that it carries his money. He never backs the right tip; and the only consolation he has is to quarrel with luck, and call it hard names. These had been Philip Durnford's experiences of the "glorious uncertainty of the turf" for seven miserable weeks of the worst season for backers the oldest turfite could remember. Undreamt-of outsiders were always coming in first, till the very ring-men avowed that they were tired of winning. The slaughter had been great, and complaints of default were loud and deep. Doncaster had punished some, the first and second weeks at Newmarket had settled others. This noble lord's and that honorable gentleman's accounts were absent from Tattersall's on settling-day. Backers could not stand against such luck, it was said in excuse. There was a pretty general stampede for the Levant among the shaky division. But Philip's little account had always been forthcoming till after the Newmarket Houghton. He had taken his shovel, and dug away manfully at his little heap of sovereigns, and paid his debts every week to time; but that last week in Cambridgeshire was a facer. It had settled him. When he added up his book after the first day of the meeting, he knew he had wagered and lost more than he could pay if he sold the coat off his back. Then he smiled the bitter smile of defeat, and, in the language of the sport, "went for the gloves" — that is, he had five days' good hard gambling, well knowing that if the result of the week's work was against him he could not settle. So, being desperate, he was foolish, and betted in amounts three times heavier than he was in the habit of doing.

"Ma boy, take ma word, the captain'sh going for the glovesh;" said a discreet Hebrew, placing his dirty jewelled paw on the shoulder of another of his tribe. "I don't bet no more with him. I'm full agen any think at all."

"Vy, Nathan, vy? Misther Vilkins settled for him all right last veek."

"I'll tell you vy, Jacob, ma boy. Ven I see a young feller as alvays used to be satisfied vith havin' a pony or fifty on the favorite for a sellin' race a bettin' in hunderds all of a suddin, I know vat it means. Look, there's Nosey Smith a layin' him two centuries agen Bella. Not for me, that's all. Mark me, now, he'll go. And nobody knows nothink about him. I've looked in the peerage: there isn't no Durnford in it as I can find. They'll book any think to anybody now, bless me if they von't! Hallo, hallo, hallo! Who'll back any think? Any pricesh agen some o' these runners! Full, Capt. Durnford, sir, agen all the fav'rits."

For Philip had not done with Bella yet, and asked her price of Mr. Nathan Morris, diamond merchant, of Bishopsgate-street Without, money-lender and leg in any part of the world he might happen to be in.

And Mr. Morris was right. Philip was betting all to nothing, for if he lost he would not pay; and he laughed as he pencilled down the name of Bella till two openings of his book were filled with it. Then there was the fun of watching the race, and seeing Bella struggle past the post.

"Of course," thought Philip; "beaten by a head just on the post, by what I always thought was the worst animal in training."

Then he rode off to while away a few minutes with luncheon,—partridge pie, washed down with champagne—coming into the ring again with a smile on his face, and filling more pages of his book with the name of another loser.

He had no money, but he had credit; and credit is a very wonderful thing. It is the only substitute for wealth. To borrow a quotation from Defoe, "Credit makes the soldier fight without pay, the armies march without provisions, and it makes the tradesman keep open shop without stock. The force of credit is not to be described by words. It is an impregnable fortification, either for a nation or for a single man in business, and he that has credit is invulnerable, whether he has money or no." And there is nowhere in the world where credit will do more, or where there is more of it to be had, than in the betting-ring. It enabled Philip to "keep open shop without goods" till the next settling-day.

That day came, and Mr. Durnford's account was absent from the clubs. His name was mentioned pretty often in the course of that Monday afternoon. He was wanted very badly. Then people began to wonder who he was, what he was, why they had booked bets to him. Well they might wonder. This tendency to trust every man who has paid ready money with his bets for one month at most is one of the most remarkable things about the professional layer. Very often he does not know the address of his debtor, or even that the name he bets in is the one he commonly makes use of. The layer must pay every week, or his living is gone. The profession is propped up by this solitary kind of honesty. The bookmaker always pays; but the hacker may retire at any moment, as Philip did after going for his gloves without getting them.

The ring-men used some very bad language when the next Monday after his default came, and there was no news of him. Nobody had seen him "about" that week either. One little man had drawn a fiver of him in the street, having met him casually in Chancery Lane. This speculator took a hopeful view of things, and thought all would be right. You see, he was out of the mire. The others swore, and said they should be careful in future whom they trusted, &c.; but they had often said so before, and it only wanted a young adventurer to pay up regularly for three or four weeks, to be able to do with them exactly what Philip Durnford had done.

When the fatal week was over, and he came to reckon up the cost of his recklessness, he wished he had never done it; but it was too late. He was neither more nor less than a welsher. So men would say, he knew. And he had still left some of the feelings of a man of honor. So, for a day or two, he shut himself up at home,— moody, very irritable, and very wretched, but safe. He blessed his stars that only one of the pack of ravening wolves knew his private address. If he had had the means he would have paid that man, under promise that he would not tell his whereabouts to the rest.

When, after a day or two had passed, he ventured out, he expected every moment to be stopped, or to meet some emissary from the ring,—to be insulted, jeered, hooted at, as a thief and a welsher. But he was safe enough: the ring-men were plying their busy trade a hundred miles from where he stood. So he got over his fear, and showed his face pretty much as of old. Then came the chance of retrieving all. Kingdon clashed with a popular Midland meeting. Not three of the bigger men who wanted him would be there. He would go, but keep out of the ring, and bet in ready money. They could not stop him from doing that; and he had been very lucky at Kingdon in the summer.

His hansom drove along the muddy road at a good speed, for he had covenanted to pay the driver "racing-price" for the day's job. They passed the last straggling rows of suburban houses, and got into the open country of the "way down Harrow-way," halting at all the recognized hostelries on the road. "Half-way houses," the driver called them, where he could just rinse the horse's mouth, and — what was equally necessary — his own. Philip drew his Dutch courage from a private fountain of inspiration in his breast pocket. An unpleasant fear of recognition kept him in his seat; but the honest cabman spent his fare's small silver for the good of the house at every port they put in at. And it is almost superfluous to add they touched at all they passed, or that to the sturdy sons of Britain this is more than half the pleasure of a day in the country. As Philip furtively peeped out through the oval side windows of his cab, he saw nothing to alarm him. He was recognized, too, by a few friends, and by some of the small fry of the professionals. These people, it was plain, had not heard of his little mishap. It gave him courage to go into the ring when he got to the course. He paid his six shillings at the gate, not with the air of the expatriated wretch he was, but more like his former self,— the loving patron of a noble sport. He was early in the field. The ring was thin. He mounted the wooden steps of the Grand Stand, and hid himself safely away in the farthest corner of the top shelf. From this eminence he watched and waited, drank in the undulating landscape with his gaze, or scanned the faces of the ring below through his glass. The clearing-bell sounded; the numbers of the runners were hoisted on the board, — he ticked them off on his card; the riders' names were added to the numbers; the saddling-bell rang; the horses streamed out of the enclosure.; the roar of the odds began in the ring down below. He pricked his ears, as the war-horse at the smell of powder, or the veteran hunter at the tongue of hounds, and forgot his luck as he strained his ear to catch, in the roar of the Babel, a notion of what it was they were making favorite, and how the market was going.

"How do they bet?" he asked, as one after another pushed up the steps to where he stood.

He was satisfied the worst favorite could win at the weights, if it was only trying. To assure himself of this, he edged and dodged his way through the ring out to the lists. Not a hungry creditor to be seen: only the small scoundrels who infest the metropolitan gatherings were assisting at Kingdon. The big rascals were away, a hundred and twenty miles off, in the Midlands.

He had begun to feel safe, and confident in his judgment, when he saw some well-known sharps putting down the money in small sums at the lists on his own selection.

"She'll win," he said, with an excited chuckle, as he pressed forward in the crowd with as springy a step as the mud round the boxes permitted.

"Good goods — the old mare is," he heard an ex-champion of England whisper in the ear of a sporting publican.

"Going straight?" inquired the confidant, putting his dirty hand before his greasy mouth. "Party got the pieces on?"

"Hold yer jaw. 'Er 'ead's loose — that's enough for you; be quick and back her, before it's blown on."

Philip profited by what he had overheard, rushed to the nearest list, wrenched a crumpled fiver from his inside pocket, and reached up to the man in the box.

"Corinthian Sal!"

The fist of the burly ruffian seized his note, squeezed it up and shoved it into his bag, calling to his clerk behind —

"Fifty to five — Corinthian Sal."

"Right!"

"Here's your ticket."

Philip took it, and in trying to get away from the list-man's stand he was met by a hurrying crowd. There was a rush from the ring to back the good thing, outside; but the men who wanted to do it were well known. In an instant the pencil was run through the "10" before the name of Corinthian Sal on all the lists in the gambling thoroughfare.

In vain the excited regiment from the ring plunged through the mud and mire, proffering their money to the list-keepers. They were answered everywhere, "Done with." The secret was out. The little Selling Plate was squared for the seven-year-old daughter of Corinthian Tom.

"Another ramp! And I've just laid fifty to five agen her," groaned the man Philip had bet with.

"Ain't they hot on these selling-races?"

"He's a hot member as I've laid it to. These swells don't come outside unless they know something."

When Philip managed to get back to his old stand, he met with a friend or two who wanted to hear "what he had done," and whether he "knew any thing;" and he had the pleasure of telling them he was "in the know," appearing to be much wiser than he really was, and letting them think he had backed the mare for a good stake.

When he saw her canter past the post, hands down, an easy winner, he inwardly cursed his luck at having won when, comparatively, speaking, he had "nothing on."

"Just my luck," he said, as he pocketed the fifty-five pounds he had drawn; "but let us hope it has taken a turn."

He patronized the refreshment booth, drinking some champagne with his friends; and then turned his attention to the next event, reduced to a match, as only two of the seven horses entered came to the post. The talent were some time in making a favorite. It was even betting between the two weedy screws that cantered down to the starting-post. Philip, thinking it prudent to keep for the present out of the ring, for fear of any little *contrétemps* that might arise from meeting somebody who wanted him, went out to the lists, and at last betted the fifty pounds he had won, in several small bets, posting the money. He backed the favorite, laying fifty to forty on it, — and lost.

Is it necessary that I should ask my reader to follow the fortunes of Philip through the two days' racing at Kingdon? To him who is initiated in the mysteries of the turf my narrative will be intelligible, but probably uninteresting, for it is a tale he knows by heart. To the uninitiated this chapter must be to a great extent unintelligible, therefore uninteresting; but the exigencies of my history — as will be seen from what is to follow — seem to demand that I should give a brief outline of Philip Durnford's doings on this last appearance of his in the charmed circle devoted to the interests of dishonesty and dirt. Apologizing, let me comply with the necessity, offering only, as some sort of excuse, the plea that I draw from the life.

After losing the fifty pounds he had won, Philip had still his little capital in his pocket intact. Three succeeding races relieved him of three-fourths of it.

"What forsaken luck!" he laughed bitterly, being desperate. "Fifty left! One more flutter, I suppose, and then"—

"Halloo, old Durnford!" a friendly voice sounded in his ear. "Well, how are they using you, old man,—eh? I have just landed again."

"I should say I had the Devil's own luck," replied Philip, "except for the curious fact that fellows say that indiscriminately of the best luck and the worst."

"Well, we'll say you have the Devil's worst luck, then."

They chatted till the numbers of the next race were run up.

"The good thing of the day," cried Philip's friend. "I know three or four of the clever division that have come down on purpose to back this. It was backed down to level money this morning in town."

"We shall get no price about it," said Philip.

"I'll see what they offer. Shall I do any thing for you?"

Philip hesitated—only for a moment.

"Yes."

"I'm going to put the money down upon it, I can tell you."

"Put on a century for me."

Then he stole out to the lists, and emptied his pockets. The odds he took against Triumpher were six to four. With the hundred his friend had put on by this time, he stood to win nearly two hundred pounds. With a beating heart he made for his place of vantage on the top of the wooden steps. As he ran in at the ring-gate he was stopped by a man who had often seen him bet, but with whom he had had no dealings before.

"What do you want to do, Capt. Durnford? Let me have a bet with you this time—come."

"Triumpher?" said Philip, raising his eyebrows in a careless way, and chewing the end of his pencil.

"Fifty to forty, sir."

"No." And he made a move to go on, feeling sure the odds would be extended.

"Sixty to forty, sir?"

"Not good enough."

"Here, I won't be be't by you," cried another ring-man. "I'll lay the gentleman eighty-five to seventy."

"All right," said Philip.

"Twice, sir?"

"Twice."

As he asked the man's name and wrote it down in his book, there was a general hoarse laugh among the book-makers, for they saw intuitively what he had failed to see—namely, that he had refused six to four and taken a fraction over four to three and a half; but the laugh, when Philip had left them, was turned in quite the opposite direction, when an acquaintance called out to the man who had done the clever trick:—

"So help me, you've gone and done it, you have!"

"Ha, ha!" laughed the lawyer.

"The cap'n ain't paid for a fortni't. Now!" The "Ha, ha!" now became "Oh-h, oh-h!"

"I'll off the bet. Where is he?"

But Philip had altered his mind, and was gone right away across the running track to the other side, opposite the stand. He was sitting out, dangling his legs over the white railing, and looking at his muddy boots. Oh, the exquisite pleasure of seeing the flag drop, the runners go down into the dip, come sweeping up the hill!

Ruined or made! His heart sank.

Curse the boy! why does he not bring the horse out of the ruck? He's shut in."

Hope at zero. Ruined.

"No, by Jove, he's got him out!" He's done it! Hur-ray-y-y!"

Up went his hat, high in the air.

"Triumpher!"

Yes, the judge sends up "No. 21," and Phil drove home nearly happy, with a mind full of resolutions to win on the morrow.

Wednesday morning broke in happy uncertainty as to whether to be wet or fine; but by twelve o'clock in the day the rain fell fast. But nothing short of the crack of doom—hard frost excepted—will stop a race-meeting. All the difference the weather apparently made to Philip was that, instead of spending two sovereigns in going down by road, he spent two shillings in going to Kingdon by rail. Wrapped in his mackintosh from head to foot, he felt in better heart than on the day before; and all went on well till he was recognized on the road, and insulted, by one of his forty-seven creditors for debts of honor.

"Well, what will *you* do?" asked Philip angrily.

"You show your face in the ring, and you'll see what I'll do. Call yourself a gentleman? I call you a welsher."

He shouted the last word; and, as there were a lot of people about, Philip rushed for a fly, and swore at the man for not driving on in a moment. He did not pay for admission to the ring. He knew the man would keep his word, so he played the undignified part of an outsider, and was, besides, in constant dread of being hooted by his enemy. There is no charge easier to bring, or more difficult to rebut, than the charge of "welshing," on a race-course; and the mob has a nasty habit of hunting the victim, half-naked, into the nearest pond, and hearing the evidence some other day. This unpleasant practice made the young man careful whom he met. Altogether things were unpleasant. There were seven races on the wet card. They were run in a pouring rain. There was no trusting to form, for the horses could not act in the wet, and all calculations were upset. Of the first four races on the card, Philip won two and lost two. Then he sat out and looked on once without a bet, — sad, weary, and dripping.

On his fancy for the last two races he staked all the money he had in the world — and lost it.

"Well, old fellow," said an acquaintance whom he met on the platform at King's Cross, seizing him by the shoulders, and giving him a friendly shake, "if you've been backing horses in red mud you've come off a winner, and no mistake: you've got plenty of it sticking about you. What a day it has been!"

Philip muttered, "Damnable," in an undertone, and, getting a cab, directed the man to drive him home. As they left the station-yard, he put his hands into his pocket, and pulled out the only coins he had left: they were just enough to pay his fare.

CHAPTER XXV.

SOME of my readers — I am writing for both worlds — have very likely been hanged. They will remember, that, on the morning of the day for which this unpleasant operation — surrounded by every thing most likely to increase the unavoidable discomfort — was fixed, they slept sweetly and soundly, awaking early in the morning with dreams of childhood's innocence. This was the case with Philip on the morning after all this disaster had fallen upon him. He woke at twelve from a dream of perfect peace and happiness — awoke smiling and at rest. Suddenly the thought of all his misery fell upon him, and he started up, wide awake, and wretched. He could not lie any longer but got up, dressing hurriedly and nervously. All, every thing, gone: more than all. Dishonor before him, and ruin already upon him. In this evil plight, what to do? He thought of Arthur; but he could not bear to go and tell him, his younger brother, the story of his ruin. And then he looked back, and saw with what fatal folly he had gone deeper and deeper, hoping against hope, living in the fool's paradise of a gambler.

He went down stairs, and found Laura, fresh and bright, reading quietly in the window. She looked up, rang the bell, and sat down again. No word of welcome for him, none of reproach; for, as her husband grew colder, the young wife retreated more and more within herself. Laura's face has changed in the last three months. The old look has passed away, and another has taken its place. It is a sad expression, an expression of thought and reflection, that sits upon her face. She has found out her great and terrible fault. Between herself and Philip there is nothing in common; and she trembles, thinking of the future that lies before, and a life spent as these last three months have been. For she has no friends, no visitors, no acquaintance. No one but Philip and Mr. MacIntyre ever speaks to her. She is alone in the world; and yet she knows, in her heart, that there is one friend to whom she may go, with whom she will find forgiveness. Of that she is certain. Philip's breakfast was brought up. He sat down, exasperated with himself, with his wife because she took no notice of him, with every thing. He poured out a cup of tea, and looked at it. Then he broke into a fit of irrepressible wrath.

"Damn it all!" he said, "the tea is cold."

His wife looked at him in surprise. It was the first time he had ever lost his temper before her.

"Philip! Why, it is just made."

To prove his words, he tasted it, and scalded his lips. Then he pushed the tray back, swearing again. Laura watched him with astonishment.

"I will have no tea and trash. Give me some brandy."

"Not in the morning. Philip, you are very strange. Are you ill?"

He went to the cellaret, and helped himself, saying nothing.

Just then the maid came, bearing a small blue paper, — a missive from the butcher.

"Philip, give me four pounds, please. The man wants his money."

"I have no money."

"Mary, tell the butcher to call again to-morrow," Laura said, flushing with shame. "What is the meaning of this, Philip?"

"Nothing. If there were, you would not care, you would not understand. Do you care any thing at all for what concerns me? Have you ever cared?"

"At least, I may know if it is any thing in which I can help."

"You cannot help. You can only make things worse. If you loved me, you might; but, there, what is the use of talking?"

She was looking quite coldly in his face.

Love? — of course she had never loved him; but why — why did not conscience, who so often slumbers when she ought to be awake and at work — why did not conscience remind him then, even then, of all the girl had given to him, and all of which he had robbed her? He might have remembered her sweet and innocent trust; the confidence which came from perfect purity of soul; the nights when he had awakened, her head upon his breast, his arms round her neck, to listen to her sweet breath rise and fall, to catch the murmur of her dreams; and, for very shame's sake, he might have thought of the friend from whom he had torn her, — the disgraceful lies and deceits with which he had surrounded her. But he thought of none of these things; he thought only, that, at all risks and hazards, this, at least, must be put an end to.

"What is it, Philip?" she asked, with frightened eyes.

"I have been thinking," he said, looking on the carpet, and lighting a cigar with trembling fingers, "for some time, that we should come to an understanding."

"What about?"

"About every thing, — our marriage especially."

I believe, that, when he got up that morning, nothing was farther from his thoughts than this villany; but a drowning man catches at a straw; and the ruined man saw, that, by getting rid of Laura, he should at least be free to act. The power of impecuniosity to make men do vile and abominable things has never been properly stated by poet or novelist. In the Lord's Prayer, after the petitions for bread and forgiveness, comes the equally important one that we may not be led into temptation — amongst other things, by an empty purse.

Laura suspected nothing, understood nothing.

"I told you two months ago, Laura, that perhaps you might, some time or other, make another attempt to recover Mr. Venn's friendship. I think the time has come."

"I may write to him, Philip? You mean it? — you really mean it?"

"I think I would not write to him, if I were you, because you might mislead him on one or two important points. I think you had better go, and see him."

"Mislead him? How am I to mislead him?"

He looked up, and met the clear, deep eyes of his wife; and his own fell. His voice grew husky.

"When you met me — that is, when I took you to the lodgings of the man in Keppel Street" —

"Where we were married?"

"Where, Laura, — there is no use in hiding things any longer, — where the man pretended to marry us."

She looked full at him, unable to take in, all at once, the whole force of his words.

Philip, the fatal shot once fired, felt emboldened to proceed; but he was very pale.

"MacIntyre was not a properly qualified clergyman. He had no power to marry us. He says he is a clergyman of the Scotch Church. If that is any consolation to you, believe it. The man is an accomplished liar; but he may sometimes speak the truth. We are no more married, Laura, than if we had never met."

"You knew this all along, Mr. Durnford?"

"All along. I should have married you regularly, because I was so infatuated with your beauty; but you insisted on being married on that particular Wednesday or no other. It was not altogether my fault. I thought perhaps" —

"Yes," said Laura, sitting down.

Neither spoke for a space. The cigar went out between Philip's lips, and these trembled and shook. His face was white, with a look of terror: a man might have it when he suddenly realizes that all the nobleness has gone out of him.

Presently he moved forward a step. She started back, crying, —

"Don't touch me — don't come near me!"

"Laura, in spite of your coldness, — though you have never loved me as I once loved you, — I should have kept this secret but for one thing. I am utterly ruined. I not only have no money, but I owe hundreds of pounds more than I can pay; and I shall be a dishonored man. I must leave the country, if I cannot raise the money. We must part."

"Yes," said the girl, "we must part, Why did we ever meet? By what cruel mockery of fate did you ever cross my path? Part! Man, if you were to touch me, if I were to feel your breath upon me, I should die. You, who for five months have lived with this shameful lie upon your conscience — you who call yourself gentleman — you who mocked at the poor man's sins and sufferings — you! Is every gentleman like this?"

He did not answer, looking down upon the hearth-rug. There were, then, some remains of shame upon him.

Laura poured out a glass of water, and drank it. Then she took off her wedding-ring, kissed it, and laid it gently on the table.

"Holy symbol," she said, "I must not

wear you any longer. Why did you find me out to ruin me, Mr. Philip Durnford? Are there not enough poor women crying in the world, but you must bring sorrow and shame to another? And — and — O God! is heaven so full that there is no room in it for me?"

Then she turned upon him like a tigress, so that he shrank back, and cowered.

"You, for whom I prayed night and morning! you, that I thought all nobleness and honor; so that I laid bare all the secrets of my soul to you, and told every thing that was in my heart! I am ashamed when I think that I have so talked with you. I am more ashamed of this than of any thing. And, oh! what will Mr. Venn say when I go back to him, and tell him all the shameful story? How shall I tell it him — how shall I tell it him? Philip Durnford, keep out of his way; and tell that other man, your accomplice, to keep out of his way, and hide himself, or it may be worse for him. I don't want any punishment to fall on you — except, I suppose, God does sometimes make wicked people feel their wickedness; but nothing can make their victims again as they have been. When your turn comes, Philip, when you go from bad to worse — when you find yourself at last upon your death-bed, with this behind you, you will think of me, — you will think of me."

Philip was a little recovered by this time.

"Of course," he said lightly, "I expected a little unpleasantness at first. You will see, when we get older, that I could not act otherwise."

"As a *gentleman* — no."

"I will not be irritated," he went on, being now as calm as if he were doing a virtuous action, — "I will not be irritated. The sale of this furniture " —

"Thank you — you are thoughtful."

Then she left him, and went to her own room, where she locked the door, and threw herself upon the bed.

Philip, left alone, wiped his forehead, and breathed more freely. One source of expense was gone, at any rate. There was comfort in that thought, — a ray of sunshine in the tempest of his mind. As for what might be said or thought of him, he was profoundly indifferent. Only it occurred to him that the news might have been broken in a different manner, less abruptly, through a third person, by letter. However, it was done, and nothing could undo it. Misfortune to some men is a kind of Ithuriel's spear: it reveals the real nature of a man —

"No falsehood can endure
Touch of celestial temper, but returns
Of force to his won likeness."

Then the brave man becomes a coward, the large-hearted man mean, the godly man ungodly, the virtuous man vicious, the noble a lache. The women of the family generally have the best opportunities of finding out the truth; but they cover it up, hide it, and go about flaunting their colors of loyalty to the great and good man whom all the world admires; and, after the first agony of shame, fall into that cynicism which sits so ill on woman's nature. As for the men, I think their thoughts may arrange themselves in the form of a collect, a prayer for every morning of the year, as thus: "Lord, the helper of sinners as well as of saints, let not the smugness of our reputation ever decrease; but replenish us, above all things, with the bulwarks of wealth and honor, so that the virtues with which we are credited may never be called into exercise." And there are some — Philip Durnford was one — who deliberately believe themselves to be chivalrous, delicately honorable, brave, manly, and great; though all the time every thought and every action might go to prove the contrary. The mirror in which men see themselves — what we call conscience — is distorted; and while the real man performs duties and absurdities in folly and sin, the mirror shows another Sir Galahad, marching with lofty crest, along the narrow path of honor, while in the sunshine glow the battlements which guard the Holy Grail.

Such was Philip in his mirror. All of a sudden, when Laura left him, there was an instant flash of lightning in his soul which showed him a thing he was never to forget, the real creature he was, — no Sir Galahad, but a mopping and mowing antic, crawling ignobly down the slope of Avernus. He started to his feet, and stood for a moment staring into space. Then he seized the brandy bottle, and drank a wine-glassful; and behold, Sir Galahad again! — only with a sort of blurr and haze around his noble form, evermore to grow more blurred as the memory of this guilt eats into his soul. Perhaps this illusory image will some day be wholly gone, and his real self be seen with clearer eyes. Then may he cry aloud to be delivered from the body of this death, and God's punishment be upon him — the punishment of forgiveness. Is there no punishment in repentance and self-abasement? Cannot revenge itself be satisfied when the sinner is prostrate, crying, from shame and remorse, "Lord, I have sinned — I have sinned"?

Laura, in her bedroom, sat silent for a while, trying to think. Then she fell upon her knees, and tried to pray; but no words came. Only as she knelt a thought came across her soul, which was, perhaps, the answer to her prayer. For she arose swiftly, and began to undress herself. Everything she had on she tore off, and threw from her, as if it had been a shirt of Nessus. Her earrings, her jewels, the cross around her neck, she laid on the table, and put with them her watch and chain, all her little trinkets,—all but a single little cross with a black ribbon, which she laid aside, for Mr. Venn had given it to her. And then she opened all her drawers, took out the contents,—the trousseau that Philip had given to her,—piled them all in a heap, and trampled on them with her bare little feet. And then, out of the lowest division, she took the dress she had worn when she was married: all that she had on that day was lying folded together, even to the stockings and the little boots. She put them on hurriedly: the dress of blue merino stuff; the little hat with an ostrich feather, Mr. Venn's last gift; the ivory cross and the locket he had given her; the brown cloth jacket, the belt with the great steel buckle, and the new pair of gloves,—the last she had received from him. In the pocket of her dress was her purse, and in it two pounds,—Mr. Venn's two pounds.

Then she took her jewel-case, placed in it all the things that Philip had given her, and descended the stairs. He was sitting there, just as she had left him half an hour before,—her handsome husband, her knight, and lord, and king! He for whom she had left the noblest of friends, to cleave to him. All the nobleness was gone out of his face. As she looked on him, she wondered where it had been; and she pitied him — yes, she pitied him — for his baseness.

He looked up, and made a motion with his lips as if he would speak; but no words came. She placed the jewel-case on the table gently.

"You will find my dresses up stairs, Mr. Durnford. You can sell them for something, I dare say. I am come to return you your other presents. There is the watch you gave me at Vieuxcamp, with a pretty speech about its lasting as long as your love: you remember it, I dare say. Here is the chain. You said that love's fetters were all golden. It was a very pretty thing to say, was it not? Here are the bracelets, and all the rest. They will do for your next victim.

"After the next mock marriage, try to undeceive the victim a little less suddenly and harshly. Let her know it in some way a little different to this.

"I wish you had died first, Philip. I wish you were lying dead at my feet, and that I were crying over your dead body, believing you to be good and true. Now there is nothing to lament; but how much worse for both of us! The last memory I shall carry away with me is of a coward and a liar. A gentleman! Look in the glass, at your own face."

It was now, though she did not know this, the face of a negro, with protruding lips, lowering eyebrows, and black cheeks.

"Have you more to say?" asked Philip hoarsely.

"I go as I came," she said. "Whatever I brought with me I take away, but nothing more. Stay, this is my own penknife."

She took a little white-handled thing from the inkstand, and put it into her pocket. It was the slightest action in the world, but it wrung Philip's heart as nothing yet had wrung it.

"Now there is nothing left to remind you of me," she said. "Mr. Venn will help me. I go back to him."

He did not speak.

"Farewell, Philip."

She turned to go. As she touched the handle of the door, her husband fell forward on his knees before her, and caught her by the hand, with tears and sobs.

"Laura, Laura," he cried, "forgive me! All shall be as it was. We will be married again. Forgive me, Laura. I am mad this morning. Only stay"—

But she slipped from him, and was gone.

After all, the memory of her husband was not altogether that of the hardened wretch she might have thought him.

CHAPTER XXVI.

ABOUT two o'clock, Mr. MacIntyre called upon his patron, and found him in a state of mental irritation which indicated the necessity of prudence and tact. He was sitting where Laura had left him, glowering over the fire, — her bracelets and trinkets on the table; and the black cloud upon his face, with this disorder, was quite sufficient to teach the student of human nature that something had happened. A curious phrase, this, if we may be allowed a digression. It surely indicates a strong belief in the malignity of fate, when the phrase, "something has happened" means misfortune; as if nothing was ever given unexpectedly except kicks and buffets. So far as my own experience goes, the voice of the people is right.

Mr. MacIntyre assumed an expression, designed to illustrate the profound sympathy working in his breast, took off his hat, and sat down in silence.

"What is the matter, Phil?" After a pause.

Philip made an impatient gesture.

"Mrs. Durnford"—

"Damnation!" cried Philip, starting to his feet, and walking backwards and forwards.

Mr. MacIntyre was silent. Presently, preserving the same sympathetic look, he rose, and, moving softly,—after the manner of one who respects trouble,—he proceeded to the well-known cellaret, whence he drew a decanter of sherry. Helping himself to a glass, he drank it off with a deep sigh. Then he shook his head solemnly, and offered the decanter to Philip.

"Drink!" he cried. "It is all you think of. Is there a misfortune in the world that you would not try to cure with drink?"

"None," said MacIntyre: "I think there is none. Drink makes a man forget every thing. But what is it, Philip? What has happened?"

"Why have you not been near me for a week?"

"Because I have been busy about my own affairs. What *has* happened, then?"

"I have been losing about as fast as a man could lose, for seven or eight weeks"—

"Eh, man! luck will"—

"I have no luck but the Devil's, I suppose. Listen: you blew the spark into a flame,—you and your wonderful secret were at the beginning of it. 'The mighty lever that can make us meellionnaires.' You recollect?"

"I can't but say I do."

"Well, the lever's broke into little bits, that's all. I owe more hundreds than I can tell you over what I can pay. I have not bothered to add up the sum total of the book over the Houghton meeting. I can tell you this, though: before Kingdon, I had forty-seven creditors; now, I suppose, I've got three or four more. They'd like to meet me, I have not the least doubt. They won't. I'm scratched for all my engagements. Broken down badly. It is not one leg in my case, it's all four."

He laughed. His mind was easier since the anxiety of how he should find the money to pay with had been removed. He had decided not to pay; been desperate, and gambled without much hope of paying; come off second-best at the game, and had not paid. His desperation had brought some sort of relief with it. Only the reckless man can laugh as he did. Mr. MacIntyre, now many degrees removed from the feeling of recklessness, saw no cause for making merry, and opened his eyes as wide as it was possible to do, putting on his most sympathizing mask, at the same time that he ejaculated a pious, "Hear that, now!" as his young friend's narrative proceeded.

"See there," Philip continued, tossing his betting-book across the table to Mr. MacIntyre, "turn over the pages, and satisfy yourself. There is a line scored through the wins. You won't find many. I backed fifteen horses in the last two days at Newmarket without scoring one win."

"I doubt," said Mr. MacIntyre, shaking his head, and handing back the book, "I doubt you did not keep to the seestem. Ah, now"—

"I did not. Nobody ever did keep to a system. They mean to at the start; but they forget they even meant till they come to add up a losing account. I thought when you saw what a succession of facers backers have had, you would have guessed what was the matter."

Here he picked up a newspaper a week old, and read, "The complaints of absent accounts were loud and deep, and no wonder. Even bookmakers don't like to be shot at; and two noble lords, besides a baker's dozen of 'untitled noblemen,' have gone in the last few weeks."

"'Untitled noblemen,' MacIntyre. that's for me. After that awful Monday came, I was frightened at my own shadow for a few days, and hardly dared to look into the paper of a morning. I expected to find my name at the head of the sporting intelligence, or in the agony column with the people wanted. They don't do that, I find; but one fellow has written, after calling about twenty times at the club, to say he shall post me at Tattersall's. Much I care if he does. It will be a *poste restante*, but I am not likely to be called for."

"Ye don't know that," said MacIntyre, wisely wagging his head.

"I do," said Philip, with his bitter, scornful, hollow laugh. "All is lost,— honor, money, all. If I raked together every thing I have in the world, I don't suppose I should be able to pay a shilling in the pound. But this is not all. I've had another loss," he went on. "I told that girl the whole truth, and she has left me."

"Is she gone? I am sorry," said MacIntyre. "I've always been vera sorry for the poor little bonnie thing."

"She is gone, and will never come back to me. So that is finished. Let us talk about other things. I suppose, MacIntyre, that the marriage was all a farce?"

The reverend gentleman took two bits of paper—the famous marriage certificates —from his pocket-book, and handed them to Philip.

"The mock certificates," he said. "Yes, Philip, you can do what you like with them. Best tear them up."

Philip threw them into the fire.

"But you told me"—

"Eh, now? Don't let us have a bletherin' about what I told you. You were in one of your moral moods that day, you see; and I always suit my conversation to circumstances. I just thought it best to make the most of what we did. Perhaps I was never an ordained clergyman at all. Perhaps I pretended. I have preached though, on probation. It was at Glasgie. They said I wanted unction. Eh, sirs, what a man I might have been, with unction!"

Philip took him by the shoulders, and held him at arm's length.

"MacIntyre, you are a precious scoundrel! I am bad enough, God knows; but not so bad as you. I have the strongest desire at this moment to take you by the throat, and throttle the life out of you."

The philosopher looked up for one moment in alarm, but speedily smiled again.

"You will not, Phil. First, because it would be murder, and you would not like to be hanged. Second, because you would not be such a fool as to hurt the only man who has it in his power to help you."

"You!"

"And third, because your wrath is like a fire of chips. It burns out as soon as it is lighted."

Philip let him go.

"If you are the only man to help me, why the devil don't you, instead of drinking sherry, and telling me what a liar you are?"

"I'm going to," said the little man, sitting down with an air of great dignity, and beginning to tremble, because he was at last going to play his great card. "I'm going to. Sit down, Phil, and listen. Let us first face the position. What is it?"

"Ruin and disgrace."

"For want of a few hundreds, which I will put into your hands at once, with plenty more to the back of them."

"Go on, man. Are there any more lies at the bottom of all this?"

"Do not pain me unnecessarily, Philip. You will be sorry afterwards. This is a very grave and serious matter. Do you remember a conversation I had with you after your father's death?"

"I do."

"I hinted then at the possession of certain documents which might or might not be found useful in proving you the heir to certain property."

"Go on, MacIntyre. Do get on faster."

"I afterwards obtained those proofs. During all the years of my wandering, I have kept them releegiously in my pocket-book, in the hope that they might one day be of use in restoring you, my favorite pupil, to your own."

He dropped his voice from nervousness. Suppose, after all, the plan should fail? It seemed to Philip that his accents trembled with emotion.

"The papers prove you beyond a doubt—I mean, mind, beyond a legal doubt—to be the sole heir of your father's property, the estate of Fontainebleau, in the Island of Palmiste."

"Arthur's estate? I will not believe it."

"Do not, if you prefer to believe to the contrary. It brings in at present about £4,000 per annum, clear profit, in good years. There is not a mortgage on it, and it is managed by the most honest man in all the island. Philip, I offer you this, not in an illegal way, not in a way of which you will hereafter be ashamed, but as a right, your right. I offer you fortune, escape from all your troubles; and, Philip,—not the least—I offer you legitimacy."

"The proofs, MacIntyre—the proofs."

"Wait, wait. First read and sign this document. It is a secret agreement. It is not possible to receive the sum named by any legal procedure,—I trust entirely to your honor; and, if you do not obtain the estate, the agreement is not worth the paper it is written on."

Philip read it. It was a paper in which he pledged himself to hand over to MacIntyre, as soon as he got the Fontainebleau estate, the sum of £5,000.

"It will be a cruel thing to turn out Arthur," he said.

"You can settle with all your creditors," said MacIntyre significantly.

"At the worst, I can but starve," said Philip.

"Hoots toots!" said the philosopher. "I've tried it: you would not like it. Of course you will not starve. Sign the paper, and we will proceed."

Philip took a pen, signed it, and tossed it back.

MacIntyre folded the document, and carefully replaced it in his pocket-book. Then he took out three or four papers, wrapped in a waterproof cover. They were clean enough, though frayed at the edges, and the ink was yellow with age. He handed them solemnly to Philip. Three of them were letters written by George Durnford, beginning "My dearest wife," and ending with "Your most affectionate husband, George Durnford."

"Obsairve," said Mr. MacIntyre. "The

dates of all are *before* that of his marriage with Mdlle. Adrienne de Rosnay. The letters themselves are not sufficient. Look at this."

It was a certificate of marriage between George Durnford and Marie ——, no other name.

"And this."

The last paper purported to be a copy of a marriage register from the Roman Catholic chaplain of St. Joseph. To it was appended a statement to the effect that the marriage had been privately solemnized in Mr. Durnford's house, but that the register was duly entered in the churchbook.

Philip's eyes flashed.

"If you had told me that you were yourself the Roman Catholic priest, I should not have believed you. MacIntyre, if those papers are what they pretend to be, I am a legitimate son."

"Of course you are. I've known it all along; but I waited my opportunity."

"Who are the witnesses to the marriage?" said Philip.

"See those signatures. I am one. I was present on the occasion. The other is Adolphe, brother to Marie, the bride. The clergyman is dead, and I suppose the other witness by this time. But you can inquire in Palmiste if you like. The ways of what we call Providence are obscure. They may appear to be winding. They are, in reality, straight."

Philip made an impatient gesture, and he stopped.

Mr. MacIntyre had played his last card, his King of Trumps, and it looked like winning. He breathed more easily.

"I believe, MacIntyre," said Philip coolly, "that there is not a single thing in the world that you would not do for money."

"There is not," replied the tutor with readiness. "There is nothing. And why not? I look round, and see all men engaged in the pursuit of wealth. They have but one thought, — to make money. I, too, have been possessed all my life with an ardent desire to be rich; but fortune has persecuted me. Ill-luck has dogged me in all that I have tried. I am past fifty now, and have but a few years to live. To have a large fortune would bring with it no enjoyment that I any longer greatly care for; but to have a small one would mean ease, respectability, comfort for my declining years, nurses to smooth my pillow, considerate friends. This is what I want. This is what you will give me. I have looked for it all these years, and bided my time. With my five thousand pounds, which is two hundred and fifty pounds a year, I shall go to some quiet country place, and live in comfort. My antecedents will be unknown. I shall be respectable at last."

The prospect was too much for him, philosopher that he was. He went on, in an agitated voice, walking up and down the room, —

"Money! Is there any thing in the world that money will not procure? Is it friends? You can get them by the bribe of a dinner. Is it love? You can buy the semblance, and win the substance. Is it honor? You can buy that too, if you have got enough money. Is it power? Money is synonymous with power. Is it comfort? Only money will buy it. Is it health? You may win it back by money. Is it independence? You cannot have it without money. Money is the provider of all."

"It won't help you to get to heaven."

"I beg your pardon. Without it I am, — I am damned if you will get to heaven."

"A curiously involved expression," said Philip, looking at the man with astonishment.

"Answer me this, Phil. Did you ever hear of a poor man repenting, unless it was when he was going to be hanged?"

"I really have not given the subject any consideration."

"You never did. It is only the rich who have leisure to repent. What is a poor man to think about but the chance of to-morrow's dinner? Great heavens! Phil, when I think of how wretchedly, miserably, detestably poor my life has been, my wonder is, not that my life has been so bad, but that it has not been worse. Do you know what grinding poverty is? Do you know what it is to be a poor student at a Scotch Univairsity? Do you know what it means to take up a sacred profession which you are not fit for, — to disgrace yourself, and lose self-respect, before you are five and twenty, — to be put to a thousand shifts, — to invent a hundred dodges, — to lose your dignity as a man, — to be a parasite, and fail in that, — to take to drink because the years of your manhood are slipping by, and a miserable old age is before you? Tell me, can you guess what all these things mean? Youth! I had no youth. It was wasted in study and poverty. I dreamed of love and the graces of life. None came to me. No woman has ever loved me. Not one. I have always been too poor even to dream of love. Philip, I like you for one reason. You have kicked me like a dog. You have called me names: you despise me; but you and I are alike in this, that we owe the world a grudge. I rejoiced when I saw you ruining yourself. I stood by at the last, and let it go on, because I knew that every hundred pounds you threw away brought me nearer to my end; and that is the five thousand pounds that you will give me."

Philip said nothing. He saw in part what this man was whom he had believed to be a simple, common rogue; saw him as he was, — pertinacious, designing, cynically unscrupulous. He recoiled before a nature stronger than his own, and felt abashed.

"The money," MacIntyre went on, "will not come a bit too soon. I am nearly at the end of the hundred pounds I had. Arthur told me I should have another fifty, and then no more. What should I do when that was gone? You remember what I was when you met me in the street? — a poor, famished creature, on one and three pence a day. A few more weeks would have finished me. Even now the effects of that bitter winter are on me; and I wake at night with the terror upon me that those days are coming back, — that I shall have to return to the twopenny breakfast, and the fourpenny dinner, and the miserable lodging where I sat at night, gloomy and drinkless. Money! He asks me if I would do any thing for money! I, with my memories! Philip, I swear there is no act of dishonesty I would not commit to save myself from this awful dread of destitution that hangs over me day and night. After my miserable life, compensation is due to me. I say, sir, it is due."

His face grew black and lowering.

"If I am not paid what is owing to me, I shall take what I can get. For the forced hypocrisies of my youth, for my servile manhood, for my ill-fortune, my wretched condition of last year, I swear that compensation is due to me. Honesty! The wise man guides himself by circumstances. Well, I've prayed — yes, you may laugh, but I have prayed till my knees were stiff — for some measure, even the smallest, of success in the world, for just a little of that material comfort which makes life tolerable. As well pray for the years to roll back as for fate to be changed. Whatever I do henceforth, I claim as my right. It is my compensation for the sufferings of the past."

He sat down. Philip noticed how shaky he was, how his legs tottered, and the perspiration stood in great beads upon his nose, — the feature where emotion generally first showed itself with this philosopher; but he answered him not a word.

"Go now," he said, "and show these papers to Arthur. He ought to see them."

MacIntyre put on his hat.

"Don't come back here," said Philip. "Find me at the club. I shall choke if I slept a night in this house."

CHAPTER XXVIII.

WHEN Arthur heard MacIntyre's story, he was amazed.

"Why did you not tell me all this before?" he asked at last.

"You have known it all these years, — why did you not tell it when my father died? Let me look at the letters again. They are in my father's writing. Is there some villany in this?"

"The extract from the register, ye'll obsairve," said the philosopher, passing over the injurious nature of the last words, "is certificated by a firm of respectable solicitors, and enclosed to me by their agents in London."

"Why not tell the story before?"

"Loard, loard! it is a suspicious world. You will remember, Mr. Arthur, that I was once violently assaulted by your brother?"

"I remember."

"It was because I hinted at this secret; for no other reason. Therefore, as I was not personally interested in either of you getting the money, — though I certainly always received great consideration from Philip, — I held my tongue. The time has now come, when poor Phil is ruined."

"Ruined! How?"

"He has lost his money on the turf. He has now nothing. This being the case, I found it time to interfere. Here are my papers, — here my proofs. It's vera hard for you, Mr. Arthur, after so many years o the pillow o' luxury, and ye will commence to remember some of the maxums" —

"What does Philip say?"

"He told me to bring you the things, and tell you the story."

"It seems incredible, — impossible. And yet the letters and the certificate."

"You can fight it, Mr. Arthur, if you please. You will have to put me in the box; and I shall, most reluctantly, have to represent to the world the secrets of your father's life."

Arthur recoiled in dismay.

"It is not a question of fighting. It is a question of doing what is right. If only your story is true. Pray, Mr. MacIntyre, what is the price you have put upon it?"

He smote his chest.

"Go on, Arthur, go on. You into whose young mind I poured treasures of philosophy. Insult your aged and poverty-stricken tutor, — and a Master of Arts of an ancient and " —

"You sold me an address."

"Pardon me. I borrowed forty pounds of you, and, with a kindness which I regret not to see rated at its real worth, I *gave* you Miss Madeleine's address. I hope you have made good use of it."

"What does it matter to you, sir, what use I have made of it?"

"Not at a', not at a': let us come back to our business. The story is not mine alone, Arthur. It rests on the evidence of the Church. Man tells lies: church registers are infallible. I suppose that Marie died in England before the second marriage"—

"Mr. MacIntyre, do you want me to wring off your neck?"

"The facs of the case,— the facs of the case only. Your elder brother, sir, received my communication without any of the manifestations of temper which you have shown. Naturally, there is a difference between you."

"You should have told us ten years ago. You should have told us even three months ago. Why did you not?"

"To begin with, I saw no reason for speaking at all, till my friend, as well as old pupil, lost his money. This was yesterday."

"And why next?"

"Because I did not choose."

This was the only outward mark of resentment at Arthur's suspicions which the sage allowed himself.

He gave a long sniff of satisfaction, and went on,—

"There may be a weakness in the evidence. The law might be evaded by a crafty counsel. You can fight the question, if you like. But the *right* of the case will remain unaltered. Arthur Durnford, you are only the second son of your father."

Arthur was silent for a while, leaning his head on his hand.

"Come into the city with me. Do you object to bring your papers to my lawyer's?"

"Not at a', not at a'. Let us go at once," answered MacIntyre, apparently in great good humor. "And don't be overmuch cast down, Arthur, at this temporary revairse of circumstances. Philip will give you enough to live upon. If not, there are several lines of life open to you. You may be a private tutor, like me. Then, indeed, my example will not have been wholly in vain."

He pursued this theme as they drove into the city in a cab, illustrating his position by reference to passages in his own life, wherein he had imitated the magnanimity of Themistocles, the clemency of Alexander, the continence of Scipio, and the generosity of Cæsar.

"Poor I may be," he said, "and certainly am: but at least I can reflect — the reflection alone is worth a bottle of Isla whiskey — on temptations avoided and good effected. I forgive you, Arthur, for your hard words; and remain, as I always have been, your best friend."

Arthur answered little, and that in monosyllables. He was so much pre-occupied, that the man's prattle dropped unheeded on his ears.

What was the right thing to do.

The lawyer heard what Arthur had to say, read the documents carefully, — from time to time casting a furtive glance on MacIntyre, who sat with an air of great dignity, and even virtue, in his countenance, and occasionally rubbed his nose.

"You are the only surviving witness, Mr. MacIntyre?"

"I am," returned our Alexander. "That is, the only one, I believe, surviving. 'Flesh is grass.' The priest was younger than myself; but, you see, he is gone first. Adolphe might be found, perhaps, though I think he is dead too."

"It is now twenty-seven years since this marriage, according to your certificate, was contracted. Would you kindly tell us more about it?."

"With pleasure. It took place in Mr. Durnford's own house at Fontainebleau, in the dining-room. You remember our lessons, — those delightful lessons, — which used to take place in the dining-room, Arthur? It's vera sweet to recall old days. It was in the evening. Marie left her mistress's house in the afternoon. No one knew where she had gone except myself. I helped her to escape."

"Oh!" said the lawyer, "you acted as — as the uncle of Cressida. It was a creditable position for you to occupy."

"Perhaps," said MacIntyre, with all that was left of his power of blushing mantling to his nose, — "perhaps. The necessities of the stomach have on several occasions obliged me to take part in actions of which my conscience disapproved. The needy man has no choice. I approve the better cause, even when fate, armed with the weapon of hunger, has obliged me to follow the worse. In the words of the Latin poet, — I hope, sir, you have not entirely neglected the humanities, — 'Dum meliora probo'"—

"My dear sir," interrupted the lawyer, "pray get on with your story."

"Marie required a good deal of persuading," he went on, gaining courage as he began to unfold his web of fiction. "Mr. Durnford, a young man at the time, had conceived a violent passion for her. She was as white as a European, and had no marks at all of her descent, except her full black hair. Her mother, indeed, was a mulatto; and perhaps her father was a white man, — I don't know. On the evening when I drove her over to Fontainebleau, I had got Father O'Callinan to ride up in the afternoon. He knew what he was to do. It was promised to Marie; and there in the sitting-room, with myself and Adolphe, a half-blood brother of Marie, who was sworn to secrecy, the marriage was performed, and these papers signed. A year and a half later, after her boy was born, Marie went away to Europe, and Mr. Durnford married Mademoiselle Adrienne de Rosnay."

"And pray how did the papers come into your hands?"

MacIntyre for a moment hesitated, and a violent effusion of red mounted to his nose.

"After the death of Mr. Durnford, I went through his papers."

"As a legally appointed agent?"

"No. As a confidential friend of the family, in which I had been a tutor for many years," said MacIntyre.

"In other words, you ransacked my father's desk?" asked Arthur.

"Do not put an injurious construction on the proceeding," said MacIntyre. "I searched the drawers for some papers of my own, and found not only my own private documents, but also these letters."

"Oh!" said the lawyer. "Dear me! Would you be good enough to step outside? Stay, though, what has become of — of — Marie?"

"She went to Europe, and was lost sight of. I suppose she died."

"Thank you," said the lawyer, opening the door. "You will find the papers in the next room. Mr. Thompson, pray give this gentleman 'The Times.' Now, Mr. Durnford, this is an ugly case. Tell me what you know of this man."

Arthur told him every thing.

"He is evidently a rogue. And I believe that the whole thing is a forgery. Do you know your father's hand-writing?"

"Yes: the letters are his."

"Well, well, it may be. Still, observe that in the only place where the word Marie occurs, the writing looks to me uncertain, and the word laps over beyond the line. It may possibly have been put in afterwards. Are you sure that the dates are in the same writing as the letters?"

"They look so. Besides, there is the church register."

"Registers *have* been tampered with, especially in novels. But what does the man mean by it all: the secrecy for ten years, — the suddenness of the revelation? *What does he get for it?*"

"Philip, I am sure, would not pay for his secret."

"Humph! I don't know. The church register is the only thing to fear. Fight it, Mr. Durnford."

"It is not the winning or losing," Arthur replied. "That seems the least part of it."

The lawyer stared at him.

"To Philip it means legitimacy. He *must* fight."

"My dear sir, it *may* also mean legitimacy to you."

"I think not. I am *quite* sure that my father would not have married a second time, except with the clearest proof of his first wife's death. That is to me a conviction. I have nothing to fear on that ground. But there is another thing. How can I drag my father's life and character into open court?"

"Would you sacrifice every thing for the mere sake of hiding scandals five and twenty years old?"

"If they are my father's — yes."

"Well, well — let us see."

He went into the outer office, and requested permission to see the papers again, holding them up to the light to see the water-mark. Mr. MacIntyre watched him steadily, with a twinkle in his eye distinctly resembling a wink. The lawyer returned the papers, and went back.

"He's a crafty rascal, at least. The water-marks are all right. Mr. Durnford, there is villany in it. Do nothing rashly."

"Philip will press on the case. I only begin now to understand what it may mean to him — what the past has been for him. I shall not fight with my brother."

"You will acknowledge every thing?"

"No," said Arthur, straightening himself, as one who is doing a strong thing, "I shall hide every thing. I may be a coward, but I *will not* have my father's name hawked about in public, and the story of his youth — and — and — perhaps his sins, told to the whole world. Let Philip have all the money. I retire. Let Philip have all the money. I shall not starve, I dare say."

"Nonsense, nonsense. As your lawyer, I protest against it. My dear sir, the time for Quixotism has passed away. People will ask questions too. What will you say?"

"Nothing. Let them ask what they please. The secret is mine — and Philip's — and this man's. Not one of us will speak of it."

"As for Mr. MacIntyre, certainly not — provided his silence is bought. Will your brother buy it?"

"I shall not ask. I should excuse him if he did."

"Take advice, Mr. Durnford, take advice."

"I will take advice. I will put the whole facts into the hands of a third person, and be guided by the counsel I get from her."

"If it is a lady," the lawyer returned, laughing, "I give you up. But come and see me to-morrow."

Arthur went out by the private door, forgetting all about Mr. MacIntyre, who still sat behind "The Times," waiting. The time passed on — an hour or two — before the lawyer came again into the outer office. Perhaps he kept his man waiting on purpose, after the sweet and gentle practice of a Bismarck, " letting him cook in his own juice."

"What!— you there still, Mr. MacIntyre? I thought you gone long ago, with Mr. Durnford. Come in again, — come and have a glass of sherry. Now, then, sit down, — sit down. We are men of business here, and shall soon understand each other. You will find that, Mr. MacIntyre, if you are a judge of sherry; and I have no doubt you are a very excellent judge " —

"Pretty well — pretty well. I am better at whiskey."

"Aha! very good — very good, indeed. Reminds me of a thing I once heard said. But never mind now; let me give you another glass. Dry, you observe, but generous. A fat wine. A wine with bone and muscle. I knew you'd like it." He sat down opposite his visitor, clapped him on the knee, and laughed. "And now let us talk about this affair which you have been the means of bringing to light."

"Under Providence."

"Quite so. Under Providence, as you say. You know, I feel for Arthur Durnford's position in this case."

"I am but an instrument," said MacIntyre, with a solemn face and another pull at the sherry — " a vera humble instrument. But life is so. The moral philosopher has often called attention to the curious way in which our sins become pitfalls for our children. I could give you some striking passages indirectly bearing upon the point from Stewart and Reid. But perhaps, Mr.— I forget your name — you are not a parent ? "

"He crossed his legs, and brought the tips of his fingers together.

"Another time, my dear sir, another time. By the way, is it not *rather* unusual for an Englishman to marry a mulatto ? "

"Most unusual. Nothing ever surprised me so much. I have often obsairved, in my progress through life, that " —

"Yes. The circumstance will tell in court."

Mr. MacIntyre visibly started.

"You will go into court ? "

"Doubtless," returned the lawyer, watching his man, in whom, however, he saw no other sign of emotion. " Doubtless — your own evidence will be the main chain, so to speak. I hope you don't mind cross-examination."

"When a medicine, however disagreeable, has to be taken, it must be taken."

"Quite so. They will probably inquire into all your antecedents — eh ? — ask you all sorts of impudent questions — ha! ha! Whether you ever got into trouble ? We, the lawyers for our side, will make it our business to hunt up every thing about you."

" What trouble ? "

"Into the hands of the law, you know — eh ? Oh, most absurd, I assure you! I remember a similar case to this, when the principal witness was obliged to confess that he had sold his information. The case was lost, sir — lost by that simple fact. Now, you see, what an ass that man was! Had he gone to the lawyers on the other side, a respectable firm like ours, — had he come to me, for instance, in a friendly way, and said 'My dear sir, I have certain papers — I am a needy man. There they are. We are men of the world.' Had he, in fact, behaved as a man of sense, he would have been, sir — for in losing the case he lost his reward — he would have been " — here the speaker looked sharply in the face of Mr. MacIntyre — " a thousand pounds in pocket."

He remained stolid — only helping himself to another glass of wine.

" Very good thing, Mr. — really, I have not caught your name."

"Never mind, sir — never mind my name. It is on the door-plate, if you wish to read it. But your opinion now as to my man's stupidity ? "

"Well, you see — it may be, after all, a question of degree. I am myself induced to think, that, if you had offered him ten thousand, he might have accepted. Money down, of course."

The cool audacity of this indirect proposal staggered the lawyer. He put the stopper in the decanter of sherry, and rose.

"I should like to see you again, Mr. MacIntyre."

"Mr. Arthur has gone to see Philip. Do you know Arthur Durnford, sir ? "

"I believe I do."

"Not so well as I do. I will tell you something about him. He is ready to do any thing that he thinks honorable, even to strip himself to the last shilling; and he is jealous that no word should be breathed against his father. He is now gone to consult Miss Madeleine. I know what her advice will be."

"Well ? "

"And do you know Philip ? No — not

so well as I do. I left him a ruined man. That you know, perhaps. He will do any thing for money when it is wanted to save his honor. He wants it now for that purpose. And he would do any thing in the whole world to remove the stain of illegitimacy and black blood. The latter is impossible The former can now be arranged. Ten thousand pounds, sir? Good heavens! If an estate is worth more than four thousand a year, and if you have got three times ten thousand accumulated — Do you know the story of the Sibyl, Mr. — really, I forget your name. Never mind. You remember the story, sir? Probably you had *some* humanities when you were a boy. She came back, sir, again and again; and the third time her price was three times that of her first."

"In point of fact, Mr. MacIntyre, you want to sell your information for ten thousand pounds. It is a disgraceful" —

Mr. MacIntyre started, and opened his eyes.

"The absence of the reasoning faculty in England is vera wonderful. Man! I was talking of general principles. I was giving you my opeenion on the creature that would not sell his information. I would have you to know, sir, that I am not in the habit of selling any thing. I am a Master of Arts, sir, of an ancient and honorable Univairsity — the Univairsity of Aberdeen. And I wish ye good-morning, sir."

He put on his hat, and stalked away with dignity.

CHAPTER XXIV.

ARTHUR went to Madeleine for advice, being one of those who, when they have made up their minds to a line of action, are not satisfied without being fortified in their design by their friends.

He called after dinner, and found the two ladies alone, — Mrs. Longworthy asleep, and Madeleine reading.

"Coming in here," he said, in a low voice, "is like coming into a haven of repose. You are always peaceful."

"Yes, — a woman's conflicts are below the surface mostly. And my own troubles lie two miles away, as you know. When are you really going to make up your mind to come and help us?"

"What am I to do? Teach science again?"

"No; lecture, start clubs, give concerts — you play very well — write tracts, do all sorts of things that will help the people to raise themselves."

"I am afraid I should not do for it, Madeleine. But I will try to join you. Only first give me your advice on a very serious matter."

He told his story.

"Your father married to a mulatto girl? Arthur, it is impossible."

"So I should have said; but it seems true. There are the certificates of marriage, duly signed and attested. And not by the man MacIntyre himself — or we might suspect them — but by a legal firm of Palmiste. You know them. There can be no doubt whatever. And Philip is my brother."

"I always knew it," murmured Mrs. Longworthy, waking up to enjoy her lazy triumph. "I told you, Arthur, that your father had no brothers."

"I suppose," Arthur continued, "that by some accident this mulatto girl, my father's first wife, died early, and that on hearing of her death my father married again. But MacIntyre knows nothing of this: he only knows that Marie — we will go on calling her Marie — went away to England."

"And the result of the whole?"

"Would be, if the claim were substantiated, that I have nothing: I am a beggar. All the estate, and all the accumulations, go to Philip."

"Have you seen Philip?"

"Not yet. I shall go and see him in the morning. I have not seen him for more than four months. You know, we were three months in Italy; but I have heard one or two stories about him. I am afraid he has lost money betting."

"What are you going to do?"

"The lawyer says fight. What ought I to do, Madeleine?"

"Fighting means further exposure of old scandals, and raking up private histories which may as well be left buried. Is there no middle way?"

"None. Either he is the rightful heir, or I am. To Phil it means not only fortune, but also legitimacy. I know now — I have known for some little time — what it is that has made Phil what he is. It is not the love of that fast life to which he belongs, so much as his constant sense of his birth, and the tinge of the black blood. Can you not understand it, Madeleine?"

"But if the certificates are correct, and not forgeries, there can be no doubt whatever of the thing."

"There can be none, — Philip is the heir."

They were silent for a while, Mrs. Longworthy only giving to the group that feeling of repose which is caused by the long breathing of one who slumbers.

"If it will make you work, Arthur, whispered Madeleine, "it will be a good thing for you. Let it go, my friend; let your mother take it, and raise no further questions about your father's private history. It may be all a forgery, put together by that creature, your Scotch tutor; only be very sure that Philip knows nothing about it. Go out into the world, and work with other men. It will be better for you. Or come and work with me."

"That is impossible, Madeleine," he whispered, — "except on one condition."

She flushed scarlet for a moment, and then she answered directly, and to the point.

"I know what your condition is. We have known each other so long, Arthur, that I am afraid."

"What are you afraid of?"

"I am afraid that our old brother and sister feeling may be all that you can have for me."

"Listen a moment, Madeleine. When I saw you first, — I mean six months ago, — I was afraid of you. You were so queenly, so beautiful, so unlike the child I loved so many years ago. When I came here day after day, and found you always the same, — always kind, thoughtful, sisterly, — the old feeling arose again, and I felt once more that, as of old, we were brother and sister; but when I was with you abroad, when we were together every day and all day, that feeling died away again, and another has sprung up in its place. Madeleine, I cannot work with you as you wished, because I love you. If you were another girl, if I did not know you so well, I should make fine speeches about coming to you as a beggar, now that I have lost all my money; but you do not want these. Let me go, or bid me stay; but, Madeleine, whatever you do, do not let me lose your friendship."

"You are sure you love me, Arthur," she murmured between her lips, — her eyes softened, her cheeks glowing.

"Am I sure? Do you know that I have sprung into new being since I found I loved you? My blood flows faster, my life has quickened. I can feel, I can hope. Madeleine, I can work. Before, what was my very existence? It was life without life, light without sunshine, work without a purpose, days that brought neither hope nor regret. Do I love you, Madeleine?"

"Then, Arthur," she whispered, leaning forward so that her lips met his, "I have always loved you. Take me, I am altogether yours."

It was then that Mrs. Longworthy showed the real goodness of her heart. She had been awake for some moments, and was taking in the situation with all her eyes.

Now she rose, and, gathering her skirts round her, she swept slowly out of the room, remarking as she went, —

"You will find me in the dining-room, my dears, as soon as you have done talking."

They sat and talked together, hand in hand, of the life that they would lead, of the perfect confidence there should be between them, of all high and sweet things that a man can only tell to a woman. Young fellows whisper to each other something of their inner life, — it can only be done between eighteen and twenty-two, — and ever after there is a bond of union between them that is always felt, if not acknowledged. Sometimes, too, at night, on the deck of a ship, when the moonlight is broken into ten thousand fragments in the white track, and the stars are gazing solemnly at us with their wide and pitying eyes, men may lay bare the secrets of their soul. One of the many whom I have known — he is ten thousand miles from here — in my wanderings abroad — I spent six months beneath the same roof with him — was wont to rise at dead of night, and pace the veranda for an hour or two. If you heard him, and got up to join him, he would *talk* to you. The memory of his talk is with me still. I remembered it in the morning, but he did not. Which was the real man, which was the false, I never knew. One lived by day, and one by night. I think the man of the night — he who showed me his thoughts — was the true man. He is the one whom I love to recall.

While they talked, Mrs. Longworthy slumbered by the table in the dining-room.

Outside, Laura was wandering in the cold and pitiless streets.

At the house at Notting Hill, Philip and MacIntyre were drinking together, — Philip to drown his excitement, which had absolutely driven Laura, for the time, out of his head; Mr. MacIntyre, to drown his anxiety. If he lost this stake! But it looked like winning.

Between the two were a couple of champagne bottles, empty. At stroke of ten, MacIntyre rang the bell for tumblers. At twelve, Philip went to bed too drunk to speak. At one, Mr. MacIntyre fell prone upon the hearth-rug, and slumbered there. In the morning, at seven, he awoke, and, finding where he was, got up, rubbed his nose thoughtfully, and went home to Keppel Street.

"It's wonderfu'," he remarked when he got back to his lodgings, and sat down to breakfast, " what a restorer is the morning air. When I go down to Scotland I shall always get up early, to shake off the whiskey of the night. Elizabeth, my lassie, I think you may bring me another rasher of bacon."

CHAPTER XXV.

"I GOT this address of yours from MacIntyre," said Arthur, calling on Philip at midday. "Why have you been hiding away so long?"

"There has been no hiding," said Philip, half sullenly.

Then both men paused, thinking of the words that were to be spoken between them.

Arthur was the first to speak.

"Of course you know what MacIntyre came to tell me,"

"Of course I know it."

"Whatever happens, Philip, let us be friends still. If it is clear that my father married — was married — before he married my mother, there is nothing more to be said."

Both flushed scarlet.

"You see, Arthur, I have known since I was fifteen years old, — no matter how, — that I am your half-brother. This question is more to me than property. It is legitimacy."

"I know."

"But, go by what your lawyer advises. Let us make a legal question of it all."

"My lawyer says fight."

"Then fight."

"Fighting means bringing the private life of our father into public, making known things that ought not to be revealed. I think I cannot fight, Phil."

"But I *must*, Arthur."

"Yes, and I must give way. After all, Phil, it matters very little to me, so far as the money goes. I shall have to work; but I am a man of very simple habits. You will make a better planter than I. You will go out, and do great things for Palmiste."

"Not I. I fight for my legitimacy. I shall do no great things, either here or in Palmiste."

"Let me tell you about the property, Phil. No, — it is best that you should know. It is a very good property. In ordinary years, when there is no hurricane, it is worth more than four thousand pounds a year. I do not spend one-fourth of that amount. There are consequently large accumulations. I should think I am worth thirty thousand pounds, — that is you are worth."

"It is not the value of the property"—

"I know. Still you ought to learn all that is at stake. This is yours. I surrender it all, rather than go to law over our father's grave."

"I must prove my legitimate birth, if I can, Arthur. Think of it. Think what it is to me, who have all along been weighted with my birth, to be made free, — free and equal to all other men."

"I do think of it. I think a great deal of it If I were in your place, nothing should persuade me to forego the chance of setting this right. Still, I believe you have always exaggerated the importance of the point."

"It may be so. I do not think so."

"And now, Phil, let us talk it over completely. I am in your hands. The whole estate will be yours as soon as the transfer can be made; but you will not let me go quite empty-handed!"

"Good heavens, — no!" cried Philip. "I believe you are the most chivalrous man in the world. Empty-handed! no: take what you will."

"Give me what you have yourself, and I shall be content."

"You mean what I had, I suppose. Make it double, Arthur, and I shall be content, — content in a way. How is any man to be contented who has the slave blood in his veins? Look here." He pulled his short, curly black hair. "This comes from the negro wool. And look here." He held out his hand. "Do you see the blue below the nails? That comes from the negro blood. And look at my eyes. Do you see the black streak beneath them? Negro blood, I tell you. And generation after generation may pass, but these marks never pass away. My face, at least, is like my father's. I am more like him than you are, Arthur."

"You are too sensitive, Phil. Do you really seriously think the old prejudices are founded in reason? Do you imagine that you are the least worse for having this little admixture of race in your blood?"

"I do," said his brother. "I know that I am worse. I feel it. When white men are calm, I am excited. When they are careless about their superiority, I am anxious to assert mine. When they are self-possessed, I am self-conscious. When they are at ease, I am vain. I know my faults. I can do things as well as any man, but I can do nothing as well as some men. That is the curse of the mulatto, the octoroon, or whatever you call him. Unstable as water, we never excel. So far we are like Judah, the son of Jacob, founder, you know, of the celebrated tribe of that name."

They were silent for a while.

"Even now I have made myself a greater fool, a greater ass, than you would conceive possible. If ever you hear stories about me, Arthur,—by Jove, you are sure to hear them!"—he suddenly remembered Venn, and his friendship with Arthur,—"think that I am more than sorry; not repentant, because I do not see any good in repentance. Milk that is spilt, eggs that are broken, money that is spent, sins that are committed, are so many *faits accomplis.* Well, never mind. Let us return to business. You will take the accumulated funds."

"No: I will take ten thousand pounds, and I shall be rich."

"Have what you like. And now take me to your lawyer's, and let us tell him what we are going to do; and if at any moment, Arthur, either now or hereafter, you wish to rescind your transfer, you shall do it, and we will fight. By gad, the prodigal son always gets the best of it! The good man toils and moils, and gets nothing. Then, you see, the scapegrace comes home. Quick, the fatted calf,—kill, cook, light the fire, make the stuffing, roast the veal, broach the cask, and spread the feast."

So he passed, in his light way, from repentance to cynicism, happy at heart in one thing,—that now he could face his creditors and meet his engagements.

It was a week after this that MacIntyre, who had been calling every day at the Burleigh Club, and at Notting Hill,—being a prey to the most gnawing anxieties he had ever known,—at last found Philip at home.

He was greeted with a shout of laughter, —not, it is true, of that kind which we are accustomed to associate with the mirth of innocence. Perhaps Philip's joyousness had something in it of the Sardinian character.

"Come, Prince of Evil Devices, and receive your due."

"You are pleased to be facetious," observed MacIntyre.

"Haven't I a right to be facetious? Do not I owe it to you that I have got rid of a wife, and come into a fortune? Sit down, man, and let us have a reckoning. My engagements are met. It is all settled. Arthur retires, and the heir-at-law steps in. Rid of a wife,—with dishonor saved, and honor gained,—what do I owe you? Five thousand is too paltry a sum to speak of."

MacIntyre turned perfectly white, and shivered from head to foot.

"The papers are signed,—the transfer is completed. I am in possession of the estate of Fontainebleau and fifteen thousand pounds in stocks. It is your doing, MacIntyre. You shall have the money bargained for. Give me up the agreement."

He took it from his pocket, and handed it over, with trembling hands. He was unable to speak, for very astonishment. He grew faint, and staggered against the table.

Phil caught him by the arm.

"Why, what is the matter, man? Will you have some brandy?"

"Not now, Phil,—not now. Let me sit down a moment, and recover myself."

Presently he started up again.

"Now," he cried,—"at once; let me have no delay. The money, Phil,—the money. Let me handle it. Ah! At last, —at last! I have been anxious, Phil. I was afraid that there was some link missing,—some possible doubt; but it is all right. I have won the prize I worked for."

"You have won the compensation you were talking about the other night."

"Yes," said the philosopher,—"the compensation,—ah, yes, the compensation! It has come."

"And without any of the little hankey-pankey that the world has agreed to condemn,—isn't that so?"

"Surely,—surely!"

He looked at Philip with steady eyes, but shaky lips.

"A righteous man, you know, never begs his bread."

"I've begged mine, like the unrighteous —or next door to it. The next door to it, may be, was not included in the text."

"Obviously, the inference is that you are a righteous man. But, come,—one word of explanation first. You know when I met you in the street?"

"As if I shall ever forget the time."

"You had those papers in your pocket then?"

"They have never left me since I took them away from Palmiste."

"Why did you not produce them at once?"

"Because the risk was too great. I wanted to sell them. I wanted to see how you would take the chance. It was one I could not afford to risk. When I saw you going down hill, I knew that I had only to wait for the end. Every thing helped me. You became more and more involved. I became more and more certain; but it was not till the very end that I dared bring them out."

"And then you thought you could win?"

"I did. I knew that under the cloud of misfortunes any of the old misplaced generosity to your milksop of a brother would be finally put away and done with, and that the lure — legitimacy and a fortune — would be too much for you to withstand. I rejoiced, Philip — I rejoiced."

Philip was silent. By all the rules he should have kicked this man then and there. But he was accustomed to the calculating and unscrupulous ways of the creature. Besides, he half liked him. The very openness of his wickedness was a kind of charm. It was only one more confession, — a confession already more than half made.

"You have won, then. Let that be your consolation. And now tell me, MacIntyre. Swear by all that you hold sacred, — Stay, is there any thing you hold sacred?"

"Money — I will swear by money. Or drink — I will swear by drink."

"Swear, then, anyhow, that you will tell me the truth. Did my father write those letters?"

"He did, Philip — I swear it. He did, indeed."

Only the smallest *suppressio veri*, — only the dates that were added long afterwards by himself.

"And the marriage. Is that register really in the church book?"

"I swear it is there. Did you not see the attestation of the Palmiste lawyers? It is really there!"

So it was. He might have added, to complete the truth of the attestation, that he had himself placed it there.

"Then I am the lawful heir. I have not defrauded Arthur."

"You have not. What does Arthur get out of it?"

"Ten thousand."

"And vera handsome too. Double of my share. Arthur has done well. Now give me my money, Phil."

Philip gave him a bank pass-book.

"I have paid into your account at this bank the sum of five thousand pounds, — you can see the note of the amount. Here is your check-book. Go, now, man, and be happy in your own way."

"Yes, I will go. You are a rich man. I am as rich as I wish to be. My old maxums will no longer be of any use either to you or me. It pains me only to think that I must not, with my experience, dissemble my convictions and go over to the other side, preaching in future that honesty is the best policy. I may vera likely give lectures to show how merit is rewarded, and steady effort always commands success. Steady effort has been, as you know, of great use to me. Industry is the best thing going. We always get what we deserve. Every thing is for the best. Whatever is, is right. The prosperous man goes back to the copy-books for his philosophy, and all his reading is thrown away. Now, my experience is the contrary. It is only the clumsy sinners who get punished. The innocent man very often receives the flogging. Therein the moral world differs from the natural. For if you run your head against a post, you infallibly get a headache. He who would be rich must also be cautious. If he can escape detection, he will acquire money, and therefore happiness. My dear pupil, a word of parting advice."

"No," replied Philip. "Go. I hardly know whether to thank you or to curse you. I think I must curse you. You have poisoned the atmosphere of life for me. I have got riches without enjoyment. I can never be happy again, with the memory of the past — your doing."

"Poor little leddy," sighed MacIntyre. "I'm vera sorry, indeed, for her hard fate. I wish it had never been done. Eh, Phil, — it was an awfu' piece of wickedness" —

"It was. God forgive us both! But it can never be forgiven."

"I'm vera sorry, Phil. It was a clumsy thing; but there — we won't talk about it. What was it I was telling you some time ago, Phil? The poor man never repents, — it is only the rich. See, now — I am rich, and I begin to repent at once. Eh, man, it is a terrible time I have before me! There's just an awfu' heap to repent for; and pocket handkerchiefs, too, very expensive. As soon as I get settled, I shall begin. But where? Phil, I think I shall work backwards. It will come easier so. Obsairve. He who tackles his worst foe at once has little to fear from the rest. The drink, and the troubles at Sydney, — all these things are venial. But the lassie, Phil, the lassie, — I must begin my repentance with the lassie."

"You will never begin your repentance at all. You will go on getting drunk till you die."

"Philip Durnford," returned Mr. MacIntyre magisterially, "You pain me. After an acquaintance of nearly twenty years — after all the maxums I have taught you, and the corpus of oreeginal and borrowed philosophy that I have compiled and digested for you — to think that you could say a thing like that. Know, sir, once for all, that the man at ease with fortune never drinks, save in moderation. The philosopher gets drunk when his cares become too much for him. He changes his world when the present is intolerable. Some poor creatures commit suicide. The true philosopher drinks. He alone is unhappy who has not the means of getting drunk. When I was between the boards, I am not ashamed to confess, I used to save twopence a day. That made a shilling a week. With that I was able to get drunk on Sunday, by taking two pennyworths of gin and porter in alternate swigs. And that is all over. Philip, my pupil, I shall go away. I shall go back to Scotland, among my own people, as an elder of the kirk, which I intend to be. I shall set an example of rigid doctrine, sabbatarian strictness, and stern morality. After a', it is good for the vulgus — the common herd — to be kept to strict rules. But drink — no sir. Intoxication and Alexander MacIntyre have parted company. I'm far from saying that I shall not take my glass whiles — the twal' hoor, especially, — that is but natural; but intemperance! sir, the thought degrades me."

He buttoned up his coat, and put on his hat.

"Farewell, Philip! you will never see me again. As for that poor young thing"—

"Do not provoke me too much," said Philip, growing pale.

"I was only going to say, that, if you can take her back, it is your duty. I'm vera sorry. She was bonnie, she was kind, she was *douce*, she was faithful. Ah! Phil, Phil! it is a terrible thing to think of — the wickedness of the world! I must go away at once, and begin my repentance."

He shook his head from side to side, seized Philip by the hand, and disappeared.

And this was the last that Philip Durnford ever saw of his old tutor.

CHAPTER XXVI.

LEAVING the house, poor little Lollie walked quickly away into the dark November mist, and down the road. She had no purpose; for as yet she had but one thought to get away, — to see the last of a house which had witnessed her shame and suffering; to take herself somewhere — it mattered not where — till the dull, dead pain in her brow would go away, and she should feel again able to see things clearly, — able to go to Mr. Venn, and tell him all. As she went along the streets, and passed the lighted shops, it seemed that every woman shunned her, or looked at her in contempt, and every man stared. In all the passers-by she detected the glance of scorn. The very beggars did not ask her for alms; the crossing-sweepers allowed her to pass unnoticed.

It was only two o'clock, and she had more than two hours of daylight before her. She pulled down her veil, and walked on, her fingers interlaced, like a suppliant's, feeling for the lost wedding-ring. She passed down the long Edgware Road, which seemed to have no end, and where the noise of the cabs nearly drove her mad. At last she came to the Park, where the comparative quiet soothed her nerves; but she walked on, and presently found herself in Piccadilly. She hurried across the road here, and got into the Green Park, which was even quieter and more deserted than the other. And so at last into St. James's, the best of the three, beyond which arose the intolerable noise and tumult of the streets. She sat down on one of the benches. It was the very same bench where she had once sat with Philip, talking over the meaning of love and marriage. Alas! she knew by this time what one might mean, but not the other. For as she sat alone, and the early evening closed round her, she felt how, through all, her marriage was but a mockery of every thing, — of love, because she never loved him; of a real ceremony, because the man was no clergyman. How there was no religion in what she had done, no duty, no prudence, — nothing but a vain and ignorant desire to please her guardian. And, after all, he had turned her off.

But as yet she could think of nothing clearly.

Two hours since she left him, — only two hours! — and it seemed an age, and the last three months a dream of long ago. And as she tried to think, the stream of her thoughts would rush backwards in her head, as if stopped and turned by some sudden dam.

Big Ben struck four. Presently there came to her a policeman, with hirsute countenance and kindly eyes.

"The Park gates shut at half-past four, miss. Don't you think you had better not sit any longer under this dripping tree?"

She got up at once — submissive. Poor little Lollie, always obedient, always *douce*.

"I will go if you like."

"Hadn't you better go home, miss?"

She made no answer, but looked at him sadly for a moment, and then, drawing her veil tighter over her face, went slowly through the gates, and passed through the Horse Guards. In the Strand, the shops were all lit up, and things looked brighter. She went down the street slowly, looking into every window as she passed, trying to think what it was she wanted to buy. Here were chains, gold watches, and silver cups; and here — what is it makes her heart leap up within her, and her pale cheek glow? — a tray of wedding-rings. She hurried in, she held out her finger to be measured without saying a word, and pointed to the tray. The ring cost her a guinea, and so she had nineteen shillings left. But she came out relieved of a little of the pain that oppressed her, and went on happier, as if something had been restored to her.

It was nearly six when she came to Chancery Lane; and as she saw the old familiar, ugly street once more, a great yearning came over her heart, for was it not the street that leads to Gray's Inn?

"I will arise and go unto my father," said the poor prodigal, — say all of us, when sorrow and punishment fall upon us. "I will go to Mr. Venn," thought Lollie.

She quickened her step, and came to the familiar portals. No one saw her go in. She mounted the stairs — ah, how often had she run up before! — thinking what she should say. Alas! when she got there, the outer door was shut, and Mr. Venn was not at home.

Then her heart fell; and she burst into low wailings and tears, leaning her cheek against the door, as if that could sympathize with her trouble. It was the hour when every man in Gray's Inn was gone to dinner, and no one was on the staircase to hear her.

She might have known, had she reflected. But she could not think. Time had no more any meaning for her. She thought that Mr. Venn was gone away altogether, and that she had no longer a single friend left in the whole world. So, when the paroxysm of tears, the first she had shed, had passed, she crept down stairs again, and turned away to go out at the north gate, by Raymond's Buildings. Alas, alas! had she taken the other turning she would have met Venn himself, almost as sad as she was, returning home to his desolate chambers.

Seven o'clock, — eight, — nine. The shops are being shut now, and the streets not so crowded. There are not so many carts about, which is good for her nerves; but the rain is pouring upon her. She is somewhere about Regent's Park — walking, walking still. The rain falls heavily. Her dress is wet through, and clings to her limbs; but she staggers on mechanically.

Hartley Venn is in his chambers, sitting over the fire, brooding.

Philip is drinking, and playing cards.

Men pass by and speak to her. She does not hear, and takes no notice.

Twelve o'clock, — one o'clock. The passengers in the street are very few now.

A rush of many people and of galloping horses. There is a fire, and the cavalcade of rescue runs headlong down the street, followed by a little mob of boys and men. They are always awake, these boys and men, ready for plunder.

Then silence again.

Two o'clock. The street is quite empty now. Then from a side street there are loud screams and cries, and a woman rushes into the road with a wild shriek. She passes close to Lollie. Her face is bleeding, her clothes are torn. She waves her arms like some wild Cassandra, as one who prophesies the woe that shall fall upon the city. But it is nothing. Only the wail of despair and misery; for she is starving, and her husband in a drunken rage has struck her down, and trampled on her. Oh! brothers and sisters, how we suffer, how we suffer for our sins!

Three o'clock. She is in Oxford Street, the stony-hearted. It is quite empty. Not even a policeman in sight. Her eyes are heavy and dim; her head is burning; an unnatural strength possesses her limbs; her shoulders have fallen forward. Is this Hartley Venn's little girl? This with the bowed head, the draggled dress, the weary gait? O Hartley, could you have seen her then, it would have been bad for Philip and his tutor! But Hartley is sound asleep, and so is Philip; so, too, is Mr. MacIntyre. They are all asleep and comfortable in their beds, and only the tender and delicate girl is wandering about in the night under the rain.

The city is sleeping. A strange hush has fallen over London. Not the sound of a single wheel, not a footstep. The silence strikes her; for it seems to have come suddenly. She lifts her head, and looks round, with a moan of weariness and agony.

After her there creeps silently, on bare feet, a creature in the semblance of a man. He is tall, nearly six feet high, lean and emaciated. His scanty clothes are rags; his trousers are so tight that the sharp bones seem projecting through them. His arms are too long for the ragged sleeves of his tattered coat. He has no hat. His face is black with dirt, and wisps of a fortnight's beard are sticking in patches over it. His hair is long and matted. His eyes are sharp. It is the wolf of London, — the wehr-wolf of civilization. In what lair does he crouch all day? Where does he hide while honest folk are up and doing.

She does not hear him as his naked feet press close upon her. As he gets nearer, he looks round quickly and furtively, like a beast of prey before he makes his spring. No policeman is in sight. His long fingers clutch her shoulder, and she feels his quick breath upon her cheek. She starts, and turns with a shriek of terror.

"Have you got any money?" he hisses. "Give it to me, — give it to me quick, or I will murder you."

She stared for a moment, and then, understanding so much, put her hand in her pocket, and drew out her purse. He looked up and down the street, and then, snatching it from her hand, swiftly fled down a court and was lost.

Then the great, bare streets filled her with terror, and she turns out of it. Perhaps there are no wolves in the small streets.

So, presently, she finds herself in Covent-garden Market. Light, activity, noise. The early market carts are arriving. She goes under the piazza, and, sitting on a basket, falls fast asleep in the midst of it all.

She sleeps for nearly two hours. Then she is awakened by a rough but not unkindly touch of her arm.

"Come, young woman, I want my basket."

She sprang to her feet, trying to remember where she was. Two or three people were staring at her. A great red-faced woman among the rest, — a coarse, rough, rude, hard-drinking creature.

They were speaking to her, but she could not understand. It seemed a dream.

"Leave her to me," said the woman. "You go about your business, all of you. I know a lady when I see her. You leave her, all of you, to me. Come, my dear, don't try to say a word. Don't 'ee speak now, or else ye'll begin to cry. Wait a bit — wait a bit."

She put her arms round Lollie's waist, and half led half carried her, to a coffee-stall, of which, indeed, she was the proprietor.

"Now, me darlin', sit ye down on my seat, and taste this."

Laura had eaten nothing since breakfast the preceding day, say eighteen hours. The coffee restored her to a sense of reality, for she had fallen into a state almost of *coma*. She drank the cup, and handed it back to her new friend.

"Now, my dear, another, and a bit of bread and butter. Don't 'ee say a word, now, or ye'll begin to cry."

She took a little bread and butter; and then, overcome with weariness, her head fell upon the tray where the bread and butter stood, and she was asleep again.

The good soul covered her with a shawl, — not the cleanest in the world, but the only one she had, — and went on with her early coffee trade. At seven she awakened her.

"I must go now, my dear," she said. "I'm an hour almost behind my time, and the childer want me; but I wouldn't waken you. Are you better now?"

Lollie felt in her pocket for her purse.

"I remember," she said, "a man robbed me last night of all I had. It was nineteen shillings. "Stay," she added, taking off her locket, — Venn's present — "take this for your kindness."

"I won't," said the woman stoutly.

"You must. Please take it. I think I should have died if it hadn't been for you. You are a good woman."

"Don't 'ee, now, miss," she answered, taking the locket, — "don't 'ee, now, miss, or you'll cry."

And then she began to cry herself; and Lollie left her, and slipped away.

On the Embankment, while the day slowly breaks, and as the light returns, the poor child begins to realize the desolateness of her position. She leans upon the low wall, and tries to think what she will do. Only one thing occurs to her. She must go back to Gray's Inn, and find out where Mr. Venn is. She has no money to buy breakfast, she has nowhere even to sit down; and her limbs are trembling with fatigue. She was almost staggering now as she reached the gate of the Inn. From the other side of the road, she saw the porter and the people who knew her face, standing in the gateway. So she went round by the side entrance in Warwick Court to the door. This time, at least, she would find him in his chambers. Alas! no. The door was still shut, as the gate of Paradise was to the Peri; and her courage died away within her. Inside lay Hartley, sound asleep; for it was but nine o'clock. Then she slowly and sadly descended the staircase. Should she go and ask the porter where he was? Not yet, — presently. She would wait a little, and make one more trial. And so, down Holborn and into Long-acre, with a dazed idea of finding her way to Covent Garden, where there might be another basket to sit upon.

But as she crawled along, her cheeks blanched, her eyes heavy and dull, neither seeing nor feeling any thing, some one passed her, started, ran back, and caught her by the arm, crying —

"Miss Lollie, Miss Lollie!" And she fell fainting forwards.

It was no other than that Mary of whom mention has already been made. Mary the sinful, you know. She was on her way to rehearsal at Drury Lane. For there was the grandest of all grand spectacles "on," and she was one of the most prominent of the ladies engaged specially — a dignified position nearest to the lights — in the joyous dance of village maidens. She also had to appear as one of the queen's personal attendants, in a procession which beat into fits any procession ever made on the stage or off it. She was going along with a friend, engaged in the same line, talking of her boy.

"And the notice he takes,—it's wonderful. Only two years old, and he understands every thing you tell him. And the words he can say; and good as gold with it all. I'm making him a little pair of— Oh, good gracious, it's Lollie Collingwood!"

She lived close by, in the pleasant seclusion of a two-pair back King Street, Longacre.

The two lifted Laura between them, and half carried her, half led her, to the door, and dragged her up stairs, because now she gave way altogether, and lay lifeless in their arms. They placed her on the bed, and waited to see if she would recover. Presently she opened her eyes, gave a dreamy look at them as they leaned over the bed, and closed them again.

"Who is it?" whispered the friend.

"Hush! Don't make any noise! It's Mr. Venn's little girl. Oh, dear! oh, dear! and she so pretty and good! See, she's got a wedding-ring on. Go down, and get the kettle, my dear; and go on to rehearsal without me. I shall be fined; but I know who will pay the fine. And bring Georgie up. Perhaps the sight of him will do her good,—it always does me; and come back, my dear, when rehearsal's over, I shall want you."

She took off Lollie's hat and jacket, her boots and wet stockings, covering her poor cold feet with blankets; and then smoothed and tidied her hair, hanging dank and wet upon her cheek as if she had been drowned.

But Lollie made no movement, lying stupefied and senseless.

Presently came up the other woman, bearing tea in one hand, and little Georgie, making a tremendous crowing, in the other.

"Is she come to?" whispered the girl.

"No; but she will presently. Go you; or you'll be late too; and don't forget to come back as soon as you can. Where's the sugar? Georgie, boy, you've got to be very quiet. Sit down and play with the spoon, and mother will give you sugared bread and butter."

The child immediately sat down, and assumed the silence of a deer-stalker.

"Did you ever see such a boy?" his mother went on. "As good as gold. Now the milk; and ask Mrs. Smith to trust me another quarter-hundred of coals. I must have a fire for this poor thing. Tell her there's them as will see it paid."

She made up the fire, tidied the room, so that it looked at least clean and neat; and then, pouring out the tea, brought it to the bedside.

"Lollie, my dear," she whispered,—"Lollie, my little darling, open your eyes. It's only me,—it's only Mary, that you helped three years ago. Take some tea, dear; and lie down, and go to sleep, and I'll send for Mr. Venn."

At this name the girl opened her eyes, and half lifted her head, while she drank the tea. Then she lay back, looked round the room, pressed her hand to her head as if in pain, and shut her eyes again.

She lay like one dead, but for the light breathing to which her good Samaritan listened from time to time.

At two o'clock the friend came back, and Mary began to hunt about in drawers, in pockets, everywhere.

"I knew I'd got a piece left somewhere," she said at last, triumphantly producing a piece of note-paper the size of a man's hand, the remnant of a quire, the only purchase of note-paper she ever had occasion to make.

"I knew I'd got a piece left, but there's no ink. A pencil must do."

With some pains, for she was not one of those who write a letter every day, she indited a letter to Mr. Venn:—

"DEAR MR. VENN,—Come here as soon as you can. If you are out, come when you get back. Never mind what time it is. If it's midnight you must come.

"MARY."

"Take that," she whispered, "to Gray's Inn. If he is out, drop it into his letter-box; if he is in, tell him not to be bringing the old grandmother round. Laura don't want to see her, I fancy, so much as him."

On the bed the patient lay sleeping through all that day; for Mr. Venn did not come. A sudden shock makes one stupid. So long as it cannot be understood, one can go to sleep over it. It is only when the dull, slow pain succeeds the stupefying blow that we begin really to suffer. Lollie's sleep was what Mr. MacIntyre might have called a compensation due to her. And in her dreams she went back to her husband, and mixed up, with the little house at Notting Hill, her former happiness with Mr. Venn.

The hours sped, and the afternoon came on. Mary had her dinner, and put something on the hob for Lollie if she should wake. Then came tea-time; but she slept still, and the boy had to be put to bed. Then it was Mary discovered that Lollie was sleeping in clothes wet through and through.

She half raised her, pulled them off, and laid her back, with her own warm flannel dressing-gown wrapped round her.

No Mr. Venn.

Then Mary sat down by the fire, prepared to watch, and keep herself awake.

CHAPTER XXVII.

But where was Venn?
He was engaged at a funeral; no other, indeed, than that of Mrs. Peck herself. The old lady was dead, — not in consequence of her grand-daughter's elopement; because when she found that little difference would be made in the allowance, she was a good deal more comfortable without her than with her. She died of some disease more common-place than a broken heart,— one for which the doctor brought her little phials of physic, and Hartley Venn pint bottles of port. As for the disappearance of the girl, that affected her chiefly in lowering the position she had hitherto held in the row. The transportation of a son or the disappearance of a daughter is held in some circles to be as much a disease as the scarlet fever. It is a thing which happens, somehow, in many most respectable families, and is not to be accounted for, or fought against.

The old woman grew worse instead of better, and presently kept her bed. Then Hartley got a nurse for her, and used to look in once a week or so to see how she was getting on. One day the inevitable message from across the river came to the dame in bed; and she immediately sent for Hartley, in great trouble lest she should have to begin the journey before he arrived; but he was in time.

"Is it about Lollie?" he asked, expecting some message of forgiveness or love to the girl.

"No — no," she answered. "Drat the girl, with her fine learning and her ways! It's myself this time, Mr. Venn, and time enough too, I think. All the things I've seen you give that child, and never a thing for me."

Hartley almost burst into a fit of laughter, it was so grotesque.

Here she was seized with a fit of coughing that nearly finished her off altogether.

"Oh, dear, dear! The time's come, Mr. Venn, when you can make amends for your selfishness, and give *me* something too."

"My good soul, haven't I given you every thing you want? Do you want more port wine?"

"Better than that," she gasped. "I want a funeral. I haven't complained, have I, sir? Not when I see the child decked out that fine as the theayter couldn't equal it, I haven't murmured; because, says I to myself — oh, dear! oh, dear! — Mr. Venn, he's a good man, he is. He means it all for the best; and the time will come. And now it has come. I want a funeral. If I was to die to-night," she went on, "you'd save all the 'lowances, and the port wine. Think of that, now."

"I don't see what you want. A funeral?"

"When Peck died we had a trifle saved and put by, — that was fifteen years ago; and we did it properly. His brother came from Hornsey, and his two cousins from Camberwell; and we all went respectable to Finchley. After the funeral — it was a cold day — we went to the 'Crown,' and sat round the fire, and cried, as was but right, and drank gin and water hot. Oh, dear! and we all enjoyed ourselves. Let *me* have a funeral, too, Mr. Venn."

He promised; and she died that very night, chuckling over the great happiness that had come to her. The two cousins from Camberwell, who had not been seen since the demise of the late Mr. Peck, could not be found; but the brother from Hornsey turned up: and Venn, anxious that the old man should really have a good time of it, went to the funeral himself, and gave him after it more gin and water than he could carry.

This pious act accomplished, he went to the club, and dined, going afterwards to Lynn's, where he sat till twelve, discoursing of funeral ceremonies of all nations; so that it was after midnight when he got Mary's missive. He trembled when he read it. The blood rushed to his head, because it could mean but one thing, — his little girl; and as he hurried down the streets to her lodging, he could find no formula for the prayer of his heart, which was for her safety and — for her purity.

"Everybody had gone to bed; but Mary heard his step at the door, and let him in herself.

"What is it?" he whispered, as she proceeded quickly to bolt the door again and put up the chain; "what is it, girl?"

"Hush!" she answered. "Pull off your boots. I'll carry them. She's up there, and asleep."

He crept up. On the bed there lay, still sleeping, her face upon her hand, her cheek all pale and blanched, her long hair streaming back upon the pillow, wrapped warm in all Mary's blankets, his Lollie, — his little girl. He made a movement towards her, but Mary held him back.

"Not yet — wait. She has been sleeping since one o'clock this morning. Let her be. Something dreadful has happened to her. Sit down and wait.

"Notice, Mr. Venn. She's got the same clothes on as she used to have. She must have been going back to you. Poor thing! poor thing! See here — her jacket, and hat, and blue frock, and all — I know them every one. And look here."

Very softly she laid back the blanket which covered her left hand. On the third finger was a wedding-ring.

Hartley bent down, and kissed the ring. His tears fell fast upon the little fingers.

"When will she wake?" he whispered.

"I don't know, — any thing may wake her."

"I shall stay here," he replied; and sat down by the bed, in the only chair in the room.

Mary hesitated a moment, and then lay down on the extreme edge of the other side of the bed. Hartley noticed then that between her and Lollie lay the child.

In two moments she, too, was asleep; and the watch of the night began in earnest. Hartley saw how Mary had laid all her blankets and wraps upon his child, and left herself with nothing, not even a shawl. He took off his own great-coat, — he was ever a kind-hearted man, — and laid it over her shoulders, with a corner of a blanket across her feet, and then sat down again, shivering, — the fire was quite out, and the room was getting cold, — and waited.

Presently the candle went out suddenly, and then there was darkness and silence, save for the breath of the sleepers.

The tumult of his thoughts in this stillness was almost more than his nerves could bear. It was not till the girl left him that he had at all realized the hold she had upon his affections and her place in his life. He had been very lonely without her. He had longed with all his soul to see her again. There was no moment, now, when he was not ready to forgive every thing, nor when his arms were not open to her. The love he had for the girl was the outcome of so many years. She had so twisted and twined the tendrils of affection round him, that when she went away he was like some old tower from which its ivy, the growth of centuries, had been rudely and roughly dragged away. With the child coming every day, full of fresh thoughts, and eager for knowledge, there was always some compensation for the neglect of the world. Laura was his family: she it was who preserved his life from utter loneliness and disappointment. While he watched the growth of her mind, he forgot that his own was, as he was fond of calling it, a wreck. While he listened to her ideas, he forgot that his own were ruthlessly consigned to waste-paper baskets; and with her bright face and child-like ways, he had forgotten that he was getting on for forty, — a poor man still, and disappointed.

All these things crowded into his mind as he sat there, and a great hunger seized his heart to have all things back again as they were before. He had been growing weary of late; the old things ceased to please him; there was little interest left in life; he felt himself getting old; he awoke in the morning without the former feeling that another day would bring its little basket of pleasure; he lay down at night with the new feeling that here was finished another of those gray-colored days which go to make up the total of a sad life. Would that all could be as it had been, — that the step of the child could be heard again upon the stairs, and the lessons renewed where they left off; but the waters run not back to the mountains. Old Mrs. Peck was lying buried in Finchley Cemetery. Laura was a woman; a wedding-ring was on her finger; her long eyelashes lay wet with tears upon her cheeks, — those cheeks that never knew a tear while he was there to kiss them. She moaned in her dreams who had once only smiled; and nothing could come back but the old, old, inextinguishable love.

So, minute by minute, the slow night passed along. Hartley sat through it motionless, in the dark, catching the breathing of the sleeper, though he could not see her face. After many hours, there came through the window the first faint streaks of a November dawn, growing stronger and stronger. When it fell on little Georgie's face, it half roused him from his sleep; and, reaching out his arms to find his mother, the boy laid his little hand on Lollie's neck, and she awoke. Woke with a start, and a rush of thoughts that made her half sit up and stare at the figure of Hartley, indistinct in the morning gloom, with strange, wild eyes.

"Where am I?—where am I?" she murmured, sinking back.

Hartley bent over, and raised her head, kissing her brow in his quiet, old-fashioned way.

"Open your eyes, my little girl. You are come home again. Thank God! you are come home again," the tears raining thick upon her face.

She hardly as yet comprehended; but at last, sitting up in bed, she looked about the room, trying to remember. The bitter knowledge came at last; and, throwing her arms about his neck, she laid her face against his, crying pitifully, —

"O Mr. Venn, Mr. Venn!"

This was all her prayer. Hartley could not trust himself to answer. He clasped her in his arms, he held her face to his, and covered it with kisses, he called her a thousand names of love and endearment, — his child, his Lollie, his little daughter. And then Mary showed herself to be a young woman of really a high order of feeling; for, awakened by the voices, she got up from the edge of the bed on which she had slept all night, and, catching up the still sleeping boy, disappeared to some other part of the house, — I fancy to the back kitchen below, — and left them alone.

Presently, as the light grew stronger, Lollie recovered herself a little, and, in a quick, nervous way began to tell him her tale. Hartley listened with grinding teeth. She told all, extenuating nothing, hiding nothing, save some of the cruelty of her husband's last words. He stopped her then.

"You wrote to me from the place where you were married, my dear?"

"Yes. Mr. MacIntyre was to take the letter."

"And again from Vieuxcamp?"

"I wrote twice from Vieuxcamp."

"I got no letters at all, poor child, — not one. They suppressed them all. Go on. It was the day before yesterday. Where did you go when you left him?"

"I walked — I don't know. I walked all night. You were not in your chambers. It rained. I walked about all night. Somebody took away my purse. What was I to do, Mr. Venn? Where was I to go? A women in Covent Garden gave me some coffee" —

"Tell me her name, Lollie, — tell me her name."

"I don't know. She had a stall at the corner of Bow Street."

"She had a stall at the corner of Bow Street," he repeated.

"And she went home at seven o'clock."

"Home at seven?" he said. "All night, Lollie? — all the cold, wet, dark night? O child, child! why did you not come to my rooms, and sit on the stairs till I came home?"

He held her close to his heart.

"All night — all night! Lollie, Lollie, my heart is breaking for you. One thing you have forgotten. Tell me the name of your husband."

"Philip Durnford."

"Arthur's cousin!"

CHAPTER XXVIII.

PHILIP DURNFORD, — Arthur's cousin, of whom he was always speaking. It seemed a new complication. Venn sat back in his chair, pondering.

"Promise me something, Mr. Venn, — promise me something. Do not harm Philip."

"Harm him!" he answered, with a fierce light in his eyes.

"For my sake, do not try to see him. Do not go in his way."

"My poor child!"

"But promise."

"Lollie, you ask too much. But what harm can I do him? I cannot go round to his tent with a knife, as a child of Israel would have done, and stab him till he die. I wish I could. I cannot even ask him to fight a duel. I would if I could. My aim should be steady, and my eye straight. Tell me what harm I can possibly do to him. True, I could go to him with a stick, and so relieve myself."

"No, Mr. Venn, you will not do that."

"Do not talk about him, child — do not talk about him. Let us talk of other things. And, first, to make you well. My child, how hot your head is! I will go and send a doctor to you. Lie down, and sleep again."

"I should like some tea," she said, sinking back exhausted. "I am thirsty. My hands are burning, and my head swims. Send me Mary, please."

He hurried down stairs, and brought up Mary; and then, promising to return in the afternoon, went away to send her a doctor. That done, he returned to his chambers, feeling lighter and happier than he had done for months past. So happy was he, that he set to work and burned no less than three immortal essays, because he suspected that they were deficient in joy and thankfulness, — two qualities which he now regarded as essential to a well-balanced mind. That sacrifice completed, he sat down before the fire, and fell fast asleep, thinking of how the good old days were to be restored to him.

When he awoke it was three o'clock, and he had had no breakfast. This was a trifling consideration, because coffee can be always made. He broke bread with a sense of happiness and gratitude that almost made his modest meal a sacrament, and then went back to his patient.

But on the stairs he was met by Mary.

"You can't come in, Mr. Venn. Lollie is very ill, and the doctor is with her. Don't be frightened. She's had too great a shock. You may come to-morrow."

He turned away, all his joy dashed. As he shut the door behind him, he ground his teeth savagely, and stood still for a moment.

"If my child" — shaking his hand at the silent heavens — "if my little girl does not get better, I will kill him — I will kill him! A life for a life. I will kill him!"

Then he wandered about the streets, following as nearly as he could the wanderings of Lollie during that night, and trying to imagine where she would stand for shelter. The fancy seized him to find out the man who robbed her. It was from a court on the north side of Oxford Street. He went along, turning into every court he could find, and prowling up and down with a vague sort of feeling that he might see the man, and know him by his long legs, his bare feet, and his crouching like a wolf. There were a good many wolf-like creatures about, but none that quite answered Lollie's description; and he desisted from the search at last, calling himself a fool, and so went home.

Then another notion seized him. He ordered the night porter to call him at four o'clock, and so went to bed.

At four he was awakened, and got up. "Most extraordinary," he murmured, shivering, and lighting a candle, "the sensation of rising in the night. I quite understand now why the laboring classes, who always do it, never take tubs."

He dressed hastily, and went out into the court. The very last light had disappeared in the square. The last roysterer was gone to bed. The last student had knocked off work for the night.

"It gives one," he said to himself, "an Antipodean feeling. I feel as if I were on my head. Now I begin to understand why agricultural laborers are never boisterous in their spirits. This is enough to sadden Momus!"

Not a soul was in Holborn when he passed through the gate. He buttoned his great-coat tighter across his chest, and strode up the street, his footsteps echoing as he went.

"I wish it would rain," he said, "then I should understand the misery of it better."

He left Holborn, and, passing down the by-streets, made directly for Covent Garden. There he found the market in full vigor, — the carts all seeming to come in at the same time. He peered about in the faces of the drivers and workmen.

"An expression of hope," he said, "or rather of expectation. We have had our bed: they seem as if they were always looking for it. Very odd! Life pulled forward, — breakfast at four, dinner at ten, tea at two. Bed, if you are a Sybarite, about seven; if you are a reveller, at nine. Where is my coffee-woman?"

He came to a stall, where a fat, red-faced woman was ladling out cups of coffee to an expectant crowd. He stood on one side, and let the crowd thin, and then humbly advanced.

"A cup of coffee, if you please, ma'am." She poured it out for him.

"Drink it, and go home to bed," she said. "You ought to be ashamed of yourself, stayin' out all night this fashion."

"I am only just out of bed," said Venn meekly. "I got out of bed to see you."

"And pray what might you be wanting to see me for, young man? I don't owe you nothing."

"On the contrary, it is I who owe you a great deal," he replied, sitting on the shafts of her coffee cart. "Tell me, my good soul, you were here the night before last?"

"I am here every night."

"Then you remember the young lady who came here."

"I should think I do remember her, — the pretty lamb."

Venn took her great rough hand in his, and held it.

"She gave you a locket. Have you got it with you?"

"Yes, it's in my pocket. Wait a bit, — wait a bit. Here it is. What do you want with the locket?"

"She has sent me to buy the locket back," he replied, "and to find out where you live. She is with her friends now. You must not ask any thing about her, — why she was out alone; but she is with her own friends, — those who love her. She is ill too, — God help her!"

"Amen," said the woman, "and good she was, I swear."

"As good as any saint. See, give me the locket, and tell me where you live. She shall come soon to see you herself. And here is the price of the locket."

He laid five pounds in her hand. The woman looked at the gold, — it was as much as ever she had had in her possession, all at once, — and then held out her hand again.

"If she's poor, take it back, I don't want it, — the Lord love her! If she's rich, I'll keep it for the childer."

"I am rich," said Venn, "because I have her back. Keep the money. And now tell me where you live."

She shook her head again, and turned away.

"I can't go to bed," he said. "I've had my breakfast too: what time shall I want lunch, I wonder? Where am I to go now?"

It was not quite six o'clock. He strolled along the streets, making mental observations, watching how the traffic began and how it slowly increased. Then he went on the Embankment.

"I have never yet seen the rosy-fingered dawn. Let us contemplate one of Nature's grandest phenomena."

A dense fog came rolling up with the

break of day, and there was nothing to see at all.

"I am disappointed," he said to himself. "From the description of that lying tribe, the poets, I had expected a very different thing. Alas! one by one the illusions of life die away. Let us go and look after our patient."

The worst was passed; and though Laura was hanging between life and death, the balance of youth and strength was in her favor.

After a day or two, they allowed Venn to enter the sick room and help to nurse. Never had patient a nurse more careful and attentive. In the morning, when Mary went to rehearsal, and in the evening, when she went to the theatre, he took her place, and watched the spark of life slowly growing again into a flame. She was light-headed still, and in her unconscious prattling revealed all the innocent secrets of her life. What revelations those are of sick men in the ears of mothers and sisters who have thought them spotless!

Venn learned all. He heard her plead with her husband for permission to tell himself, to write, to try and see him. He saw how, through it all, he himself lay at her heart; and, lastly, he heard from her lips the real and true story of the last cruel blow that drove her out into the street. What could he do to this man? How madden him with remorse? How drive him and lash him with a scourge of scorpions?

One morning he found her sitting up, half-dressed, weak and feeble, but restored to her right mind. Then Hartley Venn did a thing he had not done for nearly thirty years,— you so easily get out of the habit at Eton,— he knelt down by the bedside, her hand in his, and thanked God aloud for his great mercy.

"When I get well again, Mr. Venn," whispered Lollie, "we will go to church together, will we not."

Then he sat down by her while she told him all the story again, till the tears ran down both their cheeks; for Hartley Venn was but a great, soft-hearted baby, and showed his feelings in a manner quite unknown to the higher circles.

"But what are we to do with you, Lollie?" he asked, when he had told all his news,—how Mrs. Peck was gone, and there was no house anywhere for her. "You could not possibly have gone to live with your old grandmother any more. What shall we do for you?"

"I don't know, Mr. Venn. Do something for Mary. See how good she has been."

"Mary don't want any thing, child. When she does she knows where to go for help."

Then he told her all about the coffee woman.

"I will take you to see her," he said, "as soon as you are well. Here is your locket, my dear, back again. We are to go in the day-time, and I am to prepare her for your visit first. But what am I to do with you? Stay. I will go and ask Sukey? She always knows what ought to be done."

It was really a serious question. What was he to do with her? He might get her lodgings. But then his own visits would have to be few, so as to prevent talk. He might take a house for her, though that hardly seemed the best thing. But as he walked along to Woburn Place, a brilliant thought flashed across him. Sukey should take her. A comfortable house, the care of a lady, surrounding circumstances not only new, but new enough to have a charm, and a life beyond the reach of any malicious tongues. Nothing could be better. But, then, Sukey might object. He smoothed his face into its sweetest lines. He would diplomatize.

Sukey was in a state of great nervous excitement, in consequence of having been excommunicated. She was of High Church proclivities, and loved, in moderation, the exercise of those observances appointed by her advisers. Naturally, too, she was fond of the society of her clergyman, a gentleman who held rigid views as to fasting and feasting, observing the periods of the former courageously,— but with grief and pain,— and the latter with undisguised joy. Both states of feeling he regarded as conducive to a sound spiritual state. And so far he was followed by Miss Venn, who hated a vegetable diet as much as she loved a good dinner. In an evil hour, having been presented with an Angola cat, she christened it St. Cyril. Her director, on discovering this piece of levity, treated it as an offence quite beyond the venial sins common among mankind, and not only ordered her to change the name to Tom, but also enjoined as a penance an octave of cabbage. At this tyranny her whole soul revolted, and she flew into open rebellion; going over to the enemy's camp, a neighboring Low Church establishment, where as yet no surplice was flaunted in the pulpit, the Psalms were read, and the service finely rendered.

Thereupon she was excommunicated.

CHAPTER XXIX.

VENN, on the following morning, called upon his sister.

She burst forth with all her tale of trouble as soon as she saw him. Hartley judiciously gave her the reins, only occasionally murmuring sympathetically.

"Why, Sukey," he said, when she had quite finished, "you can do nothing better than persist. It is the most outrageous tyranny. And such a beautiful animal too! St. Cyril, come here. Sh—tsh! A lovely cat."

"I thought you hated cats, Hartley."

"As a rule, I do, but not such a superb creature as this. St. Cyril,—what a beautiful name for a cat! Suggestive of howlings on the chimney-tops,—I mean, of purrings on the hearth-rug. My dear sister, you have a genius for giving names. When I was a child—when we were children together—you used to call me Billabelub for short, I remember well."

Sukey began to purr too, falling into the trap baited by flattery, as innocently as any creature of the forest.

"I think I chose a good name, in spite of Mr. De Vere. Take a glass of wine, Hartley, and a biscuit. Why do you call here so seldom?"

"The sherry, by all means."

He poured out two glasses.

"Hartley, you know I never take wine in the morning."

"As it is poured out, you may as well drink it: besides, it will do you good."

She drank it, and appeared to like it.

"But I came to tell you some good news, Sukey," he went on, seeing that the moment had arrived. "My little girl has come back to me."

Sukey said nothing, but looked up sharply.

"Yes. Her husband has ill-treated her."

"Her husband! She has a husband, then?"

"Sukey! Why, how else should she have left me?"

This was a facer. Hartley followed up the advantage.

"Her husband, it appears"—

"Who is her husband, Hartley?"

"Mr. Philip Durnford, lieutenant in the —th Regiment, cousin of Arthur Durnford, whose father used to be a pupil at the rectory. You remember him thirty years ago?"

"My dear brother. As if I could remember any thing so long ago as that."

"True, I forgot. Philip Durnford, I am sorry to say, is not a good man. He made her conceal the marriage, destroyed the letters she wrote to me, forbade her writing any more, and at last ruined himself, and turned her out of doors. Lollie has had a hard time, Sukey."

"Where is she now?"

"She had nowhere to go, wandered about trying to find me in my chambers, kept on missing me, and at last was picked up by a girl whom she befriended two or three years ago, who took her in like a Samaritan, and we nursed her through a fortnight of dangerous illness. She is still almost too weak to be moved."

"You must see her husband at once."

"I think not."

"Then, where can she go? Hartley, you must not begin that old business of having her up in your chambers."

"No, certainly not—that must be put a stop to. I have thought it over. She must go, Sukey"—here he became very impressive—"she must go to the house of some lady, a little, but not too much, older than herself, of a kind and affectionate disposition—my child is dreadfully broken and weak, Sukey—where her wounds may be healed, and we can teach her to forget some of her troubles; where she will have no reproaches, no worries, no hard words."

"Where will you find her such a guardian?"

"Where? Here, Sukey, here,"—he took her fat little hands in his,—"here, my dear. I know no other woman so good and kind as yourself, and no house which will so entirely fulfil all the conditions as your own."

"Mine? Oh, goodness gracious!"

"Yours, Sukey. For there is, I am quite sure, no one in the world whose heart is so soft and whose house is so comfortable as yours."

She sat silent.

"You know Lollie too. It is not as if you were strangers. Remember how you used to kiss her when she was quite a little thing."

"I do," said Sukey. "The child's lips were always sticky with jam."

"They were; and it shows," said Hartley, "the kindness of your heart to treasure up this trifling circumstance. Women alone know how to touch the chords of feeling. She was always extravagantly fond of jam. I remember, too, how you used to spread it for her, on bread and butter, careful not to give her too much butter for fear of biliousness. The old days, Sukey, the old days!"

He was silent, as if overcome. Then he went on,—

"And it is really kind—more kind than I know how to thank you for—to accede at once to my suggestion. I feel as if it came from you. Believe me, sister, I am very grateful."

He kissed her forehead; and the caress, so exceedingly rare from her brother, brought a glow of conscious benevolence to Sukey's cheeks. She almost felt as if she had really suggested the step. Then her heart sank again.

"Well, you know, my dear Hartley, I am the last person in the world to think of my own comfort."

"You are, indeed, Sukey," he murmured with a glance at the sherry, "the very last. Always self-denying."

"But what will Anne think?"

Hartley rang the bell, and Anne appeared.

"My sister, Anne, — upon my word, Anne, you are getting younger every day, — wants to take, for a little while, a young lady into the house. Mrs. Durnford, who is unhappily separated from her husband. You remember her, — my ward, Miss Collingwood, that was; but she is a little afraid that it will put you out."

Anne looked troubled.

"Not a young lady who will give trouble or any extra work, but one who wants a comfortable place, and thoughtful people like yourself about her."

"If Miss Venn wants it," said Anne.

"Of course she wants it."

"Then I'm not the one to make objections; and I'm sure the house wants a little brightening up. And you never coming in but once in three months, Mr. Hartley."

"I shall come every day now, Anne; but haven't you got Mr. De Vere?"

This was the clergyman with whom Anne did not hold.

"Mr. De Vere, indeed!" and Anne retreated.

"Then we will lose no time," said Hartley. "I don't think you could have her to-morrow; but the day after, perhaps."

"The day after? O Hartley! will she be wanting gayety and fuss, and every thing?"

"Lollie? My dear Sukey, she wants quiet; but, would it not be a nice thing — a graceful thing — if you would bring her here yourself?"

"If you prefer it, Hartley. Where is she?"

"Where she has been for the last three weeks. With Mary."

"Mary has got a surname, I suppose. Pray, what is the profession of Mary?"

"Mary — I mean, Mrs. Smith, whose — ahem! whose husband has gone to —to"—

"Where is he gone to?"

"How should I know where he is gone to?" replied Hartley, a little irritably, for he did not like being off the rails of truth. "Gone to Abraham's bosom, I suppose. So Mrs. Smith, you know, dances at the theatre, and supports her child in a creditable way."

"Now, Hartley, I will not — the granddaughter of a Bishop, and all — go to the lodgings of a dancing person."

Hartley repressed an inclination to refer to the ancestral glue manufactory, and only meekly replied that there was no need.

"Bring Laura to your chambers the day after to-morrow," said Sukey, "and I will come and fetch her."

"Do, Sukey, come to breakfast, — kidneys, sister. You shall take her away afterwards in a cab. You will be kind to her, Sukey?"

"Of course I will. Oh, dear! there is nothing but trouble. Now we shall have to make things ready. Well, go away now, Hartley: you will only be in the way. I will come at ten."

Two days afterwards Hartley brought his ward back again to the old chambers. Mary hugged and kissed her; but when Laura promised to call and see her soon, she only shook her head, and said it was better not, and began to cry; and then she went back to her room again, and found it cheerless and dreary indeed.

Hartley helped Laura up stairs, and installed her in her old place, the old chair by the fire.

"It looks like what it used to be, Lollie," he said; "but it is not. It never can be again."

"Ah, no! It never can be again. My fault, my fault."

"Never again, never again. The waters are troubled, dear, and we shall be long in getting them clear. But think no more of the past. You are always my little girl, remember; and if you were dear to me before, Lollie, when you were but a child, you are doubly dear now, when you come back in your sorrow and trouble. There are to be no more lessons and talks and walks. I must not see you very often, and never here, because people might talk. But never doubt, my child, that I love you."

He kissed her forehead, and caressed her face in his old calm way, while the tears were standing in his eyes. She dropped her face in her hands, and wept unrestrainedly.

Miss Venn appeared at this juncture. She had walked to Gray's Inn, making up her mind to be kind, but yet severe; for elopement should always be visited by coldness of manner, at least. Besides, meditation of forty-eight hours had revealed to her, the cunning manner in which her brother had entrapped her into a generosity of which she half repented.

But at sight of her brother's sorrow, and the weak, wasted figure in the chair, her resolution gave way; and almost before she had got the girl well in her fat motherly arms, she was crying over her, and kissing her, with a vehemence which did infinite credit to the family.

Hartley left them, and presently returned with the kidneys, cooked in his bedroom. Nobody could do kidneys so well as Hartley, or brew such splendid coffee; and sympathy brings its own reward in the shape of appetite.

After this she took Lollie away with her, laid her on the sofa, and, with Anne, made much of her.

I have only to add that the public appearance of Laura, and the way in which she was carried off by Miss Venn, entirely re-established her in the eyes of the Gray's Inn functionaries, and effectually drowned the voices of those who had said evil things about her disappearance.

CHAPTER XXX.

VENN went with a troubled mind to find Arthur Durnford. He knew nothing as yet of his changed fortunes, and had, indeed, only heard of Philip as a cousin of whom Arthur spoke little.

"Arthur," he said, shaking his hand, "something has happened to me."

"A great deal has happened to me," said Arthur, laughing; "but I hope your accident is not so serious as mine. It's a long story; but you shall have it."

He told all, from the very beginning.

"I gave up the fortune at once," he said simply, "because it seemed to me clear and beyond any dispute that my father was actually married to this girl, who must have died in Europe before he married again, and when Philip was a year old. He is only two years older than myself. I might have fought the case, my lawyer said; but it would have been at the cost of publishing my father's early history, perhaps raking up old scandals, — all sorts of things. This I couldn't do; and Philip, who is the most generous man alive, insisted on my having double the sum which my father had given him. You see, my father never intended him to be his heir. Of that I am quite certain. On the other hand, by his will, Philip is the heir. And the decision of the case means legitimacy to him."

"I see," said Venn; "I see. Nevertheless, I do not believe. This man who supplies the proofs — I will tell you something about him directly."

"You can tell me very little that I do not know already. That MacIntyre is a scoundrel, an unscrupulous man, bound by no laws of honor, religion, or morality, I know already, — partly from his own confession."

"He sold his proofs, I suppose?"

"I suppose so. I have not asked Philip what he asked or got for them."

"Tell me his address, if you know it."

"I know the street, but not the number. He is in lodgings in Keppel Street, Russell Square."

"Keppel Street? I know it. Yes — Keppel Street."

Over his face there stole a look of thankfulness, expressed by the movement of his sensitive lips. His color rose just a little, but he was outwardly calm.

"You want to see him?"

"I think I shall probably call upon him to-day."

"But what has happened to you, Venn? I am so full of my own troubles that I am selfish, and forget yours."

"Mine are not all troubles, Arthur. My little girl has been restored to me."

Arthur did not dare say a word. He was afraid to ask the question that rose to his lips.

"Spotless, thank God, and pure. You shall learn presently how. But tell me first about this new-found brother of yours."

"What about him?"

"Is he, for instance, a man of honor?"

"I would stake my own upon Phil's honor."

"And truth?"

"Surely, my dear Venn, you have nothing to say or to suspect against Philip, have you?"

"And a man, you think, of generous leanings, of chivalrous feeling, of lofty sentiments, of — Well, Arthur, I am going to give you a greater shock than the loss of your fortune. Listen to me. I used to tell my child, in a thoughtless way, that I should like, above all things, to see her married to a gentleman. She, my innocent and ignorant Lollie, brought up with me and me only, knew nothing about love, marriage, any thing else that is common and practical. She and I lived among our books, and fed our minds on the words of old writers. Well" — he paused for a moment. "One night, when she left me, she was insulted in the street. A gentleman came to her help. Of all this she told me. She did not tell me the rest, because he persuaded her not to, — that he met her again, that he told her he loved her, and begged her to marry him. She thought it would please me. She accepted him to please me. She kept silent to please me. You think it is impossible? You do not know how I had kept the girl from knowing the world and its wickedness. The day before the marriage, she told me she had a secret, and wanted to tell it me. I, though I saw her distress, blinded by my own ignorant conceit, bade her keep her secret, and refused to hear it. The next day she was privately married by a Scotch clergyman — living, Arthur, in Keppel Street."

"Heavens, Venn! Do you mean MacIntyre? It was not Philip — it could not be Philip."

"Was the man ever a Scotch clergyman?"

"Who can know? He is a mass of lies. He would say so for his own purposes, whether he was or not."

"And yet you allowed him to take your fortune from you!"

"Not on his own evidence, Venn; but go on."

"The man who married Lollie took her to Normandy with him. Before leaving the house in Keppel Street, Lollie wrote me a note, telling all. MacIntyre promised to take it himself to Gray's Inn. *He never did.* When they got to Normandy, she wrote me a long letter, — I can fancy what my little girl would say to me in it. Her husband took the letter to the post. *It never came.* She waited a week, and then she wrote again. Her husband took the letter to the post. The second letter *never came.* Then her husband brought her back to England, put her in a small house near London, and forbade her to write to me any more. You understand so much."

"It cannot be Philip," Arthur said.

"Wait. There is more. This was in June: it is now November. For nearly five months, then, she lived there. She was absolutely alone the whole time. Her husband left her in the morning, and usually came home at night. She dined alone, sat alone, had no visitors, no companions. All the time he was, as I gather, betting on horse-racing, gambling, — losing money every day. Once or twice Mr. MacIntyre came to see her. Once her husband had a large party of men in the house. Then he sent her to her own room, and there kept her awake all night, singing and laughing. My little Lollie! When I think of it all, Arthur, I feel half mad! Wait, don't speak yet: there is more. It is now ten days ago. He came home very late; he rose at mid-day; he cursed at the breakfast; and then, without a word of regret, without a word to soften the blow, he turned upon his wife, told her that he was a ruined man, that he had nothing left at all, that she must leave him, because they never had been married at all. What do you think of that man, Arthur Durnford?"

"Finish your story."

"She left him, — left him with nothing but what she had when she married him; and all that night, that bitter, wretched, dismal night, with the wild wind and rain driving in her face, the poor girl wandered, wandered in the streets. Think of it, Arthur, — think of it! My little girl walked about the streets all night long, — never stopped, never sat down, never ate or drank. All night long! do you know what that means? The rain beating upon her, her wet clothes clinging to her, her brain confused and troubled, stupid with suffering; while the hours went on, one after the other, creeping for her, flying for us. Good God! and I in my warm bed, asleep, unthinking. My dear, my little darling! If I only had but known!"

He was standing over Arthur, as the latter sat looking at him with pained and troubled face. Venn's eyes were heavy with those tears which do not fall, and his voice was shaken as he spoke.

"There is more still, Arthur. She wandered so, — where, she does not know. In the morning a woman, a humble child of Samaria, gave her a cup of coffee. I have found that giver of the cup of coffee, Arthur. Then she thinks she sat down, somewhere, just before it grew light; and then she began to wander again. From noon till noon, twenty-four hours of walking in the streets. She was to have been, — she might have been, — Arthur, a mother. Think of it. Then, if you like it put that way, God was good to her, and sent in her path a girl, a poor starving girl, whom I had helped two years before at Lollie's own prayer, — her own prayer, mind, not any charitable act, — when she was ignorant of what the girl had done, what it meant, and why her father had turned her away. Mary found her wandering down the street, and took her home, fainting and weary to death, not knowing what was being done to her. Then she sent to me. Lollie has been ill since: that was to be expected. At death's door: that, too, was to be expected.

"Now you know, Arthur, what has happened to me. Is my little girl blameless?"

"Surely, yes, Venn."

"And the man, Arthur, — what is to be done with the man? I made her tell me his name, on the promise that I would not harm him. To keep that promise, it is necessary that I should not see him; but what is to be done with the man, I say? How can we make him feel what he has done? Is there any way — any way?

I see none. A man whose sense of honor is so delicate that you would exchange it for your own; who is the soul of truth, of honor, of nobility; who is — alas! alas! my friend — your brother Philip."

Then Venn took up his hat.

"I must go now," he said. "Shake hands, Arthur. Tell me again you think my little girl is pure and spotless."

"Before God, I think so," said Arthur. "She is my sister."

"Thank you, friend. You shall see her. Now I go. I am bound on a pleasanter journey than when I came here. I am going to pay a little visit. Yes, you are quite right, I am going to Keppel Street. I am going to see the Scotch clergyman."

He put on his hat, and went away.

He had not been gone half an hour before Philip himself came, radiant, happy, light-hearted. Some sinners are so. Then wise men say they live in Fools' Paradise. Perhaps; but I do not pretend to solve these difficulties. My own idea is that when a man has done such things as ought to take away all his self-respect, there is always some of it left so long as things are not found out. You can hardly expect self-respect in a gentleman who has stood in the dock, for instance, and heard the judge pronouncing sentence upon him. But the jury, how eminently self-respectful they are! One or two even, perhaps, of these might fairly stand side by side with the criminal. So, too, — but I am plagiarizing from Venn's essay, "On Being Found Out;" and, as the world will perhaps get this work some day, I must stop.

Arthur looked the criminal certainly; for he flushed scarlet, stammered, and refused to notice the hand that Philip held out.

"I have heard something, Philip."

"It must be something desperately solemn, then," said his brother. "Is it any thing new about the — the late business of ours?"

"Nothing. It is much worse than that. Mr. Hartley Venn has been here."

Philip had, for the moment, utterly forgotten Venn's existence. He, too, changed color.

"Well?"

"The rest you know, I suppose. Your wife" —

"Come, come, Arthur, be reasonable."

"I am reasonable. I say your wife — Good heavens, sir! what makes a woman a wife? What are the laws of the country to the laws of honor, honesty, truth? Did you not pledge your faith to her? Did you not"—

"Arthur, I will not be questioned."

"Answer me, then, one question. You have done — you, Philip, you — you have done all that Venn has told me. Learn that your wife, my *sister-in-law*, is lying ill. She has been close to dying. You will, at least, make her your wife in the eyes of the law?"

"Oh, dear, no!" said Philip lightly. "I do not justify myself, my dear fellow. Of course it is extremely wicked and improper. I am very sorry to hear about her illness. Tell Mr. Venn that no money arrangement that is at all reasonable will be objected to — that " —

"Philip, stop — I won't hear it."

"Won't hear what? You were not born yesterday, I suppose, Arthur? You know that such things are done every day. We all do them."

"We all?"

"Yes — *we* all. Bah! the girl will get over it in a month."

"And this man is my own brother," said Arthur, recoiling — "is my own brother!"

Philip's face grew cloudy. There was no longer any thing in him but the animal.

"Let us have no more of this nonsense," he said. "Tell this man Venn that he may do what he likes, and go to the devil. And as for you, Arthur" —

"Philip, you are a villain. Leave my room. Never speak to me again. Never come here. Let me never see your face any more. We have been a family of gentlemen for generations; and now you are our representative! It is shameful — it is dreadful!"

Philip left him. As he opened the door, he turned and said, —

"When you apologize to me for this language, you may, perhaps, expect to see me again. Till then, never."

It was a poor way of getting off the stage; and Philip afterwards reflected that he might have finished with at least more fire and effect if he had gone off swearing; but the best things always occur to us too late to put them into practice.

CHAPTER XXXI.

"IT is indeed a dreadful story," said Madeleine, when Arthur told her.

"What is to be done? Advise me, Madeleine."

"Who can advise? Mr. Venn's plan of assuming the marriage to be legal, without asking any questions, and letting Philip alone altogether, seems the best; unless, which I very much doubt, we can bring your brother to a better frame of mind. You, of course, have done as much mischief as was possible. Men are always so violent."

"I told him he was a villain," said Arthur. "It is true. I have never read, never heard, of baser or more cold-blooded treachery."

"Let me go and see Philip," said Madeleine.

She went at once to the house at Notting Hill. It was now dismantled; for Philip had sent away everything but the furniture of the two rooms in which he lived. There was no one in the place but himself and an old woman. He had never been up stairs to the room which had been Laura's since she left him.

Madeleine found him, unshaven, in a dressing-gown, smoking a pipe, in gloomy disorder. It was in the afternoon. On the table was an empty soda-water bottle, an empty tumbler, and a brandy bottle.

Philip, surprised to see her, made some sort of apology for the general disorder, and, putting aside his pipe, brushed the hair back from his forehead, and waited to hear what she would say.

She began by abusing him for living in such a mess.

"Why do you do it?" she asked. "Brandy and soda in the daytime — not dressed — rooms in the most dreadful litter. Philip, you ought to be ashamed of yourself."

He only groaned impatiently.

"Is that all you have come to see me for, Madeleine? Do not worry about the rooms and me. I've got something else to think of besides the disorder of my rooms. You shall blow up the old woman if you like. She is within hail, — probably sitting with her heels under the grate and her head in the coal-scuttle."

"I have a great deal more to say, Philip. First of all, do you know that I am going to be your sister? I am to marry Arthur."

"Arthur is a happy man, Madeleine. I envy him; but he always had all the luck."

"Don't call it luck, Phil. But we shall see a great deal more of you, shall we not, when we are married?"

"No — a great deal less. I have quarrelled with Arthur."

"I know, I know. But hasty words may be recalled; and — and hasty actions may be repaired, Phil, may they not?"

"If they could be undone, it would be worth talking about. Do not beat about the bush, Madeleine. I suppose you know all about that girl, and are come here to talk to me, and pitch into me. Well, go on. I cannot help what you say."

"Indeed, I do not come to pitch into you, as you call it, at all. I cannot bear to think that my own brother, my husband's brother, could do this thing in cold blood. Do tell me something."

Philip was silent for a while.

"I will tell you the exact truth, Madeleine. You may call it excuse or defence, or anything else you like. It shall be the exact truth, mind. I would tell no other living soul. I care nothing for what the world says; but I care something for what you think.

"You cannot understand the nature of a man. You will not comprehend me when I tell you that I was devoured with love for this girl. There was nothing I could not have done — nothing, mind — to get possession of her. There came a time when I had to marry her on a certain day or not at all. I got the special license, but forgot all about speaking to any clergyman till it was too late. Then MacIntyre pretended that he could marry us; and we were married. A fortnight ago, I found myself a ruined man. Worse than ruined, for I had not money to meet my debts of honor. I was on the point of being disgraced. I was maddened by my difficulties. She understood nothing of them, never entered into my pursuits, cared nothing for my life. I was maddened by her calmness. Then I lost command of myself, and told her — what, mind, I did not know till after — that the marriage was a mock one, and — and — Well, you know the rest. That is all."

"And your love for her, Philip?"

"My love? Gone — gone a long time ago. It was never more than a passing fancy, and all this business of the last fortnight put her out of my head entirely until Arthur reminded me of her. She is gone to her friend, guardian — what is it? — a Mr. Venn, who lives in chambers, and enacts the part of the universal philanthropist. I only keep on in this house, where it is torture to me to live, in order that he may not say I ran away from him. Here I am, and here I shall stay to face him — not to excuse myself, you understand. I stoop to defend my life to you alone."

"Philip, you are not so bad as he thinks; but I may tell you at once that he will not come. When Laura told him your name, she made him at the same time promise to do you no harm, — to take no revenge on you."

"I am not afraid of that, Madeleine."

"No; but you need stay here no longer. She has gone for the present to live with Miss Venn. I am going to call upon her myself. I am anxious to make the acquaintance of Mrs. Durnford."

"Mrs. Durnford!"

"I am told that she is a young lady,

very beautiful, very carefully educated, most sweet-tempered and affectionate."

"She is all that, Madeleine; but she never loved me. She was always pining after Mr. Venn. That reminds me — I told you I would give you the exact truth. I destroyed the letters that she wrote to him, without telling her. That was because I was jealous of him. I would have no man in her heart except myself. I am extremely sorry I did that, because it was an error of judgment, as well as a " —

"A wrong act, Phil, was it not?"

"It was, Madeleine, — a dishonorable thing. Have I abased myself enough before you, or do you want more of the confessions of a man about town? I have lots more relating to other events in a riotous career. Would you like to hear them? By Jove! I wonder if the prodigal son ever beguiled the winter evenings, sitting round the fire, with tales of the things he had done? The name of the other son is not given in the original narrative, but I believe it was Arthur."

"No, Philip. I want no more confessions. I want an act of reparation. See, Phil," she pleaded, " God only allows us to be happy in being good. Be good, my brother."

"I can't, Madeleine. I'm much too far gone."

"Then undo the evil you have done."

"How can that be?"

"I know you better than all the rest of them, Phil. I know that you are easily influenced, that you act without thinking, that you are easily moved, that your heart is not selfish. I know how you are repentant in spite of your light words. But think of the girl, Phil."

"I do think of her. I think of her day and night. I cannot sleep. I cannot do any thing. She is always before my eyes."

"Then marry her, and take her back, if she would come."

"She would not, Madeleine. There was a look in her eyes when she left me that told me all was over. No woman can have that expression in her face, and ever come back to love and confidence. She would never come back."

"Then marry her, Phil. In the eyes of the law, at least, let her be your wife."

Philip was silent.

"I love her no longer," he said. "There can be no longer any question of love between us. But see, you shall do with me what you will, Madeleine. Ask me any thing for Laura, and you shall have it. Keep my story, — keep what I have told you to yourself. Do not even tell it to Arthur."

"Philip, you promise?"

"I promise, Madeleine. Give me your hand. I swear by your hand, because there is nothing I know so sacred, that I will obey you in all things as regards Laura."

He kissed her fingers. Over his mobile countenance there passed the old expression of nobility, as if it had come back to settle there for good.

"And Arthur?" Madeleine began.

The bright look vanished.

"Arthur has used words to me — I have used words to Arthur — which can never be forgotten. Tell him so. I desire to meet him no more. Farewell, Madeleine. Write and tell me what I am to do; and I will do it. And let us part now, never to meet again. I do not know what I shall do with my future. Make ducks and drakes of it, I suppose. But I shall be out of my path. I shall be happy enough. The slopes that lead to Avernus are broad and pleasant. You may hear us singing as we go down them — you may see us dancing. Oh, it is a pleasant life, the life I am going to lead. Good-by, Madeleine."

She took his hand, his face was clouded and moody; and then, grateful for the promise she had got, she left him, and drove back to her own house.

And the same day she, with Arthur, made a formal call upon Miss Venn. Sukey, little accustomed to visitors who came in their own carriage, was not above being flattered.

"We are not come wholly for the pleasure of seeing you, Miss Venn," said Madeleine. " I want to make the acquaintance of my future sister-in-law, Mrs. Durnford."

"Laura?" She looked curiously at Madeleine, but it was Arthur who was blushing. "Laura? She is in her own room. Would you like to go up and see her?"

"If I might. You are too kind, dear Miss Venn. May I go up by myself, without being announced?"

Sukey took her to the door, and left her. Madeleine gently opened it.

On the sofa by the fire, wrapped in a dressing-gown, lay a fair young girl, thin, pale, wasted. Her head was lying among the pillows; and she was asleep.

Madeleine bent over her, and kissed her.

She opened her eyes. She saw a tall and queenly woman in silks and sealskin, and half rose.

"Don't move, my dear," said Madeleine: " let me kiss you. I am to make your acquaintance. Shall I tell you who I am? I am Madeleine de Villeroy; and I used to know your husband when he was quite a boy. Now I am going to marry your husband's brother; and we shall be sisters. My child, you shall be made happy again. We shall all love you."

"My husband? He said — he said"—
"Forget what he said, my darling,— forget all that he said, and, if you can, forgive him. Now, sit up, and let us talk."

She sat with her for a quarter of an hour, and then went away, promising to call again soon.

In the drawing-room there was rigid discomfort. For Sukey, the moment she got back, had seized the bull by the horns, and attacked Arthur.

"You are the brother of Mr. Philip Durnford?" she began. "You are the brother of a bad man, — a bad man, Mr. Arthur Durnford. Tell him not to come to this house, for I won't have him. Remember that"—

"Indeed, Miss Venn, he will not come here."

"If he does, Anne will take the tongs to him — I know she will. She did that much to a policeman in the kitchen. Tell him not to come."

"My brother and I, Miss Venn, are not on speaking terms at present."

"Indeed. I'm glad to hear it, — I am very glad to hear it."

Then they both relapsed into silence; and Sukey glared at poor Arthur, by way of conveying a lesson in virtue, till he nearly fell off the chair.

Madeleine relieved them; and, after asking Sukey's permission to come again, took away the unfortunate Arthur.

"Why didn't you ring for the sherry, miss?" asked Anne, presently coming up stairs.

"I gave it him. Anne — I gave it him well." Sukey shook her head virulently. "That was Laura's husband's brother. I told him if his precious brother came here you'd go at him — with the tongs, I said."

"So I would — so I would," said Anne.

"Sherry, indeed! They are always wanting to drink. We don't drink glasses of sherry all day. I dare say it was sherry drove that abandoned brother of his to bad courses. I hope, for that sweet girl's sake, he isn't like his brother. He doesn't look it, Anne; but you never can tell. They are all alike,— waste, drink, eat, and devour. Why isn't the world peopled with nothing but women?"

"'Deed, then, miss," replied Anne, "the end of the world wouldn't be very far off."

CHAPTER XXXII.

MR. MACINTYRE is sitting in his easy-chair at home, in those respectable lodgings of his in Keppel Street. He is meditating on the good fortune that has come to him. Perhaps he is too much inclined to attribute his success to merit rather than fortune; but in this we may pardon him. It is but two o'clock in the day; but a glass of steaming whiskey-toddy is on the table, and a pipe in his mouth. In spite of the many virtues which adorned this great man, I fear that the love of material comfort caused him sometimes to anticipate the evening, the legitimate season of comfort.

Nursing his leg, and watching the wreaths of smoke curling over his head, he meditated; and, if his thoughts had taken words, they would have been much as follows:—

"After all my shipwrecks, behold a haven. I have been in prison. I have been scourged by schoolboys. I have been tried for embezzlement. I have starved in the streets of London. I have been usher, preacher, missionary, tutor, retailer, sandwich man. I have, at last, found the road to fortune; not by honest means, but by lies and villanies, by practising on the honor of others. I have five thousand pounds in the bank, eleven pounds ten shillings and threepence in my pocket. Nothing can hurt me now; nothing can annoy me but ill-health and the infirmities of age. I have ten years, at least, of life before me yet. I shall go back to my own people. The Baillie will hardly refuse to receive me now that I have money. I shall be respected and respectable. 'Honesty is the best policy!' Bah! it is the maxim of the successful. I know better. Cleverness is the best policy. Scheme, plunder, purloin, cheat, and devise. When your fortune is made, hold out your clean white hands, and say 'Christian brethren, I am a living example that honesty is the best policy.' I shall join this band; and, at the kirk on the sawbath, and among my folk on week days, I shall be a living sermon to the young of the advantages of honesty. Respected and respectable, Alexander MacIntyre, retire upon your modest gains, and be happy."

Just then a knock was heard at the door.

The visitor was no other than Hartley Venn. He had strolled leisurely from Arthur's lodgings, smoking all the way, with a smile of immeasurable content, and a sweet emotion of anticipation in his heart. Having once ascertained the address of the philosopher, he lost no time in making his way to the street. On the way he stopped at a shop, and bought a gutta-percha whip, choosing one of considerable weight, yet pliant and elastic.

"This," he said to the shopman, "would curl well round the legs, in tender places, I should think?"

"I should think it would," said the man.

"Yes; and raise great weals where there was plenty of flesh, I should say. Thank you. Good-morning. It will suit me very well."

He poised the instrument in his hand, and walked along. When he got to Keppel Street, he showed his knowledge of human nature by going to the nearest public-house, and asking for Mr. MacIntyre's number. The potboy knew it.

Hartley presented himself unannounced, and, with a bow of great ceremony, — one of those Oriental salutations which were reserved for great occasions: he had not used it since his last interview with the master of his college.

"I believe I have the honor of addressing Mr. Alexander MacIntyre," he began.

The tutor confessed to owning the name, and began to feel a little uneasy. However, he asked his visitor to take a chair.

"Thank you — no, Mr. MacIntyre. Shall we say the Reverend Alexander MacIntyre?"

"No."

"We will not. The business I have to transact will not detain me long, and will be better done standing. You are, I believe, acquainted with Philip Durnford?"

"I am. May I ask"—

"Presently, presently. You are likewise acquainted with Mrs. Philip Durnford?"

It was MacIntyre's chance, but he neglected it.

"The young person calling herself Mrs. Philip Durnford has, I believe, run away from him."

Venn gave a start, but restrained himself.

"One more question. You have often, I doubt not, reflected on the wisdom of that sentence of Horace, which might be inspired were it not the result of a world's experience. In that sense, too, you would perhaps urge, and very justly, that it might be considered as divine, since experience is a form of revelation. I offer you a paraphrase, perhaps too alliterative, —

' Lightly the sinner leaps along the way,
 Lamely limps after he who bears the cane;
 Yet, soon or lete, there comes the fatal day
 When stick meets back, and joy is drowned by pain.'"

"Go on, sir," said Mr. MacIntyre, seriously alarmed, "and let me know your business. Who are you? What have you to do with me? I have never set my eyes on you before."

"Do not let us precipitate matters. Patience, Mr. MacIntyre, patience. Although you have not seen me, you have, perhaps, heard of me from Mrs. Philip Durnford. I am her guardian. My name, sir, is Hartley Venn."

The philosopher, among whose prominent defects was a want of physical courage, fell back in his chair, and began to perspire at the nose.

"Having learned from my ward the facts of the case, — that you exercised practices undoubtedly your legal right in Scotland, and married her to Durnford by a special license in this very room; also, that you suppressed the letter she sent me; and, further, that you have been the prime agent and adviser in the whole of the business, — it was but natural that I should desire to make your acquaintance. In fact," he added, with a winning smile, "I really must confess, that I had imagined your breed to be now totally extinct, gone out with the Regent, and belonging chiefly to the novels of his period. For this mistake I humbly beg permission to apologize. I obtained your address, partly from Arthur Durnford, an admirer of yours, — I wish I could say follower, — and partly from the potboy who supplies your modest wants. I hope you will remember the claim of gratitude which that potboy will henceforth have upon you. I had a struggle in my own mind — διανδιχα μερμήριζον; for while I ardently desired to converse with you myself, I had yet a feeling that the — the penalty should be left to some meaner person; but I bore in mind the distinction of rank. You are, I believe, a graduate of some university?"

"Sir, you are addressing a Master of Arts of the Univairsity of Aberdeen."

"Aberdeen is honored. I wish we had had you at Cambridge."

Venn took the riding-whip in both hands, passing his fingers up and down tenderly. MacIntyre saw now what was coming, and looked vainly round the room for a means of escape. Before him stood his tormentor. Behind the tormentor was the door. It is cruel, if you are to hang a man, first to stick him on a platform for an hour or so and harangue him; but perhaps, in the cases of lighter punishment, the suspense should be considered a part of the suffering. This was in MacIntyre's mind; but he did not give it utterance, sitting crouched in the chair, looking at the whip with a terrible foreboding.

Venn went on moralizing in a dreadful way, suggesting the confidence of one who knows that his game is fairly caught.

"The chastisement I am about to bestow upon you, Mr. MacIntyre, is ludicrously disproportionate to the offence you have committed. You will reflect upon this afterwards, and laugh. On the highest Christian grounds, I ought, perhaps, to forgive you; and I dare say I shall, if I know how, after this interview. On the other hand, I have little doubt that the slight horsewhipping I shall give you will be considered by the powers leniently, perhaps even approvingly. Let me for once consider myself an instrument."

He raised his whip above his head. MacIntyre crouched down, with his face in his hands.

"I beg your pardon," said Venn, pausing, "I have something else to say. You will remark that I have passed over the question of disgrace. No disgrace, I imagine, could possibly touch you, unless it were accompanied by severe personal discomfort. It is this curious fact — by the way, do you think it has received the attention it deserves? — which leads me to believe in the material punishments of the next world. You will remark, — I do hope I make myself sufficiently clear, and am not tedious."

"Ye are tedious," groaned the philosopher, looking up.

"I mean, there comes upon a man in the development of a long course of crime and sin — say such a man as yourself — a time when no disgrace can touch him, no dishonor can be felt, no humiliation make him lower than he actually is. He has lost not only all care about the esteem of others, but also all sense of self-respect. He is now all body and mind — no soul. Therefore, Mr. MacIntyre, when a man reaches this stage, on which I imagine that you are yourself standing now, what is left for him? How, I mean, can you get at him? I see no way of attacking his intellect, and there remains then but one way, — this!"

Quick as lightning, with a back stroke of his hand, Venn sent the whip full across MacIntyre's face. He leaped to his feet with a yell of pain and fear, and sprang to the door. But Venn caught him, as he passed, by the collar; and then, first pushing the table aside, so as to have a clear stage, he held him firmly out by the left hand, — Mr. MacIntyre was but a small man, and perfectly unresisting, — and with the right administered a punishment which, if I were Mr. Kingsley, I should call grim and great. Being myself, and not Mr. Kingsley, I describe the thrashing which Mr. Venn administered as at once calm, judicial, and severe. A boatswain would not have laid on the cuts with more judgment and dexterity, so as at once to find out all the tender places, and to get the most out of the simple instrument employed.

But it was interrupted; for, hearing the door open, Venn turned round, and saw a lady standing in the room watching him. He let go his hold, and MacIntyre instantly dropped upon the floor, and lay there curled in a heap.

A lady of middle age, with pale face and abundant black hair, dressed in comely silks. For a moment, Venn thought he knew her face, but dismissed the idea.

"Mr. MacIntyre?" she asked hesitatingly.

"He is here, madam," replied Hartley, indicating with the whip the recumbent mass beneath him.

The lady looked puzzled.

"I am extremely sorry your visit should be so ill-timed," said Hartley politely. "The fact is, you find our friend in the receipt of punishment. His appearance at this moment is not dignified, — not that with which a gentleman would prefer to see a lady in his rooms. Perhaps, if your business is not urgent, you would not mind postponing your call till to-morrow, when he may be able to receive you with more of the outward semblance of self-respect. We have not yet quite finished."

"Don't go," murmured the prostrate sage.

Venn spoke calmly, but there was a hot flush upon his cheeks which spoke of intense excitement.

"Pray, madam, leave us for a few moments together, — I am still in high spirits."

"I prefer ye in low spirits."

This was the voice of MacIntyre, lying still crouched with his face in his hands.

"Really, sir," said the visitor, "I think I ought to remain. Whatever Mr. MacIntyre has done, you have surely punished him enough."

"I think not," said Venn. "As you are apparently a friend, — perhaps a believer in Mr. MacIntyre, — I will tell you what he has done."

He told her, in a few words.

The lady looked troubled.

"The other one, you observe, madam, a young fellow of six and twenty, had still some grains left of morals and principles, — they were sapped by Mr. MacIntyre; he had still the remains of honor, — they were removed by Mr. MacIntyre; he still called himself a gentleman, — he can do so no longer, thanks to Mr. MacIntyre. Do you want to hear more?"

"And the girl, — where is she?"

"She is with me, madam. She is my ward."

"Perhaps, sir, Mr. MacIntyre would get up, if he were assured that there was no more personal violence intended."

Mr. MacIntyre shook a leg to show that he concurred in this proposition, and was prepared to listen to these terms.

"Get up," said Venn sternly.

He slowly rose, his face and hands a livid mass of bruises and weals, and staggered to his feet. His coat was torn. His eyes were staring. His face, where the whip had not marked it, was of a cold, white color. He stood for a moment stupidly gazing at Venn, and then turned to the lady. For a moment he gazed at her indifferently, then curiously, then he stepped forward and stared her in the face; and then he threw up his arms over his head, and would have fallen forward, but Venn caught him, as he cried,—

"Marie!"

They laid him on the floor, and poured cold water on his forehead. Presently he revived and sat up. Then they gave him a glass of brandy, which he drank, and staggered to his feet. But he reeled to and fro, like unto one who goes down upon the sea in a great ship.

"It is Marie," said the lady. "It is more than five and twenty years since we met last. You were bad then,—you are worse now. Tell me what new villany is this that you have committed?"

"Marie!" he began, but stopped again, and turned to Venn. "Sir, you do not understand. Some day you will be sorry for this outrage upon a respectable clergyman, who cannot retaliate, because his cloth forbids. Let me go and restore myself."

He slipped into the back room, his bedroom, and they saw him no more. Had they looked out of the window, they might have seen him slip from the door, with a greatcoat about him and a carpet-bag in his hand, his face muffled up and his hat over his eyes. He got round the corner, and, calling a cab, drove straight to his bank.

"Can I help you in any way, madam?"

"I called here to ask for the address of a Mr. Philip Durnford."

"That at least I can procure for you. For Mr. Philip Durnford is none other than the man of whom I have spoken."

She sat on a chair, and answered nothing for a while.

He, wondering, looked on silent.

"Oh, there must be a mistake! Philip would never do it. O Philip, my son, my son!"

The words seemed extorted by the agony of sharp pain.

"Your son?" cried Hartley.

"Ay, my son. Let the world know it now. Let it be published in all the papers, if they will. My son, my son!"

Then she seemed to regain her composure.

"Sir, you have the face of a gentleman."

"That must be the bishop's doing," murmured Venn, "not the glue-man."

But she did not hear him.

"You may, perhaps, keep a secret,—not altogether mine. I am Madame de Guy-on,—yes, the singer. I am a native of Palmiste. Philip Durnford is my son."

Venn sat down now, feeling as if every thing was going round with him.

And here let me finish off with Mr. MacIntyre, from whom I am loth to part.

His lodgings knew him no more. The things he left behind paid for the rent due. He drove to the city, drew out all his money in drafts on an Edinburgh bank, and went down to Scotland that very night by the limited mail. As soon as his face was restored to its original shape and hue, he went to his native town and took a small house there, after an interview with the Baillie, his cousin, who, finding that he had a large sum to deposit in the bank, received him with cordiality, and even affection.

He lives there still, respected by the town, as is right for one who left the country, and returned with money. He is consulted on all matters of finance, speculation, education, doctrine, morals, and church discipline. He holds views, perhaps, too rigid, and his visitations on minor offences are sometimes more severe than the frailty of the flock can altogether agree with. He is never seen drunk, though it is notorious that he drinks a good many tumblers of toddy every evening. He spends the mornings in his garden,—a pursuit which has always attracted great men in retirement; and on wet days in his study, where he is supposed to be elaborating a grand work on metaphysics. In conversation he is apt to deal too exclusively with principles of an abstract nature; and his friends complain that, considering he has been so great a traveller, he tells so few tales of his own experiences. Palmiste Island he never mentions. As for the story of his life, no one knows it but himself, and no single episode has ever got down to his native town. In all probability he will go on, as he said himself, respected and respectable, till the end,—a living example of the truth of the proverb that "Honesty is the best policy."

CHAPTER XXXIII.

MARIE, when she told George Durnford that she had a great voice, spoke less than the truth. She had a magnificent voice; a voice that comes but once or twice a century; a voice that history remembers, and that marks an epoch in the annals of music. With the money that Durnford gave her, she devoted herself to its cultivation. She did not hurry. In Italy she studied long and diligently, until, at the age of six and twenty, she was able to make her first appearance in London. She had hoped to please her old lover, and interest him in her success; but he answered hardly any of her letters, and only coldly acquiesced in her schemes for the future. For George Durnford's love had long disappeared from his heart: it vanished when he married Adrienne. He looked on poor Marie as a living witness of a time that he repented. He wanted, having assured her against poverty, neither to hear from her nor to see her again. He was fated not to see her; and when she wrote to him, telling of the great success of her first appearance, he tore the letter into shreds, and inwardly hoped that she would never come back to Palmiste. It is not exactly cowardice, this sort of feeling; nor is it wholly shame. It is, perhaps, the feeling that prompts one to put away all signs and remembrances of sickness and suffering. We do not like to be reminded of it. There are thousands of respectable, godly, pure-minded fathers and husbands, who have a sort of skeleton in the closet, hid away and locked up, as it were, in their brain, not to be lightly disturbed. In providing for Marie, and taking charge of her son, Mr. Durnford had done, he thought, enough. There was no longer any possibility of love — let there be no longer any friendship. And so her letters worried and irritated him, and his answers grew colder and shorter. From time to time he read in the papers of her success. Madame de Guyon appeared at the Italian Opera. She was described as of French descent, — some said from Martinique; none thought of Palmiste. She was said to be a young and strikingly beautiful widow. Her reputation was absolutely blameless; her name was widely spread about for those graceful deeds of charity which singers can do so well. And when, after a few years of the theatre, she withdrew altogether from the stage, and it was stated that henceforth she would only sing at oratorios and at concerts, everybody said that it was just the thing that was to be expected of a singer so good, so charitable, and so pious.

He once wrote to her, advising her to marry again; nor did he ever understand the bitter pain his letter caused her.

For women are not as men. It seems to me that women can only give themselves wholly and entirely to one man. To other men they may be thoughtful, and even tender; but one woman is made for one man, and when she loves she loves once and for all. Marie had told her old lover that she loved him no more, — that what had been could never come again. *It was not true.* What had been might, at any time, have come over again. The old idol of her heart was not shattered. It was erect, and stronger than ever, — strengthened by the thought of her boy; fostered by the memories which ran like a rivulet through the waste and loneliness of her life, filling it with green things and summer flowers; and held in its place by that constancy of woman which is proof against time and circumstances and absence and neglect. George Durnford loved her no longer. He did not, it is true, understand her. That magnificent nature, which had been like some wild forest plant, unchecked in its luxuriance, when he knew it best, was developed by training and sorrow to one of the most perfect types of womanhood. What more splendid than the full maturity of her beauty when she swept across the stage? What more perfect than the full rich tones of a voice that thrilled all listeners as she sang? And what — could he only have known it — more precious than the riches of the thoughts which welled up in her mind with no listener to impart them to, no husband to share them? But George Durnford died; and only when she heard of his death was she conscious of the space he occupied in her mind. She saw it in the papers; for no one wrote to her, or knew of her existence. Then she got the Palmiste papers, and read first of his funeral, and the fine things that were said about him, and then of his will; and next she saw the names of the two boys as passengers to England. And presently she began to live again; for she hoped to meet her boy, and — after many days — to reveal herself to him, and get back some of the love she lavished upon him in imagination. She did not hurry. She preferred, for many reasons, to bide her time. First, because she thought him ignorant of his birth; secondly, she thought that it would be better to wait till he was a man, and could better bear what would certainly be a bitter blow, — the stigma of his birth; and, lastly, she was afraid. George Durnford had said but little about him. He was growing tall and handsome; he was strong and clever; he was a bold rider and a good shot. All this she learned from his letters, but nothing more. In the last letter he had ever written to her, he mentioned that Philip was going into the army. And after some time she bought an Army List, and read with ecstasy the name of her son in the list of ensigns. She never attempted to see him, but she saved her money — she had made a good deal of money by this time — and laid it out judiciously for the future benefit of her son. If Philip had only known!

She lived in her own house, near Regent's Park, where she saw but few friends, and those chiefly of her own profession. Her life was not dull, however. It was brightened by the hope that lived in her. Morning and evening she prayed for her son; all day long she thought about him; at night she dreamed of him. She pictured him brave, clever, and handsome; she made him her knight,—young Galahad, without stain or blemish of sin; and she trembled at the thought of meeting him—not for fear he might fall below the standard she had set up, but for fear of her own unworthiness. She was to go to him, some day, with the bitter confession of his mother's sin. She was to say, "You are separated from other men by a broad line. They may rejoice in their mothers: you must be ashamed of yours." She was to ask him, not for that love and respect which wives can get from their sons, but for love and pity and forgiveness. She was to blight his self-respect and abase her own. No wonder that she hesitated, and thought, year after year, that there was time enough.

But one day, looking at the familiar page in the Army List, she saw that her son's name was missing; and, on looking through the "Gazette," she found that he had sold out. This agitated her. Something must have happened. He had abandoned his career. He might have married. How could she face his wife? Or he had met with some misfortune. How could she ascertain what? She did not know what to do or to whom to apply. The weeks passed on. She was in great anxiety. At last, unable to bear any longer the suspense of doubt, she went to a private inquiry office, and set them to work to find Mr. Durnford's address. It was quite easy to ascertain where he had lodged before he sold out, but impossible to learn where he was now; only the lodging-house people gave the address of his friend, Mr. MacIntyre, and his cousin, Arthur Durnford. This was all she wanted. Of the two, she would first try MacIntyre. She knew him of old. He was unscrupulous, she well knew, and still poor, as she suspected. She would bribe him to give her Philip's address, unless he would do it for nothing.

All this is by way of explanation of her sudden appearance at a moment so inopportune, when dignity was utterly out or the question, and her old acquaintance showed to such singularly small advantage.

The shock of Venn's intelligence was for the moment too much for her.

"I fear I have hurt you," said Hartley. "Pardon me, I was careless of my words. Did I understand him rightly? He said that—that"—

"Where is he?" asked Marie. "Bring him here."

Venn opened the door of the bedroom and looked in, but no one was there.

"He is gone, madame. Pray let me be of assistance to you. I can give you Mr. Durnford's address. It is at Notting Hill that he lives."

"Stay. First, the young lady you spoke of, sir—your ward. Could I see her?"

Venn hesitated.

"She is ill—she has just lost her husband. Would it do any good if you were to see her?"

Marie looked him straight in the face.

"I have not seen Philip Durnford for twenty-five years, and I am his mother." She blushed like a girl. "It is twenty-seven years ago," she murmured. "I am a native of the Palmiste Island."

"Good God!" said Venn, thinking of Arthur.

"I put my story into your hands, though I do not even know your name. You may, if you please, publish to the world the shame and disgrace of a woman that the world has always believed pure and good; but I think you will not do that."

"I?" cried Venn. "Great heavens! why should I? My name is Venn, Madame de Guyon. My father was Mr. George Durnford's tutor, and I am a friend of Arthur Durnford. My ward—the little girl that I brought up and made a lady of—is the grand-daughter of my old laundress. Your son made her acquaintance—and—it is best to let you know the whole truth—made her promise to hide the fact from me; brought her here to these very rooms, one evening, six months ago, when MacIntyre married, pretended to marry them,—I don't know which. Then he took her to France. She will tell you the rest, perhaps, herself."

"Advise me what is best to do," cried Marie, in deep distress. "Oh, sir, if I have but found my son to lose him again!"

"At all events, you shall see his wife," said Venn. "You will be very kind to her? Yes, I see you will. But there are other complications."

Then he told the story of the transferred property, just as he had heard it from Arthur an hour before.

"But I was never married," said Marie simply.

"Then Mr. MacIntyre, who is really a scoundrel of quite the ancient type, and, as one may say, of the deepest dye, has been forging the letters; and we shall, perhaps, have the pleasure of seeing him in the felon's dock before long."

"Promise me again," cried Marie, alarmed, "that you will keep my secret, whatever happens."

"I have promised already," said Venn.

"Not even Arthur Durnford shall hear a word. But it seems a pity to let the MacIntyre go."

"Then take me to your ward," Marie asked him.

"She is staying at my sister's house. Do not tell my sister, if you see her, any thing. She is a most excellent woman, Madame de Guyon, and as silent as death on unimportant matters; but, in the matter of secrets, I believe she is too confiding. She imparts in confidence all that is intrusted to her in confidence, and considers she has kept a secret when she has not proclaimed it at church. Just now, however, she is not likely to be inquisitive, because she is greatly excited at being excommunicated."

"Excommunicated?"

"Yes: she gave her cat the name of St. Cyril. On her refusal to change it, her clergyman, who holds rigid views, has excommunicated her. It is the greatest excitement that has ever happened to her, and she attends all those ordinances of religion from which she is debarred by her own director at an adjacent Low Church, where the clergyman parts his hair at the side, wears long whiskers, and reads the prayers with solemnity and effect. But I beg your pardon, Madame de Guyon, for inflicting these family details upon you. Let me get a cab for you."

He returned in a few minutes, and they drove to Miss Venn's house. His sister was out. As he afterwards learned, there had been a prayer-meeting at the evangelical clergyman's school; and, as nothing irritated the Rev. Mr. De Vere so much as a public prayer-meeting, she went there ostentatiously. By the greatest good luck, he was passing as she went in, and saw her; so that she enjoyed her meeting extremely.

Laura was lying on the sofa, reading. Her pale cheeks brightened up when Hartley came in.

"What is my ward doing?" he asked.

"Not reading too long, I hope. I have brought you a visitor, Lollie. Madame de Guyon, this is my ward, Mrs. Philip Durnford."

Laura looked appealingly at Hartley; but was more astonished when Marie went straight to the sofa, and, kneeling down, took her face in her hands, and kissed her, with tears in her eyes.

"I had better leave you, Madame de Guyon, I think," said Venn. "I shall wait in the dining-room for you."

Left alone, Marie began to tremble.

"My dear, I ought not to have kissed you. I ought, first, to tell you who I am."

"Who are you?" asked Laura. "I am sure, at least, you are very kind."

"My dear child, I hear that you have suffered. I want, if I can, to soothe your sorrow, and, if it be possible, remove it."

"Ah, no one can!"

"We shall see. Have you patience to listen to the story of a woman who has also suffered, but through her own fault; while you have only suffered through the fault of others?"

She told her own story. How poor and ignorant she had been; how George Durnford had made her proud and happy with a love of which she realized all the passion and happiness and none of the guilt; how he had told her, one day, that it was to be in future as if they had never met; how he had taken her boy, at her own request, and given her money to come to England; and how she had studied long and hard, and learned to make the most of a gift which is granted to few; and then her voice softened as she told how she had made fame and got fortune, and toiled on companionless, cheered by the hope that some day she might find her son, and pour into his heart some of the love with which her own was bursting.

"My dear," she said, "I found not my son, but his evil adviser,—not his friend,— Mr. MacIntyre. And my son is your husband."

Laura buried her face in her hands.

"Yes, I know it all. Mr. Venn has told me. Only, dear, you are not to blame. You are a wife: I never was. Let me find in you what I have lost. If I cannot win my son, let me win a daughter."

"O madame!" Laura replied, stroking back the thick brown hair that covered her face, "you are a lady, I am only a poor girl. How Philip could ever love me, — he did love me once, — I do not know. I am only Mr. Venn's little girl; and you are the only lady, except Miss Venn and Madeleine, who has ever spoken to me at all."

"My dear, and I was only a singer at the theatre."

"But you are a great singer; and I — O madame! and what will Philip say?"

"We will not care what Philip says."

"And then — oh, I am so unhappy!"

And she began to cry.

Marie cried too; and the two found consolation in the usual way.

Then Laura began to whisper.

"You have had some comfort, — you had a child."

"We will get you back your husband. Philip cannot be very bad, dear. He loved you once, at any rate."

She brightened up; but the moment after, fell back upon the sofa, and burst into fresh tears.

"I shall never get him back. I *could* never see him again. You do not know what he called me, — me, his wife. I *am* his wife, am I not? I could never look Mr. Venn in the face again if I were not."

"Yes, dear, you are his wife, surely you are; but I will go and see him."

"Take Mr. Venn with you: let him speak for me."

"Would it be wise? No, — I will go alone. If he will not hear me, he will certainly not hear Mr. Venn. And now, I must go; but, dear, my heart is very heavy. I am oppressed with a sense of coming evil. Tell me, — if Philip, if my son, should not receive me well, if, after all these years of forbearance, he greets me with coldness and distrust — oh, tell me what he is like!"

Laura told her as well as she could.

"But Philip is passionate," she concluded; "and I think he has lost some money lately, and Mr. MacIntyre makes him do reckless things."

"I can manage Mr. MacIntyre," said Marie. "Besides, he is not likely to forget the lesson Mr. Venn has taught him to-day."

"What was that?"

Marie told her of the scene she had witnessed.

Laura, usually the mildest of her sex, set her lips together, and clasped her hands.

"Oh, I am so glad — I am so glad! Was he hurt? Did he cry? Tell me all over again," she said.

Marie only smiled.

"Let me finish, dear. I have only one proposition to make to my son. If he will not agree to that, I have one to make to you."

"What is that?"

"Would you like to go back to Philip?"

She clasped her hands, and began to think.

"He was so cruel! If I only could. If he would only take me. But I *am* his wife."

"And if he will not, will you come with me, child? My heart is empty: I long for some one to love. Come with me, and be my loved and cherished daughter."

Laura threw her fair young arms round her neck, and Marie kissed her passionately.

"I must go now," she said, after a few minutes. "I do not think I can go to your husband's — to my son's house to-day. I must wait till to-morrow. Write down his address, dear, on my tablets. And now, good-by. Ask Miss Venn to let me come to see you. Tell her only that I am your husband's old friend; and remember to keep my secret till I see you again."

She went away. Presently came back Miss Venn, in a high state of exhilaration at the discomfiture of the Rev. Mr. De Vere, who, seeing her open act of rebellion, must have gone home, she concluded, in a furious state of indignation. This, indeed, the reverend gentleman had actually done. And she called loudly for St. Cyril, — her cat, — and sat down and made herself comfortable, and gave her brother a comfortable little dinner.

CHAPTER XXXIV.

"WE have not had a chorus for a long time," said Venn. "All these excitements have been too much for us. Sit down, Arthur. Jones, consider this a regular night."

"I have been reading," said Jones presently, "with a view to understanding the great secret of success, some of the poetry of the period; and I beg to submit to the Chorus a ballad done in the most approved fashion of our modern poets. May I read it? It is called 'The Knightly Tryste,' or, if you will, 'My Ladye's Bidding,' which is more poetical : —

'Between the saddle and the man,
Ah me! red gleams of sunlight ran;
He only, on his Arab steed,
Left all the streaming winds behind.
Sighed, "Well it were, in time of need,
A softer place than this to find."

The twinkling milestones at his side
Flushed for a moment as he passed;
Small thought had he of joy or pride,
Groaned only, "This can never last."
And more and more the red light ran
Between the saddle and the man.

"Woe worth the day," he gasped by times,
"My lady fair this fancy took;
And Devil take her prattling rhymes
About the willows and the brook;
For this I suffer what I can,
Between the saddle and the man."

Still rode the knight: the dewy beads
Stood on his brow, but on he spurred;
Ere compline bell doth ring it needs
He meet the lady by her word;
And great discomfort then began
Between the saddle and the man.

There came a moment — o'er a gate,
Five-barred, close shut, the destrier flew;
He also — but his knees, too late,
Clutched only mosses wet with dew.
Ah, me! the ever-lengthening span
Between the saddle and the man.'"

Jones read and looked round for applause. None followed.

"It won't do, Jones," said Venn, — "it won't do. You had better stick to the old school. The grotesque and the unreal won't last. Write for posterity, if you must write poetry."

"I don't care so much for posterity as I

did," said Jones. "I want things that pay. Now, I really think an able editor ought to give something for those lines."

"Low and grovelling aim! Look at me, — I write for nothing but the praise of my fellow-countrymen, as soon as I can get published."

"I sometimes think," Jones continued, "of taking up the satirical line. Are you aware that there is not such a thing as a satirist living? We want a Boileau. The nation asks for a man of sense. Something must be done soon."

For once Jones looked melancholy.

"What is it, Jones?" asked Venn. "More disappointments. Remember the banquet of life, my boy?"

"I do," said Jones, with an effort to smile. "In the words of Hannah More, —

'For bread and cheese and little ease
Small thanks, but no repining;
Still o'er the sky they darkling lie, —
Clouds, with no silver lining.'

Come," he went on, "the Chorus is unusually dull and silent. I will sing you a song made for the occasion: —

'I am an unfortunate man,
Bad luck at my elbow doth sit;
Let me tell how my troubles began,
If only my feelings permit.

The spoon that my young lips adorned
In infancy's hour was of wood:
No freaks, then, of fortune I mourn'd,
And for pap it was equally good.

To school I was sent, and the first day
I was caned with the rest by mistake;
But each morning that followed, the worst day
Seemed still in my annals to make;

For I laughed when I should have been weeping;
I cried when I ought to have smiled;
And the painful results still are keeping
Their memory green in this child.

The other boys sinned at their leisure;
They could do what they liked and escape;
But I, for each illicit pleasure,
Still found myself in a new scrape.

Now in London I linger, and sadly
Get shoved on my pathway by fate:
Hope dances before me, and madly
Shows fruits that are only a bait.

For I am an unfortunate man;
But fate, which has taken the rest,
Has given, to console when she can,
Good spirits still left in my breast.'"

"That's not very good, Jones," said Lynn. "What has put you into this dejected and miserable frame, unfit for the society of a decent and philosophical Chorus? First you read a bad poem, and then you sing a comic song."

"A letter I got this morning," he answered with a groan. "Let me talk, you fellows, and I'll tell you a story. Call it a vision if you like, — a vision of two lives.

"The two lives were once one. They thought the same thoughts, and had the same ambitions. They had the same chances, they won the same successes, dreamed the same dreams. No two friends were ever so close; for the two minds were one, and dwelt in the same body. I saw in my vision that there came a time — the boy was almost grown to the age of manhood — when the two separated. It was at Oxford that this disunion first took place. And in my vision it seemed to me that the one which remained in the boy was as myself; and the other, that other self which I might have been."

Jones paused, and pondered for a few moments, with grave face.

"Yes, I — that is, the one that remained behind — was seized with a kind of madness of vanity. All my noble dreams, all my thoughts of what might be, gave way to a desire to amuse. I, that is — of course" —

"Go on saying I, without apology," said Venn.

"Well, I succeeded in amusing the men of my college. I succeeded as an actor — I think I was a good mimic. I sang, I made verses, I wrote little plays and acted them. I went every day to wines, suppers, and breakfasts. I was, of course, tremendously poor; and, like most poor idiots, did no reading whatever. Meantime, my old friend was very differently occupied. I used to see his calm, quiet face — like mine in features, but different in expression — in hall and chapel. He was a student. He came up to Oxford with ambitions and hopes that I shared; but he kept them, and worked for them. Mine, with the means of realizing them, I had thrown away. I used to look at him sometimes, and ask myself if this was the friend who had once been the same as myself, like the two branches of an equation in Indeterminate Co-efficients."

"Jones," said Venn, "don't be flowery, pray don't. We are not mathematical men."

"The time came when we were to go into the schools. I, my friends, in my vision, was plucked. He, in my vision, got a Double First. Curiously enough, in reality I *was* plucked in Greats — for divinity. However, after this, we took paths even more divergent. He staid behind to try for a Fellowship, which he easily got. I went up to London to try to get my daily bread in any way, however humble. He entered at the bar, — it had always been our ambition to become Fellows, and to enter at the bar. — I became a drudge to an army cram coach, who paid me just enough to keep me going.

"He, too, a year or too later, came to London. How long is it? I think it is ten years since we took our degrees, and read law. Presently he was called,—I saw his name in the Law List,—and began to get practice. I, like a stone, neither grew nor moved.

"The time goes on; but the two lives are separated, never again to meet. He is on the road to fortune and fame. He will make his mark on the history of his country. He will,—that is, after all, the cruelest part of the vision,—he will marry Mary; for, while the boy was growing into manhood, there came to live in the village where his father, the vicar, lived, a retired officer, with a little daughter eight years younger than the boy. The boy, who had no play-fellows in the village, took to the child, and became a sort of elder brother to her; and, as they grew up, the affection between the two strengthened. Mary was serious beyond her years, chiefly from always associating with her seniors. When she was twelve and the boy eighteen, she could share his hopes, and could understand his dreams. She looked on him as a hero. Like all women, with those they love, she could not see his faults; and when he disappointed all their expectations, and came back from the grand university that was to make so much of him, disgraced instead of honored, loaded with debt instead of armed with a Fellowship, she it was who first forgave him.

"He could not forgive himself. He handed her over mentally to his old friend, and left her."

"But he will see her again," said Arthur.

"I think never. He has had his chance, that would have made them both happy; and he threw it away. My friend, however, who must be making a very large income by this time at the Chancery bar, who writes critical papers in big words in the 'Fortnightly,' whose book on something or other connected with the law is quoted by judges,—he will doubtless marry her, and then they will be happy; but I—I mean the ego of my vision—shall go on struggling with the world, and rejoicing over small sacrifices, resigned to great disappointments, till the end of the chapter. I shall contemplate the visionary happiness of my *alter ego*—with Mary, whom I shall never see again. He will be Lord Chancellor; and, if I live long enough, when I die I shall think of the great works that he has done, and thank God for his excellent gift of a steady purpose and a clear brain."

Jones was silent for a few minutes.

"You were talking about women the other night,—three months ago. It makes me angry to hear theories of women. I beg your pardon, Venn, for criticising your trumpet-noses; and yours, Lynn, for getting savage over your world of the future. Women are what men make them; and if my Mary had married the future Lord Chancellor, there would have been no nobler woman in the world, as there is now none more tender-hearted and forgiving. But—oh dear me!—if women are frivolous, it is because they have nothing to do. To make them work is to unsex them; to put them through a Cambridge course of mathematics is so ludicrously absurd in its uselessness, that we need no vision of an impossible future world to show us its folly."

"And suppose, Jones," said Arthur,—"only suppose, that Mary marries the 'I' of your dream."

"I can't suppose it. He cannot drag her down to his own level."

"But she may raise him to hers."

Jones sighed. In his vision of the two lives he had revealed the story of his own,—which Venn already partly knew; and the dignity of sorrow for a moment sat like a crown on his forehead. But he shook it off, and turning round with a cheerful smile, adjusted his spectacles, and concluded his observations.

"My own verses again:—

'Gone is the spring with wings too light,
  The hopeful song of youth is mute,
The sober tints displace the bright,
  The blossoms all are turned to fruit:
I, like a tree consumed with blight,
  Fit only for the pruner's knife,
Await the day, not far away,
  Which asks the harvest of a life.

'And, for the past is surely gone,
  The coming evil still unseen,
I think of what I might have won,
  And fancy things that should have been;
And so in dreams by summer streams,
  While golden suns light every sheaf,
I take her hand, and through the land,
  My love makes all the journey brief.'"

CHAPTER XXXI.

MADAME DE GUYON sought her son's house at noon the next day. She was ill with a long night's anxiety; and her face, usually so calm, looked troubled and haggard.

Philip was at home, and would see her.

The moment, long looked for, was come at last; and she trembled so much that she could hardly mount the steps of the door. He was sitting in the dismantled room of the little cottage at Notting Hill, but rose to receive his visitor.

She drew her thick veil more closely over her face, and stood looking at her own son with a thousand emotions in her breast.

Her own son — her Philip! A man now, whom she had last seen a child of four years old, when she took him out of his cot at Fontainebleau. A tall and shapely man, with a face like that of George Durnford, only darker, and eyes that she knew for her own, — large, deep, lustrous. She gazed at him for a few moments without speaking or moving, for her heart was too full.

Philip set a chair for her.

"Madame de Guyon?" he asked, looking at the card. "May I ask what gives me the honor of a visit from, — I presume you are the lady whose name " —

"Yes: I am the singer."

"I come," she went on, with an effort, "from your wife."

Philip changed color.

"Your wife, Philip Durnford, whom you drove away from you three weeks ago. You will be sorry to learn that she is very ill, — that she has been dangerously ill."

"Tell me," he stammered, — " she is not — not dead?"

"No: grief does not kill."

"Where is she?"

"She is at present under the charge of Miss Venn, the sister of her guardian."

The old jealousy flamed up again in his heart.

"Then she may stay there. She always loved him better than me. I hardly understand, however, what my private affairs have to do with Madame de Guyon."

"I will tell you presently. First, let me plead for this poor girl."

"I am, of course, obliged to listen to all that you have to say."

"I know the whole story, the pitiful, shameful story. I know how, influenced by that bad man, you went through a form of marriage which is illegal; how you gambled away your money; how, when you were ruined at last, you let her go from your doors, with more than the truth, — more than the cruel truth, — ringing in her ears, disgraced and ashamed."

"More than the truth?"

"Yes, more; for the man was once an ordained minister of his own church, and the illegality consisted only in the place where he married you. Philip Durnford, she *is* your wife."

He answered nothing.

"I do not ask you to take her back. That cannot be yet. I say only, remove the doubt that may exist; and, as soon as she is strong enough, make her yours in the eye of the law as well as of God."

"Why do you come here? What have you to do with me?"

She laid her hand upon his arm.

"Philip Durnford, for the love of all that you hold sacred, promise me to do this. Do not tell me that you, — you, of all men in this wide world, purposely deceived the girl, and are not repentant. O Philip — Philip!"

He started. Why should this woman call him by his Christian name? Why should she throw back her veil, and look at him with her full black eyes filled with tears?

"You *had* married her. You meant to marry her. Do not let me believe you to be utterly base and wicked. Do this, if only to undo some of the past. Then let her stay on with her friends, — deserted but not disgraced. Think of it, think of it! The girl was innocent and ignorant. She knew nothing of the world, — nothing but what one man had taught her. She had no circle of friends, no atmosphere of home, to teach her what life means. She fell into your hands. You loved her, I know you loved her " —

"She never loved me."

"I want to move your heart, Philip Durnford. Think of those in the world who love you, to whom your honor and good name are dear."

She sighed and went on, —

"There must be a way to touch your heart. Think of the days you had her with you, — men have said that for the sake of those early days, when their wives were to them as angels, they love them for the rest of their lives, long after they have found them women, full of faults, and lower than themselves, — when you read that poor child's thoughts, bared before you, and you only, — when, out of all her thoughts, there was not one that she was not ready to confess to you, — when you took her out of the solitude of maidenhood, and taught her the sweet mystery of companionship. Philip Durnford, can the Church devise any form of words, any holy ceremony, any oaths or sacraments, that ought to be more binding than these things? Can any man have memories of greater tenderness, innocence, and purity than you have of poor Laura? Not a common, untaught girl, of whom you might have been tired in a week; but a girl full of all kinds of knowledge, trained and taught. No one knows the story but Mr. Venn and myself, and, — and the other man. The fault may be repaired."

"Arthur knows it, Madeleine knows it, all the world knows it by this time. We waste time in words. I loved her, — I love her no longer. I am ashamed for my folly; ashamed, if you will, of the evil temper which made me tell her all. If no one knows, why not let things go on as they are? We are both free."

"You are neither of you free: you are bound to each other. Since her departure, you have obtained possession of Arthur Durnford's estate."

"My estate, if you please. I was prepared to prove it mine in a court of law."

"I think not, because I could have prevented it. The estate is not yours by any legal claim."

"Upon my word, Madame de Guyon," said Philip, "you appear to know a great deal about our family history."

"I do know a great deal."

"But I prefer not to discuss the details with you. I return to what I said before. Let things past be forgotten."

He waved his hand impatiently.

"Let us dismiss the subject; and now, Madame de Guyon, pray gratify my curiosity by telling me how you became mixed up in the affair at all."

"Let me say one word more."

"Not one word. I have, I confess, those qualms of regret which some people attribute to conscience. I am extremely sorry that I have made her unhappy. I do not justify any part of my conduct. Mr. MacIntyre did, it is true, endeavor to persuade me that the marriage was legal. I was madly in love, and tried to believe him. Of course, it was not legal. This is not a thing that can be said and unsaid. It is a fact. Facts are stubborn things, as you know. The history of her life, together with the overpowering affection she has for the other man, are not calculated to make me desirous of turning into an indissoluble contract what was really no contract at all. If she wants money"—

"She would die rather than take money from you."

"In that case, I think there is nothing really nothing — more to be said."

"O Philip Durnford! is Heaven's wrath"—

"Come, Madame de Guyon, let us not go into theology. We met; I loved her; I deceived her; was partly deceived myself. I did not meet with any love from her. I lost my money on the turf. I lost my temper with her. We quarrel. She goes away. I sit down and do, — nothing. The religious part of the matter concerns me only. Religious matters do not trouble my head much. I am a man of the world, and take things as I find them. Things are mostly bad, and men are all bad. Que voulez vous?"

Good heavens! And this man — this libertine — was her own son, and she was sitting there listening in silence!

But the time was coming to speak.

"I cannot believe you are speaking what you think. You cannot be so bitter against the world."

"Perhaps I have cause."

"You have not, Philip Durnford. I know your whole history, — yes, from your childhood. There are few alive, — unless it be that man MacIntyre, — who knows the secret of your birth."

"There, at least, I have no reason to be ashamed. My mother was married to my father."

She bent her face forward, and was silent for a moment.

"Suppose she was not?"

"But she was. I have legal proofs. They are in my desk."

He grew impatient.

"What is this? What does it mean? You come to me, knowing all about me; you interfere in my most private relations. Tell me, I ask again, what it means?"

"I will tell you," she said. "It is a bitter thing to tell, — it is a bitter time to have to tell it. I have prayed and hoped for five and twenty years; and now I find you — ah, me! — so changed from the Philip of my dreams."

His face grew white, and his hand shook, for a strange foreboding seized him; but he said nothing.

"There was once," she went on, the tears falling fast through her veil, — "there was once a rich man and a poor handmaiden. He was kind and generous, and she loved him: they had a son. The time came when the wickedness and folly were to cease. He married, and sent her away, — not cruelly, not with harsh words, as you sent Laura away, but kindly and considerately. She knew it must come. She was one of the inferior race, with the old slave blood in her veins. The English gentleman could never marry her, and she knew it all along. She could hope for nothing but his kindness for a time, and look for nothing but a separation. She was ignorant and untaught. She felt no degradation. That was to come afterwards, — to last through all her life. Her lover practiced no deception, made her no false promises."

"Go on," he said hoarsely, when she stopped.

"He married. The mulatto girl went away. With his money she learned to sing. She is living now, rich, and of good name. No one knows her past. Philip Durnford, she never married your father, and you are her son."

She raised her veil, and looked him straight in the face. He gazed at her, white and scared.

"And you?"

She fell at his feet, crying, — .

"O Philip, — Philip! I am your guilty mother. Forgive me, — forgive me!"

And she waited for his words of love and forgiveness.

Alas! none came. After a while he raised her, and placed her in a chair.

His lips moved, but he could not speak. When he did his voice was hard and harsh.

"You say you are my mother. I must believe you. That I am still illegitimate? That, too, I must believe. The letters and church register" —

"They are forgeries."

"They are forgeries, — I believe that too. Arthur and I have been tricked and cheated. And so, what next?"

She did not answer.

"See, now, I am an unnatural son, perhaps; but I am going to take a commonsense view of the matter. Let every thing be as it was before. For all those years I have had no mother, I cannot now — not yet, at least — feel to you as I should. Go to Arthur, — I, too, will write to him, — tell him what you please. If I were you, I should tell him nothing. And let us part. I am ruined in fortune and unhappy in every relation of life; but we should neither of us be happier if I were to go home with you, and fall into false raptures of filial love. I am unkind, perhaps; but I am trying not to deceive you in any respect. My mother, we have met once. We are not acting a play, and I cannot fall into your arms, and love you all at once. I am what my life has made me. I belong to another world, — different to yours. I have my habits, my prejudices, my opinions, — all bad, no doubt; but I have them. Let me go on my road. Believe me, with such a son you would be miserable. Let us go on keeping our secret from the world. No one shall know that Madame de Guyon has a son at all, far less such a son as myself."

For all answer she threw her arms round his neck, and kissed him again and again.

The tears came into his eyes; and, for a moment, his heart softened, and he kissed her cheek. Then the frost of selfishness fell upon him again, and he grew hard and cruel.

"Let us part," he said.

"Philip," she moaned, "God punishes me very hard; but it cannot be that you should suffer for my faults. God only grant that you never feel the agony and suffering that you have caused two women who love you."

"The agony and suffering," he answered lightly, "may be put at the door of our modern civilization. I am sure you will both feel, after a while, that I have acted for the best. Let us part, and be friends. Sometimes I will come and see you."

"I am your mother still. You can say and do nothing that I would not forgive. When your heart is softened, you will come back to me. Stay" — she bent forward with fixed eyes, as of one who looks into the future, — "I feel it. The time is not far off when you will lie in my arms, and cry for shame and sorrow. I cannot make it all out. It is my dream that comes again and again. I see the place, — it looks like George's room. And now, — now, all is dark." She closed her eyes, and then looked up with her former expression. "And now, farewell, — Laura is my daughter."

He held out his hand. She drew her face to him, and kissed him on the brow. Then she let down her veil, and went away.

Hour after hour passed; but Philip still sat in the desolate room whence he had driven away the angels of his life.

CHAPTER XXXVI.

A MONTH passed by, and no message or letter was sent to Philip. He, now quite gone back to the old life, spent his days chiefly at the Burleigh Club, in the customary unprofitable pursuits of a man about town. This is not an improving course; and every day found him more ready to keep what he had got, whatever might be the truth. His mother? And if she were his mother, what duty did he owe to her? When the new year came round, he was curious to learn if the usual two hundred pounds would be paid into his account. It was not. Then he was quite certain about the sender. It was Madame de Guyon. Another thing bothered him. Nothing could be ascertained as to Mr. MacIntyre's whereabouts. No notice given at the lodgings. He had quietly disappeared. One thing was ascertainable, however: he had drawn out the whole of his money in bank-notes and gold.

"Come with me," said Venn, after telling Arthur what he had learned, — "come and see Madame de Guyon. She would like it."

Arthur went. Madame de Guyon received him with a curious air of interest. "You are like your father," she said; "but more like poor Adrienne, your mother. May I call you Arthur? You know the whole sad story, Arthur. At this length of time, thinking what I was, in what school brought up, how utterly ignorant, I have brought myself to look upon the past as few women with such a memory could. I can now, as you see, even talk about it. Have you seen Philip lately?"

"I never see Philip at all."

"I am sorry. Mr. Venn has told me all the story. I am permitted to see my son's wife. I even hope that she may come to live with me. But this estate must be given back. It is not Philip's. Cruel as the blow would be, I would even consent to go into a court, and relate my own history, if necessary, rather than let this wrong be done you."

"Philip has offered to restore the estate," said Arthur; "but he may keep it. Be at ease, madame: there will be no steps taken, and Philip may enjoy what the forgeries of MacIntyre have given him."

"I am glad. Put yourself only in my place, Arthur. After twenty-five years of effort, I am rich, I am looked up to, I have a good name."

"Indeed you have," said Arthur.

"What if all were to be lost at a blow?"

"It shall not, madame, — it shall not be lost at all. Keep what you have, the reputation that is your own. Rest assured that none of us will ever harm it."

What Marie said about her reputation was less than the truth. Of all great singers none had become so widely known for her thousand acts of charity and grace; none had a better name; none lived a life more open and observed of all; but she was not satisfied with this. She wanted to have, if she could, the friendship of Madeleine and the love of Laura.

She wrote to Madeleine: —

"You know all my life, — its beginning and its progress. You, a girl of Palmiste, can understand what I was thirty years ago, when I was sixteen years old. I was born a slave, white as I was in complexion. My mother was a slave, and therefore I was one. My people were forbidden to marry by law, — God's laws set aside for man's purposes. They could not hold property; they were not allowed to wear shoes; they were publicly flogged in the Place; they were not allowed to read and write. When I was eight years old, the emancipation came; but, though we were free, the old habits of slave-life rested with us. Think of these, if you can; for you are too young to know much about what we were. Think of what you do know, and then ask what punishment I deserve for two years of sin. Believe me, every year that has elapsed since has been a year of punishment, never so heavy as now, when my son has cast me off. You know what a position I have conquered for myself; you know, too, — I write it with a pride that you will appreciate, — that no breath of calumny or ill report has been cast upon me during all this time. No one knows who I am, what I was. I wish that no one should know. Why do I write to you? It is because you have been kind to my daughter, my little Laura, and because you are engaged to Arthur Durnford. Years ago, — the last time I saw his father, — I took the two children, my Philip and Arthur, out of their beds, one after the other. Philip turned from me and cried; Arthur laid his arms round my neck, and went to sleep. It was an omen. Part of it has been fulfilled. *Let the rest be fulfilled.* I ask for Arthur's friendship. I — yes, I — ask *you* for your friendship. It is because I hear you are unlike other girls — independent, able to think for yourself — that I dare to ask it; and I ask it for the sake of Laura, as well as myself. I want to take her to my own heart. I am a lonely woman, and hunger for somebody to love me. I cannot do this unless her friends — you and Arthur, and all — will come to my house. Tell me you can, after these years of repentance, give me your hand. Cannot a woman ever be forgiven by other women?"

Madeleine read the letter with burning cheeks. Why should she not go to see this poor woman, shut out from the world by a thirty years' old sin, that was itself but ignorance?

But she must keep her secret.

She gave the letter to Arthur to read.

"What will you do, Madeleine?"

"I will do what you wish, Arthur."

"What would you like to do? Is it to go and see her? My dear, if you only knew, she is the best of good women."

So Madeleine went.

All this time Lollie was slowly recovering her strength, under the motherly care of Sukey.

When she grew strong enough to go out, Hartley thought Philip's promise should be fulfilled. He approached the subject very delicately one day.

"I have been thinking, Lollie," he said, "that in case of any legal difficulties about your marriage" —

"What legal difficulties, Mr. Venn?"

"You see, my child, a ceremony perfectly binding in all other respects may very possibly not be in accordance with the law as regards succession to property, and so forth."

"But what have I to do with succession to property?"

"A good deal, Lollie; and I, as your guardian, must protect your interests. The best way will be for us to have the marriage done over again."

"Over again! But then Philip would have to be there."

"Philip will be there. He has expressed his readiness to be there. You need not be alarmed, Lollie;" for she began to shiver from head to foot. "He will just come for the ceremony, and go away immediately afterwards. You will not, perhaps, even speak to him, nor him to you. All that is arranged. I know, Lollie, child, how painful all this is to you; but it must be done. Believe me, it is for your own sake."

She acquiesced. If Hartley Venn had told her to go straight to the guillotine, she would have done it for his sake.

The necessary arrangements were made. An old college friend of Venn's undertook to marry them, being just told that the circumstances were peculiar, and that he was to ask no questions.

And then Madeleine wrote to Philip:—

"MY DEAR PHILIP,—You will be prepared to go through the marriage ceremony of the Church of England the day after to-morrow, at eleven o'clock, at —— Church, —— Square. It has been explained to Laura, to save her self-respect, that this will be done in the view of possible legal difficulties. She is growing stronger and better, and will, as soon as she is able to be moved, go to reside with Madame de Guyon. For everybody's sake — for hers as well as ours — old histories will be left alone, and no steps will be taken to convict the forger who deceived us all. Keep the estate of Fontainebleau, dear Philip, and be happy. You have promised to do every thing I asked you for Laura. You will first marry her legally; you will then take her into the vestry alone, and ask her forgiveness. You cannot refuse so much. I hope that as the years move on, you may love each other again, and forget the wrongs and woes of the past. I love your wife more every day I see her.

"There is one other point I should like to ask you, if I may. It is of Madame de Guyon. You know what I would ask you, and I will not name it. O Philip! if it is a good thing, as people write, for man to be rich in woman's love, how rich ought you to be! Think of all this, and do what your heart prompts you.

"You will see me at the church. Your affectionate sister,

"MADELEINE."

But the letter reached Philip at a wrong moment, when he was in one of his bitter moods; and he only tore it up, and swore. Nevertheless, he wrote to say he would keep his promise.

It was a bitterly cold morning in January, with snow upon the ground, and icicles hanging from every projection. Sukey was to know nothing of the business on hand, and was mightily astonished when Madeleine called at ten o'clock, and took out Laura in her carriage, wrapped up as warmly as could be managed. Hartley Venn and Madame de Guyon joined them at the corner of the street, and the conspirators drove to the church.

It was the most difficult thing of any that Laura had yet been called upon to do. She had made up her mind never to see her husband again. Now it had to be all gone over just as before. She remembered that last scene, when, after words sharper than any steel, Philip fell crying at her feet as she left the room, praying her to come back, and let all be as it was. But this could never be.. She knew it could never be. All the little ties that grow up between lovers — the tendrils that bind soul to soul, growing out of daily thought and daily caresses — were snapped and severed at a stroke. The ideal had been destroyed at one blow; even its ruins seemed vanished and lost. Philip had more of her pity now than of her love. No more her gallant and noble lover, the crown and type of all loyalty and honor, but degraded and fallen; his spurs struck off, his scutcheon smirched, — a recreant knight. She had forgiven him. Perhaps, too, love might have been born out of forgiveness: a rose-bush beaten to the ground will put up one or two branches, and blossom again. And woman's love, like God's, continues through sin and shame and disgrace. And then, another thing. She had lived a different life. The three women who were now her companions and friends, — Madeleine, Marie, and Sukey, — each in her own way, had taught her what Hartley Venn could never do: how women look on things; how great had been her own sin in keeping her secret from Hartley. With all these influences upon her, as she grew stronger, her very face seemed to change: she passed from a girl to a woman, and her beauty grew, so to speak, stronger and more real.

Hartley led her up the aisle. There were no bridal veils, no bridesmaids, no pealing organ. She kept her eyes on the ground; but she knew Philip was standing, pale and agitated, by the altar.

The clergyman came out.

A strange wedding. The clerk and the pew-opener stared with open eyes at each other; for the bride stood before the altar, like a culprit, — pale, thin, tearful, shivering. Beside her, Venn, his smooth cheek flushed with suppressed fury, as he stood face to face with the destroyer of his happiness. All his philosophy, his acceptance of the inevitable, his resignation to fate, seemed useless now to stay the angry beating of his heart. But for the presence of the women, he might have broken out then and there. Behind Laura, another, more deeply moved than any of the rest — the mother of the bridegroom. With her, Madeleine, anxious that there should be, above all, no scene, — the only one present to whom the whole ceremony did not appear a kind of strange, wild dream.

As for Philip, he stood, at first defiantly, looking straight at the clergyman; and, but for the hot flush upon his face, you might have thought him careless. Madeleine looked at him, and knew otherwise. Presently he had to kneel. Then, open as natures such as his are to every kind of influence, the words of the prayer fell upon his dry heart like rain upon a thirsty soil; and he was touched, almost to tears, by pity and sorrow for the gentle girl at his side, but not by love.

They stood up, face to face. For the second time their hands were joined with solemn words; and Laura started when she heard the voice of Philip — low and sad as it seemed — saying, after the clergyman, the words prescribed by the Church.

They were pronounced man and wife.

Philip took her by the hand, and led her into the vestry, shutting the door.

He placed a chair for her, and stood in front. The church service had softened him, and the better nature was again uppermost.

"Laura," he said, "I promised Madeleine to remove any doubts that might exist in any mind by going through this ceremony. That is done. We are now married so that no one, if they could say any thing before, can say a word now against the legality of our union; but one thing remains. I have done you cruel wrong. Will you forgive me?"

"Yes, Philip, I have forgiven."

"Freely and fully?"

"Long since, Philip, — long since."

"We ought never to have met, child. Tell me again, that I may take the words away with me, that you forgive me."

"Philip, in the sight of God, I forgive all and every thing."

"We must part, Laura, now, — at all events, for the present. It is best so, is it not? I shall travel. We will not even write to each other. I have not forgiven myself. Kiss me once, my wife."

She stood up, and kissed him on the lips, her tears raining on his cheeks. Then Philip opened the door and stepped into the church, where the clerk was standing open-mouthed at this extraordinary conduct.

"There are some papers to sign, I believe," he said.

They all went into the vestry. Philip signed.

"I have done what I promised, Madeleine."

Madeleine made a gesture in the direction of Madame de Guyon, who was bending over Laura.

"You have no word for her," she whispered.

He turned to his mother, hesitated a moment, then raised her hand and kissed it. She threw her arms about his neck, and kissed him passionately, whispering, —

"Philip, my son, come back to us soon."

He freed himself gently, placed her in a chair, and took his hat. Then he saw Hartley.

"You are Mr. Venn?" he asked. "I cannot ask your forgiveness, that would be too preposterous. I leave my wife and — and my mother in your care."

He left the vestry, and strode down the aisle. They heard his footsteps out of the church door, and down the street outside. Then, they, too, left the church, and drove away in Madeleine's carriage to Madame de Guyon's house.

"He asked me to forgive him, mamma," said Laura, sobbing in her arms. "He told me he was sorry. Let us pray for him together."

"This," said the clerk to the old woman who assisted — "this here is the most extraordinary and rummest wedding I ever see. First, the young man he comes half an hour early. I told him to look at the clock. 'Damn the clock,' he said, begging your pardon, Mrs. Trigg. Such was his blasphemous words, and in a church! He didn't give you much, I suppose, Mrs. Trigg? You ain't a great deal richer for this precious morning's work?"

"Not a brass farthing!"

"Ah! they *call* themselves gentlefolks, I suppose. It's a queer way to begin married life by giving the church people nothing, let alone quarrelling before ever they come near the place! However, I dessay there's nothing absolutely illegal in not giving the clerk and pew-opener their just and lawful dues; but it looks bad. It looks very bad. Mark my words, Mrs. Trigg: there will be no blessin' on this wedding."

CHAPTER XXXVII.

So Philip went his way, and they heard no more of him for a time. But a change was coming over the unhappy young man; a change for the worse. He was, as has been seen, of that light and unstable character whose good and evil never seem to end their contest, whose owner is able at one moment to resolve the highest and noblest things, and at the next to fall into the lowest and basest actions. Does this come from the fatal African blood? God forbid that we should say so; but surely it may be helped for the worse by the presence of a constant suspicion of inferiority. It is self-respect that makes men walk erect, and in a straight line. We who sin are men who esteem ourselves but lightly. Sinners there are who think no small beer of themselves — rather the finest and oldest Trinity Audit; but they are those who have framed themselves a special code of honor and morality; and, if we called things by their right names, we should not use the idle metaphors of the common jargon, saying of a man that he wants ballast, bottom, backbone, staying power, energy, but we should say that he wants self-respect. This is the quality that makes a man Senior Wrangler, Victoria Cross, K.C.B., Mayor of his town, Deputy Grand of the Ancient Order of Druids, or any other distinction we long for. This is what inspires industry, pluck, perseverance, confidence, — every thing. Dear friends, and fathers of families, make your sons conceited, vain, proud, self-believers, encourage confidence. Never let them be snubbed or bullied. See that they walk head erect and fist ready. Inspire them with such a measure of self-esteem as will make them ready to undertake any thing. If they fail, as is quite likely, no matter. They would have failed in any case, you see; and they have always their conceit to fall back upon. Lord John Russell is a case in point. Ready to command the Channel Fleet, — you know the rest of it. I know a man — the stupidest, piggest-headed, most ignorant, most conceited, and most inflated bloater of a man you ever saw. This creature, by sheer dint of conceit and vanity, which made him step calmly to the front, and stand there *just as if he were in his right place*, has a great house at South Kensington, and is director of a lot of companies. He is also, save the mark! a Fellow of the Royal Society. He got this, I know, by asking for it; and they were so astonished by the request that they gave him the distinction by mistake. He sent in his name with all the letters of the alphabet after it — those degrees which you can get for two guineas a year or thereabouts — F.A.S., F.B.S., F.C.S. F.D.S., &c.; and then F.R.A.S. F.R.B.S., F.R.C.S., &c., and after the names there came the words, in great capitals, AUTHOR OF THE WORK ENTITLED "ON THE TRITURATION OF IGNEOUS PARTICLES." You see, he once rubbed a couple of sticks together to try and make a fire, after the manner of the barbarians, and failed to do more than bark his own knuckles. Then he wrote a pamphlet, in six pages, on the subject. This was his work, to which he refers whenever a scientific point is mooted.

Pardon me, reader, whenever I think of that man and this subject, I am carried away with an irrepressible enthusiasm and admiration.

Graviora canamus. It is an easy thing to write of a man's downward course — but a sad thing. Poor Philip, seeing sometimes the things he had done in their true and real characters, was afflicted with a sense of shame and disgrace that became so strong as to drive him back upon himself. He left off going to the club. That is to say, he left off going among his fellow-men at all. He had no friends, except club-friends. Occasionally he might be met, but not in the daytime, wandering carelessly along the streets. For he could not sleep at night, and used to tire himself by long, lonely walks, and then get home to his rooms at three in the morning, and go to bed exhausted. Presently two devils entered into him, and possessed him. The first was the demon of drink. He began to drink in the morning; he went on drinking all day. At night he was sodden, and could sleep.

All this was not done in a day. A man who begins to live by himself in this great London, where it is so easy, soon drops into the habit of ceasing to care for any society. The streets are society, — the long and multitudinous streets, with the roar of the carriages and the faces of the people. The streets inspired Dickens, who would come up from the country to London, and find in the streets the refreshment that he needed. The streets possessed the soul of De Quincy. To me there is no exhibition in the world comparable to Regent Street at four, or to the strand all day long. I know a man who dropped some years since into this lonely life. He goes nowhere now; he cares to go nowhere. He dines every day at the self-same seat and the self-same place, on the self-same dinner. Then he goes back to his chambers, smokes a cigar, and presently to bed. In the daytime he goes up and down the streets.

Philip, in his bitter moods, began by going less often to the club, so that he gradually dropped out of the set. He was no longer to be depended on for a rubber. His face was missed at the nightly pool. No more bets were to be got out of him. And then he ceased to go there at all.

It was at this period, during February and March, that another fancy took him. He found out from the "Directory" where Madame de Guyon lived. It was in one of those houses that lie so thickly round the north of Regent's Park. One night he walked up there after dinner. It was a house with a little garden-ground under the windows. One room, the drawing-room, was lighted up. The blinds were not down, and the curtains not drawn. Philip stood on the pavement, and looked in through the railings. The party inside consisted of two ladies,— his mother and his wife,— and a man, Hartley Venn. Venn was lying lazily in an easy-chair; Madame Guyon was sitting opposite to him, knitting; Lollie sat in the middle, reading aloud. Philip heard her voice. She had one of those sweet, rich voices — not strong — which curl around a man's heart like the tendrils of a vine. I hate a woman with a loud voice, and I hate a woman who whispers. He could not hear what she read; but he listened to the voice, and tried to remember the past. All that blind, mad passion was dead. There was left in his heart the *power*, like a seed waiting for the spring, of waking to a higher and purer love; and now he seemed to know her better, and acknowledged within himself that she was every way worthy of the best love a man can bring.

He stood without, in the rain and cold, looking on the quiet happiness within. Presently, Madame de Guyon went to the piano, and began to sing. Her glorious voice filled the little room to overflowing, and welled forth in great waves of sound. Philip clutched the railings, and pressed his cheek against the iron. This was his mother, — this glorious queen among women, this empress of song. There was the peaceful retreat waiting for him. He knew he had but to knock at the door. It was like Bunyan's way to heaven: to knock at the door was enough.

Then the younger lady took the elder's place, and began to play, — some of the old things he knew, that she had so often played to him. She played on, with her head thrown back, in that attitude of careless grace which he had never seen in any other woman, with lips half parted, eyes half closed, while the music rose and fell beneath her fingers, and flowed, like the rising tide among the caves, within her soul. Then she, too, stopped; and Venn got up and shook hands with both. He passed out, and crossed to the other side of the street; but did not notice the man leaning against the railings, with straining eyes, staring within.

Then the blind was drawn down. A bell rang. Some one — his wife — played an evening hymn. They sang. Then a monotonous voice for a few minutes, and presently the lights were extinguished. They had prayed, and were gone to bed; but they had prayed for him. And, as he stood there, after the lights were extinguished, there were two women, in two rooms, each on her knees by the bedside, praying for him again, — his mother and his wife. Then he came to himself, and walked back as fast as he could, trying to pull himself together.

Two or three nights afterwards, he went up again. This time there were no lights. All was dark. He waited till past eleven, walking backwards and forwards in the road. Then a carriage drew up, and he saw them descend and enter the house. They had been to the theatre, and were laughing and talking gayly. That night he went home in a rage. What right had they to be happy without him?

But he went up again. Sometimes the blinds were left up, and he saw the group. Oftener blinds and curtains were drawn; and he could only hear the voices, and the sound of the piano. He knew, too, well enough, which of the two was playing; and also got to know — which filled his soul with inexpressible pangs of rage and jealousy — that Venn was there about four nights in the week.

All this time he was drinking hard, and living entirely alone. One night he went to bed earlier than usual, — about one o'clock, — and, contrary to his usual practice, went to sleep at once. At three o'clock he awoke with a shudder and a start. Opening his eyes wide, he saw, sitting by the side of the bed, — in fact on his own pile of clothes, — a skeleton. Not a skeleton of the comic order, with a pipe in his mouth, such as we are fond of drawing, but of the entirely tragic and melancholy kind: with his mouth open wide, from ear to ear, as if it was a throat cut an inch and a half too high up; a long, bony hand that pointed straight at him, and shook its finger in anger; eyes that glared with a horrid earnestness; bones, all the way down, that seemed transparent. Solitude makes men nervous; drink makes them see skeletons. Philip sat up, and glared. Then he gave a half cry, and buried his head under the clothes.

Presently he looked out again. The skeleton was gone. He turned round with a sigh of relief. The skeleton was *on the other side*. Then he covered his head again, and waited till daybreak, — till past six o'clock. By that time the spectre was gone.

The next night he did not dare to go to

bed again. And then it was that the second devil, of whom I have spoken above, took possession of him. This time it was the demon of play. Philip, who knew every thing about London, was not ignorant of the existence of one or two places — where, indeed, he had more than once been seen, — where you may find a green table, dice, and other accessories to the gambling-table. To one of these he went that night at one o'clock. There were two or three of his club acquaintances there, who greeted him as one newly returned from some long foreign travel.

He got through the night so. And saw no spectre when he awoke at mid-day.

Then he began to frequent the place regularly. It seemed to him the only place where pleasure could be found. At the age of six and twenty this young man found the fruits of the world turned in his mouth to dust and ashes. He had no longer any ambition or any hope. The long night spent over the chances of the game gave him light, companionship, excitement. To keep his head clear, he gave up the brandy and water of the day. So far this was a gain. But then he took to champagne at night, and drank too much of it. As for the play, whether he lost or won made no difference, because he never lost heavily; and fortune favored him by giving him neither great coups, nor great reverses.

This kind of thing went on for a couple of months or so. He grew thin, pale, excitable. He had not the moral courage even to go among men at all, never went anywhere except to the gaming-table, — except when he walked up to Regent's Park to catch a glimpse of the home he had abandoned. The sight of it, the occasional sight of its inhabitants, was like a lash of scorpions. If he saw them happy, his blood boiled with jealousy and rage. If he thought they looked depressed, he ground his teeth together, and cursed himself for the cause.

At first he used to have mighty yearnings of spirit, and was moved to knock at the door and ask admittance. These emotions being suppressed, day after day, grew gradually of less strength. Then he ceased to think of any change at all; and went on moodily — without any of that singing and dancing of which he spoke to Madeleine — down the slope of Avernus, the bottom of which was not far off.

He had laid his skeleton by the process of changing his hours altogether; but it was only laid for a time. Youth will stand a good deal; but there is a point beyond which you may not go. Then a disordered liver, an unhealthy brain, a nervous excitement, produce discomforts of a very rude and practical kind. There came a time, early in April, when his sleep was so tormented with terrible dreams, and his waking hours with terrible thoughts, — thoughts that he knew could belong to no sound brain, and sights that he knew to be unreal or supernatural, — that he went to a doctor, and humbly asked assistance.

"What have you been doing?"

"Nothing. Smoking, drinking, living alone, gambling. Every thing that is bad."

"Leave it all off. Go into society."

"The only society I can go into is the society of men who do these things."

"You have money? Good. Then go away. That is the only thing I can do for you. Live temperately, and go away."

"Where am I to go to?"

"Go? Go anywhere. As far as you can. Take a long sea-voyage. Come back after it, — say in two years' time, and we will see how you are. If you stay here and go on drinking, you will probably be dead in six months."

"What does it matter if I am?"

"Pardon me, my dear sir. My business is to prolong life, not to examine into the desirability of preserving it. Most of my patients prefer to live. Doubtless they consider the chances of a change dubious."

Philip went away relieved. He would go away and travel. The new thought occupied his mind all day; and for that night he slept soundly, and if skeletons danced in his room, as they did sometimes, he was asleep, and did not see them.

Where to go?

He awoke in the morning, asking himself the question. And then a happy thought struck him. He would go away for good and all; he would get out of a country where all the memories were miserable to him. The past should be shaken off like an old garment. He would begin a new life; he would go and live on his own estate, — Arthur's, by right, said his conscience, — in Palmiste.

His thoughts flew to the place. He felt again the warm breath of the summer air; he sat in the shade, deep down in the ravine, where the cool dash and plash of the mountain stream made sweet music in his ears; roamed the forest, gun in hand, while the branches sighed in the breeze. He saw the hill-tops purpling at dawn, and the heavy dew lying in great beads upon the roses. He heard the shrill voices of the coolies, and watched the Indian women pass by, with their lithe, graceful figures and their scarlet robes. And all at once a wild longing came over him to be there, and at peace.

All day long he went about, radiant with the new thought. He drove to Silver's, and ordered a lot of things to be put together at once. He drove to his agent's, and told him what he was going to do. He ascertained that the steamer left Southampton in three days, and he took his passage.

Then he went home, and dreamed of the future.

There, in that land where it is always afternoon, peace would come to him at last, and conscience be still. A pleasant life lay before him, — a life of ease and dignity. He would be a judge among the people of his estate, as his father had been before him: he would be the giver and dispenser of hospitality. He would leave behind him, and forget forever, the two women who could be happy while he was wretched; Arthur, the wronged, — all against whom he had sinned. He would forget them all, and be happy.

Alas! "*Cœlum, non animum, mutant qui trans mare currunt.*"

CHAPTER XXXVIII.

BAD indeed must be the condition of that man whom a long voyage does not restore to freshness and health. Here are no letters, no duns, no newspapers. The world goes on without you. One has no longer the fidgety feeling, like the fly on the wheel, of being essential to the march of events. Nor is there any sense of responsibility. Nothing to be done; nothing to be thought of: eating and drinking the business of the day, its pleasure to watch the waves and the skies.

For Philip there was the additional pleasure of renewing intercourse with his brother man. He lost all his spectres, grew once more bright-eyed and keen-witted, and, when they steamed into the harbor of St. Denys, had altogether forgotten the wretched being who clung to the railings of the little house at Regent's Park, and peered into the brightness within. He stepped upon the quay, — the old familiar place, — and looked around him. There were the coolies at work; the white houses of the residents stretching up the broad street; beyond, the ugly spire of the cathedral, like a gigantic extinguisher; and over all towered the mountains, blackening now with the shadows of evening. And then there fell upon him a very curious feeling, because he suddenly remembered that he should not know a single soul in the whole island : not one. During the whole voyage he had been nursed by a vague idea that he was rushing back into the arms of innumerable friends. Now he felt like Oliver Goldsmith when he went among the Hollanders with the grandest projects, and only remembered too late that he knew no Dutch. But his laughter was short; and he felt somewhat saddened as he ordered his things to be taken to the hotel.

There is a hotel at St. Denys, — in fact, there are many, but only one of decent repute. It consists of a long, low, wooden house, painted a bright yellow, with a deep veranda round it. It has two stories, the upper one containing the bedrooms; and, for coolness' sake, the partitions are not run up to the ceiling, leaving a clear space above. This not only allows the air to circulate, but also permits the guests the advantage of overhearing all the conversation that may be going on in the adjoining rooms. Lying and sitting about the veranda are a crowd of Indian boys, dressed in a suit of uniform, of white trousers and black jackets, neat and handy looking. Outside, under the thick shade of the trees, sit the happy islanders, playing dominoes. They begin this amusement at early dawn, and go on, with short intervals for business and longer ones for breakfast and dinner, till it is time to go to bed, that is, till about eight o'clock. They do this every day, including Sunday, and are never tired; and when Azrael is sent to fetch them away, they are thinking — as they have been thinking all their lives — of the last combinations of the pips. At least their lives may be called happy, because they have all that they desire.

All was as Philip remembered it years before. The waiters ran about and chattered; the players smoked cigars, drank orgeat, and chattered; and, that nothing might be wanting, a great black parrot, which had been there ten years before, was there still, stalking about with an air of being the only really superior person present. It was a parrot of infinite accomplishments; and at sight of him Philip laughed, thinking how he had made Arthur and himself laugh years before. For he had been carefully instructed in, and had by sheer force of imitative genius acquired, the art of representing all the sounds which proceed from a person affected with cold, from its earliest appearance to its most advanced stage of pulmonary consumption. Too much of him might be undesirable, but at first, he was amusing. Nothing was changed. At the *table d'hôte*, the same dinner. The principal guests were his fellow-travellers in the mail, — at all events, the most important, because they had the latest news. Of course their importance lasts only five minutes; for no one can be expected in Palmiste to pay attention to foreign news for a longer time. The concession of five minutes granted to the outer world, the conversation rolled on in its usual groove, and the latest scandal resumed its proper place. Philip noticed it all, and listened, wondering how he should get on with all these people, whom he seemed to remember in a kind of dream. It was their old manner of talk, he remembered.

He went to bed early. Just as he was turning in, he heard voices from the next room.

"*Dites moi, mon ami,*"—it was a lady's voice,—"who was this M. Durnford, who has just arrived and dined at the *table d'hôte?*"

"It is not the son of our old friend," replied her husband,—"not, that is, the son of your school-fellow, Adrienne de Rosnay. Another son altogether. Some early liaison. His name is Philip. He has bought the estate of his half-brother, and comes here to see it, I suppose. It is not probable he will live here."

"No: that is, of course, out of the question. He is a handsome young man. Pity he is a mulatto. He had much better go back to England or France, where they are not particular as to color."

There was a plunge and a heavy thud, as if some stout person was getting into bed; and in five minutes dead silence, but for a gentle breathing, which gradually deepened into a melodious snore.

But Philip was lying in bed, tossing about, and clinching his fists. On the very first night to be reminded in this brusk and brutal way, it was too much. He lay awake. Why had he come here? What cursed fate was it which brought him back to the island he had always hated?

The night was hot too; and the mosquitoes were stinging his face and hands. He got out of bed, and lit a candle, and sat at the open window, smoking a cigar. The town was silent and asleep. Not even a dog barked; but outside the moonlight bathed every thing with a flood of rich white light. The breeze from the mountains fanned his cheek. There was the solemn silence of the night on the sleeping city; but the peace of night brought no peace to him. Why, why had he come all this way to be reminded of what he had run away from England to forget? And then he cursed his fate and himself.

All night he sat brooding and wretched. As the day broke, he fell asleep, his head on the window-sill, and slept till the noise of the Indian boys recalled him to wakefulness. Then, to avoid meeting the people of the next bedroom, he ordered a carriage to be brought round, and drove, in the early morning, away to his own estate.

As he had written to no one, he was quite unexpected. The house was uninhabited, the manager and his wife living in a cottage close by. They came and welcomed him,—a bright, cheery young Frenchman, with a pretty little wife. While his own house was being set in order, would he use theirs? The manager led him over his mills, pointed out the great improvements that had been made, and then took him back to his wife, who had got a dainty breakfast, with the best claret at her command, ready for him. Then all day there was cleaning and setting in order; and then, for a few days after, novelty and strangeness, which distracted Philip, and kept him in high spirits. Then he had to go and see his lawyer, which was a day's journey, in and out of town; then to get the lawyer to come and stay a day or two with him. All this took time, and a fortnight passed away before Philip found it dull, or had a thought for the past.

After that, things began to be a little monotonous; for no one called upon him. Philip fell back upon the officers. There was a regiment whose head-quarters were stationed at a place some eight miles off. It was on detachment duty, but there were always a good many of the officers to be found about the mess-rooms. He knew the regiment, and called upon his old friends. So, at least, companionship was attained, at the cost of perpetual dinners at Fontainebleau—which mattered little, for Philip liked hospitality. But the —— th was a fast regiment, and the young fellows who went to Fontainebleau were the fastest; and the old "pace" began again, with cards, brandy and soda, and late hours.

The first event of importance, as the histories say, was a special humiliation. The estate adjoining his own belonged to a certain old French gentleman who held strong views on the subject of the mixed races. He had been a friend of Mr. Durnford père, but he abstained from calling upon his son.

Now he gave, once a year, a great hunting-party, lasting a week, to which all the island was invited,—the governor, the merchants, the officers, everybody who had the least claim to call himself some one. Philip was his next neighbor; but he did not invite him. Then his guests began to talk about putting up at Fontainebleau during the *chasse;* and it was awkward to have to say that you were not invited.

The time drew near. Philip was riding with one of his guests in the evening. They passed the house of M. de Geoffroi, who was sitting in his veranda.

"Aha!" cried Philip's companion. "Let us ride in, and call on the old boy. You'll do the talking, you know. I can't speak French."

Philip assented, and in a few moments was introduced to a white-headed old gentleman, who saluted him coldly.

"I had the honor of knowing Capt. Durnford well," he said.

"I remember you well, M. de Geoffroi. You were often at Fontainebleau when I was a boy."

"I was. And your brother, M. Durnford? He is married, I hear, to Mdlle. de Villeroy."

"He is engaged, at least."

"Yes. It was once the wish of both parents that the estates should pass into the same hands."

Philip reddened.

"That, at least, cannot be, because the estate has now passed into my hands."

"So I have been informed."

Then they talked about weather, and so forth; and presently, when they went away, M. de Geoffroi offered his hand to the other, and merely bowed to Philip.

"Must have set the old man's back up, Durnford. What did you say to him?"

But Philip did not answer; being, in fact, in a temper the reverse of amiable.

The hunting-party came off, and Philip sat at home with troubled heart. The party was nothing, but the *reason*,— the *reason* for his exclusion from it. Then he gave a great party of his own, asking all the Englishmen, who came, and as many Frenchmen as he thought would come. It was purely out of revenge; but it seemed to affect M. de Geoffroi very little.

One more event happened to him; and then he shut himself up altogether at Fontainebleau.

There came the cold season, and the time for balls and dances. Of course Philip got an invitation to the great ball of the year, at Government House, at which the governor appears in uniform,— a gorgeous suit, similar to that of a lord lieutenant; while the members of the legislative council wear wonderful coats, with gold lace in a sort of cushion just where the tails begin, too high up for use, except in a second class railway carriage, where it might protect the small of the back. Then the heads, and the sub-heads, and even the tails of departments, appear in wonderful and strange costumes, the effect of which at first, on the civilian of plain clothes, is simply bewildering, and even appalling. Of course there are also the scarlet coats of the officers. And, on the whole, a Colonial State Ball is as pretty a sight — with the ladies all in their very finest and best — as one can generally see.

Why do we sneer at the universal desire to put on a uniform? I have never worn any, not even as a volunteer private; but I can sympathize with it. I like to see a man in all his bravery. I think there is no more admirable and edifying spectacle than that of the ordinary Briton in some strange and wonderful costume, put on about once a year. He wears it with such a lordly air, as one who should say, "This is nothing to what I could look if I had on what I deserved." Then his wife admires him, and his daughters. And more than that, all the black-coated civilians who sneer at him envy him. The last is a very great point.

Philip, being an ex-commissioned officer, was above uniforms, it may be presumed; but he was not above admiration for the uniforms of the other sex. The women of Palmiste, pale and colorless, perhaps, are yet, above the generality of women, *gracieuses*. They become their uniforms. They dance with a passion and an abandon which is unknown in colder regions. It is their one great accomplishment; and the young fellow fresh from London rooms looks on with astonishment at the lightning rapidity with which the smoothly polished floors are covered. Very soon he falls in with it, too, if he be of a sympathetic mind.

Philip, long exiled from ladies' society, enjoyed it hugely; danced every thing, always with English ladies; devoured a splendid supper; took plenty of champagne. Then, as bad luck would have it, after supper one of his friends introduced him to the lady he had been dancing with, a liberty quite unpardonable by all the rules. Philip asked for the next waltz. The girl turned red, and, after a moment's hesitation, acceded, and put her arm in his. Her brother, who was standing by with frowning forehead, stepped forward at once.

"Pardon me, monsieur," he said. "My sister does not dance any more this evening."

The young lady took her brother's arm, and walked away.

The next moment he saw her whirled round in the arms of an Englishman.

All the blood rushed to his head, and he staggered with the rage which nearly stifled him. For he *knew the reason.*

He stepped across the room to where the young Frenchman was standing, and touched him on the arm.

"Will you give me a moment's conversation outside?"

The young fellow hesitated for a moment: then he shrugged his shoulders.

"As you will," he said.

They stepped down the stairs, and into the garden. No one was there but themselves.

"May I ask the reason of your refusal to let your sister dance with me just now?"

The Frenchman hesitated. Philip repeated the question.

"Really, monsieur," said the young fellow, "it seems absurd to put such a question. Can we not leave it unanswered?"

"No. I demand an answer, and the true one. I am publicly insulted: I insist on an explanation."

"Suppose I have none to give you?"

"I *will* have one."

"You shall not have one," returned the other quietly.

Philip lost command of himself, twisted his hand in the other's collar, and threw him heavily to the ground.

"Will you give me one now?"

"Mulatto, I will give you none," hissed out his enemy, lying on the ground.

Philip left him there. Going back to the ball-room, he found young Freshley, of the —th.

"Come with me for a moment," he whispered.

They went outside. In the garden was the young Frenchman, trying to repair the damage done to his necktie and collar.

"There has been a row," said Philip. "You know this man, perhaps? I have knocked him down."

"I know Mr. Freshley," said the Frenchman.

"Be my friend, Freshley. I will wait for you in your quarters."

Philip went away to barracks, leaving the two together.

"What is it, D'Auray?"

"I called him a mulatto. *Eh, bien:* it is true, at any rate. Then he put his hand to my collar, and I fell over his foot."

"Doesn't seem manners to tell a man a thing he isn't proud of, does it?"

"What business has he among ladies?"

"I didn't invite him, so I can hardly say; but you had better ask the aide-de-camp. Look here, old fellow, this is a bad business. Don't let us have any public shindy. Give me the name of a man, and I will try to make things square."

"I put myself in the hands of my cousin. You will find him in the ball-room."

Duelling has gone out of fashion in England; but it still lingers in one or two of her majesty's colonies, where, although they have the institution of a jury, the sympathies of the jury are sure to be with the combatants. Here there would surely be fighting, thought Freshley, beginning to wish he had nothing to do with the business, in case of the thing ending seriously.

He found the cousin, and put the case to him.

"I'm going home now to barracks. Find me there early to-morrow morning."

He went home, and discovered Philip walking up and down in a wild state of excitement.

"I will kill him, Freshley. By Heaven! I will kill him."

"You've knocked him down, anyhow. Now go to bed, old fellow, — it's past two o'clock. The cousin is coming to-morrow, and we shall have an apology or a challenge. If the latter — why, then, I suppose, we must fight."

"Fight? Of course I will fight. I tell you, I mean to kill him."

"Deuced easy to pack a jury if he kills you, Philip. Don't quite see my way to packing one if you kill him."

"Bah! You don't know the country. Any lawyer will do it for you."

They went to bed, but not to sleep; and at five o'clock Freshley saw Philip outside, walking up and down, clinching his fists, in the moonlight. So, with a sigh, he got up too, and, half dressing, went out and joined him. Day broke at six, and then they had coffee and a cigar.

At half-past six the cousin was seen coming to the barracks.

"It's manners for me to receive him alone, I suppose," said Freshley. "Let's look as if we had done it fifty times before. Hang it, I feel like an Irishman out of one of Lever's novels. You go in, Phil. Well, M. D'Auray, and when do we fight?"

"I think, Mr. Freshley, that — well, you see, it's an awkward business. I hardly see my way to a fight."

"Oh, very well! for my own part, I'm very glad. My man is insulted: that you will acknowledge. Your man is knocked down: that there is no getting over, is there? So you won't fight? I'm sure I'm not displeased; because, after all, yours is the most injured side, I should say. Matter of taste, — never been knocked down myself. Why can't we fight?"

"Well, your principal — I am not in the least wishing to insult or offend you."

"You forget that Mr. Durnford has had the honor of bearing her Majesty's commission."

"Not at all. That was considered. I laid the case before several of my friends. We all agreed that if he were still an officer in the British army, to refuse a duel would be to insult the English flag; but he is no longer an officer, and we cannot fight him."

Freshley whistled.

"Oh, very good, I'm sure! The knocking down is on your side, as I remarked before. Have a pick-me-up this fine morning, M. D'Auray, — a brandy and soda?"

"Nothing, thank you. I have the honor to wish you a good-morning."

"Good-morning, M. D'Auray. Perhaps your cousin would like a pick-me-up."

But M. D'Auray did not appreciate the joke, being unacquainted with the niceties of the English language.

"Now, that's devilish smart and good," said the lieutenant, left alone. "Phil, my boy, come out. They won't fight."

"Why not?"

"Don't know. Can't say. Wasn't told. Funk, I expect. I say, Phil, I asked him if his cousin wanted a pick-me-up this morning. Devilish good remark, eh? I don't know when I said any thing sharper. He'll find out what I meant by and by. Look it up in the dictionary, I suspect. Well, old boy, I'm glad we're out of it. I didn't like it at the first; and, between ourselves, I couldn't afford to lose my commission just now. Pretty fools we should look, the brace of us, in a dock, with the beak pounding away at us, saying it was the worst case he had ever known in the whole course of his professional career, — eh? and then, perhaps, chokee for six months, and a court-martial afterwards. Upon my word, I'm delighted. And now I think I shall have another nap."

But that was Philip's last appearance in public. Henceforth his days are few and troubled, and they are spent wholly on his own estate at Fontainebleau.

CHAPTER XXXIX.

MEANWHILE, in the quiet house at Regent's Park, the two women waited, — some women seem to have nothing to do except to wait. No change came to them. All they knew — and this through Arthur's lawyer — was that Philip had arrived in Palmiste, and was residing on the estate. Nothing more. As for Laura, her suffering was over.

Only she was subdued. Time, and the atmosphere of love with which they surrounded her, had cured her.

"You love him still, child, do you not?" asked Marie.

"I will tell you, as truthfully as I can, every thing," said Lollie. "You cannot tell — it is impossible for any one to know — how ignorant and foolish I was a year ago. When Mr. Venn said he should like to see me married to a gentleman, I understood nothing, — nothing of what he meant. Then I met Philip; and he asked me to marry him. Mamma, I declare that I accepted him only to please Mr. Venn, — for no other reason whatever. Then he said I was cold, and wanted me to say I loved him. Of course I could not say so, because I did not then. Afterwards we were married, and we went abroad; and he was kind. I think I began to love him then. But now I always think of the last time I saw him, when he asked my forgiveness, and looked sorry. And since then I have loved him better than ever before. Poor Philip! Perhaps if I had been fitted for him he would have been a better man."

"I think of him always, my daughter," said Philip's mother. "I lie awake, and think of him. They took him away from me when he was only one year old. I have seen him, since then, only twice in my life. Once he refused to own me, and once he refused to speak to me; but what woman can forget the little hands that curl round her neck — of her own child? Philip is my son, Lollie; and a mother's love is better than a wife's."

"I wish I loved him more, mamma, for your sake," said Lollie, caressing her.

"Nay, dear. You are the sweetest and best of daughters. My life, now its great hope has failed, would be sad indeed, and lonely, if it were not for you. And we must pray, dear, more and more, for his return to us. I know that he will one day lay his head in my arms, and kiss me himself. Don't ask me how I know it. I am certain. Only I cannot see all the future; and there seems a cloud which I cannot pierce. Somehow, you are not with me, child."

She often talked like this, pouring out what still haunted her of the old negro superstitions.

"I know where he is now, at this moment," she murmured, half closing her eyes. "It is morning with us, but afternoon with him. He is riding alone along the road. The canes are waving each side of him. His face is clouded and angry. He is not thinking of us, Lollie. Alas — alas! he only thinks of himself. The time is not yet come."

Lollie grasped her hand, and cried out. Marie started, and looked round her.

"Kiss me, my daughter. I was far away in Palmiste with my son, our Philip."

Their only visitors were Hartley Venn and his sister, Arthur and Madeleine; and they went nowhere, except sometimes to the opera, which was a necessary luxury to the singer.

"You have changed Lollie altogether, madame," said Hartley, looking at his little girl.

"How am I changed, Mr. Venn?" asked Laura.

"That is what I am trying to find out. You look thinner than you were; but it is not that. You are no taller; so it is not that. I give it up, Lollie."

Marie could have told him. The girl had been, for the first time in her life, living among ladies, and was now a lady herself—such as all the arts of Hartley Venn could not fashion or produce.

"It is only you, Mr. Venn," said Madeleine, "who never change. Oh that I could tie ropes round you, and drag you away from your chambers, and make you work!"

"He does work, Madeleine. He really works very hard," said Lollie.

"Part of your wish has been already anticipated, Miss de Villeroy; for I have met with a grave misfortune."

"What is it?" they cried.

"I have received notice to quit my chambers at the end of the year."

"Oh!" cried Lollie, "the dear old chambers!"

"I shall not have the heart to find out new chambers, and so I shall go and live in lodgings. It is sad, after so many years of occupation. I had hoped that my life would be finished there."

"Indeed," said Madeleine, "I think it a very good thing. You men get into a habit of doing nothing, going nowhere, and living three or four in a set, which seems to me destructive of every thing. Go into the world, and work, Mr. Venn."

"Really, Miss de Villeroy, you carry about so deep an air of resolution and activity that you shame us all. I *will* go into the world and work. What shall I do?"

This was easier to ask than to answer. Besides, Madeleine was at this time intently occupied in considering Arthur's future. He, too, professed a willingness to go into the world, and work; but what work? Here was a tall, strong man to be thrown on her hands for life, and what was she to find for him? Arthur said he would work; but he never made the least effort to find work, and went on burying himself in his books, while Madeleine fretted about his useless life.

"Marry me at once, Madeleine," he said, "and I will be your secretary. Will that do?"

"I don't want a secretary," she said.

But she consented to marry him at once, which was all he wanted.

This was in February. The wedding was quiet enough, for they were a comparatively friendless pair. Mrs. Longworthy was there; and in the church, as spectators, Marie and Laura. Madeleine invited them to the breakfast; but this was against Marie's rules, and Laura would not go without her.

When they came back, after a month in Paris, the old life went on just as before. Mrs. Longworthy lived on with them, being one of those old ladies whom it is pleasant to have in the house. Arthur had his study, where Madeleine repaired sometimes in the evening, for those little talks and confidential whisperings which even the most queenly of women are not above liking. But all became as it was before, and the house at Regent's Park was still a favorite place to spend an evening.

"I like it, Arthur," said Madeleine. "It is all so different from what you get anywhere else. I like Madame de Guyon, poor woman, and the noble way she bears her misfortunes. I like Lollie, with her innocent dependence upon Mr. Venn. And I like that lazy, good-for-nothing Bohemian, who is everybody's friend except his own. They are quaint, delightful people. I suppose the world would object, if the world knew all; but then the world knows nothing. And as for poor little Lollie, our sister-in-law, no one could possibly blame her."

"Surely not. If ever there was an act"—

"No, Arthur. Do not put yourself into a rage about what has been done, and cannot be helped. After all, it was mostly Mr. Venn's fault. Did ever man devise a more absurd training for a girl?"

Came again the spring, and with it the little excursions that Venn was so fond of; but they were not quite the same. The relations between himself and Lollie were altered, somehow. He could no longer kiss her in the old paternal way. Sometimes, as he thought of her, he ground his teeth, and cursed; but ever with her, his voice was soft and kind. He was always thoughtful and anxious about her. She was still, as before all this, his little girl.

Marie grew to love him as if he had been her own son; scolded him for his laziness almost as soundly as Madeleine; went to his chambers, and brought away great stores of linen, which she and Lollie amused themselves by setting in order for him; made him read her some of his numerous Opuscula, and criticised them in a way which astonished him; and gave him hints and suggestions which opened out vistas of innumerable other literary efforts, so that he formed as many projects as Coleridge.

The spring grew into summer; and then a change was to happen. For one morning the Palmiste mail came in, and Arthur received a letter from his lawyer.

"Your half-brother," he said, "is going

on, I fear, as badly as possible. It is my duty, — or, rather, I make it my officious duty, — to tell you that his only companions are the most dissipated young Englishmen of the colony, — officers chiefly. At Fontainebleau there are reported to be nightly scenes of drink and play, which will most certainly end in disaster, if not to fortune, then to health. In this climate, as you know, one has to exercise some discretion. Poor Philip has none. I liked him at first. He landed here fresh and bright, as if he had never touched a bottle of brandy; but that is four months ago, and his face is now bloated with drink and late hours. If you have any influence over him, write and expostulate. If you, or any friend, could only come out here, all might be well. Philip is open to any influence. He can resist no temptation: he is led away by every voice that he hears; but he is kind-hearted. In an evil hour he insulted little Volet, his manager, whom you remember as a boy. No better or more honest man ever lived. Volet was obliged to resign. Since he went away, Philip has been secretly sending him money to keep him going: I suppose, out of a desire to make atonement; but the estate is going to the dogs. In a few months the hot season will be upon us again, when these excesses will tell more than they do now. I may say that he always speaks of you in terms of the highest respect. He told me, what I did not know before, that the estate is only his own because you refused to fight the case. I think that you might, at least, write to him."

And so on, all in the same strain.

Arthur showed the letter to his wife.

"What shall we do?"

"You must write to him. Say nothing of the past, except what is kind. I will write too. You will remember that he did once do what I asked him."

"I know, — that was because he loved you."

"He did not really love me. He fancied he did. The only woman he ever really loved was Lollie. I am sure of it, from the way he spoke of her, the bitterness with which he remembered the poor girl's look when he cast her off."

"How can you be bitter against a woman you have ever loved?"

"I knew you would say that. It is just what a man would be sure to say. The bitterness, great stupid, was in his own breast; and he thought he felt bitter towards her. Suppose you are bilious. It is not a romantic comparison, but it will do. You see every thing yellow. That is how Philip saw things. His real nature was turned inside out. I told you, months ago, that his mind was like your old garden, all overrun with pumpkins.

"What a silly, unreasonable creature he is! Why does he hide his head in a bush, like an ostrich? He is ashamed of his mother, — he knows, my dear Arthur, that all the stupid story of the marriage is a forgery. I saw the look he gave her in the church. There was longing and repentance in it, as well as shame. He is stupidly ashamed that his mother is a great singer, as well as that she is colored. And what a woman is he ashamed of! Is there one woman in all the world more charitable, more large-hearted, less selfish, than poor Marie? Ashamed of her! He ought to be proud of her, and to thank God, who gave him such a mother."

Arthur moved his hand.

"And, O Arthur! he is more, ten thousand times more, ashamed of himself and his treatment of Laura. I believe that is the secret of all his sins. He wanted at first to make money by gambling, for her. But gambling is a hard master to serve. And then — and then — oh! my poor Phil, what a melancholy ending it all is!"

"It is not ended yet."

She shook her head.

"You do not know," she said, "but I know; because he sent me a letter before he went away, and his landlady brought it. He used to wander about at night, to drink all day. He saw no one. He used to lie on the sofa, with his head in his hands, and groan. He used to see things that do not exist in the daytime. He knew he was dishonored, poor fellow; and he tried, like a weak creature as he is, to drown it all in drink."

"I blame myself, Madeleine. I should have gone to him, in the old way, and said what I could to help him. Poor Phil is good at heart."

"Good at heart! What is the good of that? Everybody is good at heart. I want men to be strong of will. Women only love strong men."

"Then, why do you love me, Madeleine?"

"I don't know, Arthur," she said, smiling. "You know that I love you, dear — do you not? — with all the strength of my nature. But then you are strong in all good things. I believe in your nobleness, dear. God knows, if man and wife cease to believe in that, there can be nothing left. . . . Let us go and see madame."

They got there in time for luncheon. Venn was lying lazily on the sofa. He did not get up as they came in; but held out his hand, smiling."

"You come like a breath of the most invigorating breeze, Mrs. Durnford. Do not reproach me. I am hard at work, trying to make out, with Lollie here, what it is I am to work at."

"I tell him he ought to practise at the bar," said Lollie.

"So I would, but for two things. I know no solicitors, and I know no law. Bless you! if I had a brief I should be obliged to put it into a drawer for a couple of years while I read law. No: think of something else."

"What do rich men do?" asked Marie. "They seem always at work."

"They become directors. Then they make speeches. They take chairs. They do all sorts of things for nothing, which poor men get paid for. They even write for the magazines, confound them!"

"Write a novel," said Madeleine.

"Eh?" cried Venn, starting up. "Now, that is a practical suggestion. Lollie, do you remember the novel we wrote together, and buried close above Teddington Lock? That was real work, if you like. Oh, if we had not buried that novel!"

"Let us go and fish for it," cried Lollie, laughing.

"We will. We will go at once. Mrs. Durnford, you will come too. We will go this afternoon. The sun shines. The bluebottle buzzes. The lilac is in blossom. The lark will be singing. The laburnum is golden. Lollipops, put on your hat, — your summer hat, with the brightest feather in it. We will have a glorious day."

Madeleine made a sign to Marie.

"You three go," she said. "Madeleine will stay with me, and you shall have a late dinner at nine. Go away, all of you, and leave us two to make ourselves miserable together."

"What is it, dear?" she asked.

For all answer, Madeleine gave her the lawyer's letter.

Marie read it, and the tears came into her eyes.

"What are we to do?" asked Madeleine.

"I knew it was coming. I have had presentiments. I have had dreams. I dreamed that I saw my brother Adolphe — poor Adolphe, I wonder if he is living yet — putting a gri-gri under Philip's head. That is to produce disaster, you know. Every night my thoughts carry me back to Fontainebleau. George Durnford speaks to me in visions. And every night I see Philip's face averted. My dear, since I saw him, I have felt myself *en rapport* with him. You may laugh as you will; but, as he suffers, I suffer. When he is wretched, lonely, repentant, I am sad. I hide it from that poor child, who does not know what such love means, and thinks she loves Philip because she pities him; and, as I look forward, I see nothing but clouds and blackness. A great disaster is before me, — that is, before Philip. Day by day, the yearning has become stronger in me to go out and try to save my boy. If I go, I may find him in the midst of his companions, drunken and dissolute. He may drive me away with hard words. He may — but he will not, he will not, Madeleine. I feel that the hour for reconciliation is drawing near. I shall see my boy. I shall feel his cheek to mine. I shall be able to put my arms round his neck, and kiss him. O child, child! if ever God gives you a son, pray — pray — pray that you may not suffer what I am suffering now."

She was silent for a while, struggling with her emotion.

"Do you think that God is punishing me? I cannot think that. I have learned long since my sin, and been forgiven. Of that I am as sure as if a voice from Heaven had pronounced my pardon. I know it from my own heart. My Father has forgiven the sin of an ignorant childhood. It cannot be that. Then what is it? — what is it? I lived but for him. All those years when I toiled in Italy, trying to improve the defects of my education, all those years when I sang upon the stage, it was all for Philip. I lived upon nothing: my money all went into the bank for him. I waited for the day when I could say to him, 'Son, son, take all I have, and be happy. Only kiss your mother — if only it be once, and to let her go away.' I never thought to be to him what most mothers are to their children: I prayed only for a kind thought, a kind word. I got none; and now, what are all my riches worth? I have no son."

"You have Laura. You love her."

"Yes — I am wicked. I forget, in my selfish passion. I love this child, who loves me. There is no better girl in the world than my daughter. But, Madeleine, I want my own child, — my very own: the baby that lay in my lap — my own life's blood — my darling, my gallant son! Do not tell me that he has fallen from his ideal: he suffers, and would rise again if he could. Let me go to him. Let me try once more to gain his love, all alone, by the verge of that great forest where I wandered one night all alone, and saw visions of the future. Did I ever tell you? I went out, with the first money I ever earned at singing, by myself. I crept at night through the woods. I found George Durnford weeping for his dead wife, — not me, dear Madeleine. I was bitter and cruel. Then I saw poor Adrienne, white, pale, and imploring, before me; and I was softened. I saw the children. Arthur clung to me, and kissed me, in his pretty way. My own boy, my Phil, turned his face away, and cried. It was an omen, and my heart fell. I left George Durnford, and went back as I had come, through the forest. All the night, as I walked along in the black darkness, I heard voices saying to me that there should be no happiness for me, — nothing but bitterness, disappointment, and misery."

"But you have found happiness, dear Madame de Guyon."

"Yes, yes; but not the happiness I wanted. There is nothing that I desire but the love of my son, — nothing but to hear him say that he is sorry for the words he spoke."

"Play to me, dear. Soothe me with music, for my spirit is troubled."

Madeleine played, while Marie walked up and down, with fingers interlaced, trying to recover from her agitation.

Presently she sat down, close to the piano.

"Don't leave off, my dear. It soothes me as nothing else can. I am determined what to do. I will go out by the next mail. That starts in a few days, and I shall pack to-morrow, — take my ticket, and go."

As she spoke, a wailing was heard from the next house in the street, of a child. She shrank back, with a white face.

"That is the worst sign you can hear."

"Do not be superstitious," said Madeleine. "If you had heard the child cry at any other time you would have laughed."

"At any other time — yes. That I *am* superstitious is true, my dear. I can never shake it off. Call it what you please, weakness, prejudice. I was made superstitious when I was a child; and the old fears cling to me like — like the color of my birth."

They spent the day making preparations. There were not many wanted; for Marie was a woman whom stage experience had taught to be profuse in dress.

"Lollie will go and live with Miss Venn," she said. "Yes, dear, I know what you were going to offer, and it is very kind of you; but it is better for the present that she should not go into society. I do not want her to feel things."

"She would not feel any thing. She is quite convinced that she was properly married at first."

"It is not only that. People might ask who Mr. Philip Durnford was, and — and — O Madeleine! do you not see that I am right?"

"You are always right, dear madame."

In the evening the party came back — Venn, at least, happy. They had been fishing for the novel, and failed to find it. Lollie had caught a gudgeon, Arthur had caught nothing. And so on, childishly happy, as they always were when Venn was with them, — the man who never lost his delight in childish things.

And so, after their late dinner, Venn thought it was time to go.

"Stay a moment, dear Mr. Venn," said Marie. "I have something to say. Will Miss Venn take our child for a little while?"

"Mamma!" cried Lollie.

"Yes, dear. We have had a letter from Palmiste. I am going out."

Laura turned white.

"And I so happy to-day. It is wicked. Is he ill? Tell me."

"We will tell you every thing, dear," said Madeleine. "Philip is not well, and the news is not good."

Laura gave a great gasp.

"And I shall go, too, — shall I not, Mr. Venn? Who ought to be with a man who is ill but his wife?"

They looked at each other, and were silent. Venn spoke first.

"Lollie, dear, let me talk to you alone for a moment."

He took her into another room.

"Would you like to go, my dear?" he said, folding her in his arms in the old fashion, while her head leant upon his shoulder. "Would you like to go? Remember all. He has treated you cruelly"—

"But he asked my forgiveness."

"And he said himself that you had better be away from him for a while. My dear, your husband is not a good man. He has done bad things. When he comes back, with his mother, and asks to be taken into your arms again, I shall not be one to refuse him forgiveness; but he does not ask for you, or his mother either. If humiliation is to fall on the one who goes out to him, do not let it be you."

"He will think I have forgotten him, — as if I ever could forget him," she pleaded.

"Do you love him, Lollie?"

"Always the same question: I love him as I always did, no more and no less; but he is my husband."

Venn choked a spasm of intense jealousy.

"Love him still, dear. Love your husband; but you must not go to him. Will you be guided by me?"

"I am always guided by you. Whoever else have I in the world?" she said simply. "As if I did not love you better than all the world."

"My dear little girl!" he whispered, because his voice choked, — "ever my dear little girl, are you not? Nothing can part us. Nothing shall sever the love we have for each other. But you will stay with Sukey, while madame goes out and tries to recover her son for all of us."

He went back to the others, leaving Lollie there.

Then they arranged things; and next day he went to see Sukey, telling her only that Madame de Guyon had business in Palmiste, her native place. For there was sad deceit and hiding of the truth necessary; and only the little circle themselves knew all the history that bound them together with ties so sacred and so sad.

The day she went away, Marie sought Hartley Venn alone.

"I know," she said, "that evil will come to me: I feel it like the cold wind before the rain; but good will come too. See, now, dear Mr. Venn, there is but one thing I have to say. You will find at my lawyer's, in case — in case I never come back — my will. To whom should I leave my money but to my Philip's wife?"

. CHAPTER XL.

WEARIED in body and mind, Marie landed at the old familiar wharf at Port St. Denys. Five and twenty years since last she stood there, filled with the bitterness of regret, and yet the confidence of youthful hope. She recalled now the moment when, standing on the deck, she marked the mountains growing fainter and darker as the sun set, plunging them in a bath of light and color, till night came on, and they disappeared. Now she stood once more on the wharf, and marked the old things little changed. The half-naked Indians rolled the sugar-bags about, and piled them in great heaps, with their shrill cries and wild laughter, just as she remembered to have watched them as a child. Under the trees on the Place sat the same old men — or they seemed to be the same, — who had always sat there, talking and squabbling over the little politics of the day. Among the talkers under the trees, rolled and played the little naked mulatto and Indian children, as they had always done; and in long line stood the carriages waiting to be hired, as they had stood a quarter of a century since. Nothing was changed; and for a moment the years rolled back, and all her youth flashed again before her, with its happiness, such as it was, and its regrets. Only for a moment. One of the ship's officers, seeing her standing alone, proffered his assistance; and Marie woke to a sense of the dismal errand on which she had come.

"I have got your boxes on shore, Madame de Guyon," he said: "what shall I do next? You had better let me get you a carriage. Have you no friends waiting for you?"

"No," said Marie. "I am going into the country. It is a long drive. Will you kindly see that the man has good horses? I am going quite to the other side of the island."

"You are surely not going alone, Madame de Guyon?"

"Not alone! Why not? Oh, I have never told you that I was here as a girl. I know every road in the place, I believe. Thank you, Mr. Hatton, for your kindness. If you will only, now, get me a carriage."

Presently came rattling up a long, low carriage, with a pair of screws that looked like any thing in the world except going a long journey.

Marie said something to the officer, who spoke to the driver. He was a mulatto, approaching very nearly to the negro type, with woolly head, and face almost black. He was apparently about fifty, and was accompanied by a little boy, clothed chiefly in a ragged straw hat, half a jacket, and say a quarter of a pair of cotton trousers. He answered the officer's objections, laughing and protesting in a patois that made Marie's heart leap within her, for it was the patois that she had first learned to speak. She understood it all, after these long years; the intonation of the voice, the gestures which eked out the imperfections of the language, the rough, rude inflections of the barbaric tongue; and she asked herself whether, in the far past, she herself could have been as these naked children rolling in the dust, could have talked this jargon, could have been such as her driver. Getting into the carriage, however, she explained to him that she was to go to the estate of Fontainebleau.

"How, madame?" said the man. "No one lives at Fontainebleau since Mr. Durnford died."

"You know the place, then?"

"I was born there, madame. My parents lived close by." He called them his "papa and mamma," this grizzly mulatto.

"But Mr. Philip Durnford lives there now."

"Madame wants to see Mr. Philip? Oh!"

He jumped upon his box, called the boy, whipped up his horses, and went swinging down the street at full gallop. The boy kept prattling to him; but he made no answer. When they had gone some three or four miles, taking advantage of a hill, he turned round, and, poking his head into the carriage, he remarked, in a tone as if he were conveying information, —

"Madame is going to see Mr. Philip Durnford."

Some five or six miles farther on, he put his head in again, —

"Does madame know Mr. Philip?"

"Marie said she had seen him.

"A *mauvais sujet*, madame. Alphonse, take the reins. Do not whip them, my child. I will tell you, madame. Ah! brigand, you want to repose already? Up, then. Alphonse, take the whip to that *vaurien*." This was addressed chiefly to his horses. "Madame, I am about to tell you, Mr. Philip, — why do I say monsieur? — he is the son of old Mr. Durnford, who died in the cholera, and the little Marie. Pah! everybody knows that."

Poor Marie!

"Philip goes to England with Mr. Arthur. *There* was a young man, madame. Philip stays for seven, eight years. He comes back without Mr. Arthur. He says the estate is his; and he lives there."

"Who was Marie?" asked the poor mother.

"Marie? I will tell you, madame. There was a young lady, white as a lily, who lived in the great house close by my father's hut. She was lonely, and had no one to play with; and so they took my little sister, who was almost as fair as she was" —

"Your sister! You are Adolphe?"

"Madame knows my name? See, madame." He produced a sort of card, on which was printed a tariff of prices. It was inscribed with the names, in full, "Monsieur Adolphe Napoleon Rohan de Montmorenci." This he read out with unction. "How did madame know my name? My nephew, who went to the great college, gave me the surnames; for I must confess to madame, who knows every thing, that I was formerly plain Adolphe. Alphonse, with all your force, flog that *vieux scelerat* who will do no work."

The intelligent steed, hearing this, instantly quickened, and Alphonse put back the whip.

"Yes, madame," he resumed, "Marie was as fair-cheeked as Mademoiselle Adrienne herself. Only mademoiselle had light hair, and Marie black. Droll, was it not? I was as black as Alphonse here, and so was my brother Alcide; and Marie was as white as a lady. Eh, the *vieux* papa used to laugh when he looked at her. Only the priest said it was the will of God. Well, madame, Marie went to live with mademoiselle, and staid there till she was fifteen years old; then she ran away."

"Where did she go to?"

"Oh! I know, because I saw her often enough. She lived for a year in a little cottage close by Mr. Durnford's house, in the forest. There she had a baby, white as — as " — here his eyes wandered to little Alphonse for a suitable simile; but, not finding one in his brown face, he turned back to the carriage, — "as white as madame herself."

"Well?"

"Well, madame, that baby is Philip himself. You could hardly believe it, but it is so; and I who sit here am his uncle. Ha, ha, ha! Alphonse is his cousin. Ho, ho, ho! but it's droll."

"And — and — your sister?"

"Mr. Durnford married ma'm'selle, and poor Marie went away. She came back, though, and walked all the way to Fontainebleau through the forest — Alcide saw her — on the night after Madame Durnford was buried. Then she went away again, and no one has heard of her since. Poor Marie! She was too good for us, and the *bon Dieu* took her to heaven."

"Good? When she lived with Mr. Durnford?"

"Eh?" said the black, "why not? Ah! she was *gentille*. You should have seen her, madame, go to church with her white kid gloves, and her silk parasol, and a rosebud in her hair. All the white folks stared at her. Poor Marie! But the *bon Dieu* has taken her, and her son is a *vaurien*. Alphonse, if the idler does not go quicker, get down and kick him."

The idler instantly quickened repentantly.

"He is a *vaurien*, I say, madame. He drinks in the morning, he drinks all day, he drinks at night; and he goes to bed — saoul. No one goes to see him. He lives alone, he sees ghosts, he laughs and cries. The servants run away. Last week one ventured to sit up and watch him all night. He gets up, takes a pistol, and — ping! — if the boy had not ducked his head, like this, he would have been killed. Alphonse, thou laughest? *Malin!* He is very dangerous, madame. And madame is going to see him?"

Presently they left the high road, and turned down a rudely-made lane, cut through the forest. The still, quiet air recalled all the old moments to Marie. She remembered when George Durnford, her lover, made the road; and here, before it was finished, he would walk and talk with her in the evening, telling her a thousand things she had never dreamed of, opening up paths for her thoughts which she had never suspected, lifting her above the petty things that she had been accustomed to feed her mind with, and filling her mind with a happiness that was all the sweeter as it was the newer and more unexpected.

Forgetting her present miseries, an involuntary smile wreathed her lips, and her eyes glowed again with the brightness of her youth, as she thought of those days, all too brief, of love and tenderness. Do women ever repent of first love? I think not. The man repents, thinking of the wreck he has made of a woman's happiness. She weeps, not for the folly and the sin, but for the shattered image, the perished hopes, and the cruel punishment. Guilt? What guilt was there in the young mulatto girl, who, knowing that she could never be aught but the white man's mistress, yet ran willingly into his arms, and obeyed the instincts of a passionate nature that knew no religion, and had no sense of a higher duty? Thousands of times had poor Marie, in the height of her popularity and fame, pondered over the question, and, against all the dogmas of creed, had acquitted herself; and thousands of times, besides, had she willingly acquiesced in the results of the social necessity under which we are all slaves.

The road, winding through thick underwood, presently crossed a rude wooden bridge over a small ravine. Marie made the driver stop, and leaned out of the carriage, looking at a scene she remembered so well. On the steep, damp sides, towering above the tangled herbage, grew the tall tree-ferns, each with its circle of glory, clear cut against the blue of the sky; along the foot bubbled a little mountain stream over great bowlders that lay strewn about. Just above the bridge was a tiny waterfall of some three or four feet, over which the water leaped merrily, with as much fuss and splash as if it were a great Niagara. And above the fall, huddled together and gazing with suspicious eyes on the carriage, stood a herd of twenty or thirty soft-eyed deer. But not on them were Marie's eyes resting; for half hidden within the trees, stood the remains of an old cottage, the thatch half torn off and covered with creepers, the door hanging by one hinge, the door-posts wrenched out by the force of a growing tree, and the whole place presenting a dreary look of desolation. Calling Adolphe, she pointed it out to him, with a look of interrogation.

"It is the cottage of Marie, madame. That is where Mr. Durnford put her when she left ma'm'selle. He thought no one knew. But I knew, and many a time I've lain down there watching Mr. Durnford coming to call her out. Every evening he used to come; and all day long Marie used to sit and wait, looking along the path where he would come."

It was so true; and her heart was pierced to think how this poor fellow, her own brother, not ashamed of her disgrace, would lie and wait to see her lover come.

"Mr. Durnford taught her to read, madame; and then she used to sit at the window with a book all the day, and at night would tell him all she had learned. Eh? I have listened often at the window. But it did not last long. Then she went away; and then she came back. And then — I don't know where she went. The *bon Dieu* took her."

"Why do you think she is dead?"

"Madame, I will tell you. Because — how long ago? Alphonse, how old are you?"

"How should I know?" said the boy.

"Well, it was twelve years before Alphonse was born. I was down here; it was the cholera time. Ouf! what a time! No one died here except Mr. Durnford; but the night he died I was passing through this road, and in the moonlight just here, I saw two figures in white, — one was Marie and the other was Mr. Durnford. Since then, no one has passed by here at night."

"How do you know it was Marie?"

"What a droll question. As if I should not know my own sister."

They went on; and, as they drew near the house, Marie began to think what she should say to her son, and how she would be received. Her long voyage was ended, but the uncertainty of it remained yet. Nor had she ever realized until now the almost utter hopelessness of her journey. She was to save her boy. But how? By what subtle art was that ruined nature to be raised — that seared conscience to be come softened? Alas! she knew not that what she hoped to effect by pleading, the mystery of pain and suffering was even then accomplishing.

The carriage drew up in front of the veranda. She got out, and told the driver — her brother — to put down her boxes, and to drive back.

No one received her. It was strange. In the old days, when a visitor arrived, troops of servants came running. Now not one. The veranda, too, once like a well-ordered apartment, with its matting, the blinds, the long chairs and little tables, now stood stripped of all. The floor of concrete was in holes. The old ropes of the blinds hung helplessly about. Creepers climbed up the posts, and trailed along the woodwork of the roof. Outside, the pretty rose-garden was all destroyed, and grown over. The mill beyond was closed. There was no sign of work or noise from the adjacent "camp," which seemed deserted; no voice from the house within, no barking of dogs, or clattering of hoofs. A strange dread came upon Marie. She shivered from head to foot. It was too late to recall her carriage, which was now out of sight, and almost out of hearing. And with a dull foreboding of sorrow she entered the house which, four and twenty years ago, she had quitted with such repentance and regrets.

The old furniture was there, in its old places; but dust-covered, mildewed, and uncared for. No one was in the salon, no one in the dining-room. Avoiding the rooms to the right, which had been those of George Durnford, she went into the smaller bedrooms on the left, put up originally for children and guest-rooms. These, with all their old furniture, which she remembered so well, had yet a dreary and desolate look. Only, in one, provided with a deal table, a bookcase, and a few chairs, lay the relics of the days when her son, whom she had seen so seldom, was yet but a child. In one corner were the broken toys of the two boys. On the shelves lay the old well-thumbed grammars and school-books. Damp had loosened the bindings; white ants had burrowed long passages through them; the cockroaches had gnawed away the leather; and when she moved them, a whole colony of scorpions ran out, brandishing their tails in frantic assertion of their long-established rights.

She turned away sorrowfully, and, once more entering the dining-room, went in, with sinking of heart, to the great bedroom beyond. The silence and stillness of the house oppressed her. It seemed haunted with ghosts of the days gone by; and, added to this was the dread of something, she knew not what, which she might find within.

Twice she tried to turn the handle of the door; twice her heart failed her. She went to the well-known buffet in the dining-room, where water always stood, and drank a glass of it. That, at least, in its red earthenware vase, was the same as ever. Then she resolutely opened the door, and went in.

On the bed, — ah, me! the bitterness of punishment, — on the great bed which had once been her own and George Durnford's, lay, pale and motionless, her only son, stricken even unto death. Alone and uncared for. With dry, parched lips, that sometimes murmured a wail, and sometimes moved to let fall some wild words of delirium, with bright rolling eyes, Philip was waiting for the approach of death. This was written on his forehead in unmistakable signs. He was not even undressed. It appeared as if he had thrown himself upon the bed with his clothes on, and, in the passion of fever, had torn his shirt-collar open, and tried ineffectually to take off his upper clothing; and though the fever made his brow and his hands burning hot, he shivered occasionally, and his teeth chattered with cold.

Marie took in the whole at a glance. Stepping back to the dining-room, she hastily brought water, and gave him to drink, and bathed his burning face. He drank eagerly, and as long as she would let him. Then she opened the windows, for the air was stifling; and then — what hands are so tender as a mother's? — she undressed him, and managed to make him at least a little easier. And when all was done, — her patient rambling incoherently, — she knelt by the bedside, and prayed with passionate sobs and tears, that, if her son was to die, she might at least be permitted to breathe a few words — only a few — out of the fulness of her heart, into his listening ear. Presently she recovered, and went in search of help. The silence and stillness were inexplicable. At the back of the house, behind the stables, stood the huts for the servants. Thither she went. They were empty. A hundred yards from the house, close by the road, stood the huts which formed the "camp," — a little village for some eight hundred folks. It was empty and deserted. The shop was closed, the stables were empty. What could it all mean?

Coming back to the house, she went to the kitchen. This stood by itself, a small stone building. There she found a fire; and, crouching by the fire, though it was an afternoon in the height of summer, sat an Indian boy, who only moaned when she touched him. He, too, had fever. She took him up, — a light burden enough, — and carried him to a room next to Philip's, where she tended him, and laid him in the only bed he had ever slept in in his life. Fortunately, he was not delirious; and, from him, she learned something of what had happened.

The luckless Philip had taken to drinking all day long, and almost all night. He had become moody, irritable, and capricious, so that the very men who came for the coarse revels that went on there, grew tired of him, and left off coming at all. Then, having no companions and no resources, he became every day worse. Once, the nearest doctor, an old friend of his father's, rode over to see him; and after his departure Philip improved for a short time. He even sent for his lawyer, and gave him instructions to sell the estate. No purchaser came for it. The crop was put through the mill, and sent up to town; and after it, the unhappy man, growing mad with the dreadful life he lived, resolved to have nothing more to do with the estate, and actually took steps to get rid of his coolies, in which he had almost succeeded. And for two months the canes had been uncared for, the fields almost left to themselves. He said he was going back to England. As they learned afterwards, there was still a large sum of money left out of Arthur's savings. As for the estate, Philip declared, with many oaths, that, if no one would buy the place, no one should work in it; and then he reduced his private establishment. Two boys and a cook were all he kept; while for two long months he wandered gloomily about his deserted estate, and at night drank himself into a state of insensibility. And then, one night, he was stricken with fever. The cook and one of the boys ran away in terror. The other would have followed, but that fever seized him, too, and held him down.

Marie gathered this partly from the sick boy, and partly from what she heard afterwards. Going into the camp again, she found some bustle and noise. Thank Heaven! there was some one. As she learned afterwards, the whole body of the remaining coolies had struck work that very day, and gone off together — men, women, and children — to complain to the nearest magistrate about getting no wages. Now they were all returned, and, gathered in knots, discussed their grievances. Marie called a sirdar, and despatched him, with a handsome gratuity beforehand, for the nearest doctor. This done, she returned to her patients. the Indians gazing curiously at her.

The boy told her where some tea could be got, and she hastily prepared it for Philip, who lay quietly enough. He was too weak to move, poor fellow; and only murmured incessantly. He drank the tea, however, and then fell asleep, when Marie was able to leave him, and doctor the little Indian who was almost as ill as his master. Slowly the hours passed. She marked the sun set, as, long ago, she had often watched it, behind the hills in front of the house. She saw the moon rise in the dear old tropical lustre; the cigale shrieked its monotonous note; the watchman began to go his rounds, and cry, "All's well!" the same as he had always done; and, but for the heavy breathing of the poor stricken prodigal, her son, she could almost have thought the four and twenty years since last she sat there a dream. About nine o'clock a deputation waited on her. She knew the rustling of the muslin and the clink of the bangles, and went out on the veranda to receive her visitors. Some half-dozen Indian women stood there. One bore a dish of curry for madame. All wanted to know what they could do for her; all were curious to learn who she was and why she had come; and all looked on her with a sort of superstitious dread. Their husbands accompanied them as far as the garden hedge, but would go no farther; and now stood, prepared to fly, in case of any supernatural manifestations. None occurred, however. Marie asked if two of them would stay with her, and accepted the curry gratefully. It was the first thing she had taken since the early morning coffee; and a long night was before her.

The women were horribly afraid of the fever. They would do any thing for madame in the house — they would sleep on the veranda; but nothing would induce them to go into rooms of the sick. However, it was something, in her desolation, to have even them with her; and, with a sense of companionship, she went back to watch her charges. The boy at last fell asleep; and she brought a chair and sat by Philip's bedside, watching his deep breath come and go.

The two women outside, curled under a blanket, chattered for a while, and then fell asleep. The watchman at first made a great show of wakefulness, expectorating loudly every time he passed the doors of the bedroom; finally, he, too, subsided into his usual corner, and fell fast asleep, with his long stick in his hands. The dogs began by barking against each other, but gradually grew sleepy, and left off. The cocks, who disregard all times and seasons in Palmiste Island, loudly called for the sun about midnight. As he declined to appear at their bidding, they tucked their heads in again, and had another nap. And then the silence of the forest seemed to make itself felt; and Marie, her old superstitions coming back in all their force, almost gasped with the tension of her nerves. The room filled with ghosts, — not ghosts that filled her with terror so much as regret. Her long-dead mistress, Adrienne, with long, floating light hair, seemed to be hovering in white robes in the moonshine; the faces of old acquaintances laughed at her from the dark corners of the room; or the still, sleeping face of Philip would suddenly change into the face of her dead lover. Voices, too, were whispering about her, till she could bear it no longer, and went out into the open air, to pace the veranda, and look upon the old familiar scene bathed in the silver moonlight.

Then she came back, and prayed again — in the Catholic faith that had reared her — to the Madonna. What matter if no Madonna heard her? The prayer was the same to God, who hears all prayers, and seems to grant so few. Does any one ever get all he prays for? I trow not. And yet we pray, — pray against hope and certainty —

though we see the advent of the inevitable, and *know* that God will not turn it aside for any prayers or vehement calling-out of ours. But still we pray; and when the hand of death is on the nearest and dearest to us, when all that makes life sweet is to be torn from us, we betake ourselves to our knees, and so we go on praying till the world's end, despite the calm persuasion of the philosopher, and the experience of a life. Only, by prayer, we soften our hearts; and it seems as if God answers us by alleviating the blow, and giving some comfort while our sorrow is at its bitterest.

So, while Marie prayed, it seemed to her, in the dim light, as if the face of the sick man altered and softened. The fierce heat of the fever died away, his brow grew damp and chill, his hands soft and warm, and his breathing calm and regular; and for the time, she fancied that her prayers were heard indeed.

Do you know that moment in the night — the passage, as it were, from day to day — when a chill breath seems to pass over the earth, and for a space all the world is hushed as if in death? You may feel it by sea or by land. I have shivered and trembled under its spell, while gasping for breath in the sulphureous Red Sea. Or in the heart of London, should you be awake, you lie and feel that yesterday is dead indeed, and the new day not yet fully born. This is the time when feeble old men and children die; and when death seems most terrible.

At this moment Philip woke: and, at sight of his eyes, the mother's heart leapt up, and she thanked God; for one part of her prayer, at least, was answered. For the delirium, was gone, and her son was in his right mind. She did not dare to speak, while, on her knees at the bedside, she looked him face to face, and met his eyes, which gazed wonderingly into hers, so full of tears and tender love.

"There are so many ghosts," he murmured, "about this house, that I suppose you are another. You are the ghost of my mother."

"Ah, no! herself," she cried out. "No, my son, your own mother herself come to nurse you, — your own loving mother. Oh, my boy, my darling, forgive me!"

"I am weak," he said, "and my head is confused. Touch me, that I may know you are no phantom of my brain. Kiss me, my mother."

She showered a thousand kisses on his poor thin cheeks; she took his head in her arms, and bathed it with her tears, — those precious woman's tears, not all of repentance, but some of thankfulness and love, like those that once washed our Saviour's feet, till Philip's heart, softened by suffering, broke down; and he wept aloud.

But then her fears took alarm, and she quickly dried her eyes. And when he would have spoken, — when he would have answered some of her love with repentance and prayers, — she forbade him to utter a word.

"Not yet, my son — not yet," she said. "To-morrow we will talk. Now, sleep again — or, stay a moment."

She went to the old buffet in the dining-room, and found some claret, of which she made him take a few drops. This brightened his eyes for a moment; and then, overcome with his weakness, he fell asleep once more. Her heart danced within her, — she could not sit still. Leaving him sleeping, she went out again to the veranda, and watched the coming dawn.

The moon was down by this time; and save the Southern Cross, paling before the coming day, all the stars were gone. Only the bright morning star was left in the east. The birds began to twitter in the trees, just in their dreams — as she remembered long ago — before the dawn; and the sweet words of the poet came into her mind: —

"Ah! sad and strange, as in dark summer dawns
The earliest pipe of half-awakened birds
To dying ears, when unto dying eyes
The casement slowly grows a glimmering square:
So sad, so strange, the days that are no more!"

And she was sitting with the memories of by-gone days; with her dying son in his last sleep, — save the longest, — while this gray summer dawn crept slowly up the east.

Slowly; but it came. First a dull gray, and presently a silver gray; and then those long, marvellous fingers of light which spread themselves out upon the world as though they would fain seize it, and make it their own. And then the rocks, which had been black, grew purple; the mist upon the nearest peak, which had been a cloud, became a bridal veil, drawn loosely round, and falling in a thousand folds upon the woods below. And then a few short minutes of bright green, and red, and gold, and the great sun bounded into the sky with a single leap; and another day was born to the world. And then the birds all flew about to greet the sun; from the woods chattered the monkeys; the lizards woke up, and began to hunt about for the hottest places, blinking at the light; the dogs from the camp resumed their musical contest in Amœbean strains, just where they had left it off the previous night; the cocks began to crow, and make a great triumph, as if they had compelled the sun to come back by their own personal efforts; the turkeys began to strut about with a great babbling and cackle; the mules came out, and rolled in the cane straw; the mosquitoes all went away to bed; and the women's voices began, in the way she knew so well,—the women always seemed to waken first,—to rail at their lords from the huts of the camp. Her own two companions of the night shook themselves together, and greeted her kindly. She set them to make some tea, and sat with her hands crossed, looking before her at the bright and hopeful morning.

Presently she remembered her little Indian, and went to look at him in his bed. Alas! alas! the poor child was dead. Without a sound, or she would have heard it through the open door, his spirit had gone from him in the night; and he lay, cold and stiff, in the careless grace of sleeping childhood, his head pillowed on his arm, his eyes closed. Struck with terror, she turned to the other room. There, at least, was sleep,—kinsman, but not friend, of death; and, sitting patiently by the bedside, she resumed her watch.

The hours passed on, the sun grew high; but still he slept. About ten arrived the doctor,—she had simply sent for the nearest doctor; but she recognized an old friend of George Durnford's, and went to meet him as an acquaintance.

He took off his hat,—Dr. Staunton,—and, seeing an unknown lady who held out her hand, took it with great astonishment.

"Pardon me, madame, I"—

"O Dr. Staunton! you have forgotten me, then? But come in quickly."

He went in without a word, and began to listen to her account of his patient.

"It is a bad case, madame, a very bad case. I ought to have been sent for four days ago. If you are interested in him"—

"Interested? O Dr. Staunton! is it possible you have forgotten me? I am his mother."

"You — Marie? Can it be, indeed? I thought you dead. Tell me about yourself. My poor child,—I mean"—

"Never mind, doctor. People call me Madame de Guyon. But tell me about my son."

"Madame de Guyon? Is it possible that you are"—

"Yes,—I am the singer; but now tell me about my son."

"Marie—be strong,—strong to bear the worst. He cannot live. No human art can save him."

She sat down dry-eyed.

"When will he die?"

"We cannot tell. Perhaps in an hour,—perhaps in two. He will die before the evening. I will stay with you to the end."

She covered her face with her hands,—not to weep, but to keep back the hard, rebellious thoughts that surged up in her bosom. In a few moments she stood up, and began to busy herself about her boy, smoothing his pillows, and laying the sheets straight.

"I heard," she said, "in England,—Arthur Durnford told me,—that he was being led away by bad companions. I am sure his heart was good. I came out, thinking to try and save him. I find him dying. O doctor, save him! You loved George Durnford, who loved me; for his sake save him. In all his life, since he was a baby,—since I gave him up to his father,—this is only the third time I have seen him. And, Dr. Staunton, he loves me still. Oh, save him!"

"Marie, I cannot."

"And why,"—she turned fiercely upon him,—"why did you not save him before, for his father's sake? Why, when you knew that he was here, and that he was not what he should be, did you not come and reason with him? Oh!" she added bitterly, "I know the reason,—after four and twenty years of England,—that his mother was a mulatto."

"I swear, Marie," said the old doctor earnestly, "that you wrong me. I came here,—I came twice. The first time,—I must tell you,—I was insulted. I came again, and he listened to me. I have been ill myself, and could not come a third time."

"Doctor," cried a weak, thin voice from the pillow, "I thank you; and again I beg your forgiveness."

Marie was at his side in a moment, kissing and fondling him.

"What shall he have, doctor? Tea,—oh! hear it comes."

Dr. Staunton ordered him some simple things.

"I have heard what you have been saying," said Philip. "I shall die to-day."

"Oh, no, my son,—oh, no!—God will not permit it."

"God knows, dear mother, that it is the best thing I can do. Perhaps that is the reason why he lets me do it. Doctor, I have a good deal to say to my mother, and very little time to say it in. Leave us for a little; but first shake hands with me."

Left alone—

"Kiss me, mother," said Philip. "Tell me that you forgive me. Mother, in my weakness, I implore your pardon."

"O Philip! with all my heart's love, I forgive you. You did not know me. You could not know I was your mother, indeed.

It was I who was wrong. There is nothing to forgive, dear."

"But there is," he said. "I knew you were my mother, directly you told me so. I *felt* it. But I was proud, and I had just — without knowing all my wickedness, it is true — robbed Arthur of his inheritance; and I could not bear to give it back again. My heart, too, was bitter with that other wrong I had committed, — O my mother! a deeper wrong, even, than what I did to you. You may forgive me for one, but you can never forgive me for the other."

"Hush! my boy. It is all forgiven."

"All?" He hardly seemed astonished, and had forgotten how she knew.

"All. Laura told me herself. She bade me take out to you her love and pardon. She implored me to bring her out with me. She says that all she wants now is to hear one loving word from you, to treasure up, and hide the memory of all the things you did and said — when you did not know what you were saying, my dear."

Philip turned his face, and wept on the pillow.

"Wipe my eyes, mother. I am so weak that I cannot even do that for myself. And now, get some paper, and write a letter for me, but call the doctor first."

Marie went to get the paper: before she came back, Dr. Staunton had administered a restorative.

"How long?" asked Philip of the doctor.

"Don't talk too much, or you will kill yourself in an hour."

"Good!" said Philip. "Write, dear mother, —

"'DEAREST WIFE, — I have but a short time now to live. With my last breath, I ask pardon of you for the grievous wrongs I have done you. No punishment could be too great for me. My mother tells me you have sent me your forgiveness. My dear, if I could tell you how I have repented — if you knew the bitter remorse that has seized me since I have been in this place! But all is over at last. The great weight is lifted. God has sent my mother with her love and your pardon. I go into the other world. I have no excuse for myself. I have been a bad man, and have led a bad life. Only, if God lets me ask any thing'" —

"My son!" cried Marie.

"'If God lets me ask any thing, I will ask him to bless you both. This is my only prayer — I dare have none for myself. My dear — my Laura — I am very, very sorry. Think only for the future that I loved you all along. God bless you, my wife. Your most affectionate and penitent husband, —

'PHILIP.'"

He signed it with feeble fingers, guided by Marie, and then fell back.

"I should like to write to Arthur, but I cannot. Write for me, and tell him how I repented, and ask his forgiveness. MacIntyre wanted me to do it eight years ago, but I refused. You will write; won't you, dear mother?"

She promised.

"Sing to me, dear mother; you sing so well. I should like to hear your voice once more. Sing me a hymn."

It was a cruel trial. She steadied herself, and sang — his head upon her shoulder. — with all her fulness and richness of voice, so that the old doctor wiped his brimming eyes at the sound, —

"'Abide with me! fast falls the eventide:
The darkness deepens. Lord, with me abide!
When other helpers fail, and comforts flee,
Help of the helpless, oh, abide with me!

Swift to its close ebbs out life's little day,
Life's joys grow dim, its glories fade away'" —

His cheek dropped against hers. She stopped in sudden affright.

"Mother," he murmured very faintly, "is it growing dark? Is it night already?"

"O Philip!"

"I think I am dying — give my love to Laura. Kiss me, mother. Shall we meet again?"

"My boy — in heaven. I could not go there without you."

His head fell heavily forward. He was dead.

The little Indian boy was buried that same evening, in the Indian cemetery on the hillside. Small funeral rites had he, and no mourners. The man who dug his grave, and carried him under his arm to the place of sepulture, all out of the goodness of his heart and a kind of natural piety, placed a bottle on the grave, so that, should he perchance awake, there might be the means of at least slaking his thirst. And in India, perhaps his mother waited for him to come, and wondered, looking as the years went by, that he delayed so long. The life of man is short at the best; but the shorter it is, the less of bitterness he knows. Solomon said much the same thing.

Dr. Staunton staid with Marie. After the first burst of passionate grief, she began, womanlike, to find her consolation; and the thought that his last few hours were spent in love and repentance; that the memory she would have of her son would not be of cruel insult and wrong, but of tenderness and affection, made her thank God for one great mercy at least.

They buried him next day, in the nearest English churchyard, close to his father's grave. After his feverish life, it was consoling to his mother's heart to carry with her his last few words of repentance and sorrow. She treasured them up; and when she thought of them, she forgot the cruel scene in London, his harsh words, his tones of mockery and pride, remembering only his tender love at the last, and, when all was over, his calm face set with the sweet, sad, unchanging smile of death.

They buried him as the sun went down into the sea. The fierce heat of a tropical summer day was over; and night, with its perfect calm, was stealing upon the world when the last words of the funeral service were pronounced, and the mould rattled upon the coffin of poor Philip. Marie thought of his life: of the storm and hurricane when she left him with his father, and went back alone through the forest; of the blight that his birth had thrown upon him; of his wasted energies, ruined hopes, and cruel misdeeds; and of the sweet calm and peace of the end. And it seemed to her that this tropical day was an emblem of his life, with its fierce and scorching heat, its turbulent hurricanes, and its peaceful night.

The clergyman read the service, and went away. Then Marie saw that she and the doctor were not the only mourners; for, with their hats off, and kneeling on the sward, were her two brothers, Adolphe and Alcide. Stepping reverently forward, they each threw a handful of mould upon the coffin; their first and last claim at kinship. And then the two poor fellows walked slowly away, and Marie saw them no more.

She went back to the estate, the old doctor keeping her company; and though Palmiste knew that the great singer had been to their island, and was at Fontainebleau when young Durnford died, no one knew on what errand she had come, nor what was her relationship to Philip. Dr. Staunton kept the secret well. Nor did she think it necessary to tell Adolphe Napoleon Rohan de Montmorenci that Marie was not dead, after all. What would have been the use? It was not any false shame. If all the world knew that her brothers were poor blacks, gaining a living by driving a *voiture de place*, it would have mattered nothing to her. No one in England would think the worse of her. A singer is not expected to be of unblemished family, more than any other professional person. And what good could she do to her relations? They were happy; they had no wants that they could not satisfy; they had no ambition; they desired nothing, looked for nothing. Moreover, between them and herself so great a gulf was fixed that it could not be passed; and, whatever her childhood had been, she was now a lady. Lastly, there was this, — her story no one knew except one or two persons in England, and one person in Palmiste. There was no need for any one to know. She had suffered almost every thing that a woman can suffer, except what tortures women most, — the loss of her reputation. Blameless and pure in conduct, she had passed through the theatre without a reproach, whispered or spoken. She had learned, soon enough, the value of fair fame, and she was not disposed to give it up. Therefore she kept the secret to herself.

Turning over Philip's papers, she found among them evidences, not only of the power he undoubtedly possessed, but of thoughts which showed him in a better light, — which betrayed the causes of his wreck, the fatal moral wreck which his nature had sustained when he learned, through the man who was his evil genius, that he was illegitimate, and touched with the blood of the lower race.

Philip, until the last few months of his life, had been in the habit of writing; not for papers or magazines, partly because it never occurred to him to write for them, and partly because he did not write well enough. But his loose papers, heaped together in his desk, written on slips and fragments of paper, — sometimes in a few words, sometimes many — sometimes in prose, sometimes in verse, — showed that he knew himself capable of good things, and that, though he followed the worst, he approved the better.

She burnt them all but one. This she kept, and sent to Laura. It had no title, and consisted of four stanzas — rough verses enough, but not without an element of power.

"Go, dig my grave for me —
  Not where the painted sunshine lights the aisle,
  Not where, through glories of the pillared pile,
    The silver-voiced choir
  Sing o'er the sacred bones of glorious dead
    The strains of David's lyre.

Rather seek out for me
  Some village churchyard, where the world comes not;
  Where mounds ignoble cover men forgot;
    Where the black branching yew
  O'erhangs with midnight shade the moss-grown stones,
    And hides the graves from view.

Bury me there, and write
No long inscription on a marble stone:
Only a head-cross, with these words alone—
  'He dared not: therefore failed.'
Let the dishonor of a coward heart,
  So set forth, so be veiled.

Let no man weep for me:
Rather rejoice that one whose will was weak
No longer cumbers earth; and, when they speak
  (Not with breath bated), say,
God made the world for those who dare be strong:
  Well that the weak decay!"

She kept these lines only, and on his grave set up the head-cross he wished, with his own words, "He dared not: therefore failed." Under them she wrote — " P.D. Aged twenty-six."

Over his grave, and his father's, wave the tall filhaos, with the long, mournful sough, singing a perpetual lament over the sins and sorrows of the dead. In this forgotten corner of the world, — no longer a memory even in Palmiste, though few years have as yet gone by since he died, — he lies at rest. Arthur and his wife, and their children, will perhaps be laid beside him, but not Marie. Another grave is hers, — a wider one, but I think quite as peaceful.

She sent Philip's last words to Laura and Arthur by the next mail. She staid to finish what she had to do; left presents for her people, to be given by Dr. Staunton, and embarked again for England in the first homeward-bound ship, happier, if more sad, than when she arrived but a short month before.

CHAPTER XLI.

"My dearest daughter," — it was the last letter, the one letter, that Laura ever had from Marie, — "I send you Philip's last words. It is all over, my child. I cannot write about him yet; but he kissed me at the last, and we prayed together. I have given money to a man, who promises to keep his grave, and to tend the flowers that I have planted. There is a cross at its head, with his initials, and a line that I found in his desk, — 'He dared not: therefore failed.' It is the story of his life, — a poor life, a sinful life, a sorrowful life. He saw what was good, and took what was bad, because it seemed the easiest. In all his faults, he tried to make a compromise between the two. My poor boy! He looked so handsome, though he was pale and worn at the last; and, as he lay dead, his mouth was set with a sweeter smile than I had ever seen on it in life. Alas! I never saw him smile. I love to think of him so; and to feel that he is with One who is far more merciful than we two women.

"I am delayed by all this business, but I return by the next mail.

"Strange presentiments fall upon me. I cannot sleep at night. If I do, I have dreams and visions; and I feel as if I shall never see you again. But I am not unhappy. God has forgiven us both, — my boy and me. I say that again and again; and I comfort myself with thinking how my Philip laid his arms about my neck, and kissed me, at the end.

"One thing I forgot to tell you. You are now the owner of Fontainebleau. You must give it back to Arthur. Make him take it. What is mine is yours, and I am rich. Should I never reach England, all is bequeathed to you.

"I enclose you a lock of Philip's hair. I cut it from his head when I took my last look at his poor, white, dead face. I put up one of mine with it. Tie them up together, dear child, and put them in a locket. Here, too, is a flower from his grave. And, with it all, his last letter. God bless you, my daughter. Perhaps my forebodings may come to nothing.

"MARIE."

A wild day off the Cape, where the gales are fiercer, and the waves longer, than in any other part of the ocean. In the midst of the warring winds and mighty waves a gallant ship, tossing and groaning as every successive mountain of gray-green water strikes her. The sailors are holding on by the ropes, the man at the helm is lashed to his post, the captain is giving orders clinging to the davits, and all the passengers, except two or three who are on deck and watching the waves, are below in the saloon. The storm has raged without intermission for three days. They have been driven steadily south, far out of the track of any ship. It is bitterly cold. The men have been all day trying to get up cargo and lighten the vessel. The engines labor heavily. Every now and then the screw, as the ship's stern is lifted out of the water, whizzes round against the air, with a sound that seems to terrify the ship; for she gives a shiver, and then makes another bound forwards, and gallantly tries to right herself. Now and again a passenger tries to get hold of the captain or one of the officers, and essays to find a crumb of comfort in the assurance that things cannot get worse, and therefore must change soon; but the officers wear anxious faces, and the captain shakes his head when he talks to his chief. Hour after hour goes on, and things get worse, — the wind higher, the waves longer. One after the other, the passengers creep below into the saloon, and try to cheer each other, with a sickening fear at their hearts. Marie is there, sitting with clasped hands and calm face and downcast eyes. The women around her are crying and weeping; the men are sitting with haggard faces, or sometimes looking at each other with a smile; and the storm grows worse. Presently she feels a hand catching at her arm. It is a young girl, going to England to be married. She had not spoken to Marie before. Now, in her misery, she looks round, and finds hers the only face with any courage upon it. Marie rouses herself at the touch, and takes the girl into her arms.

"My poor child," she whispers.

And at the sound of her pitying voice, the girl breaks into a flood of weeping and lamentation.

"Madame de Guyon," she cries, "do you think we are going to be drowned?"

"I don't know, my dear. God knows. He will do what is best for us."

"Pray for us, Madame de Guyon."

Marie prayed, — whispering her prayer in the girl's ear. The storm grew louder and fiercer. She had to cling to the back of the saloon-seat on which she was resting; and, in the middle of her prayer, an awful crash was heard. The child — she was little more — shrieked with terror. Marie clasped her the more firmly.

"God, our Father," she whispered, "send us what is best for us."

There was a great stamping and noise upon deck, for the mainmast had been carried by the board; but it was finally cleared away; and presently more noise befell them when the foremast followed. Those in the cabin trembled and shrieked. One or two of the men got brandy, and drank freely to keep up their courage. Four ex-diggers from California sat down to have a final gamble, and, holding the cards firmly in one hand and the brandy in the other, prepared themselves so to leave the world.

But the end was not yet. This was the forenoon. The wind abated towards one o'clock; and there seemed a prospect, however distant, of getting through. The diggers gave up their gambling, and grumbled, being half drunk, over the winnings and losings. Those who had been most terrified assumed an air of valor; and the women left off crying. Only the girl clung to Marie, and begged her not to leave her again. The long day crept on. About five, a pretence was made at dinner — whatever could be found to eat being put out. But by this time a good many of the men were drunk, and lying helpless about the seats on the floor; and the women could not eat. The captain came down, — a cheery, hearty man. He looked with infinite disgust at his drunken passengers, and hastened to say a few words to Marie and the young lady.

"You seem brave, Madame de Guyon," he said; "and so I tell you, that, though we may pull through, I do not think we shall. If the wind rises again to-night, we shall have a rough time of it. Cheer up, my pretty," he said to the girl, "we must hope for the best. And here's the doctor to look after you. He can save us from a good deal, if not from storm and tempest. As for storm and tempest," he muttered, "only the Lord can save us from those; and I don't think the Lord will."

Then the doctor — a young fellow of five and twenty; as brave as if he had fifty lives — sat down and talked to them, making a rough dinner all the while, and trying to cheer up the poor lassie, but without much effect. Presently the sun set, — or, rather, the night fell, — and darkness came upon them. The stewardess lit one or two of the saloon lamps, and relapsed into a sort of torpor which had fallen upon her. The doctor tried to rouse her up. It was no use. She lifted up her head, and moaned, —

"I've been a great sinner — oh, I've been a great sinner!"

"Well, come," said the doctor kindly, — "we all know that of course; but you might as well do your duty all the same."

But she refused to move. So the doctor tried himself to minister to his two ladies, without much effect. Indeed, there was little to be done for them.

Marie raised her head, and listened. Then she whispered to the doctor, —

"The wind is rising — I feel it coming."

The doctor shuddered. He could distinguish nothing beyond the dull roar of the waves and the struggling of the ship; for the wind had almost died away. But he listened intently. Presently it came, — first a shrill whistle in the shrouds, and then a sort of heavy, dull blow to starboard; and the good ship staggered and reeled.

"God help us!" said the doctor softly. "We shall not get through this night."

Marie and the girl clung to each other.

"Come below," said Marie, "if there is time."

He nodded, and went out into the black, howling night.

"Madame," said the girl.

"Call me Marie, dear."

"Marie, call me Lucy. If there were only a clergyman."

"Let me be your clergyman, dear Lucy. God hears us in the storm as much as in the calm. We want no clergyman."

"But — but — oh! I loved him so much,

—more than God! Do you think he will forgive me? Marie, do you think I can be forgiven?"

"God forgives us all," said Marie. "He has forgiven me. And God has taken my son, and is going to take me. He has forgiven us both,—me and my boy too. Do you not think he will forgive you?"

"Pray for me again," sobbed the girl.

Marie prayed. Two or three of the women,—they were soldiers' wives, poor things, second-class passengers, who had crept aft for better shelter,—seeing the girl on her knees, and Marie bending over her, slid and crawled over to her, and kneeled round her, while Marie prayed for all.

In the midst of her prayer there was a confused rush and gurgle of waters, and the ship seemed suddenly to stop. In the roar of the tempest, they hardly perceived that it was her engines which had stopped. And Marie, looking up, saw the doctor making his way towards her. Catching one of the iron pillars of the saloon, he bent over, and whispered in her ear,—

"The ship will be down in ten minutes."

She nodded, and drew from her breast a little packet, which she handed him. He put it in his pocket; and then, with tears in his eyes, kissed her upturned face, and disappeared up the companion ladder. None of the women noticed it.

Ten minutes afterwards, he found himself clinging to a rope on the deck. Next to him was the chief officer.

"Where's the skipper?" he shouted through the storm.

"Gone overboard. All the rest, too, I think, with the almighty wave that put out our engine-fires. Doctor, don't be drowned like a heathen. Say you didn't mean what you said the other night."

"Not I," shouted the doctor. "If I've been wrong, and there is something to come, I won't go sneaking into it with a miserable apology."

The chief officer said no more; because at that moment another wave, striking the ship, washed them both off together into the black sea.

The doctor, recovering his senses, found himself clinging to some portion of the wreck. How he got hold of it, by what instinct, how in the crash and roar when his senses left him he still managed to hold to it, he never knew. It was a black night, and he was alone on the waves. He looked round, but could see nothing.

The morning found him still living. The storm had subsided, and the sun broke fair and warm.

Two days afterwards, a homeward-bound ship saw an object tossing on the sea, and made out that it was a man and a piece of wreck. They lowered a boat. The man was breathing, but that was all. They took him on board, and gave him restoratives. He came to his senses presently, and told his story. And the doctor was the only survivor of the ship. The captain and the crew, Marie and little Lucy, and the passengers, had all gone down together. When they touched at Plymouth, the doctor landed, and went straight to Venn with the packet that Marie had put into his hands. It contained nothing but a few memorials of Philip.

Laura had lost her husband and her mother.

CHAPTER XLII.

LAURA continued to stay with Sukey. She made no new friends, and no change in her life. Hartley came to see her nearly every day, and the old visit daily was so restored, with the difference that he was the scholar.

All her beauty had come back to her: roses to her cheeks, the life and lightness of youth, the sweetness and grace, doubled and trebled by the lessons of sorrow, with that additional charm for which we have no other word than ladyhood.

All were happy, except Sukey, who watched her brother day after day, with feelings growing more and more irritated. At last she spoke. He was in a particularly good temper that morning. Laura was in her own room, dressing to go out with him.

"It's ridiculous, Hartley," cried Sukey, losing all control over herself.

"What is ridiculous, Sukey?"

"I say it is ridiculous, the way you are going on. How long is it to last? And people talking. Even Anne says it's too bad of you."

"My own Sukey, what is it?"

"It's Laura. Has the man got eyes in his head? Are you stupid? Are you blind?"

Hartley turned red.

"Tell me, Sukey — speak plain. Tell me what it is you mean?"

"O Hartley! You are the most foolish creature that ever was, my dear brother." She laughed hysterically. "The child loves the very ground you walk upon. She dreams of you,—she is never happy except with you."

"Don't, Sukey, don't"— He began walking about the room. "If you should be wrong. Am I to lose the happiness I have every day?"

"Lose it! And a second time, this nonsense! I haven't patience with the man. While the prettiest and best girl in the world is dying of love for him, he talks about losing happiness!"

"Go send her here, Sukey, dear. It's true our grandfather was a bishop, and hers was a Gray's-inn laundress — no, that was her grandmother." He looked at her with a smile playing about his lips.

"It may be remarkable, Hartley," said Sukey, "to quote yourself, but it is true, that in our family there are two grandfathers, one of whom was not unconnected with the wholesale" — here she made a wry face — "the wholesale glue trade."

"Go away, Sukey," he laughed, giving her that very unusual thing from him, a kiss. He had never, by the way, been very frugal over his kisses for little Lollie, in the old time. "Go away, and send me my little girl."

She came, dancing down the stairs and singing, ready for her walk, in a dainty little costume, all her own invention, and bringing the sunshine into the room with her.

"Here I am, Mr. Venn. Are you impatient? I have only been ten minutes. Where shall we go?"

"I am always impatient, Lollie." He took her hand, and held it for a moment in his.

"Child, I am more than impatient. I am discontented. You give me all the joy I have in life; but you withhold some — the greatest."

She began to tremble, and her eyes filled with tears.

"Give me the greatest, my darling. Never to be separated from you, — to have you always with me. Give me the right to take you in my arms, as I used to do when you were a little child. Be my wife, Lollie."

She looked in his face. The eyes were smiling, — the face was grave. No wild tempestuous passion such as she might have remembered, only that memory seemed all dead. No fierce light of a burning fire in those eyes, — only the light of a full, deep love which nothing could ever destroy.

She threw her arms round his neck, and laid her cheek to his.

"Mr. Venn, — Mr. Venn, I have never loved anybody but you."

What could he say? There was nothing to say. Five minutes afterwards, Sukey, hearing no voice, opened the door. They were still standing in that same posture, kissing each other, as Sukey afterwards told Anne, "like a pair of babies."

"My dearest," said Sukey, "I have always prayed for this from the beginning. Hartley, you must tell Anne. Ring the bell. Anne, you will be glad to hear that Mr. Hartley is going to marry Mrs. Durnford."

Anne sat down, and wiped her eyes with the corner of her apron.

"Now, I'm content to go," she said. "O Mr. Hartley, Mr. Hartley! — and she never tired of hearing how I dandled you on my knees when you were a little baby a month old. God bless and keep you both, my dears!"

That evening the Chorus assembled. Lynn and Jones arrived nearly at the same moment. Both seemed strangely pre-occupied and nervous. Jones could not sit down. He walked about, upset glasses, and comported himself as one under the influence of strong emotion. Venn only seemed perfectly tranquil.

"What is it, Jones?" he asked at last.

"My play came out last night at the Lyceum."

"Oh!" said Lynn; "and failed, of course."

"Never mind," said Venn, "you can easily write another. After all, what matters little disappointments? Mere incidents in our life, giving flavor to what else would be monotonous."

"Yes," said Jones," "if one may quote Byron on such an occasion as the present —

'Oh! weep not for me, though the Bride of Abydos
  Wildly calls upon Laura to slumber no more;
Though from Delos to Crete, from Olynthus to Coidos,
  The canoe of the Corsair is hugging the shore.

Oh! weep not for me, though on Marathon's mountain,
  The chiefs are at thimblerig, as is their wont;
Though beneath the broad plane tree, by Helicon'a fountain,
  The languishing Dudu is murmuring "Don't."'"

"We will not weep, Jones. Sit down and be cheerful."

"I am a humbug," cried Jones. "Oh! why were you not there? It was a great success. The house screamed. I have succeeded at last — at last." He sat down, and his voice broke almost into a sob as he added, "I have written to Mary."

"This will not do," said Venn. "He violates every rule of this Chorus. He brings his private joys into what is sacred to private sorrows. Lynn, he must be expelled."

"Stay a moment," said Lynn. "I, too, have something to communicate."

"What? You, too? Have you then?"

"No: I have accepted a judgeship in Trinidad. I start next month."

Venn looked round him with astonishment. Then he turned red and confused.

"I, too," he confessed, "have my secret to communicate. Yes, my friends, the Chorus is dissolved. I am going to be married."

They looked at him nervously.

"I am to marry my little girl."

"Thank God!" said Lynn.

"Why, who else could I marry? There is but one woman in the world, so far as I am concerned. We shall be married immediately, and go to Italy till we are tired of it; then we shall come back again. There will be no wedding fuss, or breakfast, or other annoyances, — unless Sukey likes to come here for a final kidney."

"And the Opuscula?"

Venn winced.

"I shall begin their careful revision with a view to publication — at my own expense. Lollie is rich, you know," he added simply. "Besides, it will be good to have something to do. In the morning, we shall roam about and enjoy the sunshine. In the evening, I shall correct the manuscripts while Lollie plays to me. You see, I am not in any hurry about publishing. Perhaps in ten years' time you may see an announcement of their appearance.

"The last night of the Chorus," he went on. "My friends, there stands before us the venerable bottle of champagne which was brought in the very first night of the newly-established Chorus, now twelve years ago. This night must witness the drinking of that wine. Aged and mellowed, it is doubtless by this time in splendid condition. I would Arthur were here to join us. Jones, get the champagne glasses from the cupboard. Lynn, my boy, help me to remove the wire. Are we ready? Now, in the sparkle of the generous wine behold the brightness of the future. Our youth will be renewed. We shall live again in the sunshine of success and happiness. Behold!"

He removed his hand from the cork. It did not immediately fly out, and he had recourse to the vulgar expedient of pulling it out with a corkscrew. After great exercise of strength, it came out with a dull thud.

He said nothing; but while all three crowded round the table, he poured out the wine. It was flat, dead, and sour. Not a single sparkle in the glass.

They looked at each other.

Lynn laughed bitterly.

"It is an emblem of life," he said. "Nothing compensates. We have wasted our youth."

Venn stared vacantly at the unhappy wine, which seemed an omen of bad luck.

"I believe it was bad at the beginning," he murmured. "It came from the public-house."

Jones, however, brought his clinched fist upon the table.

"Emblem of life? Compensation? Rubbish!" he cried. "We have waited, we have suffered. What of it? The suffering is gone, the waiting is over. It is no more than the carache I had when I was a boy. Even the memory of it is almost faded. Venn, Lynn, this infernal bottle is the emblem of our hopes and disappointed ambitions. Go, cursed symbol of defeat!"

He hurled the bottle into the fireplace, and threw the glasses after it.

"And now, Venn, if you like, I will get you some new champagne, and drink to your happiness, and to yours, Lynn, and to my own. In the words of the poet, —

'Look not for comfort in the champagne glasses,
  They foam, and fizz, and die;
Only remember that all sorrow passes,
  As childhood's ear-aches fly.

At the great Banquet where the Host dispenses,
  Ask not, but silent wait;
And when at last your helping turn commences,
  Complain not 'tis too late.

And see, O Chorus of the disappointed!
  Ourselves not quite forgot;
And after aimless play and times disjointed,
  Sunshine and love our lot.'"

THE END.

www.ingramcontent.com/pod-product-compliance
Lightning Source LLC
Chambersburg PA
CBHW020248170426
43202CB00008B/275